Afoot and Afield in
San Diego County

Jerry Schad

See page 305 for 1996 Update

Wilderness Press
Berkeley

FIRST EDITION July 1986
Second printing November 1986
Third printing July 1987
Fourth printing March 1988
Fifth printing August 1989
Sixth printing April 1991
SECOND EDITION November 1992
Second printing October 1993
Third printing May 1995
Fourth printing October 1996

Design by Thomas Winnett and Roslyn Bullas
Photos and maps by the author

Library of Congress Card Catalog Number 92-27359
International Standard Book Number 0-89997-158-X

Manufactured in the United States of America
Published by Wilderness Press
                  2440 Bancroft Way
                  Berkeley, CA 94704
                  (800) 443-7227
                  FAX (510) 548-1355
                  Write, call or fax for a free catalog

Library of Congress Cataloging-in-Publication Data

Schad, Jerry.
        Afoot and afield in San Diego County / Jerry Schad. — 2nd ed.
        p. cm.
        Includes biliographical references (p.) and index.
        ISBN 0-89997-158-X
        1. Hiking—California—San Diego County—Guidebooks.
2. Backpacking—California—San Diego County—Guidebooks.
3. San Diego County (Calif.)—Guidebooks. I. Title.
GV199.42.C22S2669 1992   92-27359
917.94'980453—dc20   CIP

ACKNOWLEDGMENTS

Many people have offered their time, talents, and knowledge during the various phases of producing this book. For the first edition, Mike Fry, Don Endicott, Nick Soroka, Bob and Sharon Hartman, Jane Rauch, Jim Sugg, Bill Becker, Gene Troxell, Janet Leavitt, Pete and Cinde Nowicki, and my wife, René, shared adventures with me on the trail, and/or helped with transportation. George Leetch and Uel Fisk shared their knowledge of some of the more obscure parts of the county. Several people associated with local parks and public agencies were of assistance too; among them, Manfred Knaak, Paul Remeika, Torrey Lystra, Norm Machado, Greg Greenhoe, Susan Blankenbaker, George Kowatch, Jack Shu, and Russ Kaldenberg. Shannon O'Dunn, Mitch Beauchamp and Jeff Schaffer reviewed parts of the original manuscript, and Cathey Byrd prepared the symbols that appear at the top of every trip description.

During the period between the first publication of this book in 1986 and the present year, I had the pleasure of re-hiking many familiar routes in San Diego County—and also exploring the 28 new trails added to this current, second edition. A whole host of people have shared new discoveries with me, or otherwise assisted in making this book as complete, up-to-date, and accurate as possible. In addition to several people already mentioned above, I wish to thank Beth Davis, Paul Freiman, Richard Hughes, Peter Jensen, Carl Johnson, Rob Langsdorf, Alex Molnar, Dave Moser, Bart Ward, Cal Williams, and Joan Wynn for help with the second edition.

Portions of this book were derived from a series of articles I wrote for *San Diego Home/Garden* magazine between 1982 and 1991; I thank editor Peter Jensen for permission to reprint parts of these articles. Some of the material in the second edition is derived from my current column in the North County Focus supplement of the *Los Angeles Times* (San Diego Edition); and I thank editor Joan Taylor for permission to use that material.

At Wilderness Press, Tom Winnett superbly edited both the first-edition manuscript and the extensive revisions and additions submitted for the second edition. Final appreciation goes to my wife, René, for patience and encouragement during periods when I'm either somewhere in the mountains, or seemingly mesmerized by the glow of my computer screen.

Jerry Schad
El Cajon, California
August 1992

PREFACE

Hiking and backpacking are just two of the many satisfying recreational pursuits enjoyed year-round by anyone fortunate enough to live in the sunny San Diego region. Not all hikers, however, realize how broad the spectrum of opportunity really is. On one end of this spectrum lie San Diego County's coastal canyons, foothills, and mountain parks, laced with well-marked hiking and bridle trails. The other end of the spectrum consists of vast stretches of undeveloped land in the county's public domain—including many of our newest state and federal wilderness areas. There are few or no trails in these areas, but the potential for exploration of a rugged kind is almost unlimited.

Until the publication of *Afoot and Afield in San Diego County* in 1986, no single information source had attempted to exhaust even one end of the above-mentioned spectrum. By publishing this book, I hoped to bring into sharp focus almost every hike worth taking in the public lands of the county—hikes ranging in difficulty from short, self-guiding nature trails, to peak climbs and canyon treks that would challenge even the most skilled adventurer.

The current edition strives to do the same, with a slight shift in emphasis. Twenty-eight new hikes have been added, covering new trails, parks, and open-space lands in the coastal and mountain areas. Nearly all of the descriptions from the first edition have been at least partially rewritten for conciseness or greater clarity, and there has been much reorganization of both old and new trips among the individually mapped areas. All maps in this book have been redrawn (with the aid of a computer) and updated as well.

In order to keep this book to a manageable size, 12 trips (mostly in the desert area) have been deleted. In some cases, all or parts of the missing trips have been incorporated into the revised trip descriptions that appear in this edition. The overall result is a book containing more information in approximately the same number of pages.

A new feature appearing in this edition is a graphic symbol denoting hikes that are "best for kids." Also, the capsulized summaries for each trip now include an "agency" listing. The coded letters found there are keyed to an Appendix with names and phone numbers of parks or agencies having jurisdiction over the trails described.

Certain compromises concerning the completeness and overall scope of this book were necessarily made. The "Afoot and Afield" theme generally covers hikes of non-trivial length that are to some extent remote from civilization. Not covered here are walks on city streets, and the many "nature trails" featured in the smaller urban and suburban parks of San Diego County. Some longer or technically difficult routes I've hiked in the county were rejected for inclusion as being too tedious or unacceptably hazardous.

Absent, too, is a complete log of San Diego County's share (about 120 miles) of the Pacific Crest Trail. Since this information is adequately treated in other publications, I chose to highlight certain shorter trips on the most scenic parts of the PCT. In several of the trip descriptions, the PCT is used as a means to reach another trail or some interesting off-trail destination.

This book encompasses all public lands (and a few private lands on which the public is welcome) within San Diego County, with a few exceptions. These include the San Mateo Canyon Wilderness, a part of which intrudes into San Diego County north of Camp

Pendleton, and San Onofre State Beach, just south of Orange County. These two areas are included in my book *Afoot and Afield in Orange County*.

Certain public lands straddling the Riverside-San Diego county line, such as Bucksnort Mountain, were excluded because access from the San Diego side is awkward. On the other hand, a portion of the Jacumba Mountains, on the border of Imperial County, was included because of its freeway-closeness to San Diego.

All hikes described in this book were hiked at least once by me at one time or another, and every effort has been made to ensure that the information contained herein is up-to-date. Roads, trailheads, and trails can and do change every year, however. Recreational opportunities within the county will surely expand during the next several years. I will continue to insert fresh updates in future printings of this edition, and a third edition will undoubtedly appear in the future. You can keep me apprised of recent developments and/or changes by writing me in care of Wilderness Press. Your comments will be appreciated.

Hiking in the backcountry entails unavoidable risk that every hiker assumes and must be aware of and respect. The fact that a trail is described in this book is not a representation that it will be safe for you. Trails vary greatly in difficulty and in the degree of conditioning and agility one needs to enjoy them safely. On some hikes routes may have changed or conditions may have deteriorated since the descriptions were written. Also trail conditions can change even from day to day, owing to weather and other factors. A trail that is safe on a dry day or for a highly conditioned, agile, properly equipped hiker may be completely unsafe for someone else or unsafe under adverse weather conditions.

You can minimize your risks on the trail by being knowledgeable, prepared and alert. There is not space in this book for a general treatise on safety in the mountains, but there are a number of good books and public courses on the subject and you should take advantage of them to increase your knowledge. Just as important, you should always be aware of your own limitations and of conditions existing when and where you are hiking. If conditions are dangerous, or if you are not prepared to deal with them safely, choose a different hike! It's better to have wasted a drive than to be the subject of a mountain rescue.

These warnings are not intended to scare you off the trails. Millions of people have safe and enjoyable hikes every year. However, one element of the beauty, freedom and excitement of the wilderness is the presence of risks that do not confront us at home. When you hike you assume those risks. They can be met safely, but only if you exercise your own independent judgment and common sense.

Contents

Coastal Strip and Foothills

The Mountains

The Desert

Appendices

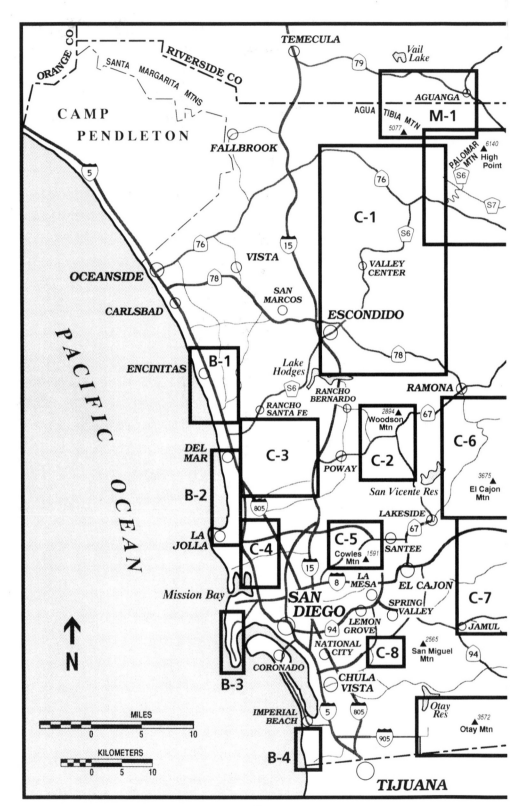

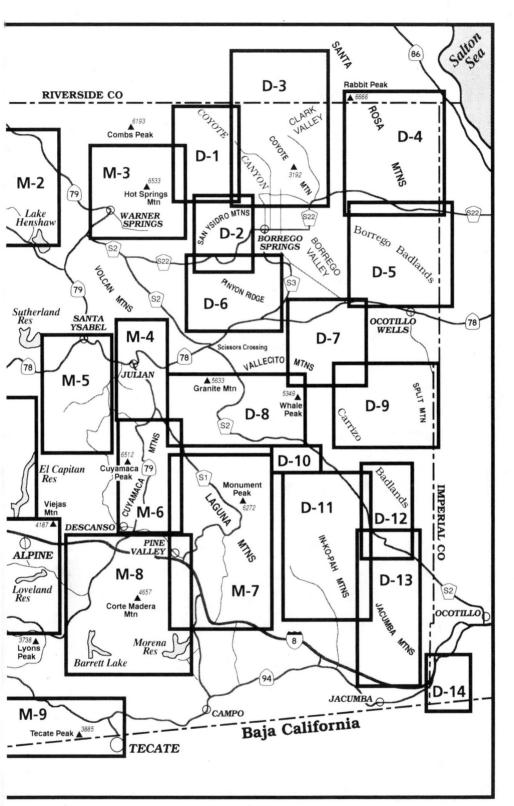

INTRODUCING
SAN DIEGO COUNTY

The San Diego region is special in that no simple description can ever hope to characterize it. Lacking any single, overpowering symbol (except, of course, the almost perpetually sunny weather), it revels instead in its remarkable diversity. The blue ocean, the tranquil bays, the sparkling beaches, the sun-splashed coastal mesas, and the rugged little coastal canyons that most San Diegans live with every day are but a small part of the whole. Beyond lies a beautiful and varied backcountry area of boulder-strewn foothills, pine-clad mountains and vast desert spaces.

For hikers, backpackers, and explorers of the great outdoors, this diversity is good news. San Diego County offers a greater variety of experiences and more opportunities to practice an unconfined type of recreation than any other similar-sized area in the United States.

Of the county's 4255 square miles, more than one-third, or a total of approximately 1550 square miles, is public land open to recreational use. Included in this total are several state parks (chiefly Anza-Borrego Desert State Park), more than 800 square miles; the Cleveland National Forest, 438 square miles; land in the public domain administered by the federal Bureau of Land Management, about 250 square miles; and numerous county and city parks.

With the expenditure of less than two hours' driving time and one or two hours' walk, a San Diego urbanite can reach any of a dozen totally different natural environments, ranging from snowy mountain peaks and fern-bedecked streams to sculpted desert badlands. Nowhere else in America is such a broad range of natural environments so close and conveniently located, and so available year-round, to a large population.

In the next few pages, we'll examine some of the remarkable aspects of San Diego County's climate, landforms, and flora and fauna. Following that, you'll find some notes about safety and appropriate behavior on the trail, and some tips on how to use this book effectively. After perusing this material, you can dig into the heart of this book's descriptions of 192 hiking routes from the coast to the Anza-Borrego Desert. Happy reading and happy hiking!

Land of Many Climates

A succinct summary of San Diego County's climate regime might take the form of just two phrases: "warm and sunny," and "winter-wet, summer-dry." In the world-wide range of climates, this pattern is called a Mediterranean-type climate, typical of less than 3 percent of the world's landmass.

Actually a lot of variation exists, a fact readily apparent to anyone traveling east or west across the county. The distribution of San Diego's sub-climates is somewhat easy to picture geographically, since they tend to run in strips parallel to the county's coastline and its roofline, the Peninsular Ranges. Without resorting to technical classification schemes, let's divide the county into five climate zones:

The westernmost zone, extending inland several miles across the coastal plain, is greatly affected by the moderating influence of the Pacific Ocean. This climate is characterized by mild temperatures that are relatively unvarying, both daily and seasonally. Average Fahrenheit temperatures range from the mid-60s/mid-40s (daily highs/lows) in winter, to mid-70s/mid-60s in summer. Rainfall averages about 10 inches annually.

The next zone, about 20-40 miles wide, covers the inland valleys and the western foothills of the Peninsular Ranges. This area, which is only partly under the influence of moderating ocean breezes, experiences more extreme temperatures: low 70s/high 30s in winter and high 80s/high 50s in summer. Precipitation averages about 15 inches annually.

The next zone east, the coolest, encompasses the highest elevations of San Diego County— the forested heights of the Palomar, Cuyamaca, Laguna and other similar mountains that form the backbone of the Peninsular Ranges. Winter temperatures average low 50s/low 30s, while summer temperatures average low 80s/high 50s. Precipitation, in the form of both rain and snow, averages about 30 inches annually.

Farther east still, on the desert-facing slopes of the mountains, is a narrow strip characterized by a "high desert" climate. This zone also includes the tops of several eastern spurs of the Peninsular Ranges that extend into the desert. Temperatures range from the low 60s/low 30s in winter to the high 90s/low 60s in summer. Precipitation averages about 10 inches per year.

The easternmost zone includes the "low desert" below about 3000 feet elevation. This area is almost completely cut off from the moderating influence of the ocean, and it experiences a relatively extreme "continental" type of climate. Temperatures range from the low 70s/low 40s in winter to 100-plus/high 60s in summer. Average precipitation is five inches or less.

No discussion of San Diego County climates would be complete without mention of some of the remarkable extremes of temperature and precipitation recorded within the county over the past century. The highest official temperature ever recorded in the county was a relatively modest 122°F at Borrego Springs (this occurred on June 25, 1990). Since some areas of the low desert outside of Borrego Springs regularly experience temperatures averaging five degrees higher, it's probable that shade temperatures above 125° can happen there.

Even the coastal area can heat up to 100° or more during a so-called Santa Ana condition. Santa Anas occur when dry air moves southwest from a high pressure area in the interior U.S. out toward San Diego County. As the air flows down mountain slopes, it compresses and becomes warmer at the rate of about 5°F per 1000 feet of descent. During strong Santa Ana conditions, which are common in early fall, San Diego or Imperial Beach or some other coastal weather station will sometimes record the highest temperature in the nation!

The lowest temperatures, and the only sub-zero temperatures, recorded in the county so far, were -4° and -1° readings at Cuyamaca Rancho State Park.

Although San Diego County and all of Southern California lie in a belt of generally dry climate, both are susceptible to monster deluges from time to time. Annual precipitation measured at San Diego over the past 140 years has ranged from 3 inches to 26 inches. Palomar Mountain, the wettest spot in the county, once received a total of 82 inches. Occasionally, a *chubasco*, or tropical storm, from Mexico will move into the desert or mountains, resulting in intense, localized downpours. A century ago, one such storm dumped 16 inches of rain on the border town of Campo in 24 hours, 11.5 inches of that total in a single 80-minute-period! In 1976, another *chubasco,* Hurricane Kathleen, wreaked havoc in southeastern San Diego County, rearranging watercourses and destroying roads, a railroad line, and half a desert town.

Despite Nature's occasional temper tantrums, more than nine times out of ten your outings in San Diego County should coincide with dry weather and temperatures in a moderate register—for at least part of the day.

Lower Penasquitos Canyon

Reading the Rocks

Some geographers think of San Diego County as being divided into three "geomorphic provinces." These provinces are not unique to San Diego County, but extend into neighboring counties and into Baja California.

The first, bounded by the curving shoreline of the Pacific Ocean and stretching no more than a few miles inland, is the Coast province. It has the form of a terraced plain, in places intricately dissected by steep-sided canyons and arroyos. This is the familiar "canyon-and-mesa" topography on which most of urban and suburban San Diego lies.

The second, the Peninsular Ranges province, consists of a series of discontinuous mountain ranges, some more than 6000 feet high. The ranges are generally parallel to one another, generally trend northwest-southeast, and are interspersed with high, sometimes narrow valleys. The bulk of San Diego County's land surface is included in this province, along with all the county's higher elevations. The province stretches north to include the San Jacinto Mountains in Riverside County and south to the tip of the Baja peninsula. The Peninsular Ranges and the Sierra Nevada range to the north are similar in topography: in rough form both are huge, tilted blocks of granitic rock, with steep east escarpments and more gradual west slopes.

The third province is called the Salton Trough. This large depression holds the Salton Sea, and most geologists would say it lies outside San Diego County. Geographers would say that some of the low-desert landscape of Anza-Borrego Desert State Park in the northeastern corner of the county belongs to this province.

The geomorphic provinces themselves are very complex. Within even a single mountain range or coastal canyon or desert basin, there may exist a dazzling variety of small-scale landforms and underlying rock types. One might want to ask: how did San Diego County's surface get to be so convoluted; and what processes were responsible for the presence of so many different kinds of rock in the county today?

First, it's important to note that California, Oregon, Washington, British Columbia and Alaska are composed largely of rock formations that were transported to their current locations from either the west or the south. This migration was accomplished by the formations riding "piggyback" atop large and small plates which, taken all together, form the earth's crust. Such grand-scale movements are still occurring today. For example, California's famous San Andreas Fault is actually just a boundary between two large plates that are gliding past each other. San Diego lies on the oceanic plate, which is drifting north with respect to the continental plate at a rate of a little more than 2 inches per year. If this rate continues, then in 14 million years, San Diego will have drifted far enough north to pass San Francisco, which lies on the continental plate. Future hikers—bring your overcoats!

With the above in mind, we begin a geologic story, as painted in broad brush strokes, back about 150 million years ago. At that time, most of the present-day San Diego County, along with much of western North America, was below sea level. Over 2000 miles to the south or southwest, a mountain-building cycle began, as an arc of volcanic islands grew in the ocean. For 50 million years or so, the volcanoes spread lava and ash over a wide area. By the end of this volcanic episode, about 100 million years ago, the arc of volcanic islands had migrated close to the mainland, and the two were now separated by a narrowing, shallow sea. After the sediments of the shallow sea floor were uplifted, they were eroded away and deposited in deltas near the coast or offshore.

Erosion also carried away the debris from the island-arc volcanoes, exposing and attacking deeper layers that had been metamorphosed by heat and pressure generated as the volcanic islands slowly rammed into the mainland.

Still more debris arriving along the coast came from erosion of a volcanic area far inland that had developed in response to the action of the oceanic plate carrying the island-arc vol-

canoes. The edge of this oceanic plate was diving beneath the mainland plate, and its rock melted when it reached a certain depth, creating magma. This magma rose within the crust, and parts of it solidified before reaching the surface, crystallizing to form granitic rock. But some magma broke through to the surface, and spewed lava and ash far and wide, constructing a volcanic landscape. (A similar process of volcanism, caused by an offshore, northward-migrating, diving plate, is occurring today in the Cascade Range of Washington, Oregon and northern California.) Much of the debris from the mainland volcanic area was in the form of erosion-resistant rhyolitic rock. It seems that during one particular period lasting several million years, cobbles of this rhyolitic rock came to our area by way of a single large river, which once flowed west through today's state of Sonora, Mexico.

Erosive forces continued to nibble away at the volcanic landscape, finally exposing, after perhaps 20 million years (80 million years ago), the underlying granitic rock, which had originally solidified about three to nine miles below the earth's surface. In time, an increasing amount of the large granitic mass, or batholith, was exposed, and the landscape acquired a different look, perhaps like that of today's mostly granitic San Diego County. The vegetation, however, was very different, in part because plants back then were different, but more important, because this area was still well south of us, located in a tropical clime.

By about 40 million years ago the assemblage of volcanic rocks and granitic rocks plus sediments from both rock types had migrated far enough north to be located immediately west of the present-day state of Sonora, on the mainland of Mexico. Later, a "mere" 10 million years ago, the Gulf of California began to form as an inlet between mainland Mexico and the sliver of land that would become Baja California.

Today, San Diego County, riding on what is known as the Pacific Plate, continues to drift northwest relative to the "mainland" North American Plate. To the east and northeast is the boundary between the two plates, the great San

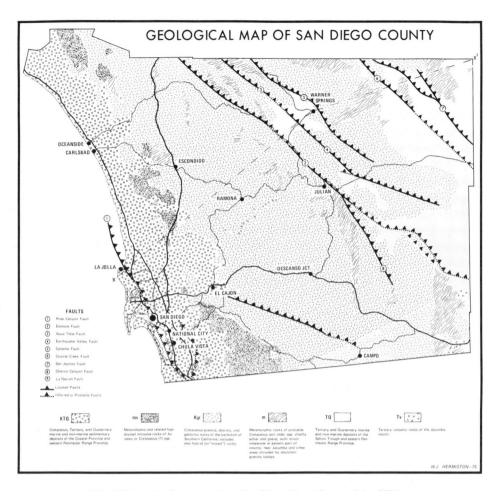

GEOLOGICAL MAP OF SAN DIEGO COUNTY

Simplified geologic map and profile of San Diego County. Line XX' on the geologic map locates the cross section of the geologic profile. From *San Diego: An Introduction to the Region*, Philip Pryde, ed., © 1976, 1984 by Kendall/Hunt Publishing Company. Reprinted by permission of Kendall/Hunt Publishing Company.

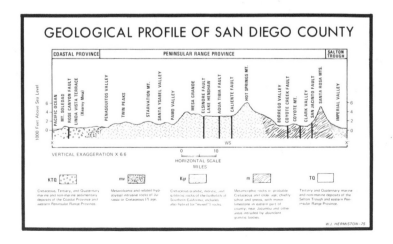

GEOLOGICAL PROFILE OF SAN DIEGO COUNTY

Andreas Fault, running beneath the eastern side of the Salton Trough and under the Gulf of California. In the county's midsection, the granitic mass continues to rise, building up mountains faster than erosive forces are currently tearing them down.

We can now begin to understand the simplified geologic map and profile on page 5. The granitic rocks (which include diorite, granodiorite and gabbro rock commonly found in San Diego County) encompass most of the Peninsular Ranges province (including what we generally call our foothills and mountains). Together all are part of the Southern California batholith—the vast mass of rock that crystallized deep beneath a tropical volcanic landscape about 100 million years ago.

Exposed on the western edge of the Penin-

Toro Peak from Collins Valley

sular Ranges province, and poking up in places through the coastal plain, is a belt of distinctly older metavolcanic rocks. This is a resistant remnant of the lava and ash that spewed out of the island volcanoes 150 million years ago, later to be metamorphosed when the islands collided with the mainland.

In the Coast province we find sedimentary deposits, both marine and nonmarine (river deposits) which were laid down in various periods from about 80 to 2 million years ago. The marine sediments are typically seen near the coast, the nonmarine sediments farther inland. In many locales you'll see exposures of sandstone, shale, and conglomerate. The rhyolitic cobbles so widely seen today on the beaches and in thick conglomerate beds through much of metropolitan San Diego were not formed where they lie today. They are the water-worn pieces of volcanic rock delivered by the aforementioned large river.

The Coast province deposits are relatively soft and easily eroded. They exhibit a record of changing sea levels and gradual uplift in the form of wave-cut terraces. The terraces themselves are in many places deeply cut by drainage channels—the coastal canyons—which are fairly recent features.

The Salton Trough, an extension of the Gulf of California, lies buried in sediments as much as four miles thick, deposited in relatively recent times, the last few million years. These sediments have been carved into spectacular forms in the badland areas of the Anza-Borrego Desert.

The geologic map shows two other less common general rock types: some volcanic rock exposures in the southeast corner of the county, and several much more widespread bands of metamorphosed sedimentary rocks. The volcanic rocks are about 20 million years in age, and mark the only period of isolated volcanic activity in the county since the great batholith cooled. The metamorphosed sedimentary rocks, which may be 100 to 300 million years old, are the altered remnants of mud, lime and sand layers deposited on a sea floor. This category includes the Julian schist, the presence of which is associated with pockets of ore con-

taining gold and other valuable minerals.

Both the geologic map and the geologic profile show several sympathetic (splinter) faults associated with the San Andreas Fault. Because of these, the land surface of the county does not move as a solid unit toward the northwest, but rather creeps differentially. Vertical and horizontal movements along these faults have fractured the Peninsular Ranges province into a series of separate blocks (mountain ranges), most of them tilted in the characteristic west-dipping fashion.

More finely detailed and colorful geologic maps can give a more vivid picture of San Diego County's geological complexities. Refer to Appendix 2 for these and other sources of information about the county's fascinating geology.

Native Gardens

About 2000 species of wild plants grow within the boundaries of San Diego County. As a single county, ours is thought to have the greatest amount of diversity of any county in the continental United States. About 10 percent of the 2000 are non-native (naturalized) plants from other places around the country and around the world.

There are two reasons for this plethora of plants. One reason has to do with physical factors: topography, geology, soils, and climate. The sheer complexity of the interrelationships among these factors has produced a wide range of possible physical habitats.

The second reason is San Diego County's strategic location between two groups of flora: a southern group represented by drought-tolerant plants characteristic of Baja California, and a northern group represented by moisture-loving plants typical of the Sierra Nevada and California's north coastal ranges. As the climate has changed, seesawing from cool and wet to warm and dry over the past million years or so, species from both groups have invaded the county. Once established, many of these species have remained in protected niches even as the climate turned unfavorable for them. Some have survived unchanged over the ages; others have evolved into unique forms. Many are present only in very specific habitats within the county.

Most of San Diego County's natural vegetation can be categorized into six general groupings, which botanists often call plant communities or plant associations. In a broader sense, these are biological communities, which include animals as well as plants. These plant communities are briefly described below in the order you would encounter them if you were to drive east from the coast, over the crest of the highest mountains, and into the desert.

The *sage-scrub* (or coastal-sage-scrub) community lies mostly below 1500 feet elevation, and extends east from the coastline to the foothills and lower slopes of the mountains. The more-open sage-scrub community intermixes readily with the dense chaparral community, especially on north slopes and in canyons along the coastal strip. The dominant species are small shrubs, typically California sagebrush, white sage, black sage, and California buckwheat. Two larger shrubs often present are laurel sumac and lemonade berry, which like poison oak are members of the sumac family. Interspersed among the somewhat loosely distributed shrubs are a variety of grasses and wildflowers. Although still relatively common, the sage-scrub community in San Diego County is fast being displaced by housing tracts and industrial parks.

The *chaparral* community is commonly found between 1000 and 4500 feet elevation on the west slopes of the mountains, and between 4000 and 5000 feet on some of the east slopes. It also occurs in a few areas along the coast. Large areas of San Diego County are still carpeted by almost unbroken stretches of chaparral. The dominant species are chamise, ribbonwood, manzanita, scrub oak, and various forms of ceanothus ("wild lilac"). These species are tough, intricately branched shrubs with deep root systems that help the plants survive during the long, hot summers. Chaparral is sometimes referred to as an "elfin forest"—a literal description of a mature stand. Without the benefit of a trail, travel through mature chaparral, which is typically 5 to 15 feet high, is almost impossible.

The *southern oak woodland* community is found in scattered locations throughout San Diego County in areas from the foothills to just below the crests of the mountains. The indicator species are broadleaf trees, such as black oaks and various live oaks. These are intermixed with abundant grasses and sometimes a sparse growth of chaparral shrubs. The southern oak woodland is very "park-like" in appearance, especially in the spring with the new growths of grass and wildflowers.

The *coniferous forest* (or ponderosa-pine forest) community exists only at the highest elevations of San Diego County—generally above 4500 feet. The common coniferous trees include the ponderosa, Jeffrey, Coulter and sugar pines; white fir; incense-cedar; and big-cone Douglas-fir. These are often intermixed with live and black oaks, various chaparral shrubs, grasses and wildflowers. This is, of course, the type of plant community most people associate with "the mountains."

The *pinyon-juniper* woodland community covers parts of the east-facing slopes of the county's higher ranges, such as the Laguna Mountains. It also exists in the form of botanical "islands" on the crests of the arid Vallecito Mountains and the Santa Rosa Mountains (within San Diego County). The two principal species are rather stunted conifers, the one-leaved pinyon pine and the California juniper. Other plants belonging to this community have rather small, leathery or rigid leaves—a water-conservation feature which is so necessary in the high desert.

The *desert shrub* (or creosote-bush scrub) community covers the desert floor and extends up the east slopes of the mountains to about 2000 feet in elevation. The indicator plant is the creosote bush, a plant not only abundant in our local Colorado Desert (a subdivision of the Sonoran Desert), but throughout the entire Sonoran and Mojave deserts. Ocotillo, many kinds of cacti, and a wide variety of drought-tolerant shrubs are also common. Displays of annual and ephemeral wildflowers are unpredictable but often spectacular within the desert shrub community.

Aside from the six fairly widespread communities above, there are others that are much

Jeffrey pine forest in Laguna Mountains

more restricted in area: *rocky shore, coastal strand, coastal salt marsh, freshwater marsh, riparian woodland, mountain meadow, desert wash,* and *alkali sink.*

Of these plant communities, the riparian (streamside) woodland, covering less than one-fifth of one percent of San Diego County's land area, is considered the most valuable. Not only is this kind of environment essential for the continued survival of many kinds of birds and animals, it is also very appealing to the senses. Live oaks, sycamores and cottonwoods, and a screen of water-hugging willows are the hallmarks of the riparian woodland. The riparian woodland all over California has steadily declined as a result of urbanization and agricultural development, and the attendant exploitation of water resources.

San Diego County has more than its share of rare, endangered, unique, or otherwise unusual

Desert sunflowers in Borrego Valley

species of vegetation. Best known are the Torrey pine, the California fan palm, and two kinds of cypress. Torrey pines are found in picturesque groves on the eroded bluffs overlooking the Pacific Ocean at Torrey Pines State Reserve, near Del Mar. These trees were widespread at one time, but an increase in aridity has caused their natural range to retreat to just this site and one other, the east end of Santa Rosa Island, which lies off the coast of Santa Barbara. Fog drip from the Torrey pine's long needles apparently provides the extra moisture it needs for its survival.

California fan palms exist in a similarly narrow niche. According to one view, they are relicts from a time when today's desert was semitropical. Increasing aridity forced them to retreat to canyons and arroyos that have an uninterrupted supply of surface or subsurface water. Their range extends across the Colorado Desert (which includes the Anza-Borrego Desert) into the southern reaches of the Mojave Desert and into Baja California.

The cypresses also have retreated to "arboreal islands." The rare Cuyamaca cypress now is restricted to a small area of chaparral-covered slopes about one mile south of Cuyamaca Peak, while the range of the more widely distributed Tecate cypress includes three San Diego County locations (Otay Mountain, Tecate Peak-Potrero Creek, and Guatay Mountain), one Orange County location, and several more in Baja California.

Spring is the best time to appreciate the cornucopia of San Diego County's native plants. Many of the showiest species, spring wildflowers, for example, burgeon at this time, and other plants show fresh new growth. Peak periods for wildflowers vary according to elevation. The low desert blooms most profusely during a rather short period centered on late March; coastal areas and foothills are usually best in April; and the high mountains are best in late April and May. Irregular summer desert thunderstorms occasionally give rise to a second period of blooming during fall in the desert and along the eastern margins of the mountains.

For more information about the wildflowers, shrubs, trees and other flora of San Diego County, see Appendix 2, Recommended Reading.

Creatures Great and Small

One's first sighting of a mountain lion, a bighorn sheep, a bald eagle, or any other seldom-seen form of wildlife is always a memorable experience. Because of the diversity and the generally broad extent of its habitats, San Diego County plays host to a great variety of indigenous creatures, including a number of rare or endangered species. People willing to stretch their legs a bit and spend some time in the areas favored by wild animals will eventually be rewarded by some kind of close visual contact.

The most numerous large creature in the county is the mule deer, with a population of several thousand. Unfortunately, the number of deer within the county has declined seriously in the past few decades, a circumstance widely blamed on loss of habitat and excessive hunting. The deer prefer areas of mixed forest and scattered chaparral, especially at the highest elevations in the county, but they can also be seen in the coastal canyons and on desert-facing slopes with moderate growths of vegetation. In places like Cuyamaca Rancho State Park, where the deer are protected from hunting, it is uncommon not to see any while out hiking the trails.

The mountain lion, once hunted to near extinction in California, has made a comeback as a protected species. Perhaps more than a hundred mountain lions roam the county today. They inhabit virtually every natural habitat, and typically travel over a large range (up to 100 square miles). Mountain lions are seldom observed, but because of their wide-ranging travels, tracks and other signs of the mountain lion are frequently seen. Conflicts between mountain lions and humans are increasing: A mountain lion had to be destroyed in Oceanside after wandering through neighborhoods there in 1992. In 1986 there were two incidents of mountain lions attacking small children in southern Orange County.

The county's most interesting large mammal

is the endangered peninsular (desert) bighorn sheep. Some 400 of these agile animals maintain a tenuous existence on the steep slopes and rocky crags of the Anza-Borrego Desert. Unlike mule deer, the bighorn sheep prefer open, rugged terrain, on which they are capable of escaping from almost any predator. They are also superbly adapted to surviving on meager supplies of water and coarse desert vegetation. Bighorn sheep tend to keep a safe distance from human activity, but sometimes seem possessed of a kind of curiosity about humans. Once accustomed to a hiker's presence, a sheep may approach quite closely and make a surprise "appearance." After three or four seconds of eye contact, the animal turns and disappears.

The county's mammals also include the coyote, which has adapted to a broad range of habitats, including the margins of suburbia; the bobcat, a creature sometimes mistaken for a mountain lion, but smaller and more common; the gray fox of mountain habitats and the kit fox of desert habitats; the opossum; the skunk; the raccoon; and various rabbits, squirrels, woodrats and mice.

Among the commonly seen reptiles are rattlesnakes, which we will discuss in the next section.

The variety of bird life in San Diego County is outstanding, not only because of the great diversity of habitats, but also because the county lies along the Pacific Flyway route of spring-fall bird migration and serves as an important wintering area for waterfowl. The undeveloped areas of the county support several species of rare or endangered birds, including the southern bald eagle, the peregrine falcon, the lightfooted clapper rail, the California least tern and the least Bell's vireo. In the years to come, the diminutive California gnatcatcher could play a pivotal role in the politics of urban development in San Diego County. If it is listed by the federal government as an endangered species, large tracts of sage-scrub habitat, on which the gnatcatcher depends, would become unavailable for development.

Mule deer, Cuyamaca Mountains

Health, Safety, And Courtesy

Good preparation is always important for any kind of recreational pursuit. Hiking the San Diego backcountry is no exception. Although most of the county's natural environments are seldom hostile or dangerous to life and limb, there are some pitfalls to be aware of.

Preparation and Equipment

An obvious safety requirement is being in good health. Some degree of physical conditioning is always desirable, even for the trips in this book designated as easy or moderate (rated * and ** in difficulty). The more challenging trips (rated ***, **** or *****) require increasing amounts of stamina and technical expertise. Running, bicycling, swimming, aerobic dancing, or any similar exercise that develops both the leg muscles and the aerobic capacity of the whole body are recommended as preparatory exercise.

For long trips over rough, cross-country terrain (there are several of these in this book) there is no really adequate way to prepare other than practicing the activity itself. Start with easy- or moderate-length cross-country trips first to accustom the leg muscles to the peculiar stresses involved in "boulder-hopping" or "non-technical climbing" (scrambling over steep terrain), and to acquire a good sense of balance. Sturdy hiking boots are recommended for such travel.

Since all hiking in San Diego County is below about 6500 feet elevation, serious health complications due to higher altitude are rare. Sea-level dwellers, of course, may find themselves breathing faster and tiring a little sooner.

Your choice of equipment and supplies on the longer hikes in this book can be critically important. The essentials you should carry with you at all times in the backcountry are the things that would allow you to survive, in a reasonably comfortable manner, one or two unscheduled nights out. It's important to note that no one ever plans these nights! No one plans to get lost, injured, stuck, or pinned down by the weather. Always do a "what if" analysis for a worst-case scenario, and plan accordingly. These essential items are your safety net; keep them with you on day hikes, and take them with you in a small day pack if you leave your backpack and camping equipment behind at a campsite.

Chief among the essential items is **warm clothing**. Inland San Diego County is characterized by wide swings in day and night temperatures. In mountain valleys susceptible to cold-air drainage, for example, a midday temperature in the 70s or 80s is often followed by a subfreezing night. Carry light, inner layers of clothing consisting of polypropylene or wool (best for cool or cold weather), or cotton (adequate for warm or hot weather, but very poor for cold and damp weather). Include a thicker insulating layer of "pile" (polyester fiberpile), wool, or down to put on whenever needed, especially when you are not moving around and generating heat. Add to this a cap, gloves, and a waterproof or water-resistant shell (a large trash bag will do in a pinch) and you'll be quite prepared for all but the most severe weather experienced in San Diego County.

In hot, sunny weather, sun-shielding clothing may be another "essential." This would normally include a sun hat and a light-colored, long-sleeve top.

Water, and to a lesser extent **food**, are next in importance. If water isn't immediately available, carry a generous supply. In the arid San

Diego backcountry, you'll need to drink up to a gallon of water during a full day's hike in 70° or 80° temperatures; and up to two or three gallons per day in summer desert conditions (hiking in these latter conditions is not recommended!) Food is needed to stave off hunger and keep energy stores up, but it is not as essential as water in a survival situation.

Down the list further, but still "essential," are a **map** and **compass**, **flashlight**, **fire-starting devices** (examples: waterproof matches or lighter, and candle), and **first-aid kit**.

Items not always essential, but potentially very useful and convenient, are sunglasses, pocket knife, whistle (or other signalling device), sunscreen, and toilet paper.

The essential items mentioned above should be carried by every member of a hiking party, because individuals or splinter groups may end up separating from the party for one reason or another. If you plan to hike solo in the back-country, being well-equipped is very important. If you hike alone, be sure to check in with a park ranger or leave your itinerary with a responsible person. In that way, if you do get stuck, help will probably come to the right place—eventually.

Taking children on hiking outings involves a special kind of responsibility. San Diego-based "Project Hug-a-Tree" (see Appendix 4) can provide you with information about training and outfitting a child to cope with the possibility of getting lost in the wilderness.

Special Hazards

Other than getting lost or pinned down by a rare sudden storm, the five most common hazards found in the San Diego backcountry are loose or slick rocks and/or steep terrain, spiny plants, rattlesnakes, ticks, and poison oak. Cross-country hiking in the desert, and to a lesser extent in the mountains and the foothills, frequently involves travel over exposed rock on steep slopes. The erosive forces of flowing water, the freezing and melting of ice, and even brush fires tend to fracture the rock into chunks anywhere in size from house-size to small pebbles. Middle-sized boulders, often poorly

anchored, are probably the most dangerous. Before you step on a boulder or pull on it with your hands, try to judge its stability. Be very cautious, too, of water-worn slabs of rock near waterfalls and along canyon bottoms—especially if the rock is wet. A good many of the injuries suffered by hikers in San Diego County have been caused by slips and falls on slick rock surfaces.

Smaller pebbles that act like ball bearings underfoot are often a problem on desert slopes, especially where cacti and the desert agave grow. The agave plant (also known as century plant) consists of a rosette of fleshy leaves, each tipped with a rigid thorn containing a mild toxin. A headlong fall into either an agave or one of the more vicious kinds of cacti could easily make you swear off desert travel permanently. It's best to give these devilish plants as wide a berth as possible.

Most desert hikers will sooner or later suffer punctures by thorns or spines. This is most likely to happen during close encounters with the cholla ("jumping") cactus, whose spine clusters readily break off and attach firmly to your skin, clothes or boots. A comb can be used to gently pull away the spine clusters, and tweezers or lightweight pliers can be used to remove any individual embedded spines.

Rattlesnakes are common in all parts of San Diego County. Seldom seen in either cold or very hot weather, they favor temperatures in the 75-90° range—spring and fall in the desert and coastal areas, and summer in the mountains. Most rattlesnakes are as interested in avoiding contact with you as you are with them. Watch carefully where you put your feet, and especial-ly your hands, during the warmer months. In brushy or rocky areas where sight distance is short, try to make your presence known from afar. Tread with heavy footfalls, or use a stick to bang against rocks or bushes. Rattlesnakes will pick up the vibrations through their skin and will usually buzz (unmistakably) before you get too close for comfort. Most bad encounters be-tween rattlesnakes and hikers occur in April and May, when snakes are irritable and hungry after a long hibernation period.

Ticks can sometimes be the scourge of over-

Diamondback rattlesnake

scrub oaks. Occasionally it is seen along well-used trails. Learn to recognize its distinctive three-leaved structure, and avoid touching it with skin or clothing. Since poison oak loses its leaves during the winter (usually January through March in San Diego County), but still retains some of the toxic oil in its stems, it can be extra hazardous at that time because it is harder to identify and avoid.

Some boulder-hopping trips in this book are routed directly down streamcourses where poison oak thickets are impossible to avoid. On these trips, you might consider taking along small garden clippers and gloves. Seldom is any major pruning necessary; just a snip here and there. Thick pants (jeans) and a long-sleeve shirt will serve as a fair barrier against the toxic oil of the poison-oak plant. Do, of course, remove these clothes as soon as the hike is over, and make sure they are washed carefully afterward.

Here are a few more safety tips:

Most free-flowing water in San Diego should be regarded as unsafe for drinking without purification. This excludes, of course, developed water sources in state and county parks. Chemical (iodine or chlorine) treatment

Poison-oak leaves

grown trails in the sage-scrub and chaparral country, particularly during the first warm spells of the year, when they climb to the tips of shrub branches and lie in wait for warm-blooded hosts. If you can't avoid brushing against vegetation along the trail, be sure to check yourself for ticks frequently. Upon finding a host, a tick will usually crawl upward in search of a protected spot, where it will try to attach itself. If you can be aware of the slightest irritation on your body, you'll usually intercept ticks long before they attempt to bite. Ticks would be of relatively minor concern here, except that tick-borne Lyme disease, which can have serious health effects, has now spread to San Diego County.

Poison oak grows profusely along many of the county's canyons below 5000 feet. It is often found on stream banks in the form of a bush or vine, and prefers the semi-shade of live and

and filtering are the most convenient purification methods, but secondary in effectiveness to boiling. A bigger problem is the availability of any water at all. Most watercourses and many springs in San Diego County are intermittent. Even some streams shown as "permanent" on topographic maps occasionally dry up.

Deer-hunting season in San Diego County usually runs through the month of October. Although conflicts between hunters and hikers are rare, you may want to confine your mid-autumn explorations to state and county parks, and wilderness areas where hunting is not permitted.

There is always some risk in leaving a vehicle unattended at a trailhead. It may be worthwhile to disable your car's ignition or attach an anti-theft device to your steering wheel. Never leave valuable property in an automobile, so as to be an invitation for a break-in. Report all theft and vandalism of personal property to the county sheriff, and report vandalism of public property to the appropriate park or forest agency.

Trail Courtesy

Whenever you travel the backcountry, you take on a burden of responsibility keeping the wilderness as you found it. Aside from common-sense prohibitions against littering, vandalism, and inappropriate campfires, there are some less obvious guidelines every hiker should be aware of. We'll mention a few:

Never cut trail switchbacks. This practice breaks down the trail tread and hastens erosion. Try to improve designated trails by removing branches, rocks, or other debris; but don't do this for unofficial trails or cross-country routes. Springtime growth can quite rapidly obscure pathways in the chaparral country, and funding for trail maintenance is often scarce, so try to do your part by joining a volunteer trail crew or by performing your own small maintenance tasks while walking the trails. Report any damage to trails or other facilities to the appropriate ranger office.

When off trail, resist the temptation to build cairns or ducks (rock piles) as route markers, except when absolutely necessary for route-finding. It is disappointing to follow a remote canyon or ridge, or a well-beaten trail, mindlessly littered with unnecessary markers. On the other hand, don't knock over cairns and ducks unless they are obviously recent and superfluous constructions. Many of the ancient Indian and early settlers' trails are marked by cairns and ducks of possible archaeological interest.

Be a "no trace" camper. Camp well away from streams and springs (there are a variety of reasons for this), and leave your campsite as you found it—or leave it in an even more natural condition. Because of the danger of wildfire, campfires are seldom allowed outside of developed campgrounds in San Diego County. Camping regulations vary considerably among the various parks and recreation lands, so be sure that you are aware of, and observe, the appropriate regulations. Look under "Agency" in the capsulized summary for each hike described in this book to find the appropriate park or agency. Phone numbers for these agencies are given in Appendix 4.

All animals, plants and minerals are fully protected in state and county parks. National forest and BLM regulations are a little more relaxed: hunting of certain animals and birds is permitted in season, for example. Rock collecting is allowed on most BLM lands.

Collecting archaeological artifacts anywhere is both ethically inappropriate and expressly forbidden by federal antiquities laws. Antiquities can include objects of rather recent origin, too, such as mining debris. Remember, never collect anything unless you've received permission from the governing agency.

It is impractical to review here all the specific rules associated with the use of the various public lands in San Diego County. You, as a visitor, are responsible for knowing them, however.

Using This Book

Whether you wish to use this book as a reference tool or as a guide to be read cover to cover, do take the time to carefully read this section. Herein we explain the meaning of the special symbols and other bits of capsulized information which appear before each trip description, and describe the way in which trips are grouped together geographically.

One way to expedite the process of finding a suitable trip, especially if you're unfamiliar with hiking opportunities in San Diego County, is to turn to Appendix 1, "Best Hikes." This is a cross-reference of several dozen highly recommended hikes in this book.

Each of the 192 hiking trips belongs to one of 35 "areas." Each area has its own introductory text and map. The areas are coded according to "regions" within San Diego County. Areas B-l, B-2, B-3, etc., are in the Beaches and Bays region of the county. Areas C-l, C-2, etc., are in the Coastal Strip and Foothills region. Letter M in the area designation refers to The Mountains region, and letter D refers to The Desert region. The index map of the whole county on pages xii, xiii shows the coverage of each area map, and the Table of Contents lists the page numbers for each region, area, and trip.

The introductory text for each area includes any general information about the area's history, geology, plants and wildlife not included in the trip descriptions. Important information about possible restrictions or special requirements (wilderness permits, for example) may appear there too, so you should review this material before embarking on a hike within a particular area.

The beginning of each area section contains an area map. On most of these maps, more than one hiking route (trip) is plotted, the numbers in the squares corresponding to trip numbers in the text. These boxed numbers refer to the start/end points of out-and-back and loop trips. The point-to-point trips have two boxed numbers indicating separate start and end points. For some hikes, the corresponding area map alone is complete enough and fully adequate for navigation; for other hikes, more detailed topographical or other maps are listed before each trip description. A legend for the area maps appears on page 20.

The following is an explanation of the small symbols and capsulized information appearing at the beginning of each trip description. If you're simply browsing through this book, these summaries alone can be used as a tool to eliminate from consideration hikes that are either too difficult, or perhaps too trivial, for your abilities.

Symbols:

 Easy Terrain: roads, trails and easy cross-country hiking

 Moderate Terrain: cross-country boulder-hopping and easy scrambling

 Difficult Terrain: nontechnical climbing required (WARNING: THESE TRIPS SHOULD BE ATTEMPTED ONLY BY SUITABLY EQUIPPED, EXPERIENCED HIKERS ADEPT AT TRAVELING OVER STEEP OR ROCKY TERRAIN REQUIRING THE USE OF THE HANDS AS WELL AS THE FEET.)

Only *one* of these three symbols appears for a given trip, indicating the general character of the terrain encountered. A trip almost entirely on roads and trails, but including a short section of boulder-hopping or perhaps nontechnical climbing, for example, will be rated as easy terrain, and the difficulties will be duly noted in the text. As the symbols suggest, light footwear (running shoes) is appropriate for easy terrain, while sturdy hiking boots are recommended for more difficult terrain.

Nontechnical climbing includes everything up to and including Class 3 on the rock-climber's scale. While ropes and climbing hardware are not normally required, a hiker should have a good sense of balance, and enough experience to recognize dangerous moves and situations. The safety and stability of heavy hiking boots are especially recommended for this kind of trip. Hazards may include loose or slippery rocks and rattlesnakes (don't put your hands in places you can't see clearly).

 Bushwhacking: cross-country travel through dense brush. This symbol is included for trips requiring a substantial amount of off-trail "bushwhacking." Wear long pants and be especially alert for ticks and rattlesnakes.

Only one of these two symbols appears:

 Marked Trails/Obvious Routes

 Navigation by Map and Compass Required (WARNING: THESE TRIPS SHOULD BE ATTEMPTED ONLY BY HIKERS SKILLED IN NAVIGATION TECHNIQUES.)

Unambiguous cross-country routes—up a canyon, for example, are included in the first category. The hiker, of course, should never be without a map, even if there are marked trails or the route seems obvious.

 Point-to-Point Route

 Out-and-Back Route

 Loop Route

Only one of these three symbols appears, reflecting the trip as described. There is some flexibility, of course, in the way in which a hiker can actually follow the trip.

 Suitable for Backpacking

Many of the trips in this book are not. Some parks and trails are closed at night, others allow night hiking but prohibit camping. Sometimes, overnight camping is permitted at some spot off the route but nearby.

 Best for Kids

These trips are especially recommended for inquisitive children. They were chosen on the basis of their safety and ease of travel (at the time they were researched by the author), and their potential for entertaining the whole family.

Capsulized Summaries:

Distance: An estimate of total distance is given. Out-and-back trips show the sum of the distances of the out and back segments.

Total Elevation Gain/Loss: These are estimates of the sum of all the vertical gain segments and the sum of all the vertical loss segments along the total length of the route (both ways for out-and-back trips).

Hiking Time: This figure is for the average hiker, and includes only the time spent in motion. It does not include time spent for rest stops, lunch, etc. Fast walkers can complete the routes in perhaps 30% less time, and slower hikers may take 50% longer. We assume the hiker is traveling with a light day pack. (IMPORTANT NOTE: Several users of the first edition of this book got into trouble by misinterpreting this specification. To save future hikers from the grief or embarrassment of late arrival, let me emphasize that "hiking time" stated in this book is for time-in-motion only. Also, hikers carrying heavy packs could easily take twice as long if they are traveling off-trail through difficult terrain. Remember, too, that the progress made by a group as a whole is limited by pace of the slowest member or members. Hiking time on routes through canyons and along streams is very difficult to quantify. Delays can occur because of such factors as rain, snow and high water.)

Optional/Recommended/Required Map(s): If no recommended or required map is given, then either the appropriate area map in this book or the optional map stated will suffice. Persons familiar with the terrain in a particular trip area may be able to do without a recommended map, as long as some other map is substituted. A required map is one that is essential for the successful navigation of a particular trip route. Most maps, whether optional, recommended or required, are U.S. Geological Survey 7.5-minute series topographic maps. These are the most complete, accurate, and up-to-date maps of the physical features of San Diego County. In some cases, the older 15-minute series maps may be substituted, but at a sacrifice in scale and detail. Even the most up-to-date topo maps (usually revised by aerial survey) omit some well-established trails and other features, so it is important to compare them with the area maps in this book. For a list of local sources of maps, see Appendix 4.

Best Times: Because of the extreme heat, the longer desert trips in this book should generally be avoided during any period except the one recommended here. Trips elsewhere in San Diego County are usually safe enough at other than "Best" times, but usually less rewarding.

Agency: These code letters refer to the agency, or office, that has jurisdiction or management over the area being hiked (for example, CNF/DD means Cleveland National Forest, Descanso District). You can contact the agency for more information. Full names, addresses, and phone numbers are listed in Appendix 4.

Difficulty: The author's subjective, overall rating takes into account the length of the trip and the nature of the terrain. The following are general definitions of the five categories:

*   Easy. Suitable for every member of the family.

**   Moderate. Suitable for all physically fit people.

***   Moderately Strenuous. Long length, substantial elevation gain, and/or difficult terrain. Recommended for experienced hikers only.

****   Strenuous. Full day's hike (or backpack trip) over a long and/or challenging route. Suitable only for experienced hikers in excellent physical condition.

*****   Very Strenuous. Long and rugged route in extremely remote area. Usually requires two days. Suitable only for experienced hikers/climbers in top physical condition.

Each higher level represents more or less a doubling of the difficulty. On average, ** trips are twice as hard as * trips, *** trips are twice as hard as ** trips, and so on.

A final note:

In the trip descriptions, mileages along the highways (example: "mile 17.4") are keyed to the mile markers posted at frequent intervals along San Diego County's state and county highways. The mileage figures are sometimes stenciled on the roadside reflectors. In the descriptions of the hikes themselves, a phrase like "at 5.8 miles" means 5.8 miles from the beginning of the hike, not from the last intersection or point of interest.

MAP LEGEND

～～～	Freeway	5	Start/end point with trip number
～～	State highway		
～	Secondary road	6533 ▲	Peak (elevation in feet)
～	Minor paved road	■	Point of interest
=======	Unpaved road		
--------	Foot trail / abandoned road	⚲	Ranger station / fire station
··········	Cross-country route	Λ	Campground
======⟍	Locked gate: no trespassing		
======⟍	Gate: hikers OK	⊼	Picnic area
～～	Drainage (canyon, creek)	⚒	Mine
— — — —	County line		
————————	Wilderness boundary	⬯	Lake / reservoir

Eroded granite near Mt. Gower

Torrey Pines Beach

BEACHES AND BAYS

Area B-1: North County Coast

North County's almost unbroken line of beaches faces the Pacific along a gentle arc about 20 miles long. Just behind this is a string of cities and beach communities—Oceanside, Carlsbad, Leucadia, Encinitas, Cardiff, Solana Beach, and Del Mar. Compared to the more densely crowded coastal areas from La Jolla south, life is a bit slower in these communities. The locals take their beach-going and ocean-watching seriously. Some have chosen to live, at some peril, on the very brink of the cliffs overlooking the Pacific.

The popular term "North County" really refers to a middle segment of San Diego County's long coastal plain, not the northernmost part containing Camp Pendleton. Many of the beaches along the North County coast are included in state or county parks. Access to all is by way of the old coast highway (commonly known as Old Highway 101) wherever it runs next to the sand, and elsewhere by stairways that descend the bluffs from back streets.

Unfortunately for beach-goers, hikers, and coastal residents alike, the North County coastline is subject to some of the most rapid erosion anywhere along the California coast. Supplies of sand from formerly free-flowing streams are now blocked by dams. A jetty built to protect an artificial harbor north of Oceanside retards the natural flow of beach sand southward along the coast. Also, powerful winter storms in past years have moved large amounts of sand to offshore sandbars, while the gentle summer waves return only a part of it to the shore. Since

the beaches have shrunk in width, the bluffs right behind some of the beaches sometimes get the full brunt of wave action during high tides and storms. Housing development on top of the bluffs has disturbed the normal drainage patterns and seems to be contributing to a faster rate of erosion.

Area B-1: North County Coast

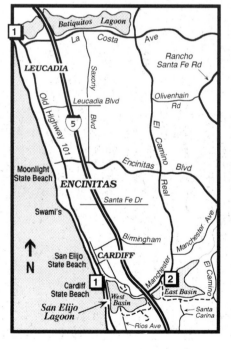

Whether the destiny of the North County coastline is to become a series of broken cliffs and pocket beaches or a somewhat stable, continuous strand of sand is not known. For the moment, at any rate, hikers can still travel many miles—at low tide—without donning wet suits and fins.

Some of North County's coastal lagoons, or estuaries, have fared better than the coastline, even though urban development continues at a rapid rate around them. San Elijo Lagoon, with its new ecological reserve and network of informal trails, stands out as the best lagoon for exploring on foot.

Trip 1: South Carlsbad to Cardiff

	Distance	5.5 miles
	Hiking Time	3 hours
	Optional Map	USGS 7.5-min *Encinitas*; or any street map
	Best Times	All year
	Agency	CP/SDC
	Difficulty	**

The finest beaches, some of the nicest surf, and the most instructive vistas along the North County coastline are seen on this beach walk. Your visit should coincide with low tide—or at least an ebb tide. During high tide, passage is restricted in at least two places by the wash of the breakers.

If you plan to walk north to south, leave one car in or near the parking area at Cardiff State Beach (opposite San Elijo Lagoon), and take the other to the south end of South Carlsbad State Beach (0.1 mile north of La Costa Avenue), where roadside parking is available.

Start by walking south along the sandy or cobbled shore. Steep bluffs rise on the left. The bulk of these bluffs is a 50-million-year-old sandstone derived from lagoon and sandbar deposits. As the sandstone erodes away, cobbles embedded in it are released and then deposited at the tide line by wave action. Most of the cobbles on this beach are metavolcanic rocks from distant sources, but some are granitic rocks apparently transported from the local Peninsular Ranges. All show the effects of prolonged tumbling and polishing.

In the next two miles you'll see many graphic illustrations of the fragility of the coastal cliffs. In winter, storm waves crash directly against the base of the cliffs, and tug at the lower underpinnings of the many private stairways that zigzag down to the beach. Some of these stairways have elaborate counterbalance

mechanisms to raise and lower them to beach level. The cliffs are fluted with both old and fairly recent landslides, including one large semicircular feature perhaps 40 years old, now almost completely revegetated.

Blufftop property owners have used every strategy and tool imaginable to stabilize the cliff faces, including elaborate retaining walls and terraces, and flexible pipes to channel runoff. Some cliff faces are coated with gunite or other impervious materials, and others wear a coat of groundcover vegetation that hopefully helps hold things together. Overwatering is a constant problem: excess irrigation water constantly percolates into the porous sandstone, and oozes from the cliffs at beach level, weakening them.

At 2.8 miles from the starting point, the cliffs draw back and the sand widens. This is Moonlight Beach, a popular sunbathing beach complete with the usual amenities (water, restrooms and a snack bar).

As you continue south, the strip of sand narrows again and you pass the "tightest" spot along this hike, an area just below the ornate Self Realization Fellowship, known as "Swami's." During a winter storm in 1941, a section of cliff collapsed here, taking with it one of the temples above. The ocean bottom off Swami's gives rise to long combers that are renowned among local surfers.

South of Swami's the strip of sand widens. This is Sea Cliff County Park, accessible from above by a long, wooden stairway. The beach remains fairly wide as you continue past the San Elijo State Beach park, with its popular campground on the low bluffs. When these bluffs dwindle to nothing and you cross the inlet to San Elijo Lagoon, the parking area for Cardiff State Beach lies just beyond.

Trip 2: San Elijo Lagoon

	Distance	1 to 3 miles out-and-back
	Optional Map	USGS 7.5-min *Encinitas*
	Best Times	All year
	Agency	SEL
	Difficulty	*

A great blue heron ambles on stilt-legs across the reed-fringed shallows, stabbing occasionally at subsurface morsels of food. Nearby, a willowy egret glides in for a perfect landing, scattering concentric ripples across the surface of the lagoon. Both birds seem oblivious to binocular-toting humans, who spy on them from a hillside a comfortable distance away.

A scene like this is repeated almost daily at San Elijo Lagoon, one of North County's most attractive coastal estuaries. Bisected by Interstate 5 and rimmed by expanding suburban development, the area has become the focus of considerable conservation effort. Local citizen groups, the San Diego County parks department, and California's Department of Fish and Game have teamed up to restore this long-neglected and formerly unappreciated resource.

West of I-5, high tides wash over mud flats and mats of salt-tolerant vegetation. Here, a dozen kinds of shorebirds can be seen on a typical day. A short trail near the site of the yet-to-be-built Nature Center off Manchester Avenue 0.5 mile west of I-5 gives direct access to the water.

From Old Highway 101, or from the north terminus of Rios Avenue in Solana Beach, you can gain access to other trails along the lagoon's beautiful south shore. These paths meander through coastal sage-scrub vegetation and copses of eucalyptus and other nonnative trees. Eroded sandstone bluffs half-hidden behind a screen of vegetation provide an impressive backdrop for the placid lagoon. Don't miss the spur trail leading south into secluded Holmwood Canyon. An abandoned apricot orchard lies tucked away halfway up the canyon's broad floor.

On the east side of I-5, runoff from Escondido Creek and La Orilla Creek supports a freshwater marsh—the East Basin. A quick access to that is by way of a flood-control dike just east of I-5. Park on the north side of Manchester Avenue, 0.3 mile east of I-5; cross Manchester (watch for fast traffic around the curves); and squeeze past a gate that keeps vehicles out. Walk past a second gate at the south end of the dike, and take the trail going left (east) toward El Camino Real. Before long the roar of traffic on the freeway fades, meadowlark songs fill the air, and your cares may disappear.

Egret at San Elijo Lagoon

Area B-2: Torrey Pines/La Jolla

Here's the San Diego coastline at its unspoiled best, with clean beaches, dramatic cliffs, and an unlikely forest of rare trees. Walking the wild stretch of beach from Del Mar to La Jolla Shores is more akin to adventuring than simply beachcombing. Exploring the caves at La Jolla Cove or looking out from the bluffs at Torrey Pines State Reserve is a sure way to forget that just inland lies the sixth largest city in America.

Try to avoid this area during summer afternoons, when tourists clog the beaches and coastal roads. Avoid by all means the traffic gridlock during weekday afternoon rush hour in the area between La Jolla and La Jolla Shores. If it's solitude you're looking for, you'll find it merely by venturing out at unconventional times—like early morning.

Torrey Pines Road, La Jolla Shores Drive, and North Torrey Pines Road are the major streets closest to the coast. Access to the beaches and coastline is frequent along these streets, except where cliffs intervene.

Trip 1: La Jolla Shores to Torrey Pines Beach

	Distance	5 miles
	Hiking Time	2 ½ hours
	Optional Maps	USGS 7.5-min *La Jolla*, *Del Mar*; or a street map
	Best Times	All year
	Agency	CP/SDC
	Difficulty	**

There are only a few places along the Southern California coastline where a person can hike for miles in a single direction and not catch sight of a highway, railroad tracks, powerlines, houses, or other signs of civilization. The Torrey Pines beaches are one such place. Here, for a space of about three miles, sharp cliffs front the shoreline and cut off the sights and sounds of the world beyond.

Plan to do this beach walk at low tide. High tides—especially in winter—could force you to walk on cobbles at the base of the cliffs or oblige you to wade in the surf. Beach sand is often carried away by the scouring action of the winter waves, but is usually replenished by currents as summer approaches.

A good place to start from is Kellogg Park (La Jolla Shores Beach), where free parking is available when you can get it. If you're making this a one-way trip, leave a second car along North Torrey Pines Road, next to Torrey Pines State Beach, or in the adjacent Torrey Pines State Reserve—or have someone drop you off and later pick you up.

Walk north under Scripps Pier and on past the rocky tidepool area. Once beyond the last of the cobbles and wave-rounded boulders, you can slip off your shoes and enjoy the feel of the fine, clean sand underfoot.

Beyond the tide pools, you may notice that some beach-goers have doffed more than just shoes. You're now on Torrey Pines City Beach,

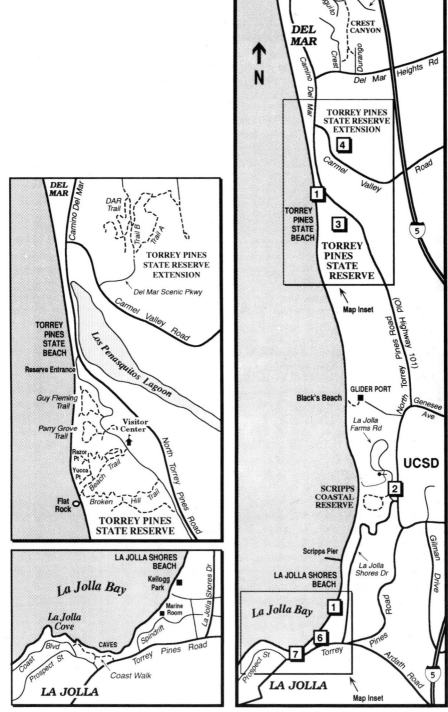

Area B-2: Torrey Pines / La Jolla

also known as Black's Beach, San Diego's un-official nude-bathing spot. The city rescinded a "clothing optional" policy for this beach in the late '70s, but old traditions have never died.

About a half mile past the tidepools, you'll see a paved road (closed to car traffic) going up through a small canyon. This is a good, safe way to reach (or exit from) the beach. There's a limited amount of 2-hour parking at the top along La Jolla Farms Road.

A bit farther ahead, where most Black's Beach users congregate, two precipitous trails ascend about 300 feet to the Glider Port, where hang-gliders launch their craft. Look up to see ant-like beachgoers lugging their gear up or down the zigzagging paths and hang-gliders soaring overhead. The southern of the two trails, recently improved and widened, is the safer one. There's plenty of free, all-day parking at the top if you want to start or end your beach walk there.

Lifeguards patrol some areas of Black's Beach during busy periods, so you can feel fairly safe about jumping into the water, which may reach a temperature warmer than 70° July through September. Elsewhere you swim at your own risk—watch out for rip currents.

At about 4 miles from Kellogg Park, you reach Flat Rock, where a protruding sandstone wall blocks easy passage. Follow the narrow path cut into the wall. From a low shelf on the far side, Beach Trail begins its ascent to Torrey Pines State Reserve's visitor center.

In the fifth and last mile, the narrow beach is squeezed between sculpted sedimentary cliffs on one side and crashing surf on the other. These are the tallest cliffs in western San Diego County. A close look at the faces reveals a slice of geologic history: the greenish siltstone on the bottom, the Del Mar Formation, is older than the buff or rust-colored Torrey Sandstone above it. Higher still is a thin cap of reddish sandstone, not easily seen from the beach—the Linda Vista Formation.

In the end, the beach widens, the cliffs fall back, and you arrive at Torrey Pines State Reserve's entrance along North Torrey Pines Road.

Trip 2: Scripps Coastal Reserve

	Distance	0.6 mile
	Hiking Time	20 minutes
	Optional Maps	USGS 7.5-min *Del Mar*, *La Jolla*
	Best Times	All year
	Difficulty	*

The Scripps Coastal Reserve, managed by the University of California Natural Reserve System, includes a small, undeveloped mesa overlooking the ocean, canyon slopes to either side of the bluff, and an underwater preserve beneath Scripps Pier. No visit to the La Jolla area is complete without a walk on the self-guiding Biodiversity Trail, which takes you along the very brink of the sea cliffs.

You'll find the trailhead on La Jolla Farms Road, 0.1 mile west of La Jolla Shores Drive. There's limited curbside parking nearby. The short trail circles the rim of the mesa, and lets you gaze over miles of spectacular coastline both north and south. So commanding is the view that gun emplacements were set up here during World War II to defend San Diego from enemy attack by sea.

At the trailhead you can borrow a self-guiding booklet that has a lot to say about the Reserve's diverse array of indigenous plants and animals. Over 200 different kinds of plants, nearly 100 birds, and a dozen mammals have been identified within the boundaries of this small reserve.

Trip 3: Torrey Pines State Reserve

	Distance	0.5- to 1-mile loops
	Optional Map	USGS 7.5-min Del Mar
	Best Times	All year
	Agency	TPSR
	Difficulty	* to **

The rare and beautiful Torrey pines atop the coastal bluffs south of Del Mar are as much a symbol of the Golden State as are the famed Monterey cypress trees native to central California's coast. Torrey pines grow naturally in only two places on earth: in and around Torrey Pines State Reserve and on Santa Rosa Island, off Santa Barbara. Of the estimated 6000 or fewer native Torrey pines, more than half grow within the boundaries of the main reserve and its detached extension area.

Torrey Pines State Reserve would be botanically noteworthy even without its pines; more than 330 species of plants have been identified there so far. Sage-scrub, chaparral and salt marsh plant communities are present in various parts of the reserve.

If you're interested in identifying plants and wildflowers typical of the coast and coastal strip, the reserve is simply the best single place to go in San Diego County. Excellent interpretive facilities at the reserve's museum make this an easy task. Besides the exhibits, you can browse through several notebooks full of captioned photographs of common and rare plants within the reserve. You can also visit the native plant gardens surrounding the museum building and at the head of Parry Grove Trail.

If you visit the reserve a number of times during February through June, you'll be able to follow the succession of flowering as the spring season progresses. Wildflower maps, updated monthly, are often available then.

A good network of trails over the eroded bluffs will take you nearly everywhere in the reserve, except into most canyon bottoms. It's important that you stick to these trails and eschew shortcuts and cross-country travel. The thin soils are easily eroded without the protection of healthy vegetation. As you'll plainly see, there are already enough instances of erosion

here, both natural and man-made.

The entrance to the reserve is on North Torrey Pines Road (old Highway 101) at the bottom of the long grade up Torrey Pines Mesa. Past the entrance a paved road goes up to a parking lot adjacent to the reserve office and museum. From there, you can walk to the beginning of any of the trails in 10 minutes or less. If the lot is full, you'll have to leave your car in the lower parking lot down near the entrance, or along the highway shoulder nearby.

The reserve has a carrying capacity of about 400 people. When this level is reached, as on certain weekends, further entry may be restricted.

After a stop at the museum for a bit of

Torrey Pines and Torrey sandstone

educational browsing, you might first explore nearby High Point, where your gaze encompasses the intriguing but currently off-limits section of the reserve known as East Grove. East Grove experienced a wildfire in 1972, and young Torrey pines are establishing a foothold on the bluffs and canyons below.

Next you might head south on the concrete roadbed of the "old" old coast highway (closed to traffic) and pick up the Broken Hill Trail. The two east branches of this trail wind through thick chamise chaparral and connect with a spur trail leading to Broken Hill Overlook. You'll be able to step out (very carefully) onto a precipitous fin of sandstone and peer over to see what, except for a few Torrey pine trees here and there, looks like desert badlands. A third (west) branch of the Broken Hill Trail winds down a slope festooned with wildflowers and joins the Beach Trail at a point just above where the latter drops sharply to the beach.

The popular Beach Trail originates at the parking lot near the museum and intersects with trails to Yucca Point and Razor Point. Fenced viewpoints along both of these trails offer views straight down to the sandy beach and surf.

The Parry Grove and Guy Fleming loop trails wind among the largest and thickest groves of Torrey pines. Unfortunately, the prolonged drought of the late '80s killed most of the trees. It's hoped that the next wet cycle will regenerate these groves, though it must be remembered that Torrey pines are probably holdovers from a wetter climate that characterized the region thousands of years ago.

The Guy Fleming Trail is mostly flat, while the Parry Grove Trail starts with a steep descent on stair steps. In spring, the sunny slopes along the Guy Fleming Trail come alive with phantasmagoric wildflower displays. Fluttering in the sea breeze, the flowers put on quite a show as several different vivid shades of color dynamically intermix with the more muted tones of earth, sea and sky.

The Torrey Pines trails can be enjoyed the year round, but they're open only during daylight hours. Ranger-led walks are featured on weekends. You can't picnic in the reserve, but after you do your hiking, you can use the tables or the beach down near the entrance. Do take water along on the trails if it's a hot day. Also bring binoculars: the soaring ravens and the red-tailed and sparrow hawks are interesting to watch, as are the hang-gliding humans you'll sometimes see.

Trip 4: Torrey Pines Extension

Distance	0.5- and 1-mile out-and-back trails	
Optional Map	USGS 7.5-min *Del Mar*	
Best Times	All year	
Agency	TPSR	
Difficulty	*	

Thanks to public donations for land acquisition, an area of natural bluffs and Torrey pine groves south and east of Del Mar is now merely surrounded—not overwhelmed—by housing developments. This is the Torrey Pines State Reserve Extension.

The extension area is farther removed from the ocean than the main reserve, but in many respects is equally interesting. The gnarled and twisted Torrey pines clinging to stark, eroded sandstone walls here seemed to have escaped the ravages of the recent drought. The extension area's narrow, ill-maintained pathways offer a sense of peacefulness and isolation you can't get along the main reserve's well-beaten trails.

Of the extension area's many entrances, the dead-end of Del Mar Scenic Parkway (off Carmel Valley Road, 1.1 mile west of Interstate 5) is perhaps the easiest to find. Park near the end of the cul-de-sac and choose either Trail "A" to the right, which goes up a sage-filled basin sparsely dotted with Torrey pine trees, or Trail

"B" to the left, which leads to the superb D.A.R. (Daughters of the American Revolution) Trail. The latter trail slants up and then along a linear ridge to the west. From the Torrey-pine-shaded south brow of this ridge, you can look across the Los Penasquitos lagoon to the bluffs of the main reserve, and out to the ocean horizon. West of this ridge, a spur trail descends into an intimate little hollow with picturesque sandstone walls and gnarled Torrey pines.

On Trail "A" you eventually climb toward a ridge capped with reddish rock. This cap is part of the familiar Linda Vista Formation, which is well represented on top of San Diego's mesas. More trails penetrate the area east of Trail "A."

In the Torrey Pines extension

Trip 5: Crest Canyon

	Distance	1 to 2 miles
	Optional Map	USGS 7.5-min *Del Mar*; or a street map
	Best Times	All year
	Agency	SDOS
	Difficulty	*

Crest Canyon, a City of San Diego open-space park, fills a bowl-shaped valley that slopes down from Del Mar Heights Road on the south to San Dieguito Lagoon on the north. On the canyon floor, native sage-scrub and chaparral vegetation mixes with African daisy, ice-plant, saltbush, and other hardy plants that were introduced years ago to solve an erosion problem. Young Torrey pines are being introduced as well, hopefully to join the handful of century-old pines that thrive higher up on the canyon's side walls.

A good place to begin is along Racetrack View Road, not far from Jimmy Durante Boulevard and the Del Mar race track. From there, a sandy road swings uphill along the canyon's broad floor. When the road peters out about two-thirds of the way up the canyon (0.7 mile), you can find and follow steep paths leading either right toward Crest Way at La Amatista, or left toward Durango Drive.

If you plan to poke around off the beaten trail—with kids especially—keep in mind a couple of caveats: Crest Canyon's cliff-like exposures of sandstone, especially on the east side, are interesting to look at (from afar), but unstable and potentially hazardous. Watch out for rattlesnakes, too, particularly in the spring and summer.

Trip 6: La Jolla Caves

	Distance	1 mile round trip
	Hiking Time	50 minutes (round trip)
	Optional Map	USGS 7.5-min *La Jolla*; or a street map
	Best Times	Extreme low tides during any time of year
	Difficulty	**

As you walk south from La Jolla Shores Beach, the wide strip of sand is soon replaced by cobbles and wave-washed cliffs. Just offshore, a major submarine canyon, La Jolla Canyon, swallows the sand that normally would migrate down the coast. This is the main reason why sandy beaches are the exception rather than the rule from La Jolla to Pacific Beach.

La Jolla lies on a step-like terrace at the foot of Soledad Mountain, an uplifted block of erosion-resistant sandstone. The precipitous north flank of this terrace faces the usually calm and deep waters of La Jolla Bay. Here, wave action from infrequent storms has gouged out a series of sea grottos, known as the La Jolla Caves.

The westernmost cave, at Goldfish Point, is well-known among tourists and natives alike; it can be reached from above by a long stairway that begins inside the La Jolla Cave Curio Shop and passes through a man-made tunnel. The half-dozen or so other grottos in the series are usually accessible only by water. Extreme low tides (minus 1.5 feet or lower), however, can bring some of these within easy reach of hikers.

Check tide tables for the most favorable low tides, and begin your hike about 30 minutes before predicted low. Start from the south end of La Jolla Shores Beach, or from the public beach access alongside the Marine Room restaurant on Spindrift Drive.

Work your way south over the cliff-hugging

cobbles, or across the newly exposed tidepools, taking care not to step on the slippery, green rocks. The tidepool areas in particular show much evidence of "biological erosion"—that is, the breakdown of the structure of the rock itself by the chemical secretions of urchins, barnacles and other sea creatures. As you walk along, you'll hear rasping noises as crabs, startled by your approach, retreat hastily into crevices. Occasionally you can find an octopus in one of the deeper pools.

The biggest grotto is enormous—about 50 feet high—at its entrance, but it pinches in toward the rear. The sandstone walls are stained with a rainbow of colors: red and orange from iron oxide, greens and grays from plant life, and purple from iodine in kelp. In the back of the cave is a low passage leading to an adjacent grotto. Enjoy, but don't forget about the incoming tide!

La Jolla Caves

Trip 7: La Jolla Coast Walk

👞	**Distance**	0.5 mile round trip (to Goldfish Point)
	Total Elevation Gain/Loss	100'/100'
🏴	**Hiking Time**	20 minutes (round trip)
	Optional Map	USGS 7.5-min *La Jolla*; or a street map
↗ 👫	**Best Times**	All year
	Difficulty	*

A stunning perspective of La Jolla Bay and the sparkling La Jolla Shores coastline is afforded on this short walk along the clifftops. You'll be walking directly above the La Jolla Caves, on or near the very brink of a 100-foot drop to the bay's calm surface.

An interesting if obscure place to begin is the small parking area (room for two cars only) at the east end of Coast Walk. This is reached by a short spur street, signed COAST WALK, that intersects Torrey Pines Road at a point 200 yards east of the traffic signal at Prospect Place.

From the tiny parking area, a cliff-hugging dirt path guides you just below the back yards of several palatial houses. A footbridge and steps span a ravine plunging directly to the blue-green waters below. Just beyond that ravine, a short spur path goes up some steps to the intersection of Prospect Place and Park Row. Keep straight. In about 200 yards you arrive at a grove of graceful Torrey pines on Goldfish Point. Although these trees grow naturally just up the coast at Torrey Pines State Reserve, they were planted here.

The path ends just beyond the pine grove, next to the La Jolla Cave Curio Shop. Some walkers like to continue by following the paved sidewalk past the pocket beach of La Jolla Cove and around the periphery of Scripps Park. Goldfish Point itself is a good place to sit and relax. You can watch the swimmers, snorkelers and divers below as they float or glide through the often glassy water. If you climb down to the edge of the water, you can look across the face of the cliffs to the east and make out the openings to several of the caves.

Evening strolls along Coast Walk are always interesting, especially during rare periods when the "red tide" (plankton) blooms and produces bioluminescence in the churning water below. Watch your step, though, night or day. Most of the cliff edges are not protected by fencing.

Brown pelicans at La Jolla Bay

Area B-3: Point Loma

The long, south-pointing peninsula of Point Loma and the spectacular curving shoreline of San Diego Bay are two of the principal elements responsible for San Diego's legendary beauty. The peninsula itself is an elongated block of sandstone uplifted about 400 feet above sea level by fault action. It serves as a natural breakwater for the once-shallow (now dredged) bay behind it.

Most of the south half of the Point Loma peninsula is reserved for military uses. Perched on its end, centered on the highest promontory, is one of America's smallest (144 acres) national monuments—Cabrillo National Monument. Because of its location adjacent to the tourist-happy city of San Diego, Cabrillo is consistently ranked as one of the two busiest national monuments in the country.

Whether you're a tourist or not, the view alone is worth the almost obligatory visit here. On the clearest winter days, you can see all the way to San Clemente Island, 70 miles offshore, and to the snow-capped summits of the San Bernardino Mountains, 100 miles north. Other attractions are the whale-watching overlook, the old and new lighthouses, the Visitor Center with its panoramic vista of the bay and cityscape, and a tidepool area located on the west (Pacific) shore. The one real hiking path in the monument—the Bayside Trail—is described below.

A new regional park at the north end of the peninsula, called Sunset Cliffs Natural Park, was dedicated in 1983. Although the park remains little-known today, we profile its small network of trails in this section as well.

Because the access road into the monument passes through a military reservation, visiting time is limited to the daylight hours, generally after 9 a.m. See Appendix 4 for more information.

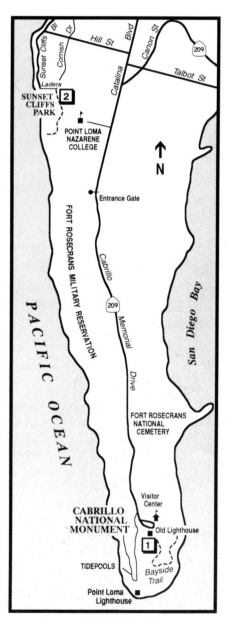

Area B-3: Point Loma

Trip 1: Bayside Trail

👟	**Distance**	2.0 miles round trip
	Total Elevation Gain/Loss	320'/320'
	Hiking Time	70 minutes (round trip)
🔲	**Optional Map**	USGS 7.5-min *Point Loma*
	Best Times	All year
🔼 🧍	**Agency**	CNM
	Difficulty	*

Coastal sage scrub and chaparral vegetation are highlighted along this trail, but it's more worth taking for the wonderful, unobstructed views of San Diego Bay, the Silver Strand, and San Diego's ever-growing skyline. You'll double your pleasure if you walk this trail on a crystal-clear day, typical of the period December through March. Note that the monument is open during daylight hours only, typically 9 a.m. to dusk.

The trail begins just east of the old lighthouse, not far from the Visitor Center. A self-guiding leaflet describes the flora, the geology, and some of the military uses of the area. The trail is simply an old asphalt road that descends gradually in a rough semicircular arc to a point about 300 feet below and east of the Visitor Center lookouts.

Point Loma's bay slope is honeycombed with the ruins of a World War II defense system of mortars, observation bunkers, generators and searchlights. You will see some of these remains along the trail. At the point where the trail ends (or rather runs into off-limits Navy property), you'll still be about 90 feet above the water surface. This is a good place to observe the sailboats and ships maneuvering in and out of the bay's narrow entrance. There are also aerial acrobatics to watch, courtesy of gulls, terns, and pelicans—plus aircraft taking off and landing at the North Island Naval Air Station across the bay.

Return to the lighthouse the same way you came. Tempting as they may be, don't take shortcuts—the vegetation is easily trampled and the soil eroded by one footprint too many. Besides, off-trail exploration is strictly forbidden within the national monument.

Point Loma tidepools

Trip 2: Sunset Cliffs Park

	Distance	0.5 to 1 mile
	Optional Map	USGS 7.5-min *Point Loma*
	Best Times	All year
	Agency	SDOS
	Difficulty	*

Stretching 1½ miles along the Pacific shoreline, Sunset Cliffs Natural Park encompasses one of the county's more impressive stretches of coastline. The northern part covers just the cliffs that separate Sunset Cliffs Boulevard from the ocean. As is the case in North County, beach-cliff erosion is very rapid here, and elaborate retaining walls that dissipate wave energy have been installed to keep the road from being undermined. The remainder of the park includes a half-mile of coastline plus some hillsides that slope upward toward the campus of Point Loma Nazarene College.

Currently there is controversy over erosion problems within the park and encroachment on park land by playing fields and parking lots used by the college. A master plan for the park has been drawn up which recommends restoring the park to a more natural condition.

Someday the park could shine as a fine example of public open space. Until then, you'll probably still enjoy following the small, informal network of trails starting at Ladera Street and Cornish Drive. These can take you up and down the hillsides and out to the tops of the low cliffs, just above where the ocean waves crash against water-worn boulders. Near sunset on clear days, a golden glow settles across the ocean and cliff faces, and Sunset Cliffs Park becomes one of the best places to toast the day's end. At nearby Cabrillo National Monument you can't usually do this, since the monument closes too early during most of the year.

During extremely low tides, which tend to occur on several afternoons each month from October through March, you can descend the steep steps at Sunset Cliffs Boulevard and Ladera Street to reach the intertidal zone below.

Below Sunset Cliffs at low tide

The tidepools here are rather poor for gazing at marine life, but it's fun to pick your way along the rocky shoreline beneath the banded cliffs.

Sunset Cliffs Park is great for kids, but little ones much be watched carefully. Most of the cliff edges are unfenced, and it's possible to slip on the hard-packed, eroded soil.

Area B-4: The Border Coast

Four square miles of marshes, tidal creeks, and sage- and chaparral-covered hillsides in and around the Tijuana River Estuary now enjoy federal protection as the Tijuana River National Estuarine Research Reserve. Included within this area is Border Field State Park, fronting the international border, and undeveloped tracts of land adjacent to the communities of Imperial Beach and San Ysidro.

For a long time now, sewage overflows from Tijuana, Mexico, have coursed through the Tijuana River and polluted parts of the estuary and beaches. Governments on both sides of the border continue to attack this problem, which grows more serious every year as Tijuana's population continues to explode.

Despite the problems with sewage, the estuary probably remains the county's richest habitat for birds. Birds congregate by the thousands here on a typical day, and over 340 bird species have been recorded to date. The reserve's best known endangered inhabitants are the light-footed clapper rail and the California least tern. Visiting birds include ospreys, golden eagles, and peregrine falcons.

Since the salt marsh surrounding the tidal creeks of the estuary receives both fresh water (from river flows and local runoff) and salt water (from tidal flows), plant life exists in tenuous balance. Plants must be able to survive in an environment that ranges from wet to dry, and from fresh to saline.

As you walk from higher elevations (a few feet above sea level), where nonnative grasses, cattails, and typical shrubs native to the coastal uplands flourish, toward lower areas along the tidal creeks, you'll notice a succession of plants tending toward greater salt tolerance: pickleweed, sea blite, sea lavender, and finally cordgrass. At the lowest levels, the soft sediment of the mudflats supports algal films, and houses worms, crabs, snails, and other small creatures which are food for the shorebirds.

When you're out exploring the reserve, stick to the designated trails to avoid trampling any vegetation. Depending on the season, you may encounter sticky mud, so its wise to wear an old pair of shoes. Parts of the beach may be closed in spring and summer to protect nesting birds such as the least tern.

Area B-4: The Border Coast

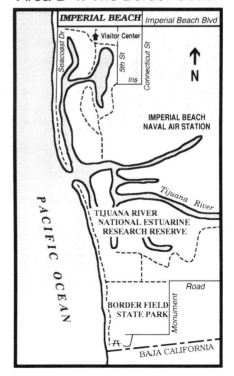

Trip 1: Tijuana River Estuary

	Distance	1 to 3 miles
	Optional Map	USGS 7.5-min *Imperial Beach*
	Best Times	All year
	Agency	TEVC, BFSP
	Difficulty	*

It's best to begin your exploration of the Tijuana River estuary and marsh with a stop at the reserve's new visitor center at 3rd Street and Caspian Way in Imperial Beach. In addition to interactive exhibits inside, a demonstration garden outside shows off about 100 species of the typical, but fast disappearing coastal sage-scrub vegetation that once blanketed San Diego's coastal mesas and hills.

From the Visitor Center, trails run south toward a tidal pond, and farther across the flat, green marsh land toward the bank of the Tijuana River. You can also start at the south terminus of Seacoast Drive for a walk along the beach, or follow a path south from the end of 5th Street, which will take you more quickly into the heart of the reserve.

Also worth a visit is Border Field State Park, which lies within the reserve boundaries. There, a picnic area atop a low coastal terrace offers a superb view of the Coronado Islands, Point Loma, and the downtown San Diego skyline, which is bisected by the Coronado Bridge. Nearby, an old stone monument, placed in 1851, commemorates the first point at which the boundary of the United States and Mexico was staked, following the 1848 Treaty of Guadalupe Hidalgo. The monument marks the extreme southwest corner of the conterminous United States, a place as significant from the standpoint of geographical trivia as Cape Flattery, Washington; Key Largo, Florida; and Madawaska, Maine.

South of the monument and the steel-mesh border fence, the goblet-shaped Bullring-by-the-Sea reaches skyward, and homes and businesses of Tijuana's Playas neighborhoods stretch for miles along the coast.

North of the monument, the landscape is mostly natural. A wide strip of sand stretches toward the mouth of the Tijuana River, and a number of trails, suitable for both hikers and horseback riders, traverse the marsh uplands. Horses are offered for rent at several of the stables you will pass when approaching the park on Monument Road or on Hollister Street.

Egret, Tijuana River Estuary

Oak woodland along San Luis Rey River

COASTAL STRIP AND FOOTHILLS

Area C-1: Escondido

A decade ago, there were hardly any designated hiking trails near Escondido. Now there are several small networks of trails within 10 miles of this city (which are described in detail below), and a major effort to piece together a 50-mile-long open-space park, centered on Escondido, is underway. When completed sometime after the turn of the century, the San Dieguito River Park will stretch from Volcan Mountain, north of Julian, to the ocean at Del Mar. The San Dieguito River Authority—a consortium of county and city governments—plans to acquire hundreds of publicly and privately owned parcels of land to complete the proposed 66,000-acre park. A decade hence, well over 100 miles of trails for hiking, mountain biking and horseback riding could permeate the park, including the Coast-to-Crest Trail which will eventually serve as the backbone for the entire network.

Following the course of the San Dieguito River and its main tributary, Santa Ysabel Creek, the Coast-to-Crest Trail will proceed from San Dieguito Lagoon in Del Mar past Rancho Santa Fe to Lake Hodges, just south of Escondido. After skirting the lake's north shore (on a 4-mile segment already open and dedicated), it will cross under Interstate 15 and continue up through San Pasqual Valley into the foothills. Passing into Cleveland National Forest, it will then follow Santa Ysabel Creek

through Pamo Valley and skirt Black Canyon and Sutherland Reservoir. The final stretch will cross Santa Ysabel Valley and climb to the headwaters of Santa Ysabel Creek on Volcan Mountain. Eventually, extensions of the Coast-to-Crest Trail may hook into other trails on public lands to the east, such as the Pacific Crest Trail in Anza-Borrego Desert State Park.

The soon-to-open Mt. Israel Recreation Area trail system near Elfin Forest (outside Escondido) will be described in detail in a future edition of this book, as will other trails (such as the Coast-to-Crest Trail) that are now in the planning stage. If you live in inland North County, stay tuned!

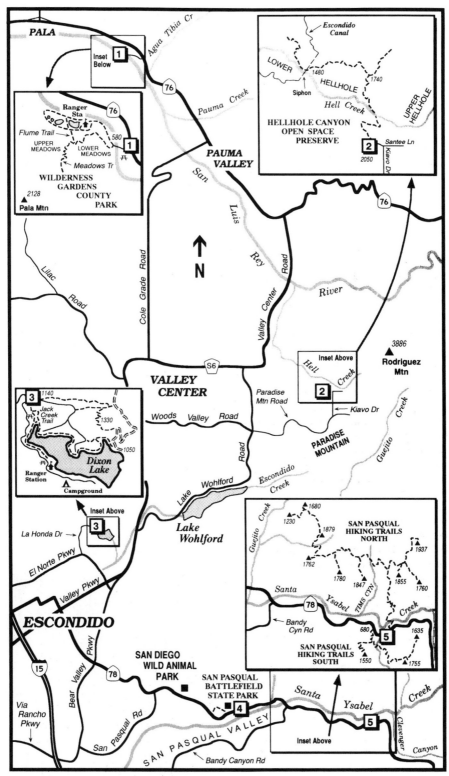

Area C-1: Escondido

Trip 1: Wilderness Gardens

👟	**Distance**	1 to 4 miles round trip
▣	**Optional Map**	USGS 7.5-min *Pala*
	Best Times	November through May
🚶	**Agency**	SDCP
	Difficulty	* to **

Wilderness Gardens County Park is a rather new addition to the San Diego County parks system. The park isn't a true wilderness, but rather the grounds of an old ranch—once the showplace of Manchester Boddy, owner of a Los Angeles newspaper and developer of the renowned Descanso Gardens in Pasadena. Today the ranch has largely reverted back to a wilderness character.

Down the middle of the park runs a wide strip of oak-woodland habitat along the San Luis Rey River. Intermixed with the oaks and sycamores are remnants of exotic plants such as silver-dollar eucalyptus, camellias, roses, shiny-leaved holly, bottlebrush, pyracantha, and oleander. Surrounding hillsides are clothed with native chaparral and sage-scrub vegetation.

Wilderness Gardens is located 10 miles east of Interstate 15 on Highway 76 (if you cross the bridge over Agua Tibia Creek, you've missed the turnoff). In addition to day hiking and exploring, the park offers overnight camping at several walk-in sites on the bank of the river.

There are at least three distinct hikes you can make in Wilderness Gardens once you arrive at the entrance. Northwest of the parking area, a short trail loops around the sunny north bank of the San Luis Rey River, passing through a sparse cover of drought-resistant, desertlike vegetation.

By following the road toward the ranger station and campground, you'll reach a series of five shallow ponds (some dry) on the south bank of the river. These are fed partly by rainwater and partly by water pumped up from the water table, which lies just below the ground surface. The larger ponds are fringed by cattails and serve as a mecca for wildlife—over 140 species of birds have been seen here and in the surrounding area.

Beyond the ponds is a loop trail through a canopy of oaks that are festooned with wild grape vines. Round trip to and from the parking lot and around the loop is about 2 miles.

The third hike is the Meadows Trail, a meandering path leading up the slope of Pala Mountain past two hillside meadows. After crossing the San Luis Rey River, bear left on the Meadows Trail. This follows a boulder-strewn, dry channel for a while, and then climbs a brush- and tree-covered slope overlooking a cluster of old buildings. Down below are the ranger's residence, an old barn remodeled as a conference center, a former chicken coop, and the remains of San Diego County's first grist mill, built more than a century ago. Sections of the trail follow the course of a flume to the old mill.

A little higher, you'll pass the lower meadow, a soft carpet of green dotted with wildflowers in late winter and early spring. After curving around the usually dry bed of an old reservoir, the trail dips and connects with a short trail to the ponds below. Bear left and continue climbing to the upper meadow, smaller than the first. Skirting this meadow, you'll pick up the switchbacks of an old road, now reverted to a narrow trail. Sugar bush, toyon, mountain mahogany, ceanothus, chamise, manzanita, and buckwheat crowd close on both sides.

After about a mile of steady ascent on these switchbacks, the old roadbed begins to veer left and descend. You've now come about 2 miles. Consider this the end of the line unless, first, you've consulted with the ranger and obtained his permission to go on to the top of Pala Mountain, and second, you still have the inclination to tackle an arduous, steep trail to the top.

As of this writing, Wilderness Gardens is currently closed for redevelopment, a process that may extend well into 1993. Future printings of this book will keep you up to date on the new changes.

Trip 2: Hellhole Canyon Open Space Preserve

👟	**Distance**	5.0 miles round trip
	Total Elevation Gain/Loss	700'/700'
	Hiking Time	2½ hours
🔲	**Optional Map**	USGS 7.5-min *Rodriguez Mtn*
	Best Times	November through May
↗ 👫	**Agency**	SDCP
	Difficulty	**

A fledgling system of trails is now open in the county's new, 1712-acre Hellhole Canyon Open Space Preserve, just east of Valley Center. Of a proposed 14 miles of trail, about 4 miles have been completed so far (1992), and a mile more has been flagged and roughed out for future construction. The county acquired this former parcel of surplus public-domain land, one of several such parcels in the North County inland area, when the BLM sought to dispose of it.

To reach the starting point, take Paradise Mountain Road 3.3 miles east from Lake Wohlford Road to Kiavo Drive, where you bear left (north). Continue another 0.5 mile north on Kiavo to the preserve's well-marked entrance and parking lot.

From the edge of the parking lot, a trail leads down along a scruffy ridgeline.The boulder-studded west rampart of 3886-foot Rodriguez Mountain lies in view toward the east; on humid days the mountain sometimes creates its own cloud cap. Perhaps you'll see a slice of ocean horizon in the northwest if the weather's clear and dry.

You then round a switchback and descend more quickly, passing a wooden bench on the right. At 0.8 mile, you come down to a secluded spot along Hell Creek that can only be described as enchanting. During winter and early spring, water happily spills over smooth boulders under a canopy of spreading live oaks and twisted sycamores. Downstream from here, a century ago, travelers sometimes had a "hell" of a time getting their wagons across the rain-swollen creek while on the Escondido to Palomar road— hence the stream's colorful name. Curiously, there's no connection between the names of Hell Creek and nearby Paradise Mountain. The latter was apparently christened by a couple of hot and thirsty prospectors after they discovered a cold spring there.

Just ahead, the trail joins an old, rock-lined canal bed and passes through one of the most charming oak glens in the whole county. Succulent live-forevers cling to the crumbling canal walls. For another 0.5 mile, the trail sticks with the old canal, which contours (or rather rises at the imperceptible rate of 10 vertical feet per mile) across a sunny, chaparral-covered slope.

At 1.3 miles, the trail veers uphill, leaving

Hell Creek

the old canal. Stay left at the trail fork 100 yards ahead (the right branch goes no where in particular at present). Up ahead, you'll traverse a grassy slope dotted with redolent wild onions. You then descend back to the canal bed, join it for a short while, and descend further to reach Hell Creek right at the point where a large metal pipe crosses over. The pipe—an "inverted siphon"—short-cuts the path of the original canal you were walking along earlier. The purpose of this canal is to shunt water from the San Luis Rey River over to Lake Wohlford, which lies on the Escondido Creek watershed.

When you have reached the siphon, you've traveled 2.5 miles from the parking lot. This is a good place to turn back. If time and energy allow, the uncompleted section of trail ahead will take you up along a steep hillside offering a somewhat distant view of a rocky declivity in the bottom of Hell Creek.

Trip 3: Dixon Lake Recreation Area

Distance	2.5 miles
Total Elevation Gain/Loss	350'/350'
Hiking Time	80 minutes
Optional Map	USGS 7.5-min *Valley Center*
Best Times	November through May
Agency	DLRA
Difficulty	**

Perched several hundred feet up in the hills just north of Escondido, Dixon Lake stores drinking water and serves as a recreational resource as well. Camping facilities, picnic grounds, playgrounds, boat rentals, and the opportunity to fish along most of the lake's shoreline are enough to draw a steady stream of visitors 7 days a week.

Newly constructed trail segments now make it possible for hikers to climb up and over a shaggy promontory just north of the lake, and then loop back to the start by way of an older, shoreline-hugging path. From the high point on this 2½-mile hike, 300 feet above the lake's shimmering surface, you may enjoy a stunning panorama stretching west to San Clemente Island and Santa Catalina Island, and south along the coast into Baja California.

To get to the lake, follow El Norte Parkway 3 miles east from Interstate 15. Turn left (north) on La Honda Drive and follow it 1 mile uphill to the recreation area's entry station.

Just beyond the entry station, you should spot the large, wooden sign marking the start of the Jack Creek Nature Trail. This half-mile-long, sometimes-steep ramble down to the lake shore and back includes 15 numbered stops keyed to a self-guiding booklet you can borrow from the ranger station. Along the way you'll become acquainted with several of the common native plants of the area—buckwheat, manzanita, chamise, California sagebrush, black sage, ceanothus, laurel sumac, toyon, willow, and live oak—and some non-native (planted) acacia and eucalyptus trees. Blue-flowered ceanothus shrubs fill the hillsides with color in March and April, while delicate, red monkey-flower plants bloom dependably from spring into summer.

With some careful, hand-in-hand guidance over several rough spots, the Jack Creek Nature Trail can be a real adventure for toddlers. The jungle-like growths of acacia, jagged rock outcrops, and rugged little stair-step inclines were enough to keep my 3-year-old son fascinated the whole way.

For the 2½-mile hike profiled here, observe the following directions: Just beyond the entry station, turn left onto the paved road that leads toward two fishing piers on the north shore of the lake. Less than a hundred yards down, pull off and park in the dirt turnout on the left. From the far corner of this turnout, start walking on the trail that cuts through the chaparral in an east direction, parallel to the road. You descend slightly, traverse a patch of riparian bottomland along trickling Jack Creek, and then climb easily through more chaparral to a junction with an old roadbed (0.5 mile). Turn right, walk downhill about 100 yards, and pick up the narrow Lake View Trail slanting up the slope on the left.

A short, steep climb through a veritable tunnel of tall chaparral takes you to the brow of a ridge offering a view of the lake, part of Escondido, and possibly the ocean. An equally steep, and rugged and rocky, descent lies ahead. At the bottom (1.0 mile) you come to a maintained dirt road.

Turn right and follow the road about 300 yards down to a "portapotty" perched above the lake, not far from the dam. From there, follow a short path on the right to join the Shoreline Trail. Veer right and stay next to the lake on the Shoreline Trail for the next mile, ignoring several side trails to parking areas above.

You'll leave the Shoreline Trail when you reach a narrow cove just beyond the second fishing pier. Look for the sign labelled TRAIL, referring to the Jack Creek Nature Trail, on the right. Climb up either branch of that trail to the paved road above and turn right to return to your parked car.

Along the Jack Creek Nature Trail

Trip 4: Battle Monument Trail

	Distance	1 mile round trip (to the ramada)
	Total Elevation Gain/Loss	240'/240'
	Hiking Time	30 minutes (round trip)
	Optional Map	USGS 7.5-min *San Pasqual*
	Best Times	All year
	Agency	SPBSP
	Difficulty	*

San Pasqual Battlefield State Historic Park recently gained a very handsome visitor center, which undoubtedly helps to snag a few of the millions of people who visit the nearby San Diego Wild Animal Park. The center features some fine interpretive displays on the 1846 Battle of San Pasqual (part of the Mexican-

American War) and on the use of the valley by Native Americans and later settlers.

You'll find the visitor center along Highway 78, 1.4 miles east of the Wild Animal Park entrance. Our recommended hike starts with the short, self-guiding nature trail on the slope just behind the visitor center. After about 0.2 mile on this, you can continue west on the Battle Monument Trail across dry slopes toward a hilltop ramada and bench. Huge thickets of prickly-pear cactus dot the slope, their ripe red fruits bulging by the hundreds during the fall season.

From the ramada the broad, flat San Pasqual Valley spreads before you. Most of the valley is a designated agricultural preserve within the city limits of San Diego—which is why it is not filled with subdivisions. In the opposite direction you can spot parts of the Wild Animal Park, and often some of the large animals that roam more-or-less-free there.

After you've had an eyeful, and perhaps lunch, at the ramada, you can head east back to your starting point. The Battle Monument Trail itself continues west down the hill to reach a state historical monument alongside Highway 78.

Trip 5: San Pasqual Hiking Trails

Distance	up to 25 miles (whole network)	
Optional Map	USGS 7.5-min *San Pasqual*	
Best Times	November through May	
Agency	SDRP	
Difficulty	* to ***	

Two of the newest additions to the emerging San Dieguito River Park are undeveloped parcels of former BLM land lying north and south of Highway 78, just east of San Pasqual Valley. Thanks to a summer's worth of labor by San Diego Urban Corps members, a 13-mile network of hiking trails was opened here in fall 1991.

Like any low-elevation route in the county's arid, warm interior, the so-called San Pasqual Hiking Trails are best explored during the cooler months. If you go on an unusually clear day, the coast-to-mountain views on these trails can be truly stunning.

The trails are divided into two networks, each with its own trailhead. To explore the easier, south trail system, start from the parking lot on the south side of Highway 78, 5.3 miles east of the San Diego Wild Animal Park entrance. You start by zigzagging 0.6 mile to the first marked trail junction. Choose the right branch for a relatively easy climb to a 1550-foot knoll. From this vantage, there's often a good ocean view.

The left branch of the trail—a more rugged alternative—begins with a short passage through a spooky ravine, replete with live oaks, mosses, and fungi. On the other side, you tackle switchbacks leading toward a prominent,

monolithic boulder on a high ridge to the east. After passing within of a few yards of the boulder, there's a side trail on the right leading to a 1755-foot viewpoint—good for another view to the west. Keep straight to continue toward a 1635-foot bump on a ridge 1/2 mile northeast (you join a dirt road briefly, and resume travel on a foot trail branching left toward the high point). That's where you get a really stupendous view of upper San Pasqual Valley, a slice of ocean horizon in the west, and the distant, blue-tinted mountains in the east. Almost straight down a thousand feet, you'll see toylike cars making their way along the sinuous gray ribbon of Highway 78.

By tracing all branches of the south trail network and returning, you cover about 7 miles with a 1900-foot total elevation gain, and the same loss.

The maze-like, north trail system involves some strenuous uphill and downhill walking—more than you might expect for any trail so close to the urban area. You start from a parking lot on the north side of Highway 78, 5.8 miles east of the Wild Animal Park entrance. If you're coming from Escondido, the turnoff comes unexpectedly; note that it is 0.3 mile beyond the parking lot for the south trails.

Exhausting the possibilities of the north trail

network in a single day is just that—exhausting. You'd have to walk 18 miles with a total elevation gain (and loss) of 4500 feet. There's something for everyone here, though—even small kids. Beautiful Santa Ysabel Creek lies only 200 feet below, 0.3 mile away by trail. There you can sit for a spell amid beautiful oaks and sycamores. Water may or may not be careening off the boulders, depending on recent rains. The trees with gray-green leaves are Engelmann oaks, a relatively rare variety whose endangered habitat centers on northern San Diego County.

The trail ahead is for peripatetic hikers only.

Dozens of switchbacks take you to a trail junction 1300 feet higher and 2.5 miles farther. At the trail fork there, decide where you want to go—right toward any of three marked viewpoints, or left toward any of six marked viewpoints.

My favorite viewpoints on the north trail maze are the 1847' knoll west of Tims Canyon, and the big boulder pile at 1762'. Both feature virtually aerial views down the length of San Pasqual Valley. Unpack your lunch at either one and enjoy a view probably superior to that from any hilltop mansion in North County.

Trailside view of upper San Pasqual Valley

Area C-2: Poway

Much of the area east and northeast of Poway, extending to the outskirts of Ramona, has been earmarked as permanent open space. This includes Woodson Mountain, one of the county's most picturesque promontories, and a swath of land to the south of it.

The upper and middle slopes of Woodson Mountain were declared open space by the City of San Diego in 1978. In the area to the south, an administrative transfer of public domain land from the BLM to the City of Poway has allowed that city to build a riding and hiking trail system stretching from Lake Poway across Woodson Mountain to Iron Mountain. This system now ties into an intricate network of horse paths being developed throughout the semirural neighborhoods of Poway.

Lake Poway serves as a hub for trails that run in several directions. A nice complement of recreational facilities has been developed along the shoreline of the lake to serve the local residents—and also non-Poway residents (they must pay a rather steep fee for parking and day use). Visitors can picnic; play horseshoes, volleyball, or softball; rent boats to fish or cruise about on the 60-acre surface of the reservoir; camp at a primitive campground accessible only by foot or horseback; and, of course, hike or ride the trails. Hours for the recreation area are sunrise to sunset, 7 days a week (the lake itself is open Wednesday through Sunday).

A scenic section of riparian bottomland below Lake Poway's dam was added to the region's protected open space in 1989 with the purchase of the 410-acre Blue Sky Ranch. The California Department of Fish and Game now runs the area as a wildlife preserve.

Sycamore Canyon Open Space Preserve, southeast of Poway, was first opened in 1988 as an undeveloped facility with one short trail. The mid-1990s should see a large expansion of the park as the adjacent Goodan Ranch, once slated for development, is added as a buffer of open space between fast-growing Poway and the city of Santee.

Ultimately the trail systems of Poway may connect to regional trails stretching south toward Mission Trails Regional Park, and east toward county-owned open space areas along Wildcat Canyon Road and into Cleveland National Forest.

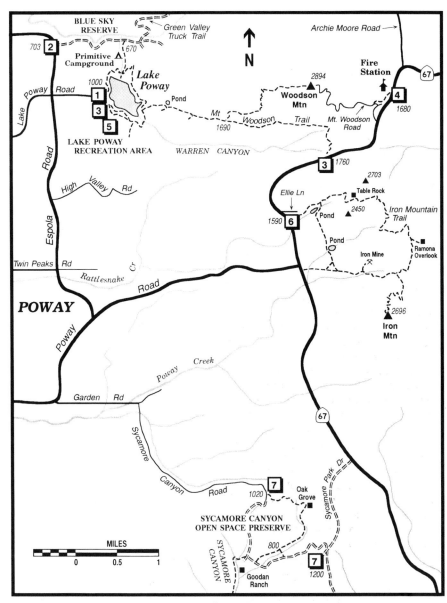

Area C-2: Poway

Trip 1: Lake Poway Loop

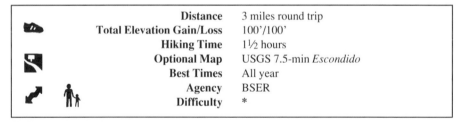

	Distance	2.5 miles
	Total Elevation Gain/Loss	400'/400'
	Hiking Time	1½ hours
	Optional Map	USGS 7.5-min *Escondido*
	Best Times	All year
	Agency	LPRA
	Difficulty	**

This loop trail around Lake Poway serves two purposes. It's an excellent exercise trail for runners and walkers, with a good mixture of flats, gentle hills, and a few fairly steep switchbacks. It is also an interpretive trail, with a leaflet (available at the lake entrance) keyed to numbered posts along way. On the trail, you'll pass through four distinct plant communities: sage scrub, chaparral, oak woodland, and riparian woodland.

Pick up the trail just beyond the lake entrance on the left (north) side of the developed area. The trail follows the west shoreline to a point beyond the dam, then drops well below the rock-fill base of the dam to cross the creek.

When you reach the dirt road below the dam, you can make a short sidetrip, if you wish, to visit a small campground. It's used mostly by horse riders, but backpackers are welcome too. Tables at vacant sites can be used for picnicking. The Blue Sky Reserve lies right below the campground; you can enter it this way if you want.

The loop trail resumes on the east side of the dirt road. Climbing by way of a long switchback segment, you gain a slope above the east end of the dam. Continue winding around the east and south shoreline, at some distance above the water, until you reach the edge of the developed area.

Trip 2: Blue Sky Ecological Reserve

	Distance	3 miles round trip
	Total Elevation Gain/Loss	100'/100'
	Hiking Time	1½ hours
	Optional Map	USGS 7.5-min *Escondido*
	Best Times	All year
	Agency	BSER
	Difficulty	*

Now that the California Department of Fish and Game has purchased the former Blue Sky Ranch along Green Valley Truck Trail, one of the finest examples of riparian woodland remaining in San Diego County will be fully preserved and protected. Never a ranch—just property held for investment—the 410 acres include typical sage-scrub/chaparral hillside vegetation and more than a mile's worth of lushly shaded canyon bottom.

After a wet winter, the whole place acquires an almost unbelievable sheen of green. Mosses,

ferns, annual grasses, and fresh new shrub growth coat everything, even the rocks. Wildflowers appear in great numbers by about April, and start to fade by June. More than 100 kinds of wildflowers have been identified here in a single year.

You'll find the entrance along the east side of Espola Road, just south of its big bend toward Rancho Bernardo and 0.6 mile north of Lake Poway Road. On foot, follow the unpaved truck trail down along the south bank of the creek. Traffic noise disappears, and frogs entertain you with their guttural serenades. Live oaks spread overhead, casting plenty of welcome shade, while willows, sycamores, and lush thickets of poison oak cluster along the creek itself. Here and there, paths diverge toward the creek, where you can spot tadpoles, frogs, and perhaps other amphibious creatures.

At 1.0 mile, a side road goes south toward the Lake Poway primitive campground. One-quarter mile farther, where powerlines pass overhead, the road splits three ways. The right branch goes up-slope to a house foundation amid a eucalyptus grove. The road straight ahead heads toward a hillside water tank. The left branch (Green Valley Truck Trail) goes across the creek and starts climbing a sunny slope toward the Ramona Reservoir. This split in the road is the end of the line for casual hiking. If you want a lot more exercise, just keep walking—all the way up to the Ramona Reservoir dam, 1.3 miles away.

Trip 3: Mount Woodson Trail

Distance	4.5 miles
Total Elevation Gain/Loss	1600'/850'
Hiking Time	2½ hours
Optional Maps	USGS 7.5-min *Escondido, San Pasqual, San Vicente Reservoir*
Best Times	October through June
Agency	LPRA
Difficulty	***

The Mt. Woodson Trail starts at Lake Poway, traverses the rugged south slopes of Woodson Mountain, and ends just below Highway 67, south of Ramona. Hand tools and human labor alone were used to forge the eastern part of this trail. Huge boulders and a massive tangle of chaparral presented constant route-finding and construction difficulties. There are sudden turns, steep up and down stretches, and, in some places, a thick canopy of ground-hugging vegetation which blots out all views. It's a real adventure to walk this trail—but only if the following caveats are observed:

Pick a cool day. (My first experience on the trail coincided with a September sizzler, with air temperatures on the sunny slopes as high as 112°!) Also allow plenty of time to negotiate the almost constant ups and downs. Although you'll be on good trail tread all the way, there are a few very steep stretches. Wear shoes with good traction.

If you can swing a ride at the east end (or set up a car shuttle), a good way to do this trail is point-to-point, as we suggest in this description. Begin at the grassy picnic area on southwest shore of Lake Poway, and follow either of two wide trails southeast (these join together after 0.4 mile). After skirting the south shore and dipping to cross Warren Canyon, you come to a trail junction, 0.8 mile. Turn right on the signed Mt. Woodson Trail and climb east on a steep grade through sage scrub and chaparral. The white-flowering ceanothus, occurring in dense patches, comes into full bloom hereabouts around March.

You'll pass another junction, with a beautiful pond on the left (filled with water in winter and spring), at 1.2 miles. Stay left and continue east. At 1.6 miles, stay left and continue east again. You then pass over a summit, descend slightly, and climb to a second summit, 2.0 miles, where a side trail branches left toward Woodson Mountain's summit.

Now, with Woodson Mountain's boulder-peppered south flank in view ahead, you begin a rollercoasterlike descent through thick brush and around huge boulders. You'll pass two picnic sites under spreading oak trees along the way. These are great spots for a break, especially in the heat. After about 2 miles' further travel

(4 miles from the start) eastward, the trail turns abruptly south and descends to a point at the foot of a fill slope created by the recent widening on Highway 67. You can then clamber up the fill slope and step over the guard rail to reach the shoulder of the highway. There's a parking turnout just west of here on the far side of the highway, at a point 1.7 miles north of Poway Road.

Sometime soon, a trail will be constructed parallel to the highway which will connect the east end of the Mt. Woodson Trail to the Iron Mountain Trail at Ellie Lane.

Trip 4: Woodson Mountain—East Approach

Distance	3.5 miles round trip
Total Elevation Gain/Loss	1200'/1200'
Hiking Time	2 hours (round trip)
Optional Map	USGS 7.5-min *San Pasqual*
Best Times	October through June
Agency	SDOS
Difficulty	**

Indians called it "Mountain of Moonlit Rocks," an appropriate name for a landmark visible, even at night, over great distances. Early white settlers dubbed it "Cobbleback Peak," a name utterly descriptive of its rugged, boulder-strewn slopes. For the past 100 years, however, it has appeared on maps simply as "Woodson Mountain," in honor of a Dr. Woodson who homesteaded some property nearby well over a century ago.

The light-colored bedrock of Woodson Mountain and several of its neighboring peaks is a type geologists call "Woodson Mountain granodiorite." When exposed at the surface, it weathers into huge spherical or ellipsoidal boulders with smooth surfaces. The largest boulders have a tendency to cleave apart along remarkably flat planes, forming "chimneys" from several inches to several feet wide. Sometimes, one half of a split boulder will roll away, leaving a vertical and almost seamless face behind. It's no wonder that local rock climbers consider Woodson Mountain (or "Mt. Woodson," as it is popularly called) to be the best place in the county for bouldering practice.

The mountain's upper and middle slopes are publicly owned open space managed by the City of San Diego. This open space surrounds a 15-acre parcel on the summit ridge reserved for communications antennae. Hikers and climbers have easy access to the slopes via a paved service road (closed to cars) serving the antenna site at the summit.

Park in one of the large turnouts on the east side of Highway 67, 3 miles north of Poway Road, opposite the entrance to the California Division of Forestry fire station. Carefully cross the highway, and follow the beaten path past the fire station to where you hook up with the aforementioned paved service road.

On most weekends, the sounds of nature will be accompanied by the clink of aluminum hardware, plus the shouts of "On belay!" and other phrases in climbers' parlance. Even if you don't see climbers, chalk marks (from gymnast's chalk) on boulders by the roadside mark their favorite routes.

Near the top of the mountain, the road passes narrowly between immense, egg-shaped boulders and split-boulder faces 20 to 30 feet high—some, perhaps, unclimbable by "ethical" means.

When you reach the top of the mountain, you'll notice the first of several cinder-block buildings. This easternmost structure was built on the site of a metal lookout tower that was removed in 1990 after several years of disuse. The metal tower was a replacement for an older structure destroyed by wildfire in 1967. That fire, which eventually burned as far west as today's Interstate 15, leaped on raging Santa Ana winds from its point of origin in Ramona to the top of Woodson in just 90 minutes!

Behind the new building is a cubical water tank with a peaked roof perched on a large boulder. On the surface of the boulder are bench marks indicating the highest (natural) point on the mountain.

From the high point you can walk west along the narrow summit ridge, past various antenna towers, to reach a vantage point overlooking Poway, the North County coastal region, and the great blue expanse of the Pacific Ocean. Santa Catalina and San Clemente islands are visible on the clearest days.

Boulders on Woodson Mountain

Trip 5: Woodson Mountain—West Approach

	**Distance**	7.6 miles round trip
	Total Elevation Gain/Loss	2300'/2300'
	Hiking Time	4½ hours
	Optional Maps	USGS 7.5-min *Escondido, San Pasqual*
	Best Times	November through May
	Agency	LPRA
	Difficulty	***

This superior, but twice-as-difficult hike to Woodson Mountain's summit (compared to the standard, east approach—Trip 4) takes you through a veritable obstacle course of gigantic boulders. The variety of shapes is amazing, from smooth and rounded, to angular or shattered.

Begin, as in Trip 3 above, by hiking the Mt. Woodson Trail to the second summit at 2.0 miles. Take the left trail from there; it rises (and sometimes falls a bit) up along Woodson's south-facing flank. A few short stretches are extremely steep—tough going up, and even tougher going down because it's hard to keep one's balance.

At 3.2 miles the trail reaches Woodson's sharply defined summit ridge and turns east toward the antenna towers. (Sometime in 1993, a new trail coming up from the Mount Woodson Estates subdivision north of the mountain will tie in here.) A final narrow and rough link of trail runs on to meet the end of a dirt service road, 3.6 miles, just short of the summit; this last link lies just outside Poway city limits and therefore receives little or no maintenance. Don't miss the remarkable, razor-sharp boulder flake on the left. Continue another 0.2 mile on the dirt road to reach Woodson's high point.

Nearing summit on Mt. Woodson road

Trip 6: Iron Mountain

🥾	**Distance**	9.5 miles
	Total Elevation Gain/Loss	1700'/1700'
	Hiking Time	5 hours
◪	**Optional Map**	USGS 7.5-min *San Vicente Reservoir*
	Best Times	November through May
↺	**Agency**	LPRA
	Difficulty	***

After five years of piecemeal construction by California Conservation Corps crews, the Iron Mountain Trail was finally dedicated and fully opened to the public in 1991. Hiking this trail on a clear, crisp late-autumn or early winter day is one of my favorite experiences—short of trips to more distant mountain and desert areas. Because it is part of Poway's multiuse trail system, the trail has become popular among equestrians and mountain bikers as well as hikers.

Although Iron Mountain's conical summit rises to nearly 2700 feet, you can start at either of two trailheads some 1000 feet lower. For the easiest way up (and then back the same way), you can start from the road shoulder of Highway 67, just south of Poway Road, where limited parking is available. The route, a dirt road at first and then a trail, proceeds directly east for 1.5 miles to join the main Iron Mountain Trail. The summit lies 1.7 trail miles south of that junction.

I prefer the longer, tougher, and more rewarding loop route starting from the main Ellie Lane trailhead (it's this one whose data appear in the capsulized summary above):

Begin at Highway 67 and Ellie Lane (0.7 mile north of Poway Road), where the trail takes off from the edge of a fenced equestrian staging area just east of the highway. In the next 1.5 miles, you'll climb through tall growths of chaparral and practically rub shoulders with boulders the size of small trucks. The boulders, which often look like oversize jelly beans or jelly-bean fragments, are the same "Woodson Mountain granodiorite" seen on nearby Woodson Mountain. The chaparral includes a lot of ceanothus, or "wild lilac," which bursts into fragrant bloom sometime around March. You'll also detect the ineffable sweetness of Cleveland sage, which permeates the air in many places along the trail almost the year round.

A large live oak spreads a pool of shade across the trail at 0.9 mile. At 1.4 miles, you bend around another large oak and soon pass Table Rock, a curious mushroom-like balanced slab of rock. From there, you'll get your first glimpse of Iron Mountain's summit, poking up over lesser ridges in the south.

Ahead, the now-primitive and occasionally very steep trail meanders down to cross a small ravine, and then zigzags sharply up along the side of a ridge. You'll catch your breath just in time to start an equally steep switchback descent into another ravine. Like Sisyphus, you must tackle yet another set of uphill switchbacks, this time alongside the bottom of the ravine.

Salvation lies at the saddle ahead (2.4 miles), with a glorious view of mile upon mile of olive-green mountains, culminating at the dark-blue wall of the Cuyamacas. Watch for an easy-to-miss switchback turn ahead—a false trail goes straight and continues for some distance, while the real trail makes a hairpin turn to the left and descends a dry, east-facing slope. At 2.8 miles, a side trail branches east and follows a ridgeline to a high spot offering a good view of the Ramona valley.

The main trail descends moderately south and swings west to reach a signed trail junction, 3.5 miles from Ellie Lane. Iron Mountain's summit—despite the posted 2 miles—is really a bit less than 1.7 miles away. The wide, well-graded trail zigzags up the mountain's north flank, offering an ever-widening view of coastal strip and the mountains to the east. Early on many springtime mornings there's no view along this stretch, as you're in the midst of the coastal stratus clouds. Just after this trail was completed, I'd invariably collect a dozen dew-drop-laden spider webs on my shirt on the way up. This no longer happens: the orb-weaving spiders have apparently learned to construct their webs so that the lowermost supporting strand lies just above the heads of passersby.

When you reach the summit, you can sign your name on the visitor's register, and sometimes admire a true panorama of the Pacific Ocean, glistening beyond the sparkle of rooftops and cars in the distant suburbs below.

Retrace your steps 1.7 miles back to the trail junction, turn left (west), and start the descent down along a ravine toward the south trailhead near Poway Road. At a point 50 yards past where you cross the ravine bottom, a side trail goes north almost straight up a hill (gaining 200 feet) to a small pit where iron ore was once mined. Dark, dense chunks of the ore lie strewn about—bring along a magnet to confirm their identity.

Close the loop by turning right on a connector trail going north. You pass by two beautiful ponds—the first on public land, the second behind a fence on private property. Both brim after the winter rains, and reflect the green-mantled, bouldered mountainsides east and north. You end up joining the trail from the Ellie Lane parking lot, your starting point.

On the Iron Mountain Trail

Trip 7: Sycamore Canyon Open Space Preserve

	Distance	2- to 4-mile hikes
	Optional Map	USGS 7.5-min *San Vicente Reservoir*
	Best Times	All year
	Agency	SDCP
	Difficulty	* to **

Sycamore Canyon Open Space Preserve currently sprawls across 2000 acres of granite-ribbed mountains southeast of Poway. San Diego County and the cities of Poway and Santee are striving to carve out a large chunk of open space that would permanently separate the two cities, which are now growing toward each other. The adjacent Goodan Ranch has just been purchased by the county for future development as a regional park. It already sees use on the weekends by model-airplane enthusiasts who fly their radio-controled craft from a shaded staging area.

Two hiking trails and a small network of dirt roads currently thread the Sycamore/Goodan park area. The older, eastern trail is accessible from the Poway side (7days a week) by way of Garden Road and Sycamore Canyon Road. In the first half-mile the trail cuts across hillsides densely covered with a mixture of chaparral and sage-scrub vegetation. Look for wild peony, its inconspicuous reddish brown flowers nodding circumspectly by the trailside. After a short, steep descent, you cross a ravine bottom shaded by overarching oaks. Ahead a short distance is the Martha Harville Memorial Oak Grove (0.7 mile), with wooden benches thoughtfully provided. It's hard to believe peaceful places like this still exist so close to the city and suburbs. The Kumeyaay Indians appreciated this spot as well. Centuries ago they processed acorn meal in the deep morteros and shallow grinding slicks indenting the surfaces of nearby rock outcrops. Watch out for poison oak, which grows large and thick here. In vine form it has embraced some of the larger oaks, forming a mock tree-canopy of foliage.

If you continue to follow the trail down along the woodsy canyon, you'll soon reach a sloping meadow, reverberating with the chirps of a hundred crickets. If you have time, turn left on a trail that goes across the top of a small, earthen dam and joins a dirt road. (By going straight, you would head toward the model aircraft area in the middle of the valley ahead.) Turn left on the dirt road and use it to climb 400 feet on a zigzag course to the large dirt parking lot on Sycamore preserve's east rim. On the weekends only, you can drive to this parking lot by way of the graded Sycamore Park Road from Highway 67.

Down near the Goodan Ranch, a newer trail goes south along the broad floor of Sycamore Canyon, and leaves county park land. This trail (which later continues on a old dirt road) can be followed down the canyon as far as the Santee Lakes (see area C-5 map), about 4 miles south. The recreation area around the lake is fenced, but by keeping either west or east of the lakes you can eventually hook up with the suburban streets of Santee.

Freshly cut trail in Sycamore Canyon

Area C-3: Penasquitos

About a third of San Diego's total share of acreage set aside as open space lies within the city's fast-developing northern sector. This area includes the suburban communities of Mira Mesa, Rancho Penasquitos, and Carmel Valley. When the urban fabric of San Diego and its northern suburbs joins together as a tightly woven tapestry in a decade or two, the wisdom of preserving these, and hopefully other, parcels of natural landscape will be very much appreciated.

One patch of open space lies on the chaparral-clad slopes of Black Mountain, the dominant topographic feature in the Rancho Penasquitos area. Hike to the summit of this peak, and you'll experience a bird's-eye view of the city, the ocean, and the mountains to the east.

A much bigger patch of open space comprises the 6-mile-long, 3000-acre Los Penasquitos Canyon Preserve, already being referred to as an "oasis amid urban sprawl." Stretching between Interstate 5 and Interstate 15, it includes both Los Penasquitos Canyon—a major east-west drainage—and a tributary, Lopez Canyon. Riparian woodland, chaparral, and grassland habitats are superbly represented in various parts of the preserve.

Most acreage in the preserve centers along the canyon bottoms and steeper canyon walls and excludes the tops of the ridges. That exclusion is how a high-speed road, Sorrento Valley Boulevard, and other major streets were pushed across the heart of the preserve in the early 1990s. In just a few years, thousands of houses popped up on the slopes north of Los Penasquitos Canyon. The next several years may see the construction of rows of condominiums along the south wall of Los Penasquitos Canyon.

Over 130 kinds of birds, 26 mammals, 22 amphibians, and 90 different plants have been identified within the preserve. Currently a herd of about 35 mule deer roam the preserve, and bobcats and mountain lions were spotted in recent years. It is not certain how the larger animals will fare after the ultimate "build-out" of the surrounding area.

Visitor facilities at the preserve now include parking/equestrian staging areas off Black Mountain Road on the east side, and next to Sorrento Valley Boulevard on the west side. Near the east entry stands the Johnson-Taylor ranch house, now the preserve's headquarters, much of which dates from 1862. In 1991, archaeologists announced the discovery that part of the ranch house is a surviving remnant of an earlier structure built in 1824 for Captain Francisco Maria Ruiz. Ruiz was commandant of the Presidio of San Diego, and the recipient of the county's first Spanish land grant. The crumbling remnants of another adobe structure, also owned by Ruiz, stand under a protective roof at the west entrance to the preserve.

Human activity within the preserve centers along the 6-mile-long dirt road through Los Penasquitos Canyon. This is a multiuse trail for hikers, horse riders, and mountain bikers. Elsewhere, the other trails (which are closed to mountain bikes) are of an informal and usually unmaintained kind.

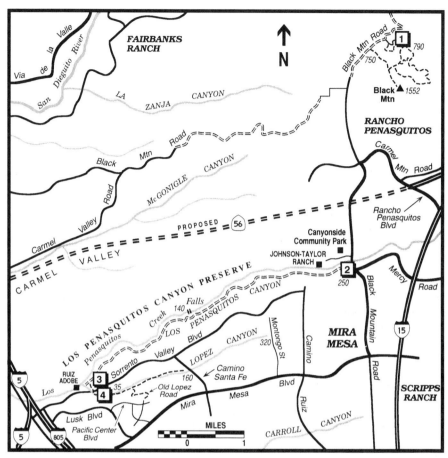

Area C-3: Penasquitos

Trip 1: Black Mountain

👟	**Distance**	3.5 miles
	Total Elevation Gain/Loss	1000'/1000'
	Hiking Time	2 hours
◪	**Optional Map**	USGS 7.5-min *Poway*
	Best Times	October through June
	Agency	SDOS
◘	**Difficulty**	**

On a really clear day atop Black Mountain your gaze encompasses a stretch of coastline from Dana Point in Orange County to Playas de Tijuana just south of the border. Mexico's Islas de Los Coronados poke up sharply beyond Point Loma to the south, while San Clemente Island and Santa Catalina Island float like mirages above low-lying coastal haze to the west. Quite often in winter you can spot the snowy summit of Old Baldy (Mt. San Antonio) in the San Gabriel Mountains to the north.

For years, local residents have been climbing Black Mountain by means of whatever old dirt road or firebreak seemed most convenient. Recently, however, about two miles of new hiking trail were constructed in the City of San Diego's Black Mountain Open Space park, which covers the north slope.

On this hike, you'll follow a 2.5-mile loop around the mountain's thickly chaparraled lower slopes. By tacking on an extra, steep, 1-mile round-trip climb, you include the top of the mountain and the wonderful view.

From the Black Mountain Road/Carmel Mountain Road intersection in Rancho Penasquitos, drive north on Black Mountain Road 2.5 miles to reach the turnoff for the open-space park. (The last part of Black Mountain Road is unpaved and possibly unsuitable for use after heavy rains). The short, paved entrance road leads to a large parking lot on a knoll overlooking a large spread of not-yet-developed land west of Rancho Bernardo. It's hard to believe the green, rolling hills below, part of San Diego's so-called urban reserve, may well be wall-to-wall subdivisions by the turn of the century.

From the parking lot, follow an old road, marked by trail signs, east. Ignore the first marked trail (old road) coming down the mountain from the right. Continue on to the narrow path that swings south up a ridge. Follow the path, generally uphill, passing three side trails—each one leading about 100 yards to an overlook. Benches have been thoughtfully placed at the second and third overlooks.

Onward past the overlooks, the trail at first sets a course for the microwave-antenna structures atop the mountain, but then it unexpectedly curves away and descends west. When you come to the next junction, an old firebreak, turn left to start the rocky, arduous 0.5-mile climb to the mountain's summit.

Even though you can't enjoy a full, 360° view from the summit in one stance, all you have to do is walk half-way around the fenced antenna structures to get the whole picture. The unique perspective afforded by Black Mountain tells a lot about San Diego's topography. To the south, overlain by seemingly endless rooftops, is a mesa-like platform called the Linda Vista Terrace. This is actually the middle level of three successive marine terraces evident in the area. A few remnants of the oldest and highest terrace, the Poway Terrace, can be glimpsed in the southeast and east. Imagine how this landscape looked sometime in the Pleistocene Epoch—with ocean waves rolling in over today's Rancho Penasquitos, Mira Mesa, and Kearny Mesa, and breakers crashing against a shoreline somewhere east of Interstate 15.

Trip 2: Los Penasquitos Canyon—East Approach

👟	**Distance**	6.5 miles round trip to falls
	Total Elevation Gain/Loss	300'/300'
	Hiking Time	3 hours (round trip)
◤	**Optional Map**	USGS 7.5-min *Del Mar*
	Best Times	All year
↗ 🚶	**Agency**	LPCP
	Difficulty	**

Take along a picnic lunch and a blanket on this hike. There are many fine places—sunny meadows, oak-shaded flats, and the sycamore-fringed streamside—to stop for an hour's relaxation. A good turnaround point is a small set of waterfalls and pools in the canyon bottom. This is about three miles out, midway through the Los Penasquitos preserve.

You begin at the parking and equestrian staging area on the west side of Black Mountain

Road, opposite Mercy Road. On foot now, head west on the dirt road. In the first mile this hugs Los Penasquitos Canyon's south wall, a steep, chaparral-covered hillside (*Los Penasquitos* means "the little cliffs").

As you pass near the Johnson-Taylor ranch (screened from view by willows and dense vegetation along the creek), you'll notice several non-native plants—eucalyptus, fan palms, and fennel, for example—introduced into this area over the past century. Next you enter a long and beautiful canopy of intertwined live oaks, accompanied by a lush understory of mostly poison oak.

Mile posts along the roadside help you gauge your progress. At mile 2 the trail winds out of the dense cover of oaks and continues through grassland dotted with a few small elderberry trees. Wildflowers such as wild radish, mustard, California poppies, bush mallow, and violets put on quite a show here in March and April. Look, too, for the fuchsia-flowered gooseberry, quite unmistakable when in bloom.

Soon after mile 2, an old road intersects and goes north across the creek to connect with a trail going along the north side of the canyon. You could follow this when you return from the falls.

At the 3-mile marker the road winds up onto the chaparral slope in order to detour a narrow, rocky section of the canyon. After the road goes down again, take one of the paths to the right (north) which lead to the canyon bottom. During the winter and early spring, a cascade of water tumbles through this constriction. Polished rock 10 feet up on either side testifies to its sometimes violent flow. These outcroppings of greenish-grey rock are a type called Santiago Peak volcanics; they're typical of the metavolcanic rock on Santiago Peak in the Santa Ana Mountains. Look for some slicks on the rock outcrops beside a shallow pool below the falls. Indians once milled and processed edible seeds there.

Author jogging in Los Penasquitos Canyon in early morn

Trip 3: Los Penasquitos Canyon—West Approach

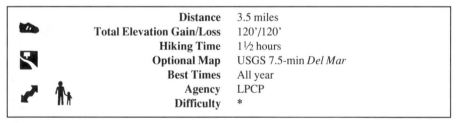	**Distance**	5.5 miles round trip to falls
	Total Elevation Gain/Loss	200'/200'
	Hiking Time	2 hours
	Optional Map	USGS 7.5-min *Del Mar*
	Best Times	All year
	Agency	LPCP
	Difficulty	**

As in the previous trip, the destination of this hike is the waterfall at the midpoint of Los Penasquitos Canyon. This time you approach from the west trailhead, just east of an industrial complex along Sorrento Valley Boulevard. Take the Sorrento Valley Road exit from either Interstate 5 or Interstate 805, follow frontage roads to Sorrento Valley Boulevard, and go northeast.

You'll enjoy the characteristic openness of this end of the canyon best if you come here on a cool day; the main dirt road stays well away from the stream most of the time, and is fully exposed to the sun. Try this hike sometime on a summer evening: plan to reach the falls by sunset, and return by the light of the moon.

Follow the trail going west under Sorrento Valley Boulevard and up broad Los Penasquitos Canyon. Sometimes fine springtime displays of lupine and owl's clover cover the steep, grassy slopes on the right. Wild radish, a plant introduced from Europe, often paints the lower slopes with shades of blue, white and purple.

At about 0.7 mile (near the 5-mile marker, measured from the east end of the canyon) the road comes close to the creek, and it's tempting to cross and explore the far bank. Do this only if the foliage along the creek is leafed out, so you can see and identify the poison oak that flourishes there.

Next, the road climbs a small hill and then descends to more grassland, dotted with small trees and shrubs such as elderberry, live oak, laurel sumac, toyon and gooseberry. Large sycamores and cottonwoods flank the creek. At a point well past mile marker 4, the road starts curving up a chaparral-covered slope. At the bottom of the next dip take one of the several small pathways leading to the waterfall area in the canyon bottom.

Trip 4: Lopez Canyon

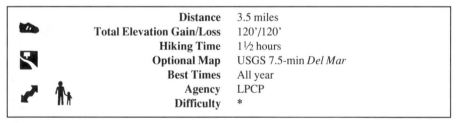	**Distance**	3.5 miles
	Total Elevation Gain/Loss	120'/120'
	Hiking Time	1½ hours
	Optional Map	USGS 7.5-min *Del Mar*
	Best Times	All year
	Agency	LPCP
	Difficulty	*

As "little brother" to Los Penasquitos Canyon, Lopez Canyon gets relatively little use, yet it could stand alone on its merit as a place worth saving. Lopez is dry most of the year, but the sights and smells of sage and chaparral and the stately sycamores down along the creekbed create a sense of a time long past when vaqueros herded cattle through this and many other coas-

tal canyons. Cattle were grazed in both canyons until the late 1980s, a tradition that stretched back to the Spanish and Mexican periods.

Begin at Los Penasquitos Canyon's west trailhead (see Trip 3 above), and walk east on the remnants of a dirt road up along Lopez Canyon's bottom. On the scenic stretch ahead, you'll spot an enormous, multitrunked sycamore tree on the right covering an area about 100 feet across.

At 0.9 mile, the Old Lopez Road (now a trail) comes down the south slope from Pacific Center Boulevard. The Lopez family homesteaded this canyon early this century and built a cabin on a little flat just north of the canyon stream. You can look for the cabin's remains next to an old pepper tree. Farther up the slope is a concrete cistern with the inscription "Ramona Lopez, Oct. 25, 1947."

After traveling about 1.7 miles up the canyon, you'll reach the last of the trees—just short of the towering Camino Santa Fe concrete bridge. This is a good place to turn around. Beyond lies a cobble-strewn, open stretch. By pressing on, you could reach Montongo Street, which crosses the canyon about 4 miles from the trailhead.

Sycamores in Lopez Canyon

Area C-4: Clairemont/University City

Aerial views of the Clairemont and University City neighborhoods of San Diego make one thing perfectly obvious: here is San Diego's "mesa and canyon" topography at its highest level of development. Geologists know this landform as an ancient marine terrace (the Linda Vista Terrace) incised by stream channels and their tributaries.

A strange kind of co-existence between unspoiled nature and full-speed-ahead development is apparent here: The mesa tops continue to fill up with a grid of housing developments and high-rise office buildings, while no more than a half mile away, a stream trickles through a canopy of oaks or a grove of sycamores in a canyon.

These once-ignored canyons, and their tributaries, or "finger canyons," have been the focus of many a fight between land developers and local homeowners. People have come to realize that canyons are valuable for their natural, educational, and recreational value. Thanks to the recent establishment of open space parks in the three largest major canyons of this area—Rose, San Clemente, and Tecolote—it looks as if the natural scenery will never be fully overwhelmed.

In recent years the canyons have become very popular among hikers, runners, and mountain bikers. If you live in Clairemont or University City, consider yourself lucky. If not, just hop on the freeway, or bicycle over on the surface streets, and you'll reach any of these canyons within minutes from most places around San Diego.

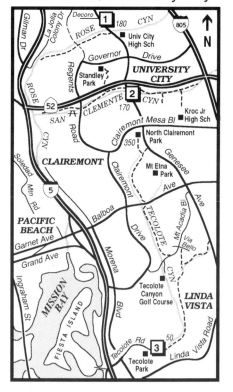

Area C-4:
Clairemont / University City

Trip 1: Rose Canyon

Distance	3.5 miles round trip
Total Elevation Gain/Loss	100'/100'
Hiking Time	1½ hours
Optional Map	USGS 7.5-min *La Jolla*
Best Times	All year
Agency	SDOS
Difficulty	*

From its outlet at Mission Bay, Rose Canyon extends north past the east brow of Soledad Mountain, and curves east toward the flat mesas of Miramar Naval Air Station. About 200,000 people unwittingly follow part of its course every day: Interstate 5 parallels the lower canyon's stream channel for about three miles, and the Santa Fe tracks (the main rail link to Los Angeles) stick with it for more than six miles. There's a proposal afoot to run San Diego Trolley tracks through here as well.

Luckily, the most picturesque and undisturbed section of Rose Canyon has been declared an open-space park by the City of San Diego. Lying only a scant mile from the Golden Triangle's high rises and traffic snarls, the park offers up a fine, smooth pathway perfect for walking, jogging, or lazy mountain-biking. Except for the Amtrak commuter trains gliding through every hour or so, the canyon resonates more with the sounds of woodpeckers, meadowlarks and crickets than with the din of auto traffic.

A convenient place to pick up the trail is along Genesee Avenue, across from University City High School. (There's no parking allowed on Genesee itself, but you'll find curbside parking space along Decoro Street, 0.2 mile north of the trail.) A large sign marks the beginning of the wide path, which follows the south side of the canyon. Dense clumps of willow and sycamore line the streambed and occasionally shade the path.

After about 1.5 miles, you'll come abreast of La Jolla Colony Drive, next to where Gilman Drive meets Interstate 5. This is a good spot to turn back and retrace your steps.

In Rose Canyon

Trip 2: San Clemente Canyon

🥾	**Distance**	1- to 4-mile hikes (out and back)
	Optional Map	USGS 7.5-min *La Jolla*, or street map
▨	**Best Times**	All year
	Agency	MBP
🧍	**Difficulty**	* to **

Eastbound in the right lane of Highway 52, the San Clemente Canyon Freeway, you can look down upon a long, slender, almost unbroken swath of natural vegetation: massive sycamores, stately live oaks, climbing vines, and tangled shrubs. This is one of San Diego County's best examples of riparian, or stream-loving, vegetation. (Recall that less than 0.2% of the county's land area consists of this type of vegetation) The decision to divert the freeway well above the canyon bottom and spare the trees, at slightly added cost, was a happy one indeed.

Much of San Clemente Canyon and several of its steep finger canyons are now included within the boundaries of Marian Bear Park, an area set aside by the City of San Diego as natural open space. Some visitor facilities are here too: parking areas, picnic tables and rest rooms off Regents Road and Genesee Avenue, and benches elsewhere.

Missing, of course, is the important element of silence. If you come here early on a Sunday morning, however, noise from the adjacent freeway is not particularly objectionable.

The easiest hiking is along the old roadbed which runs through the canopy of trees along the canyon's seasonal stream. The path stretches about three miles, is almost flat, and crosses the stream bed four times. In summer these crossings simply mean walking across cobblestones, but in winter some wading may be necessary.

The east end of the park (between Genesee Avenue and Interstate 805) offers the prettiest vegetation, the densest shade, and the biggest infestations of poison oak—which lies mostly away from the path in great tangled masses among the trees. Beginning about October, the leaves of the poison oak turn bright red in pleasing complement to the ever-green live oaks and

the yellows and oranges of the sycamores and willows.

There are several back entrances into Marian Bear Park. With the help of a city street map, you might incorporate these into a longer hike. For example:

From the west end of the main path, you can cross Rose Canyon's creek and the railroad tracks to reach the bike path paralleling Interstate 5; you can then go north to connect with Rose Canyon (Trip 1 above) or south to connect with frontage roads along Interstate 5. From a point between Regents Road and Genesee Avenue, a 0.5-mile-long trail goes north under Highway 52, follows a sage-scented ravine, zigzags through a hidden eucalyptus grove, and tops out at Standley Park in University City.

On the south side of San Clemente Canyon, an obscure pathway goes up to Cobb Drive on the mesa above. Another path follows high-voltage powerlines up toward Kroc Junior High School. These trails could be used in connection with residential streets in Clairemont to reach Tecolote Canyon Natural Park (see next trip).

Trip 3: Tecolote Canyon

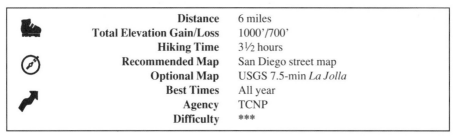

	Distance	6 miles
	Total Elevation Gain/Loss	1000'/700'
	Hiking Time	3½ hours
	Recommended Map	San Diego street map
	Optional Map	USGS 7.5-min *La Jolla*
	Best Times	All year
	Agency	TCNP
	Difficulty	***

Rustic signs along some of Clairemont's major streets call attention to one of the most valuable canyon habitats in San Diego's urban core: the 900-acre Tecolote Canyon Natural Park. On the park's patchwork of old roads and trails it's possible to poke into just about every nook and cranny. By day you're sure to spot a hawk soaring on the thermals or perching high on the crown of a dead oak tree. By night, perhaps, you might hear the yapping of a coyote or the plaintive hoot of an owl, the creature for which this canyon was named.

The title "Natural Park" refers in part to the native vegetation. The dominant plant communities are sage scrub (California sagebrush, white sage, black sage, lemonade berry, laurel sumac, monkey flower) and chaparral (chamise, toyon, scrub oak, hollyleaf cherry, redberry). Live oaks, willows, and sycamores grow along the stream channel in places where water is more plentiful. Since Tecolote Canyon has been completely surrounded by an urbanized environment for about 30 years, it's not surprising to find invading non-native plants here too. The worst "offenders" are tumbleweed, wild chrysanthemum, mustard, fennel, pampas grass, and ice plant.

For all but the most cursory exploration of this canyon, you should wear hiking boots, or at least a pair of running shoes designed for off-road traction. Be forewarned that winter rains can turn the clayey soils into sticky mud. Take along a city street map to assist in general orientation and to aid your return to the starting point via city streets, if that is your wish. Most recent-edition maps show the park's boundary.

Begin at Tecolote Park and Recreation Center, opposite Interstate 5 from Mission Bay. The smooth, dirt roadway leading up the broad, lower end of the canyon is fine for casual walking, or jogging, at first.

As you approach Tecolote Canyon Golf Course you'll start struggling up and down some steep hillsides just outside the perimeter fence. Sooner or later, on the maze of roads ahead, you should climb up the east slope of the canyon and follow the bulldozed track paralleling the high-voltage powerlines north.

Only the adventurous should continue now. Slip down a very steep section of bulldozed track to the bottom of a large eastward-heading tributary (a side trip up this fine, oak-shaded canyon to Genesee Avenue is worthwhile if you have the energy). Continue following the

In Tecolote Canyon

powerlines upward to Via Bello, go left on Via Bello for one block, then use the shoulder of Mt. Acadia Boulevard to get back to the bottom of Tecolote Canyon. Someday, the construction of a trail skirting the golf course should make this awkward detour unnecessary.

Go up the canyon now on the well-beaten path along Tecolote creek's east bank. There are good picnic spots here and there among the oaks—but watch out for poison oak!

Balboa Avenue, next, is somewhat of an obstacle. You can cross underneath the roadway in the tunnel (if reasonably dry) that carries the floodwaters of the creek, or climb the embankment and attempt to scoot across the busy lanes and over the concrete center divider—a dangerous maneuver at best. On the safe side, you could walk up the south shoulder of Balboa Avenue, cross at the traffic light on Clairemont Drive, then walk back on the north shoulder.

North of Balboa Avenue you have two choices: go up the eastern tributary to Mt. Etna Park, or thread your way up the main canyon on a well beaten path to either Genesee Avenue or North Clairemont Park.

Area C-5: Mission Trails Regional Park

Touted as the largest urban park in the country, Mission Trails Regional Park preserves some of the last remaining open space lying close to the heart of San Diego.

The concept of a new park on the east edge of San Diego was formalized in 1960, following the transfer of surplus former military reservation land to the jurisdiction of the City of San Diego. By the late '70s, the City and County of San Diego had cooperated in the purchase of 2000 acres on Cowles Mountain for preservation as open space, and a broader concept emerged—that of a 6000-acre regional park serving the diverse needs of residents throughout the entire county.

Today, while most of the park still remains undeveloped, urban development continues to press in around its perimeter. The extension of the State 52 freeway from Tierrasanta to Santee (to be completed in fall 1993) already defines the park's north boundary. On the west and east sides, the park has become hemmed in by the suburbs of Tierrasanta and Santee. There's a move afoot—currently stalled—to extend Jackson Drive along the park's west side to Highway 52. If built, this high-speed road would become the de facto west boundary, reducing in size the large block of open space now existing in the Mission Gorge area. On the south end of the park, Cowles Mountain and Lake Murray stand amid the mostly built-out communities of San Carlos, La Mesa, and Santee.

Mission Gorge along with Fortuna Mountain comprises the nucleus of the original park proposed in 1960. The visitor area overlooking the Old Mission Dam (a national historical landmark) has recently been rehabilitated, and a new campground will soon be built adjacent to Kumeyaay Lake (formerly Hollins Lake), east of the dam. Father Junipero Serra Trail, the original road through Mission Gorge, has been reconfigured with a divider down the middle: one side is for one-way traffic going northeast, while the other side has become a two-way bike path used by bicyclists, pedestrians and skaters. One of San Diego's best rock-climbing sites lies a mile southwest of the Old Mission Dam. There, climbers practice moves on several near-vertical granite walls overlooking the gorge and the San Diego River.

Cowles Mountain, centerpiece of the regional park, stands 1591 feet above sea level, the highest point within San Diego's city limits. Hundreds of people walk the main south trail to its summit daily. Several newer trails have been laid out on the east and north slopes of the mountain in recent years, so now hikers can choose among several summit routes.

The southern end of the regional park includes a golf course and Lake Murray, a city reservoir open to recreational use such as walking, bicycling, picnicking, fishing, and boating.

In February 1995, the $5.5 million Mission Trails Regional Park visitor center opened. Located on a knoll near the intersection of Father Junipero Serra Trail and Mission Gorge Road, the center features video displays, archaeological exhibits, a library, and bay-window views of Mission Gorge and neighboring peaks.

The following descriptions are suggestions for seven interesting trips in the Mission Trails Regional Park area. Aside from the routes specifically noted here, there are many other powerline service roads, firebreaks, and old jeep trails to wander along within the park.

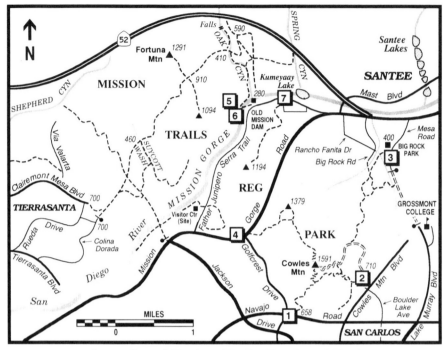

Area C-5: Mission Trails Regional Park

Trip 1: Cowles Mountain—South Approach

👟	**Distance**	3 miles round trip
	Total Elevation Gain/Loss	950'/950'
	Hiking Time	2 hours (round trip)
🔲	**Optional Map**	USGS 7.5-min *La Mesa*
	Best Times	October through June
↗ 👫	**Agency**	MTRP
	Difficulty	**

Starting from the new trailhead staging area at Navajo Road and Golfcrest Drive, this popular switchbacking trail ascends the sunny south side of Cowles Mountain, consistently offering a vista stretching from the Pacific Ocean to Mexico. The predominant chaparral and sage scrub growth rarely exceeds shoulder height, so views are unobstructed from nearly every point on the trail.

Short spur trails branch from the main trail and lead to secluded overlooks—nice places to

relax and enjoy the view, or have a picnic.

The trail was cut on mostly decomposed granite, so it is quite susceptible to erosion wherever the slope gets steep. Please don't shortcut the switchbacks, tempting as it may be on the way down, as this aggravates the erosion problem.

At a point 1.0 mile up, a trail branches right and eventually descends the east slope. Stay left and continue up the slope on the series of long switchbacks leading to the rocky summit of the mountain.

A blocky building bristling with microwave dishes obstructs the northward view somewhat, but otherwise the panorama is complete. With binoculars and a street map, you could spend a lot of time identifying features on the urban landscape. In the rift between the mesas to the west, there's a good view of Mission Valley and the tangle of freeways that pass over and through it. Southwest, the towers of downtown San Diego stand against Point Loma, Coronado, and the sparkling bay. Lake Murray shimmers to the south. The chain of Santee Lakes contrasts darkly with pale hills to the north. In all directions, you can get a sense of how populous the region has become. About four million people (on both sides of the border) now live within a 35-mile radius centered on the mountain.

On clear winter days, the view expands to include most of the higher peaks of San Diego County. Southward into Baja, you can see the flat-topped "Table Mountain" behind Tijuana, and the Coronado Islands offshore. During absolutely crystalline weather, look for the profiles of Santa Catalina and San Clemente islands, to the northwest and west respectively.

Here's a suggestion for romantics and adventurers who don't mind descending the trail by flashlight: catch the sunset from Cowles' summit when the moon is full. After the sun slides into the Pacific, turn around and enjoy the moonrise over the El Cajon valley!

Lake Murray from Cowles Mountain Summit

Trip 2: Cowles Mountain—East Approach

	Distance	3 miles
	Total Elevation Gain/Loss	1000'/1000'
	Hiking Time	2 hours
	Optional Map	USGS 7.5-min *La Mesa*
	Best Times	October through June
	Agency	MTRP
	Difficulty	**

To avoid the hordes of Cowles Mountain regulars on the popular south trail, try this loop on the east slope instead. Partly on a service road (open only to maintenance vehicles) and partly on an ill-maintained trail, the route draws relatively few travelers. Since I live relatively close to the mountain and use it as a training ground, you'll often find me jogging up either the road or the trail by the light of dawn.

When early-morning fog hugs the ground, most commonly in the fall, a quick trip up the slope allows me to punch through the cloud layer and witness a scene every bit equal to the famous sunrises over the cloud-wreathed crater of Haleakala on Maui.

Begin near the west terminus of Boulder Lake Avenue, one block west of Cowles Mountain Boulevard. Squeeze past the vehicle gate and start climbing up the service road. Footwear with good traction will help on the sometimes steep and slippery, hard-packed dirt roadway. Two level stretches relieve the uphill grind, then six short, very steep switchback legs lead to the summit.

Return to your starting point by descending the upper 0.5 mile of the main, south trail. Then veer left (east) on the lesser-traveled east trail. You bend northeast around the mountain and soon start descending on many tight switchbacks. They'll take you to a point close to the foot of the service road, which you'll be able to reach by dodging a few bushes.

Sunset from Cowles Mountain

Trip 3: Cowles Mountain—Northeast Approach

👞	Distance	4.5 miles
	Total Elevation Gain/Loss:	1400'/1400'
	Hiking Time	3 hours
🏴	Optional Map	USGS 7.5-min *La Mesa*
	Best Times	October through June
⟳	Agency	MTRP
	Difficulty	***

This most difficult approach to Cowles' summit is also the most beautiful—especially in the early spring when blooming chaparral, ground-hugging wildflowers, and bright green grass freshen the landscape.

The trails on the mountain's northeast slopes are mostly reworked versions of old roads cut for mining access or fire control. Most are very steep in places and often rocky and eroded. A veritable maze of still-obvious trails cut by motorcycles long ago makes route-finding a bit confusing here. Generally you can recognize the maintained (often unsigned) routes by looking for improvements such as water bars (rocks and dirt heaped up to keep water from flowing down the trail).

Big Rock Park (corner of Mesa Road and Prospect Avenue), Santee's most attractive city park, is a good starting point for the northeast trek to the summit. Follow the park's perimeter fence to a trail running south and parallel to a small watercourse we'll call Big Rock Creek. After passing the west end of Rancho Fanita Drive, you go up along a hillside, gradually heading away from the creek and a row of houses to the west. At 0.5 mile a trail merges from the right—it leads back down to Big Rock Creek and hooks up with the end of Big Rock Road. At a fork a hundred yards farther south, a trail diverges to the left; either fork will work, but stay right if you want to follow the more scenic path.

Work your way sharply uphill through dense, aromatic chaparral to a junction with an unmaintained trail at 1.2 miles. Stay right and follow an eroded path 0.2 mile to where you meet the wide maintenance road going up to Cowles' summit. From there, use the road to climb 0.8 mile farther to the summit and return the same way.

On the return, you can try a somewhat different tack. Retrace your steps on the eroded path for 0.2 mile, but stay right at the next junction (not left, which is the way you came up the hill). After another 0.3 mile, and just after a very steep and rocky downhill stretch, bear right. You'll descend east along a hillside, finally reaching a graded dirt road (when paved someday, it will carry traffic between Mesa Road and Lake Murray Boulevard). Follow this graded road down past a rock outcrop on the left—a beautiful mini-waterfall after lots of rain—and you'll come to your starting point along Mesa Road.

Trip 4: Cowles Mountain—Northwest Approach

	Distance	3.2 miles round trip
	Total Elevation Gain/Loss	1400'/1400'
	Hiking Time	2½ hours (round trip)
	Optional Map	USGS 7.5-min *La Mesa*
	Best Times	October through June
	Agency	MTRP
	Difficulty	***

For years, hikers have traveled up and down the north and northwest ridges of Cowles Mountain, beating down a well-worn, though very steep and rocky trail. A 1988 fire burned these slopes to a crisp, but now the chaparral and sage-scrub vegetation is returning, softening the stark appearance of the mountain.

Unless you're very sure-footed, you should rely on the stability and traction of hiking boots for this approach. Parts of the trail can get quite clogged by springtime growth, and therefore difficult to follow.

You begin along the shoulder of Mission Gorge Road, just around the corner from (east of) Golfcrest Drive. Find the obscure trail that wastes no time in going straight up the ridge ahead. Seven hundred vertical feet (and lots of heavy breathing) later, the trail quits climbing and contours across a grassy slope toward a notch just south of Peak 1379.(Two side trails

ascend toward Peak 1379's rocky summit.) From the notch, follow the path ascending south, over or past several boulder piles, to a high point at about 1380 feet. You're now more than a mile from any semblance of a road, and so high above the San Carlos and Santee suburbs that the sounds of the city traffic have become merely a muted, sonorous roar.

Next, the trail descends precipitously 150 feet to a saddle north of the Cowles Mountain summit. From the saddle, a better-defined trail takes you the remaining 350 vertical feet up to the microwave antenna structure that sits just north of Cowles' true summit.

You can retrace your steps, 3.2 miles for the round trip; or instead, for a longer, roundabout return, follow the main trail down Cowles' south side and then the sidewalk along Golfcrest Drive.

Trip 5: Oak Canyon

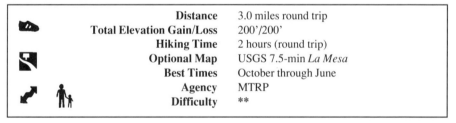

	Distance	3.0 miles round trip
	Total Elevation Gain/Loss	200'/200'
	Hiking Time	2 hours (round trip)
	Optional Map	USGS 7.5-min *La Mesa*
	Best Times	October through June
	Agency	MTRP
	Difficulty	**

Oak Canyon, a sycamore- and oak-lined ravine winding north from the Old Mission Dam, is a perfect place to celebrate the return of spring in San Diego. Heavy rains never fail to revive the canyon's intermittent stream and transform the hillside vegetation from dormant brown to festive green. By March, annual

wildflowers pop up amid the tender new blades of grass, blooming ceanothus colors the slopes, and the sweet-pungent odor of sage floats on the warm breeze.

Start at the Old Mission Dam parking area, along the paved road called Father Junipero Serra Trail, 0.8 mile west of Mission Gorge

Road in Santee. (Vehicle gates on both ends of Father Junipero Serra Trail swing shut between sunset and sunrise, so don't get caught with your car inside.) The dam was built between 1807 and 1816 under the direction of the San Diego Mission, and was considered a major engineering feat of its day. A 6-mile-long flume carried water from the dam to the mission located at the east end of Mission Valley.

From the parking area, walk west (downstream) past the old dam and across the turbid waters of the San Diego River by way of an iron footbridge. Once across the river, double back east for 0.2 mile, and then go left on the informal pathway up along the shallow bottom of Oak Canyon. In the next mile or so you'll wend your way along the banks of the trickling creek, passing small cascades and rock-bound pools (in season, of course). Small kids will need a hand in places, and they should be kept well away from the sheer drops here and there along the banks.

Oak Canyon

All will enjoy the scamperings of cottontail rabbits through the brush, and with some luck, you might flush a covey of quail. Coyotes patrol these spaces, but unless the hour is either very early or very late you'll likely see no more than tracks and scat.

At 1.2 miles the path intersects a dirt service road. Turn left, follow the road about 100 yards, and go right on a path that continues up Oak Canyon. About ¼ mile farther you'll come to a picturesque mini-chasm of water-polished rock, with a deep, narrow pool. This is about as far as it's worth going; the new Highway 52 passes over the canyon not far ahead, and military land lies beyond.

Trip 6: Fortuna Mountain

	Distance	4.2 miles round trip
	Total Elevation Gain/Loss	1000'/1000'
	Hiking Time	3 hours (round trip)
	Optional Map	USGS 7.5-min *La Mesa*
	Best Times	November through May
	Agency	MTRP
	Difficulty	***

Unlike the view from Cowles Mountain, Fortuna's expansive vantage encompasses a good deal of still-undeveloped country. Low-sun illumination delineates the rolling, sensuous texture of the parallel ridges and shallow canyons to the northeast. In the southeast, four

shaggy peaks—1094, 1194, 1379, and finally 1591-foot Cowles Mountain—lie along an almost-straight line. It's easy to see why this linear range of mountains is called "Long Mountain" on century-old maps.

On this hike, you never actually see

Fortuna's summit until you're almost within spitting distance of it. You begin, exactly as in Trip 5 above, by following the deep-cut course of Oak Canyon north from the Old Mission Dam. At 1.2 miles turn left on a dirt road built to service the power lines passing overhead. Continue 0.5 mile west, up a steep ravine to a 910' saddle southeast of Fortuna's summit. Just short of the saddle, the road becomes so steep it's difficult to keep from slipping in the dirt. Bear right at the intersection of roads on top, and proceed northwest up a steep, eroded firebreak to the 1291' summit, which is marked by a few large boulders.

Fortuna Mountain is also accessible from the Tierrasanta side. You can start at either the east end of Clairemont Mesa Boulevard or the north end of Colina Dorada. By staying on dirt roads more or less close to the high-voltage power-lines, you'll reach the 910' saddle near Fortuna's summit.

Trip 7: Peak 1194

	Distance	2.5 miles round trip
	Total Elevation Gain/Loss	900'/900'
	Hiking Time	1½ hours (round trip)
	Optional Map	USGS 7.5-min *La Mesa*
	Best Times	November through May
	Agency	MTRP
	Difficulty	**

Flanked by steep walls on all sides but one, peak 1194's platform-like top stands quite aloof from all else around it. The peak offers a unique vantage for tracing the lower San Diego River's course. To the east you'll see the river's willow-lined flood plain dividing the suburban tracts of Santee. In the west and southwest you'll see how its mighty flow (in Pleistocene times, at least) carved the granite walls of Mission Gorge.

A decently well-defined but rather steep old road/trail ascends the peak's north ridge, starting from the intersection of Simeon Drive and Father Junipero Serra Trail (0.4 mile east of Mission Gorge Road. The trail goes up and down a bit before settling into a steady grind up along the north ridge.

There's not much to find in the way of comfortable sitting spots on the summit, but you can wander east over to the top of the rock outcrops overlooking Mission Gorge Road for lunch and a great view of Santee. There are rock outcrops on the west and south sides as well. You should avoid scrambling down to the out-crops on west, so as not to dislodge rocks that could roll and injure the climbers who practice on the sheer rock faces below.

View east from Peak 1194

Area C-6: Lakeside/Ramona

Several newly opened parks and open-space preserves in the foothills between Lakeside and Ramona now beckon hikers and nature lovers. All are county-managed facilities, except for the oldest one—the Audubon Society's Silverwood Wildlife Sanctuary. All offer the city-dwelling public an opportunity to study and enjoy the chaparral, oak woodland, and riparian vegetation that are fast disappearing on San Diego County's urban fringes.

Most of the parks and preserves lie along Wildcat Canyon Road, which climbs steeply into the foothills north of Lakeside and continues through the scenic Barona Indian Reservation toward Ramona and San Diego County Estates. To reach Wildcat Canyon Road, take Highway 67 to Mapleview Street in Lakeside, go east for 0.3 mile, then north on Ashwood Street. Ashwood becomes Wildcat Canyon Road after one mile. From Ramona, you can reach the north end of Wildcat Canyon Road by way of San Vicente Road, which is the south extension of 10th Street in Ramona.

This can be mighty hot and dry country in summer—but cool and invigorating in the "dead" of winter, and green, moist and inviting during the magical months of March and April. When the right morning comes along, go ahead and "seize the moment." Make your getaway for a couple of hours or a half day of great hiking close to the city.

Trip 1: Stelzer County Park

Distance	1 to 2 miles
Optional Map	USGS 7.5-min *San Vicente Reservoir*
Best Times	October through May
Agency	SDCP
Difficulty	* to **

Stelzer County Park features 314 acres of trails, campsites and picnic areas, and a small interpretive area. The park was specially designed to attract handicapped persons, though nonhandicapped visitors and hikers are welcome as well. You'll find the park's well marked entrance on Wildcat Canyon Road, two miles up from Mapleview Street in Lakeside.

Of interest to hikers are two trails of quite different character. The Riparian Trail parallels the stream bottom of Wildcat Canyon for about 0.5 mile, ending at a secluded picnic site. It is shaded throughout by a stream-hugging canopy of live oaks, some draped with filigrees of wild-grape and poison-oak vines.

The Stelzer Ridge Trail, on the other hand, zigzags 0.6 mile toward the ridgeline south and east of Wildcat Canyon. This wide, gradually ascending trail is cut wide enough for most wheelchair use. The most recent fire swept across these slopes in 1982, so you can see the result of a decade or more of regrowth. The now-vigorous laurel sumac and toyon shrubs were among the first plants to recover.

At the top of the Stelzer Ridge Trail, there are two choices for those who wish a better view: you can go 0.3 mile southwest on a power-line access road to reach "Kumeyaay Promontory," or go 0.5 mile northeast up a steep ridge to "Stelzer Summit." Both points offer good views of the San Diego River valley and the cities of Lakeside and Santee to the south.

Area C-6: Lakeside / Ramona

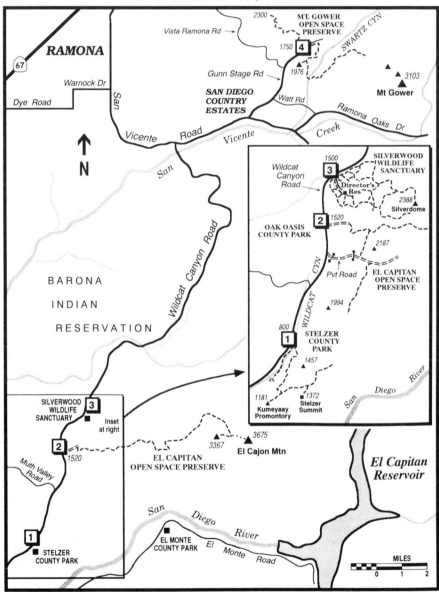

Trip 2: El Capitan Open Space Preserve

	Distance	10.0 miles
	Total Elevation Gain/Loss	4000'/4000'
	Hiking Time	5½ hours
	Optional Maps	USGS 7.5-min *San Vicente Reservoir*, *El Cajon Mtn.*
	Best Times	November through April
	Agency	SDCP
	Difficulty	****

As you walk along the granite-ribbed ridgeline, down the middle of the El Capitan Open Space Preserve, a binational panorama of ocean, islands, and innumerable mountain peaks lies in view. The broad San Diego River valley below curves beneath the sheer south face of El Cajon Mountain—the landmark informally known as "El Capitan."

The 2800-acre preserve was pieced together out of former BLM lands adjacent to the Cleveland National Forest. If you have the determination to tackle some really severe uphills and downhills, try following the main ridge-running trail—actually an old road bulldozed by miners years ago. It twists and turns over a scrubby, boulder-punctuated landscape that in spring comes alive with a blue frosting of ceanothus blossoms.

If you follow the old road to its end, 5 miles out, you'll reach a 3367-foot peak subordinate only to the slightly higher summit of El Cajon Mountain nearby. This strenuous effort involves a surprising gain and loss of 4000 vertical feet (because of various ups and downs) over the entire round trip. Still, a nice vista of the surrounding mountains can be yours even if you hike less than a mile to reach the first of the five trailside rest stops along the way.

Park in the signed lot on the east side of Wildcat Canyon Road (at mile 4.2). On the opposite side of the road is Oak Oasis County Park, which is being developed as a picnic area. From the lot, walk east 0.4 mile on a graded dirt road, past some houses, to where the trail starts a steep, zigzag ascent up a cool, north-facing slope. You soon hook up with the old mining road, and the going gets easier for a while. Once you're past a small summit, the round top and

sheer south brow of El Cajon Mountain become visible in the middle distance. Closer, on the left, rises the impressive Silverdome peak (in the Silverwood Wildlife Sanctuary), believed to be the largest granite monolith in San Diego County. As you start descending, a narrow trail forks right, leading south 1.5 miles to a dead-end (as of 1992) at the preserve's south boundary. This side trail will eventually connect with Stelzer Park's trail system.

A very steep pitch, starting at 2.6 miles, will turn you back if you're not serious about this hike. A proposed trail will one day veer south from the 2.6-mile point and follow a south ridge down to El Monte Park, 1500 feet below.

At 4.0 miles, a rock-lined spring on the left, brimming with iron-rich water, serves horses (not people) that can make it this far. At 4.8 miles, the road arrives on a saddle between El Cajon Mountain's summit dome on the left and a smaller 3367-foot peak on the right (west). Turn right on the spur road going west to reach

Old mining road in El Capitan Preserve

the latter summit, which offers a 270° view of distant horizons.

At the saddle, a sign indicates private property ahead (to the south). As an option on this hike, you can bag El Cajon Mountain's summit, which has a climber's register, by going due east. You'll soon pick up the brushy summit trail, worn in by hikers, that goes through national forest land to the summit.

Trip 3: Silverwood Wildlife Sanctuary

	Distance	1- to 4-mile loops
	Recommended Map	Silverwood trail map (available at entrance)
	Optional Maps	USGS 7.5-min San *Vicente Reservoir*, *El Cajon Mtn.*
	Best Times	October through June
	Agency	SWS
	Difficulty	* to ***

Silverwood: the name comes from the glittering effect of sunlight upon the leaves of the coast live oak. Scores of these trees, some of them 200-year-old giants scarred by fire, shade the canyon floor at the entrance to the Silverwood Wildlife Sanctuary and Nature Education Center. Owned and managed by the San Diego Audubon Society, the sanctuary preserves 700 acres of flora and fauna indigenous to the foothill region.

Silverwood is open to the public every Sunday (except in August) between 9 a.m. and 4 p.m. You'll find the entrance on the east side of Wildcat Canyon Road at mile 4.8. For your first visit, plan to attend the guided nature walk (at 10 and 1:30) to familiarize yourself with the area's natural history. Topics include plant identification, chaparral ecology, geology, bird watching, and identification of animal tracks and scats.

Several miles of hiking trails lace the area. A short and easy stroll from the parking lot to the director's house will introduce you to a cool, moist environment in the shade of the spreading oaks. Half a dozen kinds of fungi can be found clinging to fallen limbs or pushing through the leaf litter. Just beyond the house is a small cienaga, or soggy meadow, adorned in spring with blue-eyed grass and paintbrush blossoms.

The outlying trails of Silverwood are narrow, rugged, easily overgrown, and not always maintained. Some of these climb, like spokes in a wheel, to Circuit Trail, a loop trail following the rugged, chaparral-clad ridges that overlook the oak-filled valley. A single eucalyptus tree, planted next to the director's house, stands head and shoulders above all else in the valley and marks the direction of return for confused hikers.

On the relatively short (2 miles) but difficult hike around the Circuit Trail, the springtime blossoms of ceanothus, sage, coast spice bush, manzanita, and a dozen other flowering plants scent the air with sweet fragrances. There are two more remote trips possible via the Circuit Trail—the Silverspring Trail (about 3 miles round trip) and the Silverdome Trail (about 4 miles round trip)—both surprisingly arduous. These trips require the permission of the director; take lots of water and be sure you can get back before closing time.

The Silverdome Trail goes to the top of a rounded granitic dome about 500 feet high, believed to be the largest granite monolith in San Diego County. Ecologists have done a study of the biological "successional islands" on the exposed, exfoliating surface of the dome. Lichens are the first colonizers; then come certain hardy mosses—but only in crevices and depressed areas where surface flows of rainwater are concentrated, yet not too erosive. If the mosses trap dust particles and debris to form a layer of soil, succulent live-forevers (specifically a type descriptively called "lady fingers") establish a foothold on the rock. The live-forevers act as a further trap for soil, which leads to colonization of many more species, including ferns, grasses and flowering plants. Some of the richer islands on the dome exhibit, in concentric zones, the full range of succession. In other places, succession has been halted, and only lichens and mosses survive, often in mazelike patterns on the rock.

Trip 4: Mount Gower Open Space Preserve

👟	**Distance**	4- to 6-mile hikes
	Optional Map	USGS 7.5-min *Ramona*
	Best Times	November through April
🏔	**Agency**	SDCP
	Difficulty	** to ***

The 1574-acre Mount Gower preserve is one of several parcels of surplus federal land being transferred from the BLM to San Diego County jurisdiction. The preserve is being managed primarily for protection of the natural vegetation and wildlife, but public use is mandated as well. The county has been busy building a parking area and trails for the convenience of visitors. As of this writing, 5 miles of a projected 8 miles of trail have been completed. The unfinished links may lead to two proposed trail campgrounds on the west shoulder of Mt. Gower, a rocky promontory that serves as a local landmark.

To reach the preserve from Ramona, take San Vicente Road 6 miles south and east to Gunn Stage Road. Turn left (north), and continue 1.8 miles to the preserve entrance. Drive another ¼ mile on a graded dirt road to the fenced lot on the right. An informational kiosk marks the start of the trail system at the far end of the lot.

The trail system has two main branches. The meandering west trail, 2.0 miles long, leads to a 2300' viewpoint on top of a barren ridge. This is worth the climb on clear days, when you can take advantage of a view that includes the Coronado Islands, Point Loma, Mt. San Antonio in Los Angeles County, and a long roster of San Diego County high points.

The more difficult, rambling trail to the south and east currently goes about 3 miles before petering out. At 1.2 miles you reach a pleasant rest area overlooking oak-lined Swartz Canyon. From there, you can follow a short spur trail up to a 1976-foot peaklet perched strategically over San Diego Country Estates and San Vicente Valley. Past the rest area, the trail descends to cross Swartz Canyon and then ascends on zig-zags to a high ridgeline. After following this ridge for a while, you descend into a shady ravine, 3.0 miles from the start, and reach the dead end. Someday, Mt. Gower's summit may be rather easily reached by this approach, but not now—there's impenetrable chaparral ahead.

Local hikers have forged a path to Mt. Gower by way of a southern route that doesn't start in the open-space preserve. Don't try to follow it unless you're a glutton for adventure and absolutely sure you can retrace your route: Find the marked equestrian trail starting from Bellemore Drive, 0.45 mile east of Welcome Way. It skirts a couple of houses and enters Cleveland National Forest as it ascends a hillside. A side trail contours east and enters a narrow canyon cut by San Vicente Creek, while the main trail continues to rise toward another trail junction atop a saddle, 0.9 mile from the start. The trail to the left (west) continues on a more or less level course for 0.7 mile, then it swings sharply right (uphill). The rest of the now-obscure trail, marked in places by red and orange ribbons, continues north and finally east over rock slabs to reach the northernmost of three summits of virtually identical height—just over 3100 feet. From there you can look down on the secluded EA Ranch, with its quarter-mile thoroughbred track, in a valley to the north. Mt. Gower's two south summits are guarded by dense thickets of brush and are very difficult to reach.

Area C-7: Alpine/Jamul

A kind of low-density suburbia has been creeping across the rugged foothills and valleys east of San Diego as more and more people who work in the city seek a quiet, pseudo-rural lifestyle. Still, opportunities for hiking in the areas around Alpine and Jamul have actually increased in recent years.

After falling into disuse in the '70s and '80s, the California Riding and Hiking Trail, which passes near Alpine and Jamul, is once again coming to life—thanks mainly to the efforts of groups such as the San Diego Trails Council (an equestrian organization). One of the biggest obstacles has been legal access to the route. The original trail was routed in many places over private property, so it was necessary to obtain easement rights from various property owners before the trail could be signed and reopened to

Area C-7: Alpine / Jamul

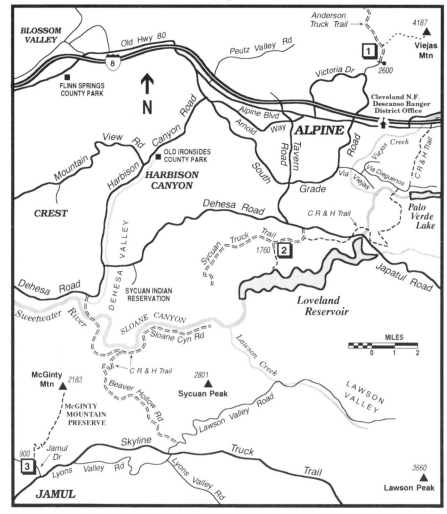

public use.

Much of the still-uncompleted California Riding and Hiking Trail is routed on dirt roads open to auto traffic, which makes it a bit tedious for walking—though good enough for horseback riding and mountain biking. The most interesting part of the CRHT mapped here goes between Japatul Road and Via Dieguenos in the Palo Verde (southeast) part of Alpine.

Just east of Alpine, in the Cleveland National Forest, the Sweetwater River cuts through a rugged little gorge ending at Palo Verde Lake. Someday the Forest Service may construct a trail through here, and perhaps another to the nearby granite-ribbed summit of Bell Bluff, which also lies in the national forest. Northeast

of Alpine, massive Viejas Mountain rises to an elevation of over 4000 feet. An obscure trail, described below, leads to its summit.

Another hike decribed below, a very short one, leads to the shoreline of Loveland Reservoir, which is largely off-limits to public use. A third hike I describe below focuses on McGinty Mountain, just outside Jamul, which is notable for the extraordinary number of rare plants found there. The Nature Conservancy picked up most of the McGinty land from the BLM in 1983, when the agency sought to dispose of isolated lands it could not properly manage. Additional land purchases increased the preserve's size to 800 acres and made it possible to construct a trail allowing public access.

Trip 1: Viejas Mountain

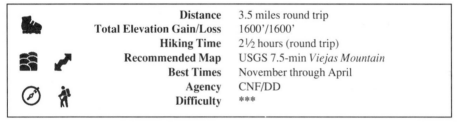

Distance	3.5 miles round trip
Total Elevation Gain/Loss	1600'/1600'
Hiking Time	2½ hours (round trip)
Recommended Map	USGS 7.5-min *Viejas Mountain*
Best Times	November through April
Agency	CNF/DD
Difficulty	***

Undistinguished by either its moderate height or its rather squat shape, Viejas Mountain is nonetheless a fairly prominent topographic feature. Standing aloof from nearby peaks, it can be seen from many parts of metropolitan San Diego as a dusky, obtusely triangular feature along the eastern horizon. A faint, partially overgrown trail up the west slope offers the only straightforward passage to the summit, a trek that is well worth the effort during crystal-clear weather.

Most San Diegans can drive to the trailhead in as little as 40 minutes. Exit Interstate 8 at Tavern Road, go south 0.1 mile, then go east on Alpine Boulevard through the town of Alpine. After 1.5 miles, turn left (north) on East Victoria Drive, passing under I-8. Proceed 1.1 miles north to Anderson Road. Turn right and continue northeast 0.5 mile to a large water tank and gate (which may or may not block motor traffic).

Park just short of the gate and continue on foot 0.3 mile uphill to a point just before where the road becomes level. To your right (east) look for the unmarked beginning of the informal trail up the brushy slope of Viejas Mountain.

The ascent is straight up the mountain at first, then slightly winding as you near the summit. You'll be in waist-to-shoulder-high chaparral the whole way. The occasional passage of hikers and coyotes is apparently all that keeps the rock-strewn path barely open. Scattered among the tangled web of chamise, scrub oak, manzanita, ceanothus and yucca are a few open areas with fair displays of spring wildflowers—woolly blue curls, prickly phlox, wild onion, and cow parsnip.

Years ago there existed on the summit of Viejas Mountain an arrangement of stones interpreted by local anthropologists to be a wintersolstice marker, used for ceremonial purposes by the Indians. The marker was a T-shaped array of stones that pointed precisely to a small peak on the southeastern horizon about 16 miles away. At winter solstice (December 21) the sun comes up directly behind this peak. On topographic maps, this peak is identified as "Buckman", elevation 4641 feet, located south of Pine Valley. Unfortunately the marker was thoughtlessly destroyed by campers in the mid-1970s. In its place is a wall of stones evidently built as a windbreak.

On exceptionally clear days the view from the Viejas summit can be stupendous—all the way from Mexico to Orange County, with the blue Pacific Ocean spread wide before you. You never quite get the feeling of being "away from it all," however, since the wide gash of Interstate 8 and the fast-spreading suburban sprawl of Alpine lie in the foreground.

Trip 2: Loveland Reservoir

Distance	1.0 miles round trip
Total Elevation Gain/Loss	350'/350'
Hiking Time	½ hour
Optional Map	USGS 7.5-min *Alpine*
Best Times	October through June
Agency	CNF/DD
Difficulty	*

Almost the entire shoreline of one of San Diego County's most isolated and pristine reservoirs, Loveland Reservoir, is off-limits to public visitation. The one exception is a small stretch of shoreline known as "Government Cove" because it lies within a piece of Cleveland National Forest land. The cove is known among fishermen, but you can also find solitude and quiet contemplation here, particularly late in the afternoon or in the evening. The current wet cycle has filled the reservoir to capacity (as of 1993), and this situation may continue into the mid or late 1990s if past rainfall patterns are any guide.

The 0.5-mile-long trail to the shore stays entirely within national forest land, which encompasses most of the southern part of section 9 (shown on the *Alpine* topo map). You start from a dirt parking area under some powerlines just south of Sycuan Truck Trail, 1.2 miles west of Japatul Road. On foot, follow the eroded and sometimes steep and slippery pathway that starts going south along a chaparral-covered ridge toward the reservoir's north shore.

Down a short way, you must cross—or rather jump across—a deep gully cut alongside a huge granite slab. A bit farther on, you come to a dirt service road that contours around the reservoir. Cross the road and continue in the same direction, downhill toward the cove, on the narrow trail. No swimming is allowed in the reservoir. There are no trash cans either, so be sure to pack out whatever you bring in.

Trip 3: McGinty Mountain

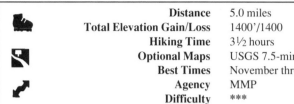

	Distance	5.0 miles
	Total Elevation Gain/Loss	1400'/1400
	Hiking Time	3½ hours
	Optional Maps	USGS 7.5-min *Dulzura, Alpine*
	Best Times	November through May
	Agency	MMP
	Difficulty	***

Rising like a scruffy whaleback above a sea of new luxury homes, McGinty Mountain hosts a rich but circumspect treasure of botanical oddities. Several rare and endangered plant species make their home here on soils derived from a relatively uncommon form of bedrock called gabbro. Over half of California's remaining specimens of Dehesa beargrass cling to the mountain's rocky spine. The endemic San Diego thornmint, its habitat reduced by 90% over the last century by urbanization, survives here, as does San Miguel savory, Perry's tetracoccus, and Gander's butterweed. Some of these plants are believed to be relict species, once common but now almost squeezed out of existence by gradual climate changes occurring over the past 10,000 years or more.

To reach the starting point for the access trail into the McGinty Mountain preserve, follow Lyons Valley Road 0.8 mile north from Highway 94 at Jamul, turn left on Jamul Drive, and proceed 0.4 mile to the gated entrance. Park on the shoulder of Jamul Drive and walk in.

Follow the dirt road north up along a shallow draw. After 0.4 mile, turn right on a switchback trail that quickly rises to McGinty Mountain's long south ridge. Trained eyes might pick out some of the rarer plants, but mostly you'll notice the typical sage-scrub and chaparral vegetation—attractively green and very aromatic if moistened by winter rains. Look for the somewhat unusual coast spice bush (a member of the citrus family) and the Lord's Candle yucca, whose tall flower stalks bear white blossom clusters in the early spring.

At 1.0 mile, you meet an old dirt road on top of the ridge. Turn left (north) to set a course for McGinty Mountain's rounded, 2183-foot summit, another 1.5 miles away. You'll be returning on the same route, so take note of any intersecting roads that might cause confusion on your way back. In a few places, this road is very steep and rocky.

Clumps of Dehesa beargrass dot the ridgeline, looking somewhat like poor cousins of the common yuccas. They can be identified by their diminutive stature and fibrous, pale green, ribbon-like leaves. As you climb up the ridge, the odor of Cleveland sage—probably the most pleasantly aromatic plant in the county—is almost overpowering, especially in springtime.

The panoramic view expands as you get higher, easily encompassing most of the border-region peaks from Tecate Peak to San Miguel Mountain. Off to the west, beyond Mount Helix and Cowles Mountain, you can sometimes spot the ocean—dark blue or glistening with sun glare, depending on the time of day.

Area C-8: Bonita

From headwaters in the Cuyamaca Mountains, the Sweetwater River flows through foothills south of Descanso, pools up in Loveland Reservoir near Alpine, and flows again through the Dehesa Valley past El Cajon and Spring Valley. After being detained by the Sweetwater Reservoir, whatever is left of the water continues 7 miles through Bonita and Chula Vista to the river's mouth at south San Diego Bay.

Urban development has yet to catch up with the rolling country south and east of Sweetwater Reservoir. It's still a place where wild oats and foxtails chafe in the afternoon breeze, hawks glide overhead, and coyotes and other small animals flourish.

Although the entire surface and shoreline of the reservoir are closed to the public, the Sweetwater River Trail, for horses and hikers, traverses the hills to the south and east. Someday it may tie into the California Riding and Hiking Trail near Alpine or into future trails north of Interstate 8, thereby establishing a trail link between the South Bay suburbs and Cuyamaca Rancho State Park high in the mountains.

Area C-8: Bonita

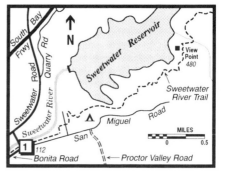

Trip 1: Sweetwater River Trail

Distance	7.5 miles round trip (to hilltop view)
Total Elevation Gain/Loss	1100'/1100'
Hiking Time	3 hours (round trip)
Optional Maps	USGS 7.5-min *National City, Jamul Mtns*
Best Times	October through June
Agency	SDCP
Difficulty	***

The most scenic, existing segment of the Sweetwater River Trail begins in the Bonita area, east of the main Sweetwater County Park and Chula Vista Golf Course. Take the Bonita Road exit from Interstate 805 and drive 4 miles to the point where Bonita Road swings left to cross the Sweetwater River on a long, narrow bridge. Park off the pavement beside Bonita Road, or on any nearby residential street.

Pick up the narrow trail underneath the bridge and follow it east along the perimeter of the Bonita Golf Club course. After 0.7 mile the trail starts zigzagging up a grassy hillside. The view of Bonita and the lower Sweetwater River valley widens, with a slice of the ocean in the distance. At 1.4 miles, you skirt the county's new Sweetwater Summit equestrian campground and soon catch a first glimpse of the reservoir. Stay on the trail—the shoreline is strictly off limits to everyone.

The trail, which is following dirt roads at this point, meanders east and north over rolling grassland, staying well back from the shoreline of Sweetwater Reservoir. At 2.3 miles the route starts going north along a wide dirt road. After another 150 yards it becomes a narrow path that veers east up a grassy hillside alongside a wire fence. Then it descends sharply, goes up a few switchbacks, drops again, and goes up to a grove of pepper trees on a hillside. It drops once more, goes through a pipe gate, contours across a scrubby hillside, and finally begins a switchbacking ascent of a prominent hill.

The top of this hill offers the best view of the lake and surrounding mountains. To the east rises 2565' San Miguel Mountain, its summit bewhiskered by several spiky radio and TV broadcast antennas. Across the lake to the north and west is the unkempt suburban sprawl of

Spring Valley and the huge Pointe Resort development now taking form. Right around you you'll notice some good examples of the fairly rare native coast cholla and coast barrel cactus, along with some common prickly pear cacti.

The hilltop is a good turnaround point. If you want, you can continue exploring the trail ahead. About a mile farther ahead, it reaches a dirt road that parallels the Sweetwater River upstream from the reservoir.

On the Sweetwater River Trail

THE MOUNTAINS

Area M-1: Agua Tibia

The 18,000-acre Agua Tibia Wilderness lies northwest of Palomar Mountain, straddling the San Diego-Riverside county line in Cleveland National Forest. Until 1984, Agua Tibia was the only officially designated wilderness area in San Diego County. Now it is joined by three others within the Cleveland forest—Pine Creek, Hauser, and San Mateo Canyon—and by several other state wilderness areas within Cuyamaca Rancho and Anza-Borrego Desert state parks. Additional lands within the county under jurisdiction of the BLM are being considered for federal wilderness designation as well, including a parcel adjacent to the existing Agua Tibia Wilderness.

Agua Tibia Mountain, one of the three distinct mountain blocks of the Palomar range, is the centerpiece of the wilderness that bears its name. Forests of Coulter pine, bigcone Douglas-fir (a.k.a. bigcone spruce), incense cedar, live oak, and black oak cover the highest elevations, while the lower slopes are scrub-covered and fluted by many steep canyons holding intermittent streams. The wilderness was named after one of these streams, Agua Tibia ("warm water") Creek.

The 16,000-acre Vail Fire of 1989 burned the north slopes of Agua Tibia Mountain to a crisp, but spared much of the oak and coniferous forest atop the highest ridges. As of the early 1990s, heavy winter rains were spurring the recovery of vegetation on the lower slopes. Spectacular wildflower displays occurred after the rains, in part because the seeds of some

plants germinate and grow best in soils enriched by ash.

Also in the late '80s, several successive drought years took their toll on the coniferous forests of Agua Tibia and Palomar (indeed on forests all over the higher elevations of San Diego County and the rest of California). A large fraction of the Coulter and Jeffrey pines were damaged or killed by infestations of bark beetles. During periods of normal or above-normal rainfall, the trees produce enough sap to protect against these natural parasites.

Wild creatures were plentiful before the fire, and they are gradually returning to the burned areas. Aside from the usual deer, squirrels, rabbits and common birds of chaparral and pine-oak forest habitats, bobcats, mountain lions, wild pigs, prairie falcons, and bald and golden eagles have been noted here.

There is only one convenient entry into the Agua Tibia Wilderness—Dripping Springs Campground, located 10 miles east of Interstate 15 on Highway 79 in Riverside County. Trip 1 below begins and ends there. An indirect entrance or exit is possible by way of the Cutca Trail (see Trip 2).

If your visit to Dripping Springs is to be a short one, you could try boulder-hopping up the bed of Arroyo Seco Creek. This often bone-dry creek bed comes alive with the sound of gurgling water in winter through spring. Sycamores, cottonwoods, alders and oaks, all recovering from the fire, line the bank, while the hillsides exhibit the fresh new growth of young sage-scrub and chaparral vegetation. This sort of excursion can be fun for kids—but watch out for poison oak, which used to grow in dense thickets along the stream. The trips described below are of a more serious nature, involving long treks over sometimes-primitive trails with no dependable water available.

All federal and state wilderness areas in the county are subject to stringently protective management rules. These rules permit free access to anyone on foot or horseback, but prohibit any wheeled devices—bicycles and carts included. You must also be in possession of a wilderness permit in order to enter a national-forest wilderness area, either for day or for overnight use. Permits for the Agua Tibia Wilderness are available at the Dripping Springs Fire Station (open approximately April through November). Better yet, call or visit the

Palomar ranger district office well in advance of your visit to obtain the permit and to inquire about the current condition of the trails. The Agua Tibia trails aren't cleared and maintained very often, and the post-fire regrowth of brushy vegetation can be incredibly rapid after prolonged rainy periods.

Area M-1: Agua Tibia

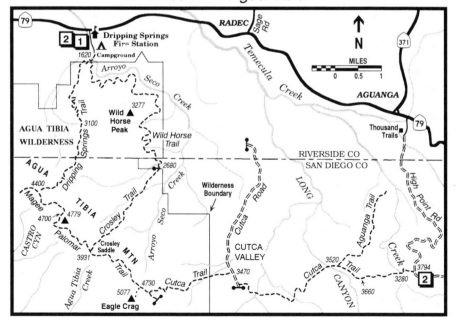

Trip 1: Agua Tibia Loop

🥾	**Distance**	20.0 miles
	Total Elevation Gain/Loss	4100'/4100'
	Hiking Time	12 hours
🧭	**Recommended Maps**	Cleveland National Forest recreation map;
		USGS 7.5-min *Vail Lake*
	Best Times	November through May
↻ 🚶	**Agency**	CNF/PD
	Difficulty	****

For two decades the Dripping Springs Trail (originally known as the Pine Flat Trail) was the only direct way in and out of the Agua Tibia Wilderness. The completion of the Wild Horse Trail in 1992 now makes possible a loop hike that allows you to discover a good fraction of the entire Agua Tibia Wilderness area.

Unless you're a real speed demon, plan this as a two-day backpack trip, with an overnight stay amid the pines and oaks of Agua Tibia Mountain. Navigation is straightforward, except when the trails become overgrown, as they periodically do. Note, also, that there's normally no water along the trail, except along the Crosley Trail as noted below.

You start from the trailhead parking area at the south end of Dripping Springs Campground, 0.4 mile south of the fire station on Highway 79. (The campground may be seasonally closed; if so you must park outside and walk in.) Just beyond the trailhead, ford Arroyo Seco Creek and begin a switchbacking ascent through sage scrub and chaparral vegetation, liberally sprinkled with annual wildflowers in March through May. After 0.1 mile, the Wild Horse Trail branches left; keep straight on the Dripping Springs Trail. At about 1.0 mile, the trail gains the top of a nearly flat ridge and proceeds south. After another mile, you start a series of switchback segments crossing an old firebreak (stay on the gradually ascending trail—don't make short cuts). Vail Lake and Southern California's highest mountains—Mounts San Antonio, San Gorgonio and San Jacinto—are visible in the north. On a clear winter day, these snow-covered summits etched against the blue sky are a memorable sight.

At about 3.5 miles (3100'), the trail crosses the head of a small creek, where, before the Vail Fire, the chamise- and ceanothus-dominated cover yielded to manzanita and ribbonwood (red shanks) shrubs. Today, lots of deerweed and a host of fire-following herbs and wildflowers dominate the scene, but young versions of the original vegetation—especially manzanita and ribbonwood—are already pushing out the newcomers. The smooth, bronzed limbs and branches of the manzanita support dark green, leathery leaves that turn edge-on to the sun on hot days, thus conserving moisture. Ribbonwood has a perpetually peeling reddish bark and feathery, light green foliage. Starting in February, the manzanita shows off myriads of tiny white or pinkish blossoms shaped like hanging lanterns. Later in the year, red berries (manzanita is Spanish for "little apple") appear. When ripe, these edible berries taste a lot like a pippin apple.

At about 4 miles (3300') you'll pass what little remains of the truly giant specimens of manzanita and ribbonwood that stood here until the 1989 fire. These century-old shrubs, up to 20 feet high, represented the equivalent of a "climax forest" consisting entirely of chaparral. The loss of this mature patch of vegetation was tragic, but it must be remembered that without the effect of fire-suppression measures enacted over the past century, the natural cycle of growth and incineration by natural causes (roughly every decade) would probably never have allowed so mature a stand of chaparral to develop.

At about 4.5 miles, the trail descends a little and crosses an area of poor soil. A view opens up to the southeast. The white dome of the Hale Telescope at Palomar Observatory gleams on a ridge about 9 miles away. After crossing a ravine, you resume climbing on switchbacks, passing the burned-out hulks of several large Coulter pines, plus their fledgling offspring. A patch of unburned live-oak forest heralds your arrival (7.0 miles) at the Magee-Palomar Trail on the crest of Agua Tibia Mountain. Turn left and follow this former fire road (now a foot trail) for one more mile until you reach a wide spot on the crest of the old roadbed just north of peak 4779. This flat area on the edge of the burn offers the best camping.

Beyond the campsite the Magee-Palomar Trail descends gradually, offering views of the coastal valleys and hills to the west and south. On most spring and summer mornings, you can look down on the top of the marine layer, which looks like a flat, white ocean of mist. Large bigcone Douglas-firs dot the unburned slopes and ridges that fall away to the south.

At 10.0 miles (2.0 miles from the campsite), you'll reach Crosley Saddle and the intersection of the recently cleared Crosley Trail, itself an old roadbed. You're now exactly half way around the loop. Follow the Crosley Trail down through an incredibly dense and magnificent live-oak forest, and back out into the sunlight at the edge of the burn (11.5 miles). You cross a shady ravine (flowing until late spring) at 12.4 miles, and come to a gate at 12.7 miles marking the edge of private property. Cross a private access road and continue (momentarily north) on the freshly cut Wild Horse Trail. After crossing another seasonally wet ravine just beyond, you briefly join another old roadbed slanting up a hillside, then depart from it.

The next 7 miles of all-new trail circuitously snake around the east and north flanks of boulder-studded Wild Horse Peak. Here and there you look down upon the rocky bed of Arroyo Seco Creek—tantalizingly close but not easily accessible. After weaving your way in and out of numerous side canyons, contouring much of the while, the trail pitches downward to meet the Dripping Springs Trail, a short distance from your starting point.

Trip 2: North Palomar Traverse

Distance	19.8 miles
Total Elevation Gain/Loss	2900'/5100'
Hiking Time	10 hours
Recommended Maps	Cleveland National Forest recreation map; USGS 7.5-min *Vail Lake*, *Aguanga*
Best Times	November through May
Agency	CNF/PD
Difficulty	****

This one-way route across Cleveland National Forest lands on Palomar's north slopes traverses some wild and lonely country—some of the most remote territory found anywhere in Southern California. Two variations of the route are possible—one via the Dripping Springs Trail, the other via the Wild Horse Trail. Both involve virtually the same distance and elevation change, so your choice between them should depend on the current maintenance of the trails. You'll cross a number of small streams that flow in the winter and spring; otherwise water isn't usually available on the route. Ask about trail conditions and the availability of water when you obtain your wilderness permit. If you're backpacking the route, make sure your permit is good for entry into the Agua Tibia Wilderness and for camping inside or outside the wilderness area on Cleveland National Forest land.

If you're setting up a car shuttle, leave one car at Dripping Springs and take the other to the east terminus of the Cutca Trail. To reach the latter, turn south from Highway 79 (just east of Aguanga) on the paved access road toward the Thousand Trails campground. From the campground entrance, continue south on the graded-dirt High Point Road (8S05) 5 miles south to the signed Cutca Trail.

Start off by descending sharply on the Cutca Trail into the shady depths of Cottonwood Creek, 0.5 mile. Climb to a saddle at 1.2 miles, then descend slightly to the Aguanga Trail junction at 2.1 miles. (The poorly maintained Aguanga Trail, which goes north, runs into private property near the Riverside County line.)

Continue over rolling terrain, through chaparral and oaks, crossing Long Canyon and two of its tributaries. These streambeds usually have water until early summer. Nearing Cutca Valley you strike Cutca Road at 5.0 miles. Walk 0.4 mile north on the dirt road, then resume westward travel on the Cutca Trail.

You now rise out of Cutca Valley, cross the Agua Tibia Wilderness boundary, and follow a shady ravine with a seasonal, trickling brook. Sword ferns on the bank flutter in the cool and languid breeze. Switchbacks take you up to a junction with the Magee-Palomar Trail (7.6 miles), which is an old roadbed following the Palomar-Agua Tibia crest. (From this junction, or from another point on the roadbed 0.2 mile west, you can make a bid for Eagle Crag, which involves a short, steep, cross-country climb through post-fire scrub vegetation. The rock pile at the apex of Eagle Crag's sheer south face offers a dramatic platform for a vista unparalleled at any other site in the Palomar range of mountains.)

Past the junction, the Magee-Palomar Trail gradually descends to Crosley Saddle (9.8 miles), where signs indicate it's 10 miles to Dripping Springs, either by way of the Magee-Palomar and Dripping Springs trails straight ahead, or by way of the Crosley and Wild Horse trails to the right. For a description of both alternatives, see Trip 1 above.

Eagle Crag

Area M-2: Palomar Mountain

Without a doubt, the rolling high country of Palomar Mountain contains San Diego County's most picture-perfect mountain scenery. Palomar's uplands, covered with thick forests of pine, oak, fir and cedar, and its gentle valleys, laced with sparkling streams, bring to mind landscapes more commonly seen in mountain ranges far to the north. With an average annual precipitation of more than 40 inches, snowfalls of up to 3 feet in winter, and vibrant spring and fall color, this is San Diego County's best answer to those who might complain about the lack of four seasons in Southern California.

Palomar Mountain is the middle of three distinctively named promontories forming the

Area M-2: Palomar Mountain

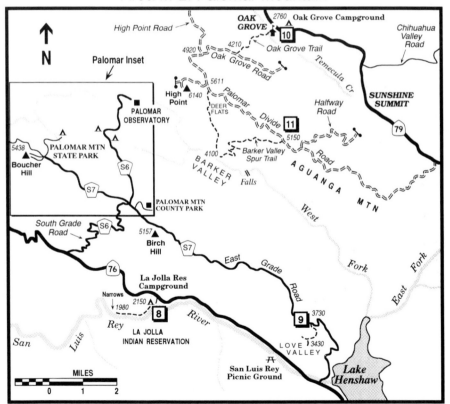

25-mile-long range often known as the Palomar Mountains. Agua Tibia Mountain anchors the range to the northwest, while Aguanga Mountain stretches to the southeast. Several faults pass through the area, including the Elsinore Fault, which parallels Highway 76 and the San Luis Rey River at the foot of Palomar Mountain.

The amount of public acreage on Palomar Mountain itself is not large. Palomar Mountain State Park spreads across 3 square miles of the finest wooded area on the mountain. The national forest is checkered with private inholdings, including a big piece of property owned by Palomar Observatory. Nonetheless, there are enough trails in both the state park and national forest to keep hikers busy for a while.

Public campgrounds are located within Palomar Mountain State Park (open year-round), at Palomar Mountain County Park (open year-round), and in the national forest (open seasonally) along the road to Palomar Observatory. Backpacking is not permitted in Palomar Mountain State Park. Backpacking and remote camping are encouraged in such areas as Agua Tibia (Area M-1) and Barker Valley (Trip 11 below).

Palomar Mountain is served by two paved highways that climb up from State Highway 76. South Grade Road (County Highway S-6) is steep and winding; while East Grade Road (County Highway S-7) offers a longer, more gradual ascent. Both offer spectacular views and fine roadside scenery. At the junction of South Grade and East Grade roads on the Palomar Mountain crest, you can turn west toward Palomar Mountain State Park (Trips 1-4 below), or north toward the national-forest campgrounds (Trips 5-7) and Palomar Observatory. The observatory houses the famous 200-inch Hale Telescope, now only the third largest in the world, but still a marvel to behold. Visitors are welcome to view the telescope and visit a nearby museum from 9 a.m. to 4 p.m. daily.

At the foot of Palomar Mountain along Highway 76, the La Jolla Indian Reservation welcomes campers to its busy campground on the San Luis Rey River. Hikers and backpackers can follow the shady river bank downstream some distance from the main camping area (Trip 8).

On the drier and warmer south and east slopes of Palomar Mountain and Aguanga Mountain, elfin forests of chaparral and park-like oak woodlands are king. From East Grade Road near Lake Henshaw you can descend into oak-filled Love Valley (Trip 9). From Oak Grove on Highway 79, you can can tackle Palomar's "High Point" the hard way via the Oak Grove Trail (Trip 10). Oak Grove also features a popular national-forest campground.

Probably the most intriguing trip below Palomar's high plateau is the descent into Barker Valley (Trip 11). This oak-dotted swale, caressed by the San Luis Rey River's West Fork, is perhaps the most isolated nonwilderness area in San Diego County.

Falls below Barker Valley

Trip 1: Scott's Cabin/Boucher Hill Loop

	Distance	3 miles
	Total Elevation Gain/Loss	800'/800'
	Hiking Time	1½ hours
	Recommended Map	Palomar Mountain State Park map/brochure
	Optional Map	USGS 7.5-min *Boucher Hill*
	Best Times	All year
	Agency	PMSP
	Difficulty	**

Like most hikes on Palomar Mountain, this one is at its very best during spring and fall, especially April-May and October-November. The route begins along an open ridge dotted with black oaks, and these trees undergo rapid color changes in both seasons.

Park at the Silver Crest Picnic Area, just beyond the state park's entrance. Walk back to the paved road and go west toward a junction of five roads. Now continue west up the ridgeline between the two roads to the left (these roads are a one-way loop around the summit of Boucher Hill), following a narrow, unmarked trail through the grass and bracken ferns. Black oaks crown the ridgeline, their gnarled limbs bare in winter, but alive with fluttering leaves during the remainder of the year. A few white firs appear as you approach the fire tower and microwave structure on Boucher Hill. From the parking area at Boucher Hill, there's a good view west down to Pauma Valley, but it's often too hazy to spot the Pacific Ocean.

Now find the Boucher Trail, which descends on a stretch of old fire road to the north. Beyond more black oaks, bracken ferns and a meadow dotted with baby-blue-eyes, the trail swings right to traverse a north slope, entering a dense, almost gloomy forest of white fir. Upon reaching Nate Harrison Road, cross and pick up the Adams Trail on the other side. You're in mixed forest now, with a few bigcone Douglas-fir trees whose wandlike limbs tower head and shoulders above all else. Winding around a sunlight-flooded ravine, you'll see beautiful specimens of dogwood and ceanothus, in bloom during April and May. In early summer, Humboldt lilies brighten up the shady areas.

When you arrive at Cedar Grove Campground, walk out to the entrance, where you can pick up the trail to Scott's Cabin. A steep climb through mostly white fir forest takes you to the modest remains of the cabin, built by an early homesteader. Complete the circle by bearing right at the next junction, taking the trail that ends up opposite the Silver Crest Picnic Area.

Bracken ferns

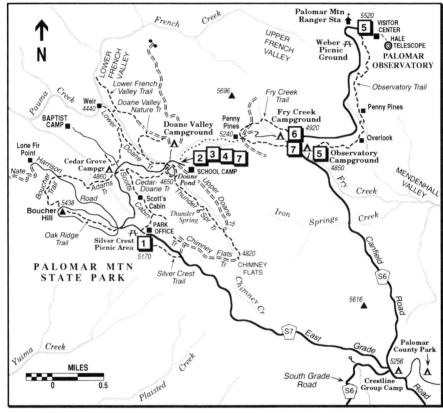

Palomar Inset

Trip 2: Thunder Spring/Chimney Flats Loop

👟	**Distance**	4 miles
	Total Elevation Gain/Loss	900'/900'
	Hiking Time	2 hours
🏔	**Recommended Map**	Palomar Mountain State Park map/brochure
	Optional Map	USGS 7.5-min *Boucher Hill*
	Best Times	All year
🔄 👫	**Agency**	PMSP
	Difficulty	**

This loop has a little of everything—a walk along a stream-edged meadow; a passage through a canopy of western azaleas (relatively rare in San Diego County); a stroll through a century-old apple orchard; a visit to an old grave; the best views in the entire park; and a visit (once more, if you've already taken Trip 1) to the old ruins of Scott's Cabin.

The parking lot at Doane Pond—the lowest elevation on this hike—is a good place to begin. Tiny Doane Pond is stocked with trout and is very popular, especially with youngsters. The buildings just east belong to San Diego's Palomar school camp. This camp, along with Camp Cuyamaca in Cuyamaca Rancho State Park, provides fifth-graders with an opportunity to experience a week of adventure and learning in lieu of regular class attendance.

Walk around the lake, then go southeast up the Thunder Spring Trail (or, if it's one of those frosty days of winter, you can drift toward the Upper Doane Trail, the parallel dirt road on the sunny side of the valley). The Thunder Spring Trail skirts a patch of skunk cabbage, then plunges into a dark forest of oaks and conifers. Alder-fringed Doane Creek on the left appears luminescent in the sunlight. A side path on the right leads to Thunder Spring, framed by four-foot-long fronds of chain fern in a shady ravine.

At the end of the valley, commence a steep climb on an informal trail up along Chimney Creek. Azalea grows thickly through here, displaying hundreds of white blossoms in mid-spring.

Next you reach Chimney Flats, an oak-fringed, bracken-filled meadow. Bear right (west) on the Chimney Flats Trail, an old fire road. Climb through the forest to another flat, this one filled with the remains of a century-old

apple orchard believed to have been tended by the man who built Scott's Cabin. At the entrance to this flat, turn left on the service road from the reservoir, cross East Grade Road, and pick up the Silver Crest Trail. On the left is "Big Willy's grave," the resting place of William Pearson, an early settler, killed by a falling tree. According to the inscription, Willy was "aged 66 Y's 1 Mo. 16 D's." The Silver Crest Trail meanders along the edge of a steep ridge affording spectacular wintertime views of the San Luis Rey River valley and the distant Pacific Ocean. Up ahead is Silver Crest Picnic Area, where water is available.

From the picnic area head east across the road and pick up Scott's Cabin Trail. Follow this past the cabin, down through the white-fir forest, then go right (east) on the Cedar-Doane Trail—formerly known as the "Slide Trail" because of its steepness. This passes through mixed forest and emerges at the shoreline of Doane Pond, your starting point. There's quite a lot of poison oak in the shade of the oaks along this narrow trail. If it's winter, avoid brushing against any twigs poking up; the twigs of poison oak contain some of the same skin-irritating oil found in the leaves.

Trip 3: Doane Valley Nature Trail

Distance	1 mile
Total Elevation Gain/Loss	150'/150'
Hiking Time	30 minutes
Recommended Map	Palomar Mountain State Park map/brochure
Optional Map	USGS 7.5-min *Boucher Hill*
Best Times	All year
Agency	PMSP
Difficulty	*

This is a trail for inspiration. Here is the Palomar forest at its best, complete with a trickling stream that seems out of place amid the generally arid mountain ranges of far-southern California.

The brochure available at the trailhead is excellent in its descriptions and sketches of trees and shrubs seen along the route. Among the more interesting species: box elder (a tree rare

in San Diego County), creek dogwood, wild strawberry, mountain currant, and Sierra gooseberry. At one point, the brochure calls attention to a massive incense-cedar towering 150 feet. If you weren't educated to its true identity, you might think it was a giant (sequoia) redwood.

You'll find the trailhead at the Doane Pond parking lot. The trail goes downhill along Doane

Doane Pond at dawn

Creek for about 0.3 mile, then curves and climbs around a hill to connect with Doane Valley Campground. Walk through the campground and down the road toward Doane Pond to close the loop.

Trip 4: Lower Doane Valley/Lower French Valley

Distance	2.5 miles round trip
Total Elevation Gain/Loss	300'/300'
Hiking Time	1½ hours
Recommended Map	Palomar Mountain State Park map/brochure
Optional Map	USGS 7.5-min *Boucher Hill*
Best Times	All year
Agency	PMSP
Difficulty	**

Unquestionably, the best time of day to make this hike is during the first two hours of daylight. At midday the landscape is bathed in a harsh, flat light. Afterward, lowland haze may blow in, diluting the purity of the light. In early morning light, however, magic is wrought. Long shadows from the treetops stab across the pillowy meadows, then recede quickly as the sun gains altitude. Subtle shades of color come alive in the foliage as light from the blue sky mixes with golden-white sunlight. Silver dewdrops glisten on the blades of grass.

As in Trip 3 above start hiking on the Doane Valley Nature Trail, but bear left at the trail fork after 0.3 mile. This is the Lower Doane Trail, following Doane Creek through stately groves of white fir and incense-cedar. Walk all the way down to the weir at the end of the trail, and

On the Doane Valley Nature Trail

admire the stone-and-mortar structure above it. This small dam and gauging station were used in the late 1920s to test the hydroelectric potential of the stream. The tests proved there was not enough flow to justify construction of a power plant. Today, the silted-in dam holds barely enough water to soak your feet in.

Some fishermen and hikers are familiar with the rugged and beautiful stretch of Pauma Creek below the weir. Currently, it's legal to scramble down the creek to the park boundary, only 0.2

mile away. Beyond this point access is strictly forbidden. The creek flows through the Pala Indian Reservation and eventually joins the San Luis Rey River in Pauma Valley. During high water, even the less-rugged stretch within the park can be quite treacherous.

From the weir, backtrack 0.2 mile and take the short connecting trail across Lower Doane Valley to the Lower French Valley Trail. Go left (north), passing into Lower French Valley. The setting is idyllic: rolling grasslands dotted with statuesque ponderosa pines, surrounded by hillsides clothed in oaks and tall conifers.

Several of the ponderosa pines are riddled with holes—some plugged with acorns. This is the handiwork of the acorn woodpecker, who uses the holes to store acorns filled with larvae. The birds retrieve these acorns and the grubs in leaner times. Listen for the repetitive, guttural call of this bird, and observe the distinctive red patch on its head and the white wing patch when in flight.

You can hike up as far as the bank of French Creek, then return along the same trail, staying left to finish the hike on the Lower French Valley Trail.

Trip 5: Observatory Trail

	Distance	2.2 miles
	Total Elevation Gain/Loss	100'/750'
	Hiking Time	1 hour
	Optional Maps	Cleveland National Forest recreation map; USGS 7.5-min *Palomar Observatory*, *Boucher Hill*
	Best Times	All year
	Agency	CNF/PD
	Difficulty	*

The Observatory Trail has won kudos as one of only four National Recreation trails in San Diego County. Since the trail roughly parallels Highway S-6 (Canfield Road), it can be walked one-way, either uphill or downhill. For the easier trip, start at the upper trailhead, just below Palomar Observatory's entrance gate, and have someone drive around to meet you at the trail's

lower end at Observatory Campground. A car-shuttle arrangement works well, too, since there's only 2 miles of highway distance in between the trailheads.

From the upper trailhead, walk first through a thicket of dense chaparral, then past pines, oaks, and incense cedars. In the sunny clearings between the trees, wildflowers dot the grassy

Mendenhall Valley overlook

slopes and bracken ferns spread like a lacy carpet at waist level.

About halfway down, the trail bends around a ravine, alive with the sound of a trickling stream until summer's heat and drought silence it. Soon after, you come to a wooden platform on the left overlooking Mendenhall Valley— one of several large meadows tucked into Palomar's rolling flanks. Mendenhall Valley sheds water into the San Luis Rey River's West Fork. The water flows east through Barker Valley, circles around to Lake Henshaw at Palomar Mountain's southeastern tip, rushes down along Highway 76, tumbles through a deep canyon on the La Jolla Indian Reservation, and emerges upon the sloping alluvial plain between Rincon and Pauma Valley.

After meandering some more under a leafy canopy, you descend to the east edge of Observatory Campground.

Trip 6: Fry Creek Trail

	Distance	1.5 miles
	Total Elevation Gain/Loss	300'/300'
	Hiking Time	1 hour
	Optional Maps	Cleveland National Forest recreation map; USGS 7.5-min *Boucher Hill*
	Best Times	All year
	Agency	CNF/PD
	Difficulty	*

This beautiful trail circles the head of Fry Creek, visiting a "Penny Pines" (planted) grove of Coulter pines atop a saddle. You'll find the signed trailhead just inside the entrance to the campground, 2 miles below Palomar Observatory and 2.7 miles north of the South Grade/East Grade road junction. Although the trail receives a fair amount of use, you may find that it is ill-maintained and a bit hard to follow.

The trail winds up along the slope north of the creek, crosses a dirt road, and continues on to the Penny Pines. You pass live and black oaks, pines, and scattered underbrush. This mix of vegetation is well adapted to the sunny, somewhat dry south-facing slopes. October and November are the most glorious months: the black oak in full autumn color delights the eye, and the sporadic pitter-patter of falling acorns pleases the ear—if not the top of the head.

In late April and early May there's a curious kind of pseudo-autumn color in these forests. When the black oak leaves first emerge from buds, they're reddish in color. They gradually acquire a shade of green as they unfold. Wherever the oaks are exposed to varying conditions of elevation and sun exposure, bands of color ranging from reddish-brown to green can be seen on the mountainsides. You can see this effect near the Penny Pines, where springtime pseudo-autumn color contrasts with the green palette of white firs, live oaks and Coulter pines.

Look for common birds such as Steller's jays, chickadees, and acorn woodpeckers. I've seen mule deer here—and once, at twilight, a striped skunk.

After you reach the Penny Pines, don't take the road to the east (a shortcut to the campground) if you want to complete the whole trail. Instead, find and follow the continuation of the Fry Creek Trail, which angles down the slope south of the creek. You thread your way amid closely spaced incense-cedar, white fir, and live oak tree trunks. Very few black oaks and no Coulter pines grow here—they seem to prefer the sunnier slopes on the other side of the creek.

Trip 7: Fry Creek to Doane Valley

	Distance	1.5 miles
	Total Elevation Gain/Loss	300'/550'
	Hiking Time	1 ½ hours
	Recommended Maps	Cleveland National Forest recreation map; USGS 7.5-min *Boucher Hill*
	Best Times	All year
	Agency	CNF/PD
	Difficulty	**

This short, cross-country route serves as the only convenient connection (for hikers) between the Fry Creek/Observatory campground area in Cleveland National Forest and Palomar Mountain State Park. The distance from start to end point via roads is almost seven miles.

From the entrance to Fry Creek Campground, walk up either branch of the Fry Creek Trail (see Trip 6) to the Penny Pines plantation. Several roads and trails diverge there. You go west down a narrow ravine with a semblance of a trail. All other paths go up, or back down toward Fry Creek. In the ravine you'll dodge fallen trees and, depending on the amount of recent use, you may have to push through scratchy brush as well.

Toward the bottom of the ravine, you'll be boulder-hopping over outcrops of gray metasedimentary rock. Back along Fry Creek, the rock is granitic. You're on one of several wedges of pre-Cretaceous metasedimentary rock that alternate with younger granitic rock exposures along the summit of Palomar Mountain.

At the bottom you come out behind the buildings of the Palomar School Camp. The parking lot at Doane Pond lies a short distance away.

Trip 8: La Jolla Indian Reservation

	Distance	3 miles round trip (to San Luis Rey River narrows)
	Total Elevation Gain/Loss	150'/150'
	Hiking Time	3 hours (round trip)
	Optional Map	USGS 7.5-min *Palomar Observatory*, *Boucher Hill*
	Best Times	All year
	Agency	LJIR
	Difficulty	**

In the heat of summer, the La Jolla Indian Reservation draws plenty of visitors to its campground and water slide. On the hot days, "tubing" down the lazily flowing San Luis Rey River (on giant inner tubes) is very popular as well. If it's peaceful and quiet hiking you're looking for, though, you'd best come during late fall through early spring when the place is practically deserted.

The campground turnoff is located at mile 41.7 on Highway 76, about 25 miles east of Interstate 15. The day-use or camping fee you pay at the campground entrance entitles you to a "trespass permit" for hiking or backpacking on the reservation.

The best hiking is downstream from the campground. The river here is graced with a dense riparian strip of willows, sycamores, cottonwoods and live oaks, nourished by steady releases of water from Lake Henshaw upstream.

Drive to the farthest camping area on the downstream side, and begin hiking along the right (northwest) bank of the river. You'll be on a fairly well defined trail beaten down by tubing enthusiasts who have to cart their tubes upriver after floating down. Poison oak appears here and there. In places you may have to scramble over rock outcrops if you don't want to get your

San Luis Rey River

feet wet.

Shady camp spots are available back from the bank. You won't want to drink the often murky river water, even after purification, so bring all you need.

At about 1.5 miles down the river, the canyon walls become steep and close in. This is a good spot for the average person to turn back. The more adventuresome can continue by making a long traverse over steep rock slabs on the right bank, or by staggering right through the river itself, which is usually about mid-thigh depth. You'll be lucky if you don't fall in, since you can't always see the bottom.

Over the next 2 miles, the canyon swings around a gooseneck and tumbles over several waterfalls two to four feet high. Beyond this stretch, a diversion dam takes virtually all the water and sends it through the Escondido Canal to Lake Wohlford, leaving a bone-dry creekbed below.

Trip 9: Love Valley

	Distance	2 miles
	Total Elevation Gain/Loss	300'/300'
	Hiking Time	1½ hours
	Optional Map	USGS 7.5-min *Palomar Observatory*
	Best Times	November through June
	Agency	CNF/PD
	Difficulty	*

After a wet winter, Love Valley holds the shimmering, upside-down image of a classic California landscape: a weathered barn nestled at the far end of an Ireland-colored meadow, rounded foothills studded with oaks, and white cumulus billowing over the dark, conifer-draped Palomar crest. By April or May, the shallow ponds in the valley bottom start shrinking, leaving in their wake an eye-popping display of yellow tidy tips.

This little-known, day-use destination near the foot of Palomar Mountain is perfect for a picnic—at least in the cooler months, when fresh daytime breezes and cold nighttime temperatures keep crawling and flying insects at bay. The starting point is easy to find, mile 3.3 on East Grade Road (3.3 miles north of Highway 76). Park in the large turnout on the south side of the road, walk around the locked vehicle gate, and continue over a low rise on the dirt road ahead.

As you descend, watch for three kinds of oak trees—black, coast, and Engelmann oaks. The 3600' elevation here is a bit too low for coniferous trees. As you curve south, Lake Henshaw comes into view, tucked into a corner of the large Valle de San Jose—which is a down-dropped basin along the Elsinore Fault.

When you reach the edge of Love Valley at 0.8 mile, you can walk straight to the old barn (which, upon closer inspection, is made of unromantic and rusty corrugated metal), or veer left toward the two ephemeral ponds on the valley floor. Choose your picnic site on the open meadow, or beneath one of the oaks. There are no facilities out there, so you must pack out whatever you pack in.

Love Valley in spring

Trip 10: Oak Grove to High Point

	Distance	14 miles round trip
	Total Elevation Gain/Loss	3600'/3600'
	Hiking Time	8 hours (round trip)
	Recommended Map	Cleveland National Forest recreation map
	Optional Maps	USGS 7.5-min *Aguanga, Palomar Observatory*
	Best Times	October through May
	Agency	CNF/PD
	Difficulty	****

How's this for a climb of Palomar Mountain from bottom to top? Start at Oak Grove, along the east base of the mountain, and climb steadily up 7 miles of foot trail and fire road to reach High Point, the highest mountain within a radius of 14 miles. Of course, with the right kind of vehicle it's usually possible to drive to High Point—but you'd miss the exercise that way. There's no water along this route, so plan accordingly.

The tiny community of Oak Grove is 14 miles north of Warner Springs by way of Highway 79. Begin at the fire station at mile 49.1 on Highway 79. Follow the "Oak Grove Trail" signs directing you over dirt roads and footpaths

behind the station. After crossing a small stream just behind the station, the trail meanders up to a ridgeline and begins cutting back and forth across an old firebreak.

You're now in the usual chaparral community of the mid-elevation mountains, where chamise, ribbonwood, scrub oak, and manzanita thrive. A few conifers cluster below in the ravines on either side of the ridge. Sunny exposures along the trail support a fair springtime growth of annual wildflowers, including wild canterbury bells, chia, monkey flower and aster. A view opens to the north toward the summits of San Gorgonio Mountain and San Jacinto Peak.

At about 1.8 miles you reach Oak Grove Road, which is closed to public travel below this point. Go uphill (west) on the road and continue toward an intersection with High Point Road at 3.9 miles. Turn left and continue uphill through chaparral and oak forest to Palomar Divide Road at 5.7 miles. Go right and head west around the north flank of High Point through a cool, shady forest of oaks and pines. At 6.7 miles you veer left on the steep road to the summit.

The 67-foot-high fire tower is one of the remaining few in San Diego County still used during the fire season. It may be possible to climb up the first few flights of steps for a better view of the surroundings. The list of peaks visible—including the one you're on—reads like a roster of the highest points in southern California. Combs Peak, whose summit is right

about eye level if you stand on the tower, is the nearest rival, 14 miles to the east. Parts of the Santa Rosa, San Ysidro, and Vallecito mountains in the Anza-Borrego Desert are visible, along with the Laguna and Cuyamaca mountains farther to the southeast. In the north are the real giants—Old Baldy, San Gorgonio, and San Jacinto. On very clear days, several of the Channel Islands are visible far out in the Pacific. A lookout here once reported a fire burning in Santa Barbara County, almost two hundred miles away.

As an alternative to the long climb up, you could have someone drop you off at the top (High Point is often accessible to sturdy vehicles via the Palomar Divide Road or High Point Road) and do this hike one-way downhill to Oak Grove. But then you'd miss the fun of coming up. Right?

Trip 11: Barker Valley

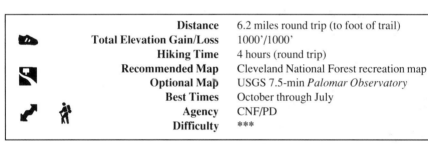

Distance	6.2 miles round trip (to foot of trail)
Total Elevation Gain/Loss	1000'/1000'
Hiking Time	4 hours (round trip)
Recommended Map	Cleveland National Forest recreation map
Optional Map	USGS 7.5-min *Palomar Observatory*
Best Times	October through July
Agency	CNF/PD
Difficulty	***

A cool current caressed my feet, erasing the memory of several long, hot miles on the trail. Sunlight scattered among a thousand fluttering leaves, and a tiny sliver of new moon glowed softly in a blue wedge of sky overhead. Water skaters flitted nervously on the rippled surface of the pool, casting fleeting shadows on a trio of small fish feeding on the bottom. Even in the warm month of July, with the creek ebbing, Barker Valley could still be delightful.

Barker Valley perches squarely in one of the more remote corners of Palomar Mountain, 3 miles by dusty foot trail and 8 miles by bone-shaking dirt road from the nearest paved road, Highway 79. At the least, you'll need a sturdy, high-clearance passenger car or truck to reach the trailhead. (Check first to see if the road is open; storms can render it temporarily un-

usable.)

Turn west from Highway 79 at a point 6.5 miles northwest of Warner Springs (mile 41.9) and continue up the unpaved Palomar Divide Road for 7.8 miles to the Barker Valley Spur trailhead on the left (west) side.

Park off the roadway and head down the trail (an old roadbed). On the way down, keep an eye out for bald eagles in the sky. A number of these raptors roost in old snags on the shore of nearby Lake Henshaw during the winter.

Hike for 1.7 miles on a gradual descent until the old roadbed switches back sharply. Continue around the U-curve, and within 0.1 mile veer to the right on a trail (completed in 1991) that lazily zigzags down a dry slope and into oak-rimmed Barker Valley. If you're looking for a campsite, they're abundant around here.

Just remember to select one at least 100 feet away from the nearest water—in this case, the West Fork San Luis Rey River. A second trail descends into Barker Valley from Deer Flats—from the direction of the metal lookout tower on High Point.

Barker Valley is notorious for cold air drainage at night. I had the interesting experience of sweating out an 85° July day, and awakening next morning to find frost along the stream.

A rugged set of falls and pools awaits adventurous hikers a mile downstream from the foot of the Barker Spur Trail. These occur just below an old stone weir and gauging station. By following rough paths traversing the steep, brushy, north canyon wall, it's possible to reach hidden swimming holes worn in the water-polished rock. Wild trout can be found in the pools below the first falls. Don't attempt to explore this area unless you're adept at scrambling over steep terrain and across potentially slippery, water-polished rock.

Cascade and pool below Barker Valley

Area M-3: Warner Springs

Some of the loftiest—and least visited—mountain country in San Diego County surrounds the resort community of Warner Springs. Hot Springs Mountain, on the Los Coyotes Indian Reservation to the east, is recognized as the county's highest point. At 6533 feet, it beats the better-known, 6512-foot Cuyamaca Peak by a whisker.

Northeast, a rather remote section of the Cleveland National Forest spreads into an even more remote corner of the immense Anza-Borrego Desert State Park. The roadless, eastern section of the national forest parcel, the so-called Caliente Wilderness Study Area, was one of two national-forest WSA's in San Diego County that did not make the cut for wilderness designation in 1984. The other is the Sill Hill WSA adjoining Cuyamaca Rancho State Park. These two WSA's remain "unroaded" and could at some future time be included in the National Wilderness Preservation System. The Pacific Crest Trail passes near Warner Springs, and two of its most scenic segments (within the county) are profiled in the trip descriptions below.

Hikers and backpackers are in on a little secret when they discover the Los Coyotes Indian Reservation. This is the largest (25,000 acres) of the 17 reservations in San Diego County, yet one of the least populated. Visitors can make use of developed camping facilities there, as well as explore the undeveloped parts on a network of graded dirt roads, 4-wheel-drive roads, and trails. Motorcycles are prohibited on the reservation and the vehicle traffic is light on the roads, so you're quite likely to find this a pleasant place to go hiking. With its network of roads and trails that seem to go everywhere, the reservation has also become popular among mountain bikers. Out of many possible hikes on the reservation, I've chosen a couple (Trips 1 and 2 below) that are well suited for a bit of challenging foot travel. Another trip in this book (Area D-2, Trip 3) starts in the reservation and ends down in the desert at Borrego Springs.

To reach the Los Coyotes reservation, turn east on Camino San Ignacio from Highway 79 (mile 35.0) at Warner Springs. After 0.6 mile, bear right on Los Tules Road and continue 4.5 miles to the reservation gate. There you pay a fee for an entrance permit and pick up a sketch map of the roads and trails. The main campground (where water is available) lies another 2.7 miles farther on via paved and dirt road. Los Coyotes is open year-round on the weekends and holidays, weather and road conditions permitting. Call or write first if you plan to visit on a weekday.

Abandoned fire lookout, Hot Springs Mountain

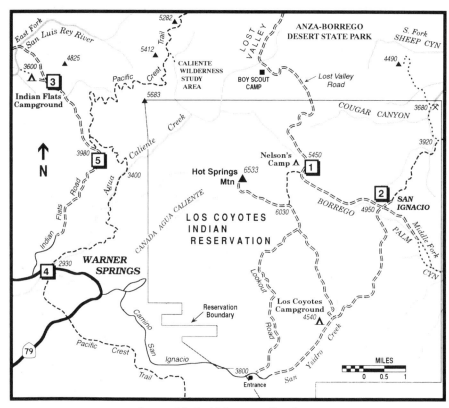

Area M-3: Warner Springs

Trip 1: Hot Springs Mountain

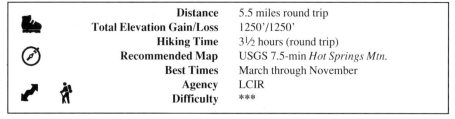

	Distance	5.5 miles round trip
	Total Elevation Gain/Loss	1250'/1250'
	Hiking Time	3½ hours (round trip)
	Recommended Map	USGS 7.5-min *Hot Springs Mtn.*
	Best Times	March through November
	Agency	LCIR
	Difficulty	***

In the mist, the ghostly, abandoned fire lookout tower appeared. We climbed the steps and reached the observation deck. Suddenly there was a radiant heat around us and a flood of light from above. A residue of tiny water droplets floated in the blue glare, and a dozen mountain peaks were unveiled—the glistening summits of San Jacinto and San Gorgonio in the north, the somber Santa Rosas to the east, the dark Lagunas and Cuyamacas southward, and more. In the chasm of Agua Caliente Creek to the northwest, a tenuous rainbow rode a billowing cloud.

That's what it's often like in winter or early

spring up on Hot Springs Mountain—uncertain weather, but clear as a bell if and when the clouds part. Summer days, on the other hand, are usually sunny and warm, but often quite hazy. Santa Ana days near the end of the year can be just about right, especially when the autumn leaves of the black oaks are falling.

Some people like to drive, hike, or mountain bike up along the 7-mile dirt road going up the mountain's south slope, but the northern approach described here is cooler, more interesting, and much shorter. This approach, however, may be blocked by snowfall during part of the winter.

Drive up Los Coyotes' main road, past the developed campground, to an intersection of roads in a valley near the top of Middle Fork Borrego Palm Canyon (6.1 miles past the entrance gate). Turn left (west) and drive up the valley on a sandy road to reach a saddle above the valley, 2.2 miles farther. Just beyond this saddle, on the left (west) side of the road, is Nelson's Camp, with campsites nestled in a shallow bowl shaded by live oak, pine and cedar trees. Picnic tables, fire rings and privies are here. (Los Coyotes permits open fires in campgrounds, but bring your own wood and make sure you observe safe campfire practices.)

Park at the camp and begin hiking southwest up along a small tributary stream that flows north and west into Agua Caliente Creek. You'll follow an old jeep trail up this drainage, still used by daring 4-wheel drivers, gaining more than 500 feet in just over a mile. At the top, you'll meet a better road that runs up the south slope to Hot Springs Mountain. Turn right (west) on this road and climb another 1.6 miles along the ridgeline to the tower. You'll pass through dense forests of black oak, Coulter pine and white fir, and across sunny meadows dotted in late spring with wildflowers.

The lookout tower, dilapidated and seemingly on its last legs, sits on the west shoulder of the mountain. You can go a bit higher on the ridge by following a faint trail through thick brush and around boulders to the true summit. A flat concrete platform, the foundation of an old radio antenna, caps the summit block.

You may use Nelson's Camp as a base for at least two other interesting trips in the northern part of the reservation. You can go north and east to explore the uppermost reaches of Cougar Canyon. Or you can go north and west down the tributary of Agua Caliente Creek to some pleasant backpacker's campsites about 1 mile away.

Trip 2: Upper Cougar Canyon

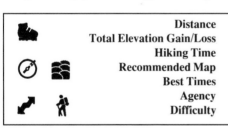

Distance	6 miles round trip (to old mines)
Total Elevation Gain/Loss	1400'/1400'
Hiking Time	4 hours (round trip)
Recommended Map	USGS 7.5-min *Hot Springs Mtn.*
Best Times	October though May
Agency	LCIR
Difficulty	***

Several challenging mountain-to-desert routes will become apparent if you spend much time exploring the northeastern corner of the Los Coyotes reservation. One such route, still marked as a trail on the *Hot Springs Mtn.* and *Borrego Palm Canyon* topographic maps, descends from upper Cougar Canyon into Indian Canyon and thence into Coyote Canyon. That route, colorfully described in Joseph Smeaton

Chase's 1919 book *California Desert Trails*, was worn into a steep mountainside by generations of Native Americans. Other routes to the desert floor—all steep and extremely difficult—are possible via the south ridge of Cougar Canyon, and down tributaries of both Sheep Canyon and Borrego Palm Canyon. The more modest, and still interesting, goal of this trip is to explore a somewhat gentle but overgrown section of upper Cougar Canyon.

Drive to the intersection in the valley above Middle Fork Borrego Palm Canyon (called San Ignacio on older maps), 6.1 miles past the entrance gate. Find a parking spot nearby off the road. Begin hiking northeast 0.3 mile over a low saddle, where a view opens up of the northern Santa Rosa Mountains and San Jacinto Peak. Descend moderately on eroded jeep tracks, past some springs at 4650 feet, to a 4534-foot knob, 1.5 miles from the start. Continue sharply downhill to a usually wet, south tributary of Cougar Canyon, shaded by live oaks, sycamores, and alders.

The road peters out; but continue north down this tributary, pushing through willow and alder thickets. Occasionally there's a snippet of road above the washed-out bank. When you reach the confluence of Cougar Canyon, you'll find a delightful grove of tall live oaks flanked by bracken and chain ferns. You can make camp on any flat spot nearby (be sure to find a fire-safe place to operate your camp stove).

Downstream about 300 yards, near some more live oaks and a couple of Coulter pines, are the remains of mining equipment including a sluice box. Beyond this point the bottom of Cougar Canyon gets quite steep and rugged, so this is a good place to turn back.

The mine can be the starting point for at least two very rugged trips down to the desert floor:

The first is by way of lower Cougar Canyon. From the mine, go down along Cougar's south wall, detouring around a rocky section with small waterfalls, until you can drop into the canyon bottom at 3400 feet. An easy section follows. Below the 3080-foot contour, the canyon becomes impassable without technical climbing equipment. You must climb south out of the canyon and make a long traverse over a

Cougar Canyon below mine

rocky ridge before dropping down to the lower canyon floor. Area D-1, Trip 4 has further details.

The second is by way of an old and mostly overgrown jeep trail from the mine to a 4490-foot peak (not labelled on the topo map) north of the reservation boundary. The pinyon-pine-dotted peak offers up an extraordinary panorama of perhaps a hundred square miles of mountains and desert—with no visible signs of the works of man, save an almost imperceptible microwave tower on distant Toro Peak. From there a determined hiker could push toward South Fork Sheep Canyon and descend through that steep and rugged canyon. See Area D-1, Trip 3 for further details.

Horned lizard in Upper Cougar Canyon

Trip 3: Indian Flats

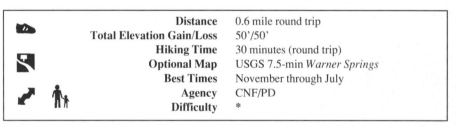

Distance	0.6 mile round trip
Total Elevation Gain/Loss	50'/50'
Hiking Time	30 minutes (round trip)
Optional Map	USGS 7.5-min *Warner Springs*
Best Times	November through July
Agency	CNF/PD
Difficulty	*

What better way is there to pique a toddler's interest in nature than to introduce him or her to a shallow, lazily flowing river, full of tadpoles and frogs? At Indian Flats Campground, you can get to the river in a matter of minutes, and also make use of the usual conveniences of developed campgrounds—such as drinking water, restrooms (no showers) and fire rings—that are nice during a overnight campout with small kids.

This no-reservation campground fills up on most weekends, so it's a good idea to either get there early on a Friday afternoon, or come up on a weekday. From the turnoff along Highway 79, 1.6 miles west of Warner Springs, drive 6.5 miles north on the partly oiled, partly graded-dirt Indian Flats Road to the campground. You'd best use a truck or 4-wheel-drive vehicle if it's recently rained or snowed.

From the far end of the campground, simply head downhill over rock slabs and decomposed granite to the bank of the East Fork San Luis Rey River. By turning upstream, you'll very quickly reach a spot where the water twists and turns through an obstacle course of boulders. Since the river doesn't have much drainage upstream, it seldom flows at a dangerous rate. Rattlesnakes are a more immediate hazard, but only when the weather is warm enough for them to be out and about.

Trip 4: Agua Caliente Creek

	Distance	8.0 miles round trip
	Total Elevation Gain/Loss	900'/900'
	Hiking Time	4 hours (round trip)
	Recommended Map	Cleveland National Forest recreation map
	Optional Maps	USGS 7.5-min *Warner Springs*, *Hot Springs Mtn.*
	Best Times	November though May
	Agency	CNF/PD
	Difficulty	***

Until about 15 years ago, the middle reaches of Agua Caliente Creek seldom saw the intrusion of humans. After the Pacific Crest Trail was routed through, it became a favorite resting spot for hikers heading north or south. This is one of only four places in San Diego County where the PCT dips to cross a fairly dependable stream, and the only place where the trail closely follows water for a fair distance. The stream—if not perennial every year—is at least alive from the first rains of fall into early summer.

Begin at the Agua Caliente Creek bridge at mile 36.6 on Highway 79. There's a turnout for parking just west (mile 36.7) and a dirt road slanting over to where the PCT crosses under the highway. Proceed upstream along the cottonwood-shaded creek, first on the left (north) bank, then on the right. In this first mile, the trail goes through Warner Ranch resort property on an easement. Near the Cleveland National Forest boundary (camping allowed past this point), water flows or trickles from a canyon mouth. The trail detours this canyon by swinging to the east and climbing moderately onto

Winter camping at Agua Caliente Creek

gentle, ribbonwood-clothed slopes. After almost 2 miles of somewhat tedious twisting and turning in the chaparral you join the creek again at the 3200' contour.

Now the gorgeous scenery begins. In the next mile the trail crosses the stream several times and passes a number of appealing small campsites well up on the bank. Live oaks, sycamores, willows, and alders line the creek. The canyon walls soar several hundred feet on either side—clad in dense chaparral on the southeast side, dotted with sage and yucca on the northwest.

After a final crossing of the creek, the trail doubles back and begins a switchbacking (and not too scenic) ascent northwest toward Indian Flats Road. This is a good place to turn around.

If you want to explore farther upstream, you can do it by boulder-hopping and wading. With prior permission to enter Los Coyotes reservation property, starting about a mile ahead, you could go all the way to Nelson's Camp. That would involve some serious scrambling around small waterfalls, possibly swimming across one pool, and doing battle with the ever-present alder branches.

Trip 5: Caliente Wilderness

Distance	12 miles round trip
Total Elevation Gain/Loss	1700'/1700'
Hiking Time	7 hours (round trip)
Recommended Map	Cleveland National Forest recreation map
Optional Maps	USGS 7.5-min *Warner Springs, Hot Springs Mtn.*
Best Times	November though May
Agency	CNF/PD
Difficulty	***

This section of the Pacific Crest Trail through the Caliente WSA winds along boulder-strewn ridges dotted with Coulter pine, and through small ravines shaded by minigroves of live oak. In the upper reaches, there's no noise other than the wind, and no signs of man other than the trail itself. Even the skies are quiet; the area seems to be removed from the flight paths of aircraft.

To reach the starting point, drive north on Indian Flats Road from mile 37.0 on Highway 79. After 4.6 miles of winding road, you'll come to a road summit and the intersection of a gated, abandoned dirt road. Park in the limited space provided, and walk up this abandoned road 0.5 mile to the point where the PCT joins from the right. Continue uphill on the old roadbed, somewhat monotonously, a mile farther to the point where the PCT tread diverges right. Make the right turn (by staying left you would descend to a seasonal spring).

The scenery improves with every step now. You wind up through scattered Coulter pines and picturesque granitic outcrops, with nice views of Lake Henshaw and the grasslands surrounding it. You lose that view as you pass north of peak 5212 and contour around the head of a ravine.

The trail continues to climb moderately and winds around another ravine, this just south of a knob also labelled 5212 feet. It then descends slightly to cross a saddle and resumes climbing on the south side of a hill. From this hill there's a wonderful vista into Agua Caliente Creek and across to the north slope of Hot Springs Mountain. From nearly every vantage point but this, Hot Springs Mountain looks like an inconspicuous bump on a ridge, but from here it looks decidedly massive. Black oaks cluster along the small drainages along its flank, flashing gold in the fall season.

Next the trail bends north and contours, with

Boulders and Coulter pines beside Pacific Crest Trail

small ups and downs, along the east side of the ridge containing peak 5412. In late April and early May, these slopes are tinted pink with the blossoms of manzanita, and blue and white with blooming ceanothus. A dozen exotic fragrances scent the air. The Coulter pines are joined by live oaks and an occasional black oak.

At a point east of peak 5412, you'll see below and to the east a grassy flat, filled with Coulter pines and black oaks, along an upper tributary of Agua Caliente Creek. This is a perfect place for a midday picnic, and even better for an overnight stay. Leave the trail at any point where the brush thins, and descend cross-country about 0.2 mile, losing 150 feet, to the seasonal creek. Water trickles through here until about June after a normal wet season.

Farther north, the Pacific Crest Trail winds over a stretch of less interesting chaparral country. This hidden glade, then, is a good place to turn around.

Area M-4: Upper San Diego River

The San Diego River and its upper tributaries drain the pastoral valleys and forested hillsides around Julian, and the rugged western slopes of the Cuyamaca Mountains. The water flows generally southwest through V-shaped canyons, and eventually reaches El Capitan Reservoir, not far from the East County suburbs. Quite frequently in the higher country, the water encounters resistant layers in the underlying igneous and metamorphic rocks. In several places it tumbles over cataracts up to a hundred feet high. The grinding of stones trapped in pockets below these falls has created deep pools, or "punchbowls."

Highways and paved roads bypass most of the upper San Diego River area, making it seem more remote that it really is. There are plenty of unpaved roads—but some, with locked gates, cross private land with no public easement. Cleveland National Forest encompasses most of the area, but several large private properties, or

inholdings, exist within the forest boundaries.

Because of the mix of public and private ownership, access to some of the more interesting spots in the canyons can be problematical. As a general guide to where you can and can't go, consult the Cleveland National Forest recreation map. Green tinted areas are national forest lands open to the public, while the white areas are private lands. You are allowed to drive or hike any public road going through private property, as long as you don't stray from the road. Aside from public easements like this, don't trespass on private land (unless you've obtained the landowner's permission first).

The following field-tested trips will take you to some of San Diego County's most spectacular and hidden spots—by legal routes. If you're planning to stay out overnight, either car-camping or backpacking, you'll need a remote camping permit. Obtain one in advance from any Forest Service office or fire station.

Trip 1: Inaja Trail

	Distance	0.5 mile
	Total Elevation Gain/Loss	100'/100'
	Hiking Time:	20 minutes
	Optional Map:	USGS 7.5-min *Santa Ysabel*
	Best Times	All year
	Agency	CNF/PD
	Difficulty	*

The Inaja Trail, one of four trails in San Diego County to have earned the appellation "National Recreation Trail," begins at the Inaja Picnic Area along State Highway 78/79, just 1 mile east of Santa Ysabel and 6 miles west of Julian. The picnic area memorializes 11 firefighters who lost their lives in the San Diego

River canyon while battling the 60,000-acre Inaja Fire in 1956.

An excellent trail brochure, available at the trailhead, gives information about the typical live-oak/chaparral vegetation seen here and elsewhere in the upper foothills of San Diego County. An overlook at midpoint in the trail

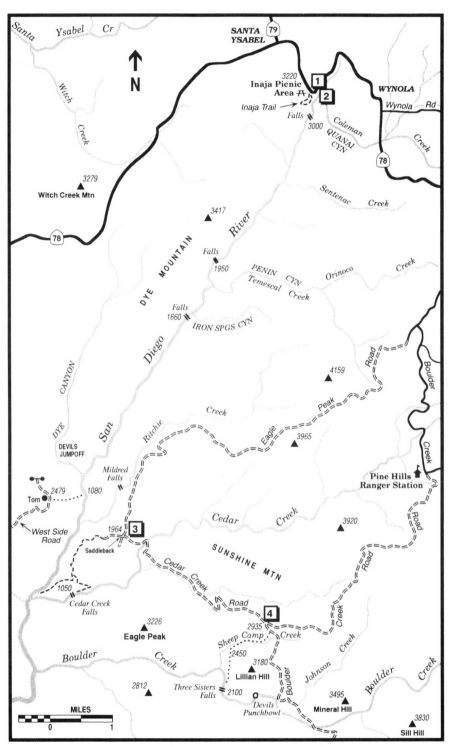

Area M-4: Upper San Diego River

gives a good view down the linear canyon of the San Diego River. At 3440 feet elevation, this overlook is often just above a temperature inversion layer that traps cooler, moist air below. On some mornings, you'll find the canyon hidden by a cottony blanket of fog, while neighboring peaks and ridges stand like islands in clear air.

Out along the north side of the trail your gaze takes in the fertile Santa Ysabel Valley, the rolling hills of Mesa Grande, and the dark, brooding Volcan Mountains.

Trip 2: San Diego River

Distance	10.5 miles
Total Elevation Gain/Loss	1400'/3000'
Hiking Time	11 hours
Required Maps	USGS 7.5-min *Santa Ysabel, Ramona*
Recommended Map	Cleveland National Forest recreation map
Best Times	November through May
Agency	CNF/PD
Difficulty	*****

A trip down this canyon in early spring is a true adventure. Runoff from winter storms fills the bed of the river with a silvery band of water. New leaves and gaily colored wildflowers brighten the banks as well as the slopes. The stream drops abruptly several times over precipices up to a hundred feet high.

Bedrock morteros and metates along the river, especially near groves of oaks, attest to frequent use of the canyon by Native Americans for hundreds of years. Contemporary human usage pales by comparison; only an occasional hiker, backpacker or hunter penetrates these canyon depths today.

Sturdy boots and a patient, cautious attitude are essential for this trip. By April or May, when hungry and irritable rattlesnakes emerge from their wintertime burrows, you'll have to be extra vigilant. Long pants are recommended, as are small clippers to prune back the branches of poison oak in a few tight spots. If you're traveling with a heavy or awkward pack, bring a 30-foot length of cord to assist in lowering it over rock faces as you detour around the waterfalls. Avoid the canyon after intense storms, when high water levels may make stream crossings difficult or hazardous. Before the winter rains come, on the other hand, there may be no water at all.

The hike as I describe it begins at Inaja Picnic Area and ends at the east terminus of Ramona Oaks Road in San Diego Country Estates. To reach the latter from Ramona, take San Vicente Road south and east about seven miles to Ramona Oaks Road; turn left and go three miles east to the roadend at the edge of Cleveland National Forest. If you're setting up a car shuttle, use the Old Julian Highway and Vista Ramona Road through the Country Estates (consult the Thomas Brothers street guide or the Auto Club's "North San Diego Area" street map for the exact details). The drive between start and end points this way is less than 30 minutes.

From the restrooms at Inaja, descend south through brush into the oak-shaded canyon bottom, a short distance below. Turn down-canyon, and at 0.5 mile arrive at the first falls, a set of two, each about 50 feet high. Traverse through brush and over tilted rock slabs on the right (west) side. If you don't like this difficult maneuver, consider giving up and turning back.

The riverbed ahead is choked with small willows and a variety of water-loving plants including wild berry vines. Live oaks and sycamores are rooted to the banks. Much time is spent dodging vegetation and stepping over water-worn boulders, mostly dark-gray and black-colored gabbro rock. At 1.5 miles, a usually wet tributary, Sentenac Creek, comes in from the east. For a while you can follow some eroded bulldozer tracks, first on the east bank, then the west.

You continue on a fairly gradual descent, boulder-hopping much of the way, until you reach the abrupt lip of a 100-foot fall at 3.2 miles (1950'). The water tumbles into an open grotto

fashioned of granite and gneiss, and collects in a shallow pool perhaps 60 feet across. Traverse on the left (south) side of the canyon, over club moss and through shrubbery, taking care not to approach the brink of the grotto too closely.

At a wide bend in the river at 3.7 miles

The San Diego River canyon

(1760'), excellent campsites can be found among spreading oaks on the bank—but watch out for clumps of poison oak (in winter, these will be leafless and hard to identify). At 4.4 miles (1660'), you come upon another beautiful fall, 30 feet high with a deep pool below about 70 feet across. This is probably your best opportunity for a refreshing dip if the weather and water temperature allow.

The vegetation thins now, and walking becomes easier over alternating stretches of sand and rocks. You'll pass more pools in the canyon bottom, with shallow water that can become solar heated on warm, sunny days. Cottonwoods appear and increase in number as the canyon gradually widens.

Watch carefully for the major tributary entering from the north at 7.6 miles. This usually dry canyon comes down from a sheer rock face (on private property) known as the Devil's Jump-off. From this point continue south down the canyon, pass a gully on the right in 0.2 mile, and then climb west up a steep ridge toward the survey point "Tom," nearly 1400 feet above. This steep, brushy climb is better done in the late afternoon, when the sun is hidden from view. Make your way up through an obstacle course of mostly waist-high chamise and buckwheat, relieved on occasion by patches of spring wildflowers. At the top of this exhausting stretch, you'll come upon West Side Road. Follow it 1.8 miles down to the end of Ramona Oaks Road.

There are other alternatives to the last part of this hike. It is possible, for example, to continue farther down the San Diego River and hook up with Eagle Peak Road, which descends toward Cedar Creek Falls (Trip 3).

Trip 3: Cedar Creek Falls

Distance	4.5 miles round trip
Total Elevation Gain/Loss	1200'/1200'
Hiking Time	2½ hours (round trip)
Recommended Map	Cleveland National Forest recreation map
Optional Maps	USGS 7.5-min *Santa Ysabel*, *Tule Springs*
Best Times	November through June
Agency	CNF/PD
Difficulty	**

Here's one of San Diego County's hidden treasures, tucked back in a tributary of the upper San Diego River, and accessible (legally) only by a circuitous drive down a long dirt road and a hike on an abandoned road. Before the construction of El Capitan Dam in the early '30s, the falls were a popular destination for Sunday outings, and could be reached relatively easily on an auto road up the San Diego River valley from Lakeside.

From the coast, drive east through Ramona toward Santa Ysabel and Julian. Six miles east of Santa Ysabel and 1 mile short of (west of) Julian, turn south on Pine Hills Road. After 1.5 miles, bear right on Eagle Peak Road. After 1.4 more miles, veer right on Eagle Peak Road (Boulder Creek Road goes left). Now you face 8.2 miles of progressively poorer road, parts of which could become slippery and muddy in wet weather. In the end, you'll come to a 4-way junction of roads (called "Saddleback" on the topo map) and a Forest Service sign announcing the old road—now a riding and hiking trail— toward the falls.

As you head downhill on foot, look up the canyon in the north to see Mildred Falls, arguably San Diego County's highest at more than 100 feet. Unfortunately, it's often little more than a dark stain on an orange-tinted cliff. In flood, however, it is truly an awesome sight.

The road winds farther west, offering a splendid view of the upper San Diego River canyon, then turns south on a long descent to the river bed. At 1.4 miles (1270'), take the spur road that goes left (southeast) over a low saddle into the Cedar Creek drainage. Descend to the bank of the creek and continue following the old road and trail down to the shallow, reflecting pool at the brink of the falls. Be extremely cautious here, as the rock is very slippery. Long-time San Diego hiker Uel Fisk remembers quite vividly watching one of his classmates fall to her death from this brink in 1926.

From a ridge on the right side, it's possible to admire the 90-foot-high cascade and the cottonwood-framed punchbowl at the bottom—some 50 feet across and 20 feet deep. After heavy rains, water thunders over the precipice, but by late summer the falls merely whisper. Many people obviously make the steep traverse down to the pool at the bottom, though the Forest Service advises against it.

There are other routes to the falls via the mouth of Cedar Creek canyon, but they necessitate crossing property owned by the Helix Water District (land below the 995' contour in the San Diego River drainage.) The Forest Service says that permission must be obtained from the landowner to cross this land.

When you've had your fill of the almost overwhelming natural beauty, return to your starting point the same way. If the spirit moves you, you can try this more adventurous, difficult route on the return: From the top of the falls, walk east along the north bank of Cedar Creek about 0.5 mile until the canyon walls close in. There you'll be forced into the creekbed. After about two hours (about 1.2 miles) of boulder-hopping, bushwhacking, and wading through a beautiful and isolated stretch of canyon, Cedar Creek Road will lie above you on the left. Climb north up the slope to Cedar Creek Road and follow it a short distance up to Saddleback, your starting point.

Cedar Creek Falls

Trip 4: Three Sisters Waterfalls

	Distance	3 miles round trip
	Total Elevation Gain/Loss	1100'/1100'
	Hiking Time	4 hours (round trip)
	Recommended Maps	Cleveland National Forest recreation map; USGS 7.5-min *Tule Springs*
	Best Times	November through June
	Agency	CNF/PD
	Difficulty	****

This triple set of waterfalls in Boulder Creek, dubbed the "Three Sisters," is an amazing San Diego County feature that few have ever seen. In full flood these cascades put on a show reminiscent of Yosemite's show stoppers—except at a reduced scale. Since some of the upstream drainage of Boulder Creek comes from Cuyamaca Reservoir, water releases there can affect the flow of water over the falls. During late summer and early fall, there may be almost none.

The falls are located in a patch of national forest incised by several private inholdings. A caretaker who lives nearby patrols the area on behalf of the local ranchers, and is quite adept at detecting trespassers. Follow the directions below to avoid trespassing.

The starting point is reached most easily via Pine Hills Road and Boulder Creek Road near Julian (see Trip 3 above). From the point where Boulder Creek Road and Eagle Peak Road diverge, go south on Boulder Creek Road 8.4 miles (pavement ends in 3.2 miles) to a hairpin turn where Cedar Creek Road joins from the west. Park there, taking care not to block traffic. You can also reach this intersection by driving 13.0 miles north on Boulder Creek Road (less than half paved) from Oak Grove Drive in Descanso.

From the intersection, walk 200 yards (about 200 paces) southeast on Boulder Creek Road. There you'll find a narrow trail on the right going southwest down a chamise-covered ridge. By going this way you'll stay within a block of national forest land in the southwest corner of Section 4. Very shortly, you'll reach the canyon bottom of Sheep Camp Creek. A poor trail threads this canyon for the next 0.5 mile. You

may have to dodge some overhanging shrubbery and clumps of poison oak. There's slick bedrock in a couple of places; be especially careful if it's wet.

When you come upon the remains of old jeep trail, follow it along the south bank (again dodging encroaching poison oak) for about 0.3 mile. Then turn south over a low saddle. You'll both see and probably hear the falls below in the V-shaped canyon of Boulder Creek. The saddle would be a good place to camp if you can't handle packing your gear down the precipitous slope ahead.

Three Sisters Falls

You'll now have to drop very steeply down the slope, in a sort of controlled fall, losing 500 feet. On the way down, enjoy if you can the superb display of spring wildflowers.

At the bottom you can either forge a path through the brush along the left side of the creek, or rock hop and wade toward the falls. Great masses of poison oak, intermixed with wild grape vines, lie along the banks. Be very cautious of slippery rocks.

When you reach the base of the waterfalls, all the previous trouble will have been worth it. The "middle sister" is impressive, with water sliding 50 feet down a smooth channel worn in the bedrock into a kidney-shaped pool about 80 feet long and at least 10 feet deep. Watch your footing—it's deceptively easy to slip on the smooth rock and perhaps be seriously injured. It's difficult and dangerous to climb up to the uppermost fall, although if you're agile it's possible to bypass it by climbing high on the left side.

A circular feature worn in the bed of Boulder Creek called the Devils Punch Bowl lies 0.6 mile upstream from the falls. You can work your way toward it on public land, but the punchbowl itself lies on private property.

Area M-5: Julian

The town of Julian enjoys a reputation far wider than its modest size would seem to call for. Tourists come in droves to this gold-mining-boom-town-turned-apple-growing-center to tour its quaint museums, buy an apple pie, bend an elbow at the soda fountain, and, of course, to walk in the pine-scented woods. Actually there isn't too much woods-walking available close to town. Beyond the little grid of streets, east of town, you can find the path leading to the site of the old Washington Mine; otherwise the land all around is private.

Hiking opportunities multiply if you drive some distance out of town. Cuyamaca Rancho State Park and the Laguna Mountain Recreation Area (Areas M-6 and M-7 in this book) offer a plethora of trails. Somewhat closer is William Heise County Park, with its small network of trails in a superb forested setting; the Banner Toll Road, a historic wagon road going through a parcel of BLM land; and the Volcan Mountain Wilderness Preserve, San Diego County's newest open-space park. All of these are profiled in the trips below.

Sometime before the turn of the century, a greatly expanded Volcan Mountain Preserve should stretch across much of the Volcan Mountains north of Julian, encompassing the uppermost reaches of the Santa Ysabel Creek watershed. This area will be a key acquisition for the emerging San Dieguito River Park, which will ultimately consist of a series of linked parks and greenways stretching 50 miles from the mouth of the San Dieguito River at Del Mar to the Volcan Mountains. Considered one of the most ambitious and innovative land-use projects in the country, the park will comprise a significant fraction of the entire watershed of the San Dieguito River and its main tributary, Santa Ysabel Creek.

The next edition of this book will doubtless feature many more opportunities for exploring the Julian/Volcan Mountains area on foot. For the latest update, you may call the offices of the San Dieguito River Park, 595-5398.

Trip 1: William Heise County Park

	Distance	1- to 3-mile hikes
	Recommended Map	William Heise County Park map/brochure
	Optional Map	USGS 7.5-min *Julian*
	Best Times	All year
	Agency	SDCP
	Difficulty	* to **

At Heise Park you can find your quintessential walk in the pine woods. The park is located in one of the most beautiful and unspoiled pockets of undeveloped land around Julian, and is just large enough to contain a significant network of footpaths.

About one-tenth of the park is devoted to meticulously maintained camping and picnic areas. These lie along the thickly wooded bottomlands of Cedar Creek and its upper

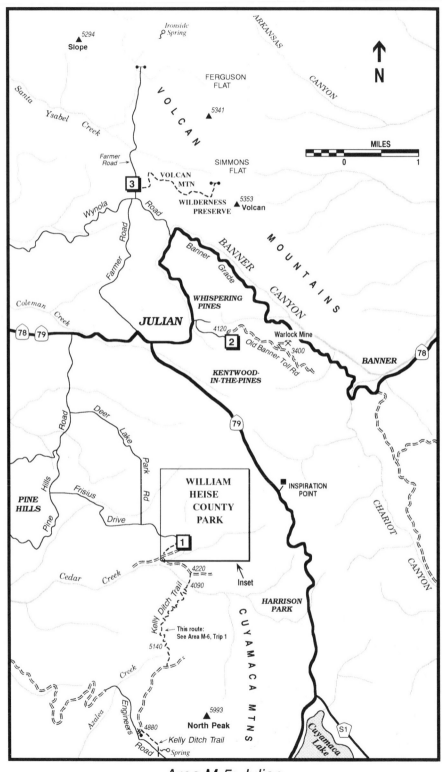

Area M-5: Julian

tributaries. The surrounding area is a virtual wilderness laced with about 7 miles of loop trails. Heise Park is also the northern terminus of the outstanding Kelly Ditch Trail, which leads into Cuyamaca Rancho State Park (Area M-6, Trip 1).

The Cedar Trail and the self-guiding Nature Trail, each a mile in length, stay beneath a shady canopy of oaks, pines and cedars. The Manzanita and Canyon Oak trails, on the other hand, climb up along steep slopes clothed with dense chaparral; in some places, the manzanita grows to 10 feet or more in height, enclosing you in a tangled net of limbs and leaves.

Glenn's View lies on a windswept ridgeline in the northeast corner of the park. The view here is similar to, but more inclusive than, that enjoyed by motorists at Inspiration Point, a half mile below on Highway 79. To the south you can look over a rolling expanse of timbered hills toward the summits of the Cuyamaca and Laguna mountains. Eastward, the Anza-Borrego Desert and the Salton Sea shimmer in the distance. On late summer afternoons, when conditions are propitious, you can watch massive thunderheads roil in as moist air flowing across the desert from the Gulf of California rises over the mountains.

The well-marked turnoff to Heise Park is one mile west of Julian on Highway 78/79. Signs direct you south on Pine Hills Road to Frisius Drive, then east on Frisius to the park entrance.

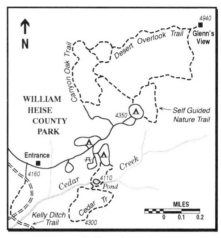

Julian inset

Oak-shaded trail in Heise Park

Trip 2: Old Banner Toll Road

🥾	**Distance**	2.5 miles round trip
	Total Elevation Gain/Loss	700'/700'
	Hiking Time	1½ hours
▧	**Optional Map**	USGS 7.5-min *Julian*
	Best Times	October through June
➹	**Agency**	BLM/EC
	Difficulty	**

Honeycombed hillsides and bits and pieces of rusted equipment—that is the legacy left behind by Julian's gold-mining heyday over a century ago. Although a few mines continue to be worked sporadically even today, most have long been abandoned. For a look at one of the first mines to be discovered (1870) and one of the last to be extensively worked, try this short hike down the Old Banner Toll Road.

Drive 1 mile east of Julian on Highway 78, then turn right at Whispering Pines Road. Immediately after, make a sharp right, then a left to connect with Woodland Road. After 0.4 mile on Woodland Road, go left at a fork (the right fork leads to a locked gate) and proceed another 0.1 mile to the end of the pavement. Park here, off the roadway.

On foot now, take the dirt road that curves steeply downward to the left (generally east). This is one of the two roads down Banner Canyon from Julian to Banner shown on a circa-1910 topographic map of the area. Nature has not been kind to this old road in recent years. Violent storms over the past several winters have caused deep washouts across its bed. As tracks show, only foot travelers, horses, coyotes, and a few intrepid motorcyclists come this way today.

Below you is the modern road through Banner Canyon—Highway 78. It appears only slightly less twisting than the road you're on, but offers a more gradual—if longer—descent to the town of Banner. Below Highway 78, near the very bottom of the canyon, there once existed even earlier routes of travel between Julian and Banner. The earliest was a "skid road" so steep that a driver descending it would have to drag an uprooted tree behind his wagon to provide enough braking power.

The linear shape of Banner Canyon is due to repeated ruptures along the Elsinore Fault. This splinter fault of the San Andreas is the most extensive fault system in San Diego County, and is believed capable of causing a major earthquake. Look across the canyon to see the fault's surface trace, which cuts low across the north wall, and also notice how some of the ravines exhibit a dogleg or offset pattern due to horizontal movements.

Old mine shafts pierce the earth on the steep slopes above and below you, but most are concealed by thick chaparral. At about 1 mile, the Warlock Mine, with its processing mill, comes into view.

The mine suspended operations in 1957 and lies in a state of advanced dilapidation. It's worth a look around though. You'll find a relatively intact ball mill, the superintendent's formerly cozy cottage with its fine view, and other buildings in a state of collapse. In 1962 the mine's shafts were declared a radioactive fallout shelter for 222 people by the Civil Defense Commission and stocked accordingly with emergency provisions. A cave-in two years later ended its usefulness in that regard. Tread carefully among the ruins, and don't enter the mine openings.

Someday the BLM may establish an interpretive station near here to introduce visitors to the history of gold mining in the Julian District, and to explain the fascinating geology of Banner Canyon.

Beyond the Warlock Mine, Old Banner Toll Road runs into private property, so it's best to turn back after visiting the mine.

Trip 3: Volcan Mountain

👞	**Distance**	3.0 miles round trip
	Total Elevation Gain/Loss	800'/800'
	Hiking Time	2 hours (round trip)
▨	**Optional Map**	USGS 7.5-min *Julian*
	Best Times	October through June
➽	**Agency**	SDCP
	Difficulty	**

Named by early Spanish or Mexican travelers for its dubious resemblance to a volcano, Volcan Mountain (called the "Volcan Mountains" on topographic maps) is really a fault-block mountain range, essentially no different from any other major component of the Peninsular Ranges. Two faults—the Elsinore and the Earthquake Valley faults—bracket the range on the southwest and northeast sides respectively.

Crowned with magnificent forests of oak, pine and cedar, the mountain has been privately owned and off-limits to public access for more than a century. In the early 1990s the county acquired approximately 800 acres on the southwest slope, and soon (pending completion of a county management plan for the area) it will be possible to walk up to "Volcan" peak, the southernmost of several knolls along the crest of the range.

A single trail (old jeep road) leads from the edge of the apple orchards north of Julian to the top. Park alongside Farmer Road, 200 yards north of Wynola Road, and walk east along a dirt road marked by a sign indicating the Volcan Mountain Wilderness Preserve. After 0.2 mile, you'll pass a carved entry designed by noted Julian artist James Hubbell, and stonework including an open-air "kiva" for use during interpretive programs. The Elsinore Fault, a major splinter of the San Andreas, passes almost directly under this spot.

On the old jeep road now, you swing north, round a horseshoe bend, and continue climbing in earnest along a rounded ridgeline leading toward Volcan peak. Along the ridge, wind-rippled expanses of grassland alternate with dense copses of live oak, and the view expands to include the townsite of Julian, its "suburb" of Whispering Pines, and the dusky Cuyamaca Mountains to the south.

At 1.4 miles beyond the Volcan Mountain Preserve entrance, you come (as of 1993) to a locked gate, and must turn back. Please do not trespass on private land in the area, which is well posted. Before heading back, enjoy watching birds of prey soaring on updrafts over the grassy slopes hereabouts, and admire the view toward the northwest of rolling hills and wooded hollows in the upper Santa Ysabel Creek drainage. Much of this landscape may one day be incorporated into San Dieguito River Park.

Area M-6: Cuyamaca Mountains

Who among those unfamiliar with Southern California would believe that such beautiful forests could exist less than 40 miles from San Diego Bay? Who would believe the intensity of the fall and spring colors? Who would believe that snow can blanket the Cuyamaca Mountains while the coastal area bakes in subtropical sunshine?

This knowledge is not lost among San Diego hikers. The Cuyamaca Mountains are probably the most popular place to hike in San Diego County. Cuyamaca Rancho State Park, one of California's largest state parks, has over 100 miles of trails and old fire roads for hiking. Anyone in San Diego willing to spend barely an hour driving up there can easily escape the pressures of the city.

The Cuyamacas have attracted humans for at least 7000 years. Until the arrival of Europeans, bands of Native Americans migrated to higher elevation such as these every summer. Then, as now, game and certain basic vegetable foodstuffs, such as acorns, were plentiful. The Indians called the area *Ah-ha-Kwe-ah-mac*, variously translated as "the place where it rains," and "rain yonder," in reference to the relatively wet climate at higher elevations— about 35 inches of precipitation a year. Dozens of archaeological sites have been identified within the park. As you explore, you'll probably discover some of the many bedrock milling sites (mortars or "morteros") that were a common feature around springs and resting areas.

In 1845 the area became a Mexican land grant, Rancho Cuyamaca. The promise of harvesting timber from the rancho was never fulfilled, and it was not until 1855 that the first non-Indian, James Lassator, settled here.

Gold was discovered in the hills around Julian and along the north edge of the Cuyamacas in the 1860s, and within a few years the influx of prospectors and miners had displaced the remaining native people. A prospect near the shoreline of today's Cuyamaca Reservoir eventually became southern California's most productive gold mine, the Stonewall Mine.

After the gold boom, the old rancho property changed hands several times until it was purchased by the state in 1933 for use as a park. With subsequent additions, today's Cuyamaca Rancho State Park now includes nearly 30,000 acres, of which about 13,000 acres have been set aside as state wilderness.

The backbone of the Cuyamaca Mountains consists of a chain of forested peaks—North, Middle, and Cuyamaca—that runs north to south. Most of North Peak is in private ownership, while Middle Peak and Cuyamaca Peak lie along the state park's west boundary. Lower and drier, chaparral-covered peaks—like Stonewall and Oakzanita—lie along the park's eastern edge.

The highest ridges are crowned with forests of live and black oak, incense-cedar, white fir, and four varieties of pine—Coulter, sugar, ponderosa, and Jeffrey. Below that are broad, treeless mesas and valley bottoms, awash in tall grasses. Sycamore, alder, and willow cling to the major watercourses. Still lower are boulder-strewn foothills densely covered with chaparral.

For better and for worse, the park is split asunder by a rather heavily trafficked (on weekends, at least) road—Highway 79. This route permits fast access from either Interstate 8 on the south or from the Julian area on the north. Since many of the trails depart from turnouts along the highway and head directly into park's back areas, you can quickly get away from traffic noise—and most people, too.

The park's camping and picnic areas include Green Valley and Paso Picacho, popular among families; and Los Caballos and Los Vaqueros, which cater to equestrians. You'll find interpretive displays at Paso Picacho and in the Indian Museum next to park headquarters. The Stonewall Mine site features some old relics of the mining days. Ranger-led walks, and lectures on the geology, wildlife, and history of the area are offered on most weekends.

Backpacking within the park is rewarding, but somewhat limited. Only two trail campgrounds in the park cater to hikers (and also horse riders): Arroyo Seco and Granite Spring. Both are available on a first-come-first-served basis by pre-registration at the park headquarters, Green Valley, or Paso Picacho. Some "environmental" (walk-in) sites are also available near Paso Picacho. Outside of these designated spots trail camping is not allowed; however, the state park shares its east and west borders with Cleveland National Forest, where remote camping (by permit) is allowed. Pure water gushes from several springs in the park, but most have never undergone the necessary, expensive tests that would certify them as officially "potable." Check with the rangers first, or plan on carrying your own water while on the trails.

There are no restrictions on day hiking, and no fees to pay if you start from one of the roadside turnouts (some turnouts have parking restrictions, however). You will have to pay a day-use fee if you drive into either the Paso Picacho or Green Valley camp/picnic areas.

The 17 trips described below hardly exhaust all possibilities. One possible trip intentionally not described in this book is a visit to the Cuyamaca cypress groves. The Cuyamaca cypress, recognized as one of the rarest trees in the world, has retreated to a small area straddling the park boundary. The park rangers may be able to help you find these trees if you express an interest in seeing them.

The Cuyamaca Mountains offer special opportunities for two other modes of travel: mountain bicycling and cross-country skiing. You can mountain bike any of the park's qualifying fire roads, but none of the trails. Qualifying roads are marked on the current Cuyamaca Rancho State Park map and brochure. Ski touring is possible on several roads and wide trails at higher elevations, but good conditions are fairly rare. When the cold, wet storms of winter strike—perhaps two or three times a year—don't hesitate to grab your skis and take off at the first sign of clearing skies.

Trip 1: Kelly Ditch Trail

Distance	5.5 miles
Total Elevation Gain/Loss	1000'/1600'
Hiking Time	4 hours
Recommended Map	Cuyamaca Rancho State Park map/brochure
Optional Maps	USGS 7.5-min *Cuyamaca Peak*, *Julian*
Best Times	All year
Agency	CRSP
Difficulty	***

The Kelly Ditch Trail, completed in 1985, is perhaps the most beautiful pathway yet built in the Cuyamaca-Julian area. This hiking/horse trail is routed partly along a century-old diversion ditch. You'll also tread over dim traces of "skid roads" where freshly-cut logs were slid down off the mountain ridges to serve as lumber and fuel for the mines and boom towns of

Julian's gold rush era.

Hiking the trail is rewarding in any season, but it's hard to beat the fall-color season which reaches its peak around late October. By then the black oaks exhibit full crowns of crispy, golden leaves, and fat, glossy acorns litter the ground. Crimson squaw bush and poison oak leaves show their stuff amid the glades of rus-

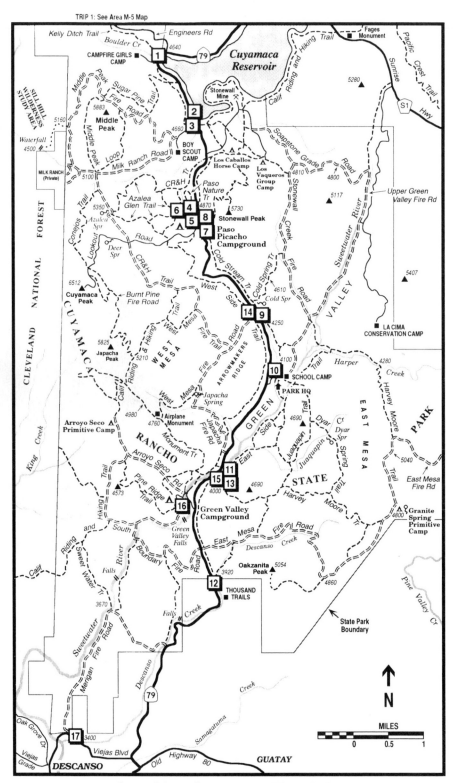

Area M-6: Cuyamaca Mountains

set-colored bracken fern.

The Kelly Ditch Trail is best hiked one-way, with the aid of a car shuttle or a drop-off-and-pick-up arrangement. The easier (mostly downhill) direction is south to north—Cuyamaca Reservoir to William Heise County Park. The starting point is on Highway 79, 8.3 miles south of Julian, near the intersection of Engineers Road and Highway 79. The trail ends at a parking lot just inside William Heise County Park.

Pick up the trail west of Engineers Road and just north of where Highway 79 crosses the low dam impounding the waters of Cuyamaca Reservoir. In the first mile you'll travel in, or on the rim of, the remnant Kelly Ditch, constructed by pick-and-shovel labor more than a century ago. Its purpose was to divert runoff from the south slope of North Peak into the then-new reservoir. Poison oak grows alongside the trail-take care to avoid contact with it.

After one mile the trail climbs abruptly out of the ditch, veers north through a sun-struck patch of chaparral, and then crosses paved Engineers Road. You pass a spring-fed horse trough, and continue a short distance to join a disused dirt road. Turn right and follow the road's gentle uphill course around the west slope of North Peak. You'll stroll past a couple of ancient sugar pines, and enter a delightful, parklike meadow, dotted with black oaks and carpeted by bracken ferns. On the clearest days, blue sky meets the blue Pacific horizon more than a hundred miles to the west.

At the next fork (about 2.5 miles from the start), you're directed left across a sunny bowl, and then up to a low ridge shaded by live oaks, black oaks, Coulter pines, incense-cedars, and white firs. From this point, the highest elevation of the hike, a long series of switchbacks leads you steadily downward (and north) to a small stream—a tributary of Cedar Creek—fringed with ferns and wild berries.

On past the creek, the trail goes up a steep ravine evidently cut deeply by some agent other than running water. This is the remnant of one of the skid roads. After a 120' gain, the trail tops a saddle and joins a dirt road. You descend to a second creek (the main fork of Cedar Creek), cross a meadow beyond, and pick up the last link of trail that leads to the Heise Park entrance.

Ranger-led bird watch in Cuyamaca Rancho State Park

Trip 2: Middle Peak

👟	**Distance**	5.7 miles
	Total Elevation Gain/Loss	1100'/1100'
	Hiking Time	3 hours
🔲	**Recommended Map**	Cuyamaca Rancho State Park map/brochure
	Optional Maps	USGS 7.5-min *Cuyamaca Peak*
	Best Times	All year
Q	**Agency**	CRSP
	Difficulty	**

If you like big trees, Middle Peak is the place to go. Middle Peak's cone-shaped bulk is crowned with the largest conifers in the Cuyamaca Mountains—and possibly in all of San Diego County.

The old fire trails that encircle Middle Peak have long been popular hiking routes. This trip description, however, introduces a variation: along with one of the older loop trails, it includes the new Sugar Pine Trail, which goes through an area added to the park in the early '80s.

Begin at the parking area just south of Cuyamaca Reservoir, mile 10.7 on Highway 79. Walk across the highway and pick up the Minshall Trail going north along the roadside. At about 0.7 mile, the trail pulls away from the highway, turns westward behind several cabins, and joins a dirt road. Continue 0.2 mile on this dirt road, then go left on the marked Sugar Pine Trail (an old roadbed) toward Middle Peak.

You climb moderately through dense forests of black oak, white fir and incense-cedar, reversing direction twice. After the second switchback (hairpin turn), ponderosa pines appear along with patches of bracken fern. A little higher, you come upon the first sugar pines; notice the long, narrow cones on the tips of the drooping branches. Some of the sugar pines on Middle Peak have diameters over six feet. Both sugar-pine and ponderosa-pine trunks exhibit "puzzle patterns" in their bark, but ponderosas are distinguished by smaller cones and shorter branches.

At 2.5 miles the road passes the foundation of an old cabin and then curves southwest to join Middle Peak Fire Road. Keep left at the intersection, go 50 yards, and then turn left, staying on Middle Peak Fire Road.

The summit of Middle Peak now lies south and about 200 feet above you. (You can make the trailless scramble to the top easily enough as a side trip, but views in all directions are screened by brush and trees.) Continue east, then south around the upper flank of Middle Peak, keeping straight on Middle Peak Loop Road (if you prefer to stay with our trip description) as Middle Peak Fire Road veers left and begins a sharp switchbacking descent toward the starting point.

In another mile you'll come to a 5-way intersection of roads and trails on the saddle between Middle and Cuyamaca peaks. Double back (left, east) on Milk Ranch Road to complete the hike. As you walk along Milk Ranch Road, you'll be treated to some superb parklike vistas of broad, rolling meadows and distant, thickly forested slopes. When the leaves of the black oaks flush a bright yellow around late October and early November, these vistas are quite reminiscent of Appalachian landscapes.

Trip 3: Sill Hill Waterfall

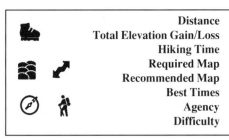

	Distance	6.5 miles round trip
	Total Elevation Gain/Loss	1400'/1400'
	Hiking Time	4½ hours (round trip)
	Required Map	USGS 7.5-min *Cuyamaca Peak*
	Recommended Map	Cleveland National Forest recreation map
	Best Times	November through June
	Agency	CRSP, CNF/PD
	Difficulty	***

This hidden grotto and 30' high waterfall lie within Cleveland National Forest, just outside the west boundary of Cuyamaca Rancho State Park. It is a part of the Sill Hill Wilderness Study Area, one of two national forest WSA's in San Diego County that have so far failed to win official wilderness designation.

Finding the waterfall and grotto is puzzle—a real challenge for those who don't mind being slightly lost part of the time. The last few hundred yards involve some fairly difficult rock hopping and bushwhacking. In addition, you must take care not to enter an island of private land lying between the national forest and the state park.

Begin at the parking area (day use only) at mile 10.7 on Highway 79. (Overnighters can inquire about parking at the resort area near Cuyamaca Dam or at Paso Picacho Campground.) From the parking area, cross the highway and go up Milk Ranch Road. After climbing gradually around the southeast flank of Middle Peak, you come to a saddle and a 5-way intersection of fire roads and trails. Con-

tinue straight (west) for 0.4 mile, then bear right (north) on Middle Peak Fire Road.

Climb for 0.7 mile through oak and pine forest until you come abreast of a barbed-wire fence on the left (west) side of the trail, precisely at the 5160-foot contour. Step over the fence, entering Cleveland National Forest, and descend west and northwest along a faint path through the oak forest.

You'll soon come upon a beautiful hillside meadow, with views stretching to the coastline. The south-pointing finger of Point Loma is visible along with much of the suburban sprawl of the coastal strip and inland valleys. This meadow is one of several conspicuous bald spots on Middle Peak that can be clearly seen from San Diego on crystal-clear days.

Since the meadow is on national-forest land outside the state park, an overnight stay (with remote camping permit from the Forest Service) is permitted.

From the southwest edge of the meadow, work your way south-southwest along the oak- and brush-covered slopes, skirting the corner of

Riding in Green Valley

the fenceline that defines the island of private land. Try to lose elevation gradually, while dodging thickets of poison oak. Within 0.3 mile of the meadow, you'll hear the sound of falling water—if you're lucky. The waterfall is located at about 4500 feet elevation along the perennial stream that arises from La Puerta Springs near the aforementioned 5-way intersection of roads and trails.

The water makes an abrupt leap over a dark cliff into a grotto shaded by oak and alder trees. It's tough to take a photo that does justice to the scene, because the sunlight never seems to fall at the right angle.

The surrounding area isn't suitable for camping, but the rocks at the base of the falls are fine for lounging or having lunch. (Safety reminder: resist the temptation to approach the lip of the falls; fallen leaves conceal a slippery rock surface.) With much effort and caution, you can explore downstream and come upon more falls sculpted into the bed of the canyon.

Probably the biggest navigational difficulty on this trip is finding your way back to the meadow. Despite your best efforts to retrace your path, there's a distinct possibility of getting temporarily lost in the brush and trees. Careful work with your compass, both going there and coming back, should pay off.

Trip 4: Paso Nature Trail

	Distance	0.4 mile
	Total Elevation Gain/Loss	50'/50'
	Hiking Time	15 minutes
	Optional Map	Cuyamaca Rancho State Park map/brochure
	Best Times	All year
	Agency	CRSP
	Difficulty	*

This short, self-guiding nature trail highlights some of the native trees and shrubs of the Cuyamaca Mountains. Look for it at the north end of the picnic area at Paso Picacho. There are 12 stations along the trail, keyed to a leaflet available at the entrance station. If you aren't, as yet, very familiar with the local flora and fauna, visit the small interpretive center (just outside the entrance to the campground) as well.

Trip 5: West Side Trail (to Morteros)

	Distance	0.7 mile round trip
	Total Elevation Gain/Loss	50'/50'
	Hiking Time	20 minutes
	Recommended Map	Cuyamaca Rancho State Park map/brochure
	Optional Maps	USGS 7.5-min *Cuyamaca Peak*
	Best Times	All year
	Agency	CRSP
	Difficulty	*

At least a dozen major Indian villages existed in the Cuyamaca Mountains prior to about 130 years ago. These were the mountain villages, or summer camps, of the Kumeyaay Indians, who divided their time between the mountains and the desert. Many of these sites are today occupied by modern campgrounds, as the presence of bedrock morteros confirms. Other sites have remained more isolated, reachable only by trail. One such place, marked by a large cluster of morteros on a granite slab, lies a short distance from Paso Picacho Campground by way of a short section of the West Side Trail.

The easiest way to reach the West Side Trail is by way of the paved Cuyamaca Peak Fire Road (Lookout Road) beginning in back of the fire station just outside the campground entrance. Beyond the gate that blocks vehicle traffic on the fire road, a sign marks the beginning of the West Side Trail—a trail that parallels Highway 79 all the way to Green Valley Campground.

After about 0.2 mile on the West Side Trail, you emerge from the forest cover and skirt the north edge of a meadow. Look for a complex of about 30 morteros near the trail. There are others nearby.

With a modest leap of imagination, it's not too difficult to picture a typical scene on a summer's day two hundred years ago: Indian women grinding acorn meal, children squalling nearby, the men off hunting small game, or perhaps fashioning stone tools or arrowheads. Unfortunately, collectors long ago carried off all the arrowheads and tools, but the well-worn pits in the granite remain as reminders of an age not far removed in time from our own.

Morteros, West Side Trail

Trip 6: Azalea Glen Trail

	Distance	3.0 miles
	Total Elevation Gain/Loss	550'/550'
	Hiking Time	1½ hours
	Recommended Map	Cuyamaca Rancho State Park map/brochure
	Optional Maps	USGS 7.5-min *Cuyamaca Peak*
	Best Times	All year
	Agency	CRSP
	Difficulty	**

Of all the trails in Cuyamaca Rancho State Park, this one is my favorite for a leisurely walk. There are dense forests, a sunny meadow, a trickling brook, Indian morteros, and a refreshing spring—all in one delightful 3-mile loop hike.

You begin across from the Paso Picacho picnic area, not far from the restrooms. Follow the trail 0.2 mile west to a split. Take the right fork to hike the trail counterclockwise—the way I'll describe it.

Contour through the mixed forest of oaks, pines, firs, and cedars, crossing three small ravines. At 0.6 mile from the split, you emerge from the shade into a cheerful, bracken-fringed meadow. It's hard to miss the fine collection of morteros on the nearby granite slabs. Leaving the meadow, you plunge into the dark forest again, and descend to the bank of a small brook, informally called Azalea Creek. Here, western azalea, thimbleberry, and other moisture- and

shade-loving plants form a delicate understory of greenery under dense stands of white fir and incense-cedar. Come in May or June to see the azaleas in bloom.

Our route joins the California Riding and Hiking Trail and turns steeply uphill through white fir forest, then through thickets of manzanita and other brush forms. After about 0.5 mile, the trail tops out, joining Azalea Spring Fire Road in a clearing. Azalea Spring is nearby, serving as a popular resting place and water stop for hikers and horses. A giant pine, with a trunk perhaps 6 feet in diameter, stands on the slope just south of the spring.

From Azalea Spring, it's back into the forest again as you descend moderately on the last leg of the Azalea Glen Trail. Let gravity pay its debt, but don't rush through: watch and listen for gray squirrels, chipmunks, chickadees, acorn woodpeckers, and the ubiquitous Steller's jays.

Trip 7: Cuyamaca Peak

	Distance	5.5 miles round trip
	Total Elevation Gain/Loss	1650'/1650'
	Hiking Time	3 hours (round trip)
	Recommended Map	Cuyamaca Rancho State Park map/brochure
	Optional Maps	USGS 7.5-min *Cuyamaca Peak*
	Best Times	All year
	Agency	CRSP
	Difficulty	***

Cuyamaca Peak, San Diego County's second highest summit, lies only a few miles from the county's geographical center. Its unique position and height make it the best land-

based vantage point for studying the topography of our county. The view from ground level on the peak is somewhat less than a continuous 360° due to the presence of some antenna structures and a few trees, but you can still take in the complete panorama in increments by simply moving around a bit.

The one-lane, paved Lookout Road ("Cuyamaca Peak Fire Road" on most maps), is closed to public vehicles, but provides a very straightforward passage to the top of the peak for self-propelled travelers—be they hikers, runners, bicyclists, or cross-country skiers. Deer Spring, a dependable and delicious source of water located fortuitously near the midpoint of the road, is an added delight.

You can pick up the road at its intersection with Highway 79 just south of the Interpretive Center, or you can wend your way through Paso Picacho Campground and pick it up just beyond the southernmost campsites. It's an uphill grind all the way, moderate at first, then steep beyond the intersection of the California Riding and Hiking Trail.

After 1.5 miles the road grade becomes flat for a short stretch and you pass Deer Spring, for years a dependable source of potable water for hikers on their way up the mountain. Sadly, the pipe that used to dispense cold water is gone and no water is available.

Views improve as you continue beyond the spring into an area still recovering from forest fires that swept through in 1950 and 1970. Some tall snags poke above the smaller trees, serving as perches for a variety of birds. By now, the vista to the north and east includes Cuyamaca Reservoir and some of the desert mountain ranges.

In the final steep stretch, you climb past some mature timber that survived the fires and suddenly arrive at the flat, antenna-cluttered summit of the peak. A fire-lookout structure stood here until a few years ago, when it was removed for lack of use.

During a Santa Ana condition in fall or winter, and after the passage of major winter storms, Cuyamaca Peak becomes a grandstand seat for views stretching into at least five counties and one foreign state. To name some of the features visible within San Diego County: the Palomar Mountains (look for the tiny white speck on the summit ridge—the Hale Telescope dome) northwest more than 30 miles away; Hot

Springs Mountain, 26 miles almost due north over the summit of nearby Middle Peak; Granite Mountain, 11 miles to the northeast; the south end of the Santa Rosa Mountains, 40 miles northeast; and Whale Peak and the Vallecito Mountains, 18 miles east-northeast.

Close in, just 10 or so miles to the southeast, are the conifer-covered Laguna Mountains. South and southwest along the international border are Tecate Peak and Otay Mountain, 25-30 miles away. The Pacific Ocean gleams in the west, with Point Loma, the Silver Strand, San Diego Bay, and Mission Bay visible from a distance of about 35-40 miles. Along an arc from west to southwest, you'll spot coastal peaks like Black Mountain, Soledad Mountain, Fortuna Mountain, Cowles Mountain, Mount Helix, and San Miguel Mountain. Along a west-to-south arc, but closer in, you'll see El Cajon Mountain, Viejas Mountain, Lyons Peak, and Corte Madera Mountain.

You'll enhance the pleasure of your stay on the peak if you bring along a good county map and binoculars.

Deer Spring

Trip 8: Stonewall Peak

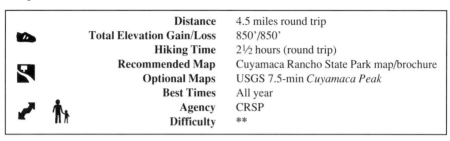

Distance	4.5 miles round trip
Total Elevation Gain/Loss	850'/850'
Hiking Time	2½ hours (round trip)
Recommended Map	Cuyamaca Rancho State Park map/brochure
Optional Maps	USGS 7.5-min *Cuyamaca Peak*
Best Times	All year
Agency	CRSP
Difficulty	**

Stonewall Peak's angular summit of white granite is a conspicuous landmark throughout Cuyamaca Rancho State Park. Although Stonewall stands some 800 feet lower than nearby Cuyamaca Peak, its unique position and steep, south exposure provide a more inclusive view of the park area itself.

Beginning across the highway from the entrance to Paso Picacho Campground, the trail climbs steadily and moderately on a set of well-engineered switchbacks up the west slope of Stonewall Peak. Thick groves of live and black oaks keep you in semi-shade most of the way.

About halfway up the trail, a view opens to the north and east. Cuyamaca Reservoir lies to the north, its level and its extent varying according to the season and the year's precipitation. When it is full, its surface covers nearly 1000 acres.

When you reach the top of the switchbacks, turn right (south) toward the summit of the peak. (The trail to the left descends sharply to Los Caballos Camp; if you prefer, this can be used as an alternate, but substantially longer, return route.) Follow the trail through chaparral and scattered trees to the base of the exposed granite cap. A series of steps hewn in the rock and a guardrail are provided in the last hundred feet or so. Small children will certainly need assistance here.

On top, you won't see any ocean views (the main Cuyamaca massif stands tall in the west), but the foreground panorama of the park's rolling topography is impressive enough. Patches of meadow along the streamcourses and the bald grassland areas on East Mesa and West Mesa change color with the seasons: green in spring, yellow in summer, brown or gray in fall, and occasionally white with fallen snow in winter. The forested slopes appear as a tapestry of color, the light green or yellow-tinted black oaks playing counterpoint to the rather dark hues of the conifers and live oaks. Direction-finders on the summit assist in the identification of major peaks in the middle and far distance.

Swallows or swifts practically rake the summit during their high-speed maneuvers, and larger birds—ravens, hawks, and even bald eagles may cruise by. Eagles, along with egrets, herons, and ospreys, are sometimes attracted to the shoreline of nearby Cuyamaca Reservoir, especially in winter.

Trip 9: Stonewall Creek/Soapstone Grade Loop

	Distance	8.2 miles
	Total Elevation Gain/Loss	1050'/1050'
	Hiking Time	4 hours
	Recommended Map	Cuyamaca Rancho State Park map/brochure
	Optional Maps	USGS 7.5-min *Cuyamaca Peak*
	Best Times	September through June
	Agency	CRSP
	Difficulty	***

This is probably the nearest to level of any of the longer hikes possible within Cuyamaca Rancho State Park. Instead of climbing a mountain or a mesa, the route follows, for the most part, the gentle valleys of Stonewall Creek and the upper Sweetwater River. Most elevation gain takes place in the first 3 miles.

Begin at the parking turnout on the east side of Highway 79 at mile 7.3. Cross the creek (Cold Stream), and go east about 100 feet to join the Cold Stream Trail. Go left (north) and continue about 200 yards to Cold Spring. From the spring, bear right on the Cold Spring Trail and follow it northeast 1.2 miles, up and over a chaparral- and oak-covered ridge. On the far side of the ridge you'll cross Stonewall Creek, whose flow becomes sluggish after the rainy season, but pools up in shallow bedrock basins until about June. Turn left (north) at the next intersection—Stonewall Creek Fire Road.

The fire road meanders along the east bank of Stonewall Creek, passing through chaparral, oaks, and pines, and finally across grassland, to a low saddle just east of the two equestrian campgrounds (a side trip to piped water sources is possible from this point).

Just beyond the low saddle is Soapstone Grade Road. Turn right (east) and skirt the edge of the broad, open valley containing Cuyamaca Reservoir. Trees stood in this valley in fair abundance before discovery of the nearby Stonewall Mine—afterward, the sudden demand for lumber caused a brief logging bonanza. The road is named for the soapstone, a talclike rock used commercially as a base for bath powders, exposed in the area.

After contouring for about one mile, the road turns sharply downhill along a scrubby hillside;

in less than one more mile, it meets Upper Green Valley Fire Road amid a fine canopy of spreading oaks. Now it's simply a matter of following the Sweetwater River downstream on the adjacent road. Your accompaniment is a riparian strip of oaks, pines, and willows, providing welcome shade on warm days, and shelter from the wind on blustery days. Stay with Upper Green Valley Fire Road for 2.3 miles, pass the lower end of Stonewall Creek Fire Road, and continue another 0.4 mile to a cutoff trail on the right. Go west on this cutoff for 0.4 mile, passing over a low ridge. Then merge into northbound Cold Stream Trail, and in just 0.6 mile you'll be back at your starting point.

Trip 10: Harper Creek

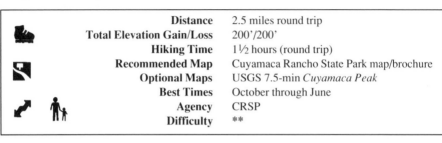

	Distance	2.5 miles round trip
	Total Elevation Gain/Loss	200'/200'
	Hiking Time	1½ hours (round trip)
	Recommended Map	Cuyamaca Rancho State Park map/brochure
	Optional Maps	USGS 7.5-min *Cuyamaca Peak*
	Best Times	October through June
	Agency	CRSP
	Difficulty	**

If you visit Harper Creek's jewel-like pools during a winter cold snap, you might be surprised to find some of them icebound. Come on a warm day in May or June, on the other hand, and you may feel like sliding into one of the pools for a bracing splash. In the heat of late summer, though, you may find only dry, sun-blasted slabs of water-polished rock here.

The parking area next to the Indian Museum and park headquarters (entrance at mile 6.2 on Highway 79) is a good point to start this hike, but parking is limited to two hours. You can park for an unlimited time (during the daylight

On Harper Creek

hours) in any of several nearby turnouts along Highway 79; the most convenient of these is right at the intersection of Highway 79 and the Indian Museum entrance road.

From the Indian Museum walk east around the buildings of Camp Cuyamaca, a San Diego city and county school camp, and drop down to the sandy bank of the Sweetwater River. Find a place to cross the shallow river, and pick up the East Side Trail on the far side.

Follow the East Side Trail northeast across a grassy bluff overlooking the river. In about 0.9 mile, the trail turns east, continues briefly along Harper Creek, and then crosses the creek. At this crossing, leave the trail and simply scramble up along the bank or the creekbed. Be careful of your footing, especially in winter, when the dark, wet-looking streaks on the rock may actually be ice.

The stream water flows over bedrock slabs, often streaked with mineral deposits, and collects in small pools, two to four feet deep, fed by mini-waterfalls. The exposed rock above the creek is almost completely covered by a gray-green mantle of lichens. High on the slopes on either side are belts of chaparral, chiefly mountain mahogany, punctuated by the flower stalks of Our Lord's Candle yucca. The best pools are about 0.1 mile up from the point where you leave the trail; but the creekbed remains interesting for another 0.2 mile.

Retrace your steps to return. Alternately, you can continue up the creekbed and pick up the Harvey Moore Trail, which parallels Harper Creek on the north. Go west on this trail and you'll be led back to the East Side Trail.

Trip 11: Dyar Spring/Juaquapin Loop

	Distance	5.8 miles
	Total Elevation Gain/Loss	800'/800'
	Hiking Time	3 hours
	Recommended Map	Cuyamaca Rancho State Park map/brochure
	Optional Maps	USGS 7.5-min Cuyamaca Peak
	Best Times	All year
	Agency	CRSP
	Difficulty	**

If water is an element essential to your hiking pleasure, you won't want to miss this hike. Dyar Spring, midway along the route, gurgles from a pipe at head-high level, offering the possibility of a cool shower. Downstream, along Juaquapin Creek, you can sit in the shade and listen to the most peaceful of sounds—the gentle flow of water over stones.

The starting point is the large parking area at the Sweetwater River bridge, between mile 4.8 and 4.9 on Highway 79. From here, take the Harvey Moore Trail south and east across a hillside, passing first through a belt of oaks and pines, then later through chaparral.

After 2.4 miles, turn left (north) on the Dyar Spring Trail and enter the domain of East Mesa, an open, grassy expanse studded with oaks. Several shallow ravines, tributaries of Juaquapin Creek, indent the surface of the mesa. Most are outlined by clumps of wild rose, squaw bush, and (in the wettest areas) stinging nettles. At a point about 0.8 mile north of the Harvey Moore Trail, a small sign directs you left (northwest) toward Dyar Spring. You'll find the spring somewhat hidden on the edge of a meadow among elderberry, willow, live oak, and black oak trees.

The East Mesa area is excellent for spotting mule deer and coyotes. Station yourself on one of the knolls above Dyar Spring, enjoy a picnic, and watch the parade of wildlife below.

Back on the trail again, go northwest over a small rise and drop steeply down a slope densely covered by chaparral. Arriving at an oak-shaded saddle, turn left (south) on the Juaquapin Trail and continue downhill along a grassy draw that leads toward the west bank of Juaquapin Creek. Good displays of wildflowers are seen here in the

spring: forget-me-not, lupine, wallflower, checker, wild onion, and more.

The Juaquapin Trail stays on a bench above the creek, and finally turns northwest around the brow of a ridge. Look for several bedrock morteros in a clump of oak trees just south of the junction of the trail to Juaquapin Crossing. (This trail is a short cut to the Harvey Moore Trail.)

Upon reaching the next junction, turn left (the right fork goes toward the Museum and park headquarters). Continue down along Juaquapin Creek and the Sweetwater River all the way back to your starting point.

Dyar Spring

Trip 12: Oakzanita Peak

	**Distance**	8.6 miles round trip
	Total Elevation Gain/Loss	1400'/1400'
	Hiking Time	4½ hours (round trip)
	Recommended Map	Cuyamaca Rancho State Park map/brochure
	Optional Maps	USGS 7.5-min *Cuyamaca Peak*
	Best Times	October through May
	Agency	CRSP
	Difficulty	***

Oakzanita Peak (a.k.a Lookout Mountain) is one of only a handful of named peaks in the Cuyamaca Mountains, yet its humble appearance—at least on approach—would not inspire most hikers to climb it. Actually, the view from its rocky summit is quite impressive on a clear day, and well worth the long hike—if done during cool weather. The name, of course, is a contraction of "oak" and "manzanita," two plant genera that complement each other well in the foothills of the Cuyamacas.

Begin at the parking turnout on the east side of Highway 79 at mile 3.1. Two trails start from there; take the one to the right (northeast). This new (opened in 1991) trail up along oak-shaded Descanso Creek joins East Mesa Fire Road after 0.5 mile. Turn right and continue east up through chaparral.

After 3.0 miles, turn right (west) on the Oakzanita Peak Trail. After traversing a grassy meadow, you end up just south of Oakzanita Peak. A brief scramble through scattered brush is necessary to reach the jumbled pile of granitic rocks on the summit. The view includes most of the Cuyamacas' southern reaches: Pine, Airplane, and Arrowmakers ridges to the northwest, and the meadows of East Mesa to the northeast. In the distance lie the dark, wave-shaped form of Cuyamaca Peak and the pointed, alabaster summit of Stonewall Peak.

Live oak tree above Descanso Creek

Trip 13: East Mesa Loop

Distance	10.5 miles
Total Elevation Gain/Loss	1300'/1300'
Hiking Time	5½ hours
Recommended Map	Cuyamaca Rancho State Park map/brochure
Optional Maps	USGS 7.5-min *Cuyamaca Peak*
Best Times	October through May
Agency	CRSP
Difficulty	***

This is what you could call a "grand tour" of the East Mesa area—and the state wilderness that encompasses it. Describing a rough circle, you follow the route of the Harvey Moore Trail up and over the rolling meadows of East Mesa and down the canyon of Harper Creek. You complete the circuit on the East Side Trail along the Sweetwater River. There's enough scenic variety on this trip, as well as elevation change, to keep things interesting. If you plan to stay overnight at Granite Spring, you'll need to contact the park rangers for a permit and to make parking arrangements.

A good starting point is the Sweetwater River bridge parking area at mile 4.8-4.9 on Highway 79. Follow the Harvey Moore Trail south and east across a hillside, passing first through a band of oaks and pines, then through chaparral. After about 2 miles, oaks and pines appear again. At the junction of the Dyar Spring Trail (2.4 miles), you'll have gained almost 800 feet, already the majority of the total elevation gain during the entire trip. East Mesa now lies ahead.

East Mesa isn't a mesa in the usual desert sense, but rather a gently inclined bench of broad grasslands interrupted by tree- and brush-covered promontories. The diversity of habitats in this area supports possibly the largest deer herd in the county.

After climbing over a low saddle you come to a junction (3.4 miles). Turn left and continue 0.6 mile to Granite Spring Primitive Camp. Of the two trail camps in the park designated for hikers and equestrians, this one is more remote from trailheads and therefore less popular.

From Granite Spring, continue north on the Harvey Moore Trail (which is now coincident with East Mesa Fire Road) for another 1.0 mile to the next junction. Swing left and follow the Harvey Moore Trail north toward the canyon containing Harper Creek. The descent is gradual at first, then quite steep on many short switchbacks. A lush growth of oaks, pines, manzanita, and other head-high brush forms provides plenty of shade. After a loss of 700 feet, you reach Harper Creek.

The trail turns west and follows Harper Creek downstream; after three crossings, it climbs abruptly up the brushy north slope to a position about 100 feet above the creek to avoid the rocky gorge below. It contours for about 0.4 mile and then drops sharply to the bank of the creek just below the gorge. Leave the Harvey Moore Trail at this point, cross the creek, and pick up the East Side Trail. It will take you directly back to the Sweetwater River bridge, about 3 miles away.

Trip 14: West Mesa Loop

👟	**Distance**	7.2 miles
	Total Elevation Gain/Loss	1100'/1100'
	Hiking Time	3½ hours
▨	**Recommended Map**	Cuyamaca Rancho State Park map/brochure
	Optional Maps	USGS 7.5-min *Cuyamaca Peak*
	Best Times	All year
℺	**Agency**	CRSP
	Difficulty	***

The forest: you're never far from it on this hike. The fluttering of oak leaves, the soughing of pine needles in the breeze, the scurrying of gray squirrels, the pungent sweetness in the air—these you can enjoy any time of year. The very best sights, sounds, and smells in this forest, however, are reserved for two special times of year—spring and fall.

The route is entirely on well-graded fire roads along the massive, but rather gently sloping, southeast flank of Cuyamaca Peak. There's more shade than sunshine along the way, and, if you're not unlucky, you'll see more deer than humans. Unfortunately, there's no dependable source of potable water.

Begin at the day-use parking area at mile 7.3 on Highway 79. Head west around a gate and continue up West Mesa Fire Road through a forest of mostly oaks and pines. After 0.5 mile you come to a junction from where West Mesa Fire Road continues southwest toward Japacha Spring and the West Mesa Fire Trail branches right (northwest). Either direction you choose at the intersection is fine since this is a loop hike, but we'll assume you're going counterclockwise. Head northwest and ascend through stands of ponderosa and Coulter pine. Staying left at the next two trail junctions, you level off at about the 5200' contour and continue around several small ravines. These are carpeted with bracken fern and other shade-loving greenery. Elsewhere, ceanothus, ablaze with white blossoms in May, complements the various shades of arboreal foliage: these run the gamut from the light green of black oaks, to the dark green of incense-cedars, to the curious dull reds and browns of flowering live oaks. You're in the middle of the biggest block of state wilderness within the park.

The Burnt Pine Fire Trail, intersecting from the right, can be used to reach Cuyamaca Peak, but it's a long and tedious haul. Beyond this intersection, the West Mesa Fire Trail starts a gentle descent across a bald spot on the mountain slope. A beautiful vista of swaying grasses, rolling hills, and distant ridges lies before you.

The descent quickens and you soon come to West Mesa Fire Road (now a trail). Turn left and continue along the top of Airplane Ridge. After 0.9 mile, round the hairpin turn (Monument Trail junction on the right) and notice the side trail on the left leading to the Airplane Monument (see Trip 15).

Continue descending, into and around the shady canyon of Japacha Creek, and in 1.2 miles from the hairpin turn come to the junction of Japacha Fire Road. Japacha Spring is nearby, accessible via a short spur trail.

Continue northeast along the edge of the broad meadow at the foot of Arrowmakers Ridge. After another 0.8 mile, take West Mesa Fire Road back to your starting point.

Trip 15: Arroyo Seco/Monument Loop

Distance	7.2 miles
Total Elevation Gain/Loss	1200'/1200'
Hiking Time	4 hours
Recommended Map	Cuyamaca Rancho State Park map/brochure
Optional Maps	USGS 7.5-min *Cuyamaca Peak*
Best Times	September through May
Agency	CRSP
Difficulty	***

"In Memory of Col. F. C. Marshall and 1st Lt. C. L. Webber who fell at this spot Dec. 7, 1922." Without this inscription, the presence of an old 12-cylinder engine permanently mounted in stone atop remote Airplane Ridge wouldn't make much sense to a hiker passing by. The Airplane Monument is just one of several interesting sights along this loop hike.

One option is to carry your overnight gear along this route and stay at Arroyo Seco Primitive Camp; if so you must park your car overnight at Green Valley Campground. Day hikers can start from the Sweetwater River bridge parking area.

From the bridge parking area, walk north over the Sweetwater River bridge and immediately turn left on a short spur trail that hooks up with the West Side Trail. Continue north about 0.4 mile, paralleling the highway, then bear left on Japacha Fire Road. You now wind uphill, following the south wall of the canyon containing Japacha Creek, and after about 0.8 mile cross the creek. Bracken fern, sword fern, thimbleberry and wild strawberry thrive in the shade of oaks and sycamores along the creek bottom. Turning northeast to follow a shady draw, you soon come to a marked spur trail to Japacha Spring. The water merely dribbles from cracks in the bedrock, but there are some flat rocks to rest upon in a shady spot nearby.

Go back down to Japacha Fire Road and follow it north to West Mesa Fire Road (now reverting to a trail), where you turn left (southwest). Climb gradually through a magnificent conifer and oak forest, and cross Japacha Creek once again. Now watch carefully for the small footpath—on the right about 0.2 mile past the

creek crossing—that leads to the Airplane Monument. Here again is a nice place for relaxation. You can sit in the shade on the stone bench, while the breeze fans across you, and look out through the trees toward Arrowmakers Ridge and Stonewall Peak.

Returning to West Mesa Fire Road, you continue around a hairpin turn, doubling back to the northwest to follow the top of Airplane Ridge. (The Monument Trail branches south from the hairpin turn, providing a shortcut to Green Valley Campground for those who wish to bail out of this trip early.) Continue for 1 mile along the ridgetop, staying left at the next junction, then leave the road by turning left on a narrow, poorly maintained segment of the California Riding and Hiking Trail. The trail descends quite rapidly on a series of long switchbacks through a dense forest of oaks (watch for poison oak here), passes an intermittent spring marked by an old water trough, and then favors a straight course through tall chaparral. Turn left at the bottom of the trail and continue downhill into Arroyo Seco Primitive Camp.

The camp lies at the south end of a wide meadow frequented by mule deer and other wildlife. To loop back toward your starting point, go downhill toward Green Valley Campground, 1.5 miles away. Before you reach the campground take the cutoff trail on the left that slants over to the West Side Trail. Then follow the West Side Trail over to the Sweetwater bridge.

Trip 16: Pine Ridge Trail

👟	**Distance**	3.3 miles
	Total Elevation Gain/Loss	600'/600'
	Hiking Time	2 hours
▣	**Recommended Map**	Cuyamaca Rancho State Park map/brochure
	Optional Maps	USGS 7.5-min *Cuyamaca Peak*
	Best Times	All year
↻ 👫	**Agency**	CRSP
	Difficulty	**

This hike is especially worthwhile during the winter months, when melting snow or soggy ground at higher elevations in the Cuyamacas can make hiking in those areas difficult. A good part of the route is open to the winter sun's southern rays, and the added warmth can be quite welcome and invigorating at that time. The hike is also short enough to be suitable for a sunrise or a sunset stroll, even during the hottest months of late spring and early summer.

Park in one of the day-use lots at Green Valley Campground, then head for campsite 38 at the southwest edge of the campground. The Pine Ridge Trail goes straight up the chaparral-covered ridge behind this site, and soon gains a foothold on a steep, south-facing slope overlooking the Sweetwater River canyon. Green Valley Falls lie below, unseen but often heard. Higher still, the trail swings to the north side of Pine Ridge and offers a spectacular view of West Mesa, Cuyamaca Peak, and the length of Green Valley. In the valley just below you can trace your return route, Arroyo Seco Road.

In the first mile, the trail has passed through only thick chaparral—mostly manzanita, chamise and ceanothus. But some timber appears as you approach the topmost knoll of Pine Ridge. These trees—Coulter pines and black oaks—cling to the north slopes of the ridge, where less sunshine permits a greater retention of ground moisture.

Past the topmost knoll, the trail zigzags down to the California Riding and Hiking Trail. Turn right (east), go 0.1 mile, and turn right again on Arroyo Seco Road. An easy return to Green Valley Campground follows. Mule deer, apparently accustomed to the human activity around the nearby campground, are often seen grazing in and around the meadow areas along this road.

Green Valley Falls

Trip 17: Sweetwater River Loop

	Distance	7.2 miles
👟	**Total Elevation Gain/Loss**	700'/700'
	Hiking Time	3½ hours
	Recommended Map	Cuyamaca Rancho State Park map/brochure
◥	**Optional Maps**	USGS 7.5-min *Descanso, Cuyamaca Peak*
	Best Times	October through June
Q	**Agency**	CRSP
	Difficulty	***

Fed by countless ravines and rivulets on the slopes of the Cuyamaca Mountains, the Sweetwater River at last becomes a watercourse worthy of the name "river"—albeit sometimes a seasonal one. Below Green Valley Campground and Green Valley Falls, the sweet, bubbling liquid slides placidly down a pleasant little gorge shaded by alders and willows. For years there were sporadic attempts to introduce beaver along this stretch of the river, so look for evidence in the form of dams made from willow saplings and mud.

The obscurely marked trailhead and parking lot, next to a ranger residence, is located on Viejas Boulevard, 0.6 mile east of the main crossroads in Descanso. You can also reach it by going 1.1 miles west from Highway 79 along Viejas Boulevard.

From the lot, walk past a vehicle gate. The Merigan Fire Road beyond takes you across a sunny meadow, then up onto a brushy slope. In springtime, the air rising along the slopes bears both the tangy fragrance of new growth in the chaparral and the humid scent of the stream-hugging willows just ahead. Blue ceanothus paints the brushy hillsides in April through early May. Mountain mahogany is conspicuous in late summer, sporting thousands of hairy seed tufts that resemble twisted pipe cleaners.

Just beyond the saddle, the first of two spur trails branches left toward the river and its accompanying strip of riparian vegetation. The second spur trail, 0.4 mile farther, leads to an artificial waterfall—a silted-in diversion dam.

After some further climbing, the road enters a magnificent grove of live oak trees and sidles up against the high banks of the creek. Down below, through a screen of willows and alders,

the ice-cold Sweetwater sparkles as it tumbles over the gravelly canyon floor.

At 1.9 miles, you reach a junction of trails in a flat area dotted with oaks and a few pines. Crossing the river there, you can pick up the Sweet Water Trail, which takes you uphill and northwest to the California Riding and Hiking Trail (3.1 miles). During March this slope is alive with the drone of bees frantically gathering nectar from the blooming manzanitas.

Make a right turn onto the California Riding and Hiking Trail, a right on South Boundary Fire Road, another right to stay on South Boundary Fire Road, and a fourth right on a trail paralleling the Sweetwater River at 4.2 miles. That trail will take you down along the east wall of the Sweetwater gorge, at times almost 100 feet above the water. At 5.3 miles you'll arrive back at Merigan Fire Road; follow it back to the trailhead.

As an alternate to the loop described above, you can try this slightly longer loop with a little less elevation gain: At 1.9 miles, continue east on Merigan Fire Road toward Highway 79. Just short of the vehicle gate near the highway, turn north and follow a recently cut trail that goes up a drainage toward South Boundary Fire Road. Take the latter down to the bank of the Sweetwater River and turn left on the trail going down the Sweetwater gorge.

Area M-7: Laguna Mountains

East of the Cuyamaca Mountains—the first great moisture-wringing barrier to Pacific storms—lies a second and slightly drier range, the Laguna Mountains. Here the storm clouds yield enough precipitation to support a patchwork forest of Jeffrey pines and black oaks. Farther east still, the land falls away abruptly. Below this escarpment lies the desert.

The human history of the Laguna Mountains closely parallels that of other mountain and foothill regions in southern California. The first peoples to arrive were bands of Kumeyaay Indians, who summered here to escape from the heat of the lowlands and gain sustenance from the natural resources of the forest. Bedrock morteros, commonly seen along the trails, are a reminder of this era.

The 1800s brought livestock ranching to the Lagunas, then mining for gold and other minerals. Mining activity peaked in the late 1800s, but it continues on a very small scale even today. Cattle grazing continues on private lands and on some national forest lands.

After the turn of the century, recreation played an increasingly dominant role. The Laguna Mountains were included within the boundaries of the Cleveland National Forest in 1893, and one of the first ranger stations in California, El Prado Ranger Cabin, was constructed here in 1911. Summer homes were erected on private land within the national forest, and on certain parcels of forest land by lease arrangement.

In recent years, the emphasis has been on serving the public-at-large through recreation such as camping, hiking, and snow play. The Laguna crest, which includes elevations of about 6000 feet, is the highest place you can reach within the county by way of a public road.

If winter snowfalls are heavy enough, the Laguna Meadow area becomes San Diego County's best playground for cross-country skiing. As the terrain here is mostly flat to gently sloping, there is probably no better area in San Diego County for easy skiing.

The higher Laguna Mountains have been placed administratively within a zone called the Laguna Mountain Recreation Area. The Forest Service—with volunteer assistance—is managing it as a heavy-use area, with campgrounds, picnic areas, and nature trails throughout. In recent years, several new trails have been added, mostly through the efforts of members of the Laguna Mountain Volunteer Association.

On summer weekends, rangers and volunteers offer interpretive walks, evening campfire programs, and other special events. On Friday and Saturday nights during the summer, San Diego State University's Mount Laguna Observatory offers visitors a chance to view various celestial objects through a 21-inch telescope and smaller instruments. Information about these and other events can be obtained at the Visitor Information Office, mile 23.5 on Sunrise Highway, or by calling the Descanso Ranger District office of the Cleveland National Forest (Appendix 4).

Currently, over 70 miles of hiking trails lace the Laguna Mountains. The biggest share of this mileage is in the form of the Pacific Crest Trail, which passes north-south over the Laguna crest. For several miles the PCT edges close to the spectacular eastern escarpment—the "sunrise" side—of the Lagunas. Nowhere else in San Diego County can you experience so dramatically the interface between mountain and desert.

Most of the trips below traverse at least some part of the Laguna Mountain Recreation Area, where camping is allowed only in the developed campgrounds. Car camping and trail camping are allowed on most national forest lands outside the recreation area—but you must be sure to obtain a remote camping permit first. For up-to-date, recorded information about the Laguna Mountain Recreation Area, phone 445-8341.

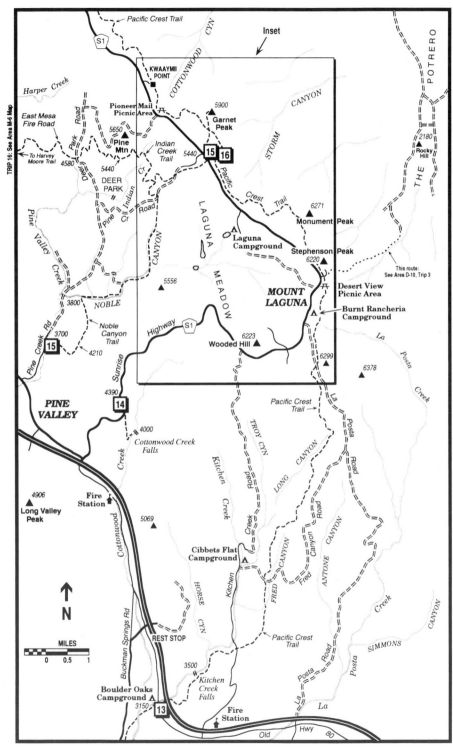

Area M-7: Laguna Mountains

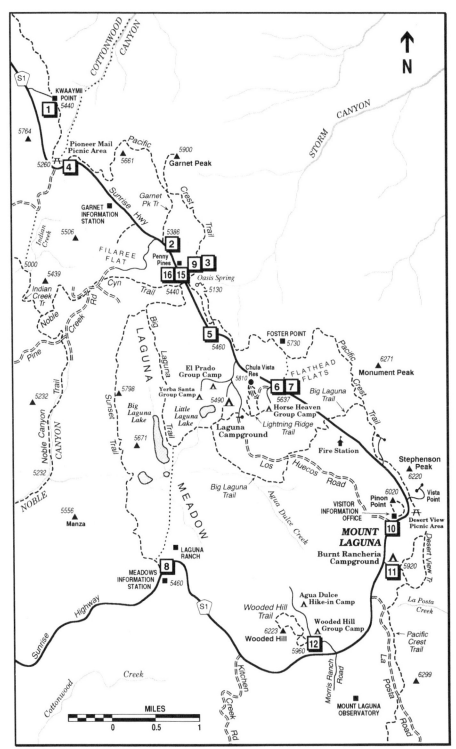

Laguna Mountains inset

Trip 1: Kwaaymii Point

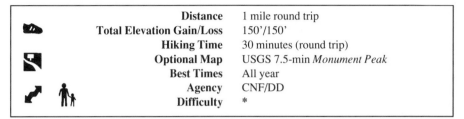

	Distance	1 mile round trip
	Total Elevation Gain/Loss	150'/150'
	Hiking Time	30 minutes (round trip)
	Optional Map	USGS 7.5-min *Monument Peak*
	Best Times	All year
	Agency	CNF/DD
	Difficulty	*

If you have no more time to spare than a half-hour during a cruise through the Laguna Mountains, at least stop at Kwaaymii Point and take this brief stroll along the eastern escarpment. Here, in the abbreviated transition zone between mountain and desert, you can peer down into the depths of the desert, almost 4000 feet below, and at the same time catch sight of cool forests on the Laguna rim.

You'll be walking on a segment of the Pacific Crest Trail incorporating an old roadbed literally chiseled into a cliff. About two decades ago, this was a hair-raising part of Sunrise Highway; but it is now bypassed by a newer, less spectacular, safer stretch of road to the west.

The starting point can be either Kwaaymii

Point (turnoff at mile 30.3 on Sunrise Highway) or Pioneer Mail Picnic Area (mile 29.3). The old roadbed between these two points skirts the lip of Cottonwood Canyon, a forbidding-looking abyss with just a hint of lushness in its deepest creases. In an effort to return the old roadbed to some semblance of naturalness, trail builders removed its macadam surface. The outer retaining walls are holding firm, but tons of rock from road cuts have fallen from above.

If you start from Kwaaymii Point, you can also walk north for less than ½ mile on the PCT to the east shoulder of Garnet Mountain, where the views of Cottonwood Canyon and the desert floor are even more panoramic.

Trip 2: Garnet Peak

	Distance	2.4 miles round trip
	Total Elevation Gain/Loss	500'/500'
	Hiking Time	1½ hour (round trip)
	Optional Maps	Cleveland National Forest recreation map;
		USGS 7.5-min *Monument Peak*
	Best Times	All year
	Agency	CNF/DD
	Difficulty	**

Although Garnet Peak isn't the highest peaklet along the edge of the Lagunas' eastern escarpment, its exposed position makes it a good place to view both the pine-clad plateau and the raw desert below. Especially rewarding is a predawn pilgrimage to observe the sunrise from its summit. Around the time of the winter solstice, the sun's flattened disk peeps up over the desert wastes of northwestern Sonora,

Mexico, some 150 miles away. On the clearest mornings at that time of year, you might witness the famed "green flash," an event occasionally seen on the horizon at sunset from San Diego's coast, but seldom seen at sunrise.

Park on the shoulder (but off the pavement) of Sunrise Highway near mile 27.8. Take the signed Garnet Peak Trail 0.5 mile north through Jeffrey pine forest to where it crosses the Pacific

Crest Trail. Continue north, out in the open chaparral now, on the rocky path that slants up along the shoulder of the peak. Lord's Candle yucca stalks, heavy with white flowers in the spring and early summer, poke through the ceanothus and manzanita brush along the trail.

The summit is crowned by a jagged cluster of layered, tan-colored metasedimentary rock, the type seen along much of the Laguna escarpment. The peak falls away abruptly, revealing a vertiginous panorama of Storm Canyon and its distant alluvial fan. Along the horizon lie the Salton Sea and Baja's Laguna Salada, both desert sinks. To the south and west, the Laguna crest, dusky with oak and pine forests and patches of chaparral, seems to roll like a frozen wave to the edge of the escarpment.

Watch your step as you move around on the summit, and hang on to your hat. This must be one of the windiest places in the county.

Trip 3: Indian Creek Loop

	Distance	8.0 miles
	Total Elevation Gain/Loss	1000'/1000'
	Hiking Time	5 hours
	Recommended Maps	Cleveland National Forest recreation map; USGS 7.5-min *Monument Peak*
	Best Times	March through June
	Agency	CNF/DD
	Difficulty	***

Here's a nice way to fit a scenic portion of the Pacific Crest Trail into a circle hike. You'll sample a variety of appealing environments—shady woodland, spice-scented chaparral, sage-dotted meadow—plus a bird's-eye view of the desert.

You can begin at the Penny Pines trailhead, mile 27.3 on Sunrise Highway, where parking is available along the highway's wide shoulder. Start by following the Noble Canyon Trail (see Trip 15 for more) west through Jeffrey-pine forest. After gaining the north slope of a hill, dropping to cross dirt roads three times, and ascending once again to circle around the north end of a ridge, you'll come to a junction with the Indian Creek Trail, 2.4 miles from the start. Turn right at this junction and descend about 0.8 mile through black oaks and chaparral to the grassy banks along trickling (or dry) Indian Creek.

You now leave the Indian Creek Trail and head north, upstream along Indian Creek, following the remnants of an old jeep road on the left (west) bank. Keep going on what becomes a better dirt road until you reach Pioneer Mail Picnic Area, 4.6 miles, on the far side of Sunrise Highway. Pick up the PCT, which passes downslope of the picnic tables, and head east.

After paralleling Sunrise Highway for a while, the PCT starts rising on oak- and pine-shaded hillsides often dotted with wallflowers, lupine, and paintbrush. Then, after contouring around a lilac-scented slope overlooking Cottonwood Canyon, you start trending south, intersect the trail to Garnet Peak, and maintain a course that takes you along the rim of the desert-facing escarpment. You can work your way east through some intervening chaparral growth to reach the very brink of the escarpment, or wait until you get to a stretch where you look straight down into the yawning depths of Storm Canyon. A final descent on the PCT through oaks and pines takes you back to the Penny Pines plantation and your car.

Trip 4: Cottonwood Canyon

	Distance	3.2 miles round trip
	Total Elevation Gain/Loss	2000'/2000'
	Hiking Time	5 hours (round trip)
	Recommended Map	Cleveland National Forest recreation map
		USGS 7.5-min *Monument Peak*
	Best Times	October through June
	Agency	CNF/DD, ABDSP
	Difficulty	****

V-shaped Cottonwood Canyon once provided Indians with a direct, but very steep passage between the desert floor and the lush meadows of the Laguna Mountains. Springs and seasonal flows of water in the canyon undoubtedly served its travelers well. For a time Cottonwood Canyon was mistakenly believed to have been the route of the Jackass Mail (part of a pioneering mail route between San Antonio and San Diego)—hence the naming of Pioneer Mail Picnic Area. Later research showed the true route of the Jackass Mail to be Oriflamme Canyon.

Like trips into the Grand Canyon, this is strictly a down-and-back-up affair. Since private land lies on the desert floor below Cottonwood Canyon, you should retrace your path after descending. Unlike hiking on the Grand Canyon trails, there's no established path, so even the downhill part is slow-going. There are lots of tricky little descents—especially if you're carrying extra gear—over small waterfalls. A 25' length of cord will serve you well for lowering or raising a heavy pack over the steepest precipices.

Start hiking at Pioneer Mail Picnic Area, mile 29.3 on Sunrise Highway. Follow the draw that descends northeast. At 0.4 mile, the "bottom drops out" and the canyon walls become steep—this first drop is a good example of what lies ahead. You won't find water here unless it's recently rained, but water usually runs at the surface farther down.

Down to about 1.4 miles, you'll stay mostly under a narrow, shade-giving cover of willows, live oaks, and bays. The cool pungency of the bay trees is rivalled by the equally sharp odors of white sage and stinging nettles. Here and

there, the banks are loaded with Humboldt lilies (in bloom around May or June). Poison oak grows in fair abundance, too.

Unfortunately, a number of car bodies, tires and various auto parts are wedged, probably permanently, in the canyon's deepest recesses. These vehicles were rolled down from the former Sunrise Highway (now Pacific Crest Trail) 20 or more years ago.

At 1.4 miles the canyon opens up, and it becomes possible to walk through the shrubbery well above the stream. You're in a chaparral belt here—a sort of transition to the desert vegetation below. At 1.6 miles you come upon a disused dirt road that could serve as space for setting up camp. According to your map you've been in Section 21, a remote corner of Anza-Borrego Desert State Park, for the last mile. Private land lies ahead in Sections 15 and 16. If you follow the old road northeast and then southeast, you'll curl over into Section 22 (BLM land), where you'll come upon a spring tucked into the north flank of the Sawtooth Range.

Trip 5: Oasis Spring

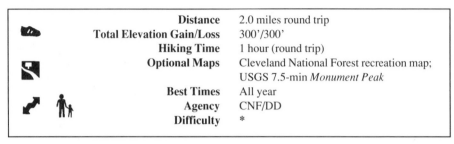

Distance	2.0 miles round trip
Total Elevation Gain/Loss	300'/300'
Hiking Time	1 hour (round trip)
Optional Maps	Cleveland National Forest recreation map; USGS 7.5-min *Monument Peak*
Best Times	All year
Agency	CNF/DD
Difficulty	*

A more restful place could scarcely be imagined. A warm breeze from the desert below wafts up the shady canyon, bringing with it the scent of sage and California bay. A lone bigleaf maple tree shimmers in the sunlight. A sparkling stream gushes out of the ground and begins a headlong rush toward the dry desert sands a half mile below. "Oasis" is a perfectly apt description of this idyllic spot.

Oasis Spring lies only 200 yards from Sunrise Highway, but about 300 feet lower in elevation. The best way to reach it is by way of a gradually descending dirt road from the south. This gated road intersects Sunrise Highway at mile 26.7, but parking is very limited here. An east-side turnout at mile 26.5 offers more room. Just below this turnout, you may pick up the Pacific Crest Trail and follow it north. After about 300 yards, the PCT dips into a shallow ravine and briefly joins the road to Oasis Spring. Stay on the road and continue descending through an elfin forest of mostly mountain mahogany.

Curving left, the road leaves the ravine and briefly traverses the abrupt face of the Laguna escarpment. From the lip of the road there's a dramatic view of Storm Canyon and the distant alluvial fans and barren peaks of the desert.

From the road's end, a trail descends on tight switchbacks through a thick growth of live oak and bay to reach an old pumphouse. Nearby is the aforementioned bigleaf maple tree. This particular specimen was evidently planted here. The natural range of the bigleaf maple within the Pacific coast states extends no farther south than the Santa Ana and San Bernardino mountains.

Trip 6: Foster Point

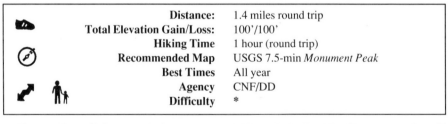

Distance:	1.4 miles round trip
Total Elevation Gain/Loss:	100'/100'
Hiking Time	1 hour (round trip)
Recommended Map	USGS 7.5-min *Monument Peak*
Best Times	All year
Agency	CNF/DD
Difficulty	*

Come to Foster Point not only for the great view, but also for a chance to identify many of Southern California's highest mountains. A direction finder, constructed by the Sierra Club, shows 17 peaks, including the Southland's highest, San Gorgonio Mountain.

Park opposite the entrance to Horse Heaven Group Camp at mile 25.7 on Sunrise Highway. Walk up the hard-to-identify remnants of an old jeep road going east into a gently sloping forested area known as Flathead Flats. After about 0.2 mile, curve left (north) and you'll soon come upon the narrow but well-defined tread of the Pacific Crest Trail (remember this spot—you'll be returning the same way). Continue north on the PCT through oaks and pines another 0.2 mile.

At this point the forest cover abruptly ends, and dense chaparral begins. Walk 50 yards past the last of the small Jeffrey-pine trees, and you'll find a little trail to the right, marked by a FOSTER POINT sign. It goes about 100 yards through waist-high manzanita, ceanothus, and chamise to the direction-finder on top of a rounded knob.

Monument Peak and its supporting ridgeline cuts off the distant view to the east and the south, but the panorama from north to northeast is excellent. If you know the way well, try coming up here on a moonlit night, when the desert down below glows ghostly white.

Foster Point

Trip 7: Lightning Ridge Trail

Distance	1.5 miles
Total Elevation Gain/Loss	250'/250'
Hiking Time	1 hour
Optional Map	USGS 7.5-min *Monument Peak*
Best Times	All year
Agency	CNF/DD
Difficulty	*

You can reach this trail from either the amphitheater at Laguna Campground or the access road to Horse Heaven Group Camp intersecting Sunrise Highway at mile 25.7. To start from the latter place, park off the pavement, taking care not to block any gates. Head west down the road to Horse Heaven Group Camp. At a fork in 100 yards, take the dirt road to the right. This goes to Chula Vista Reservoir, a water tank on top of the forested hill ahead of you. After another 0.2 mile, go right on the unmarked footpath—the Lightning Ridge Trail. This will take you to the

View of Laguna Lakes from Lightning Ridge Trail

top of the hill in a more leisurely fashion.

The panoramic, tree-framed view from the reservoir includes Little Laguna Lake and a long stretch of Laguna Meadow. The water in the lake rises, falls, and vanishes according to the vagaries of the weather. In spring, the brimming surface can be like a mirror, reflecting the greens and blues of the surrounding forest and sky. In the southwest, ridge after forested ridge leads the eye out to the distant, haze-shrouded coastal foothills.

The Lightning Ridge Trail continues downslope toward Laguna Campground. You can follow it as it switchbacks through a confusing maze of false trails and short cuts to the bottom of the hill, then continue around the south side of the hill to reach Horse Heaven Group Camp: or you can drop only halfway down the hill and cut back to reach the reservoir access road at the point where you first left it.

Trip 8: Sunset Trail

	Distance	7.2 miles
	Total Elevation Gain/Loss	700'/700'
	Hiking Time	4 hours
	Optional Maps	USGS 7.5-min *Monument Peak*, *Mount Laguna*
	Best Times	October through June
	Agency	CNF/DD
	Difficulty	***

The new Sunset Trail (under final development as of this writing) permits easy access by foot to the entire west rim of the high Laguna Mountain plateau. Like its analogue to the east—the sunrise-facing Pacific Crest Trail—the Sunset Trail offers sweeping views, but on the "sunset" side. You'll almost invariably get the most out of this trail if you start early. As the sun rises unseen in the east, you can look down on what is often either an immense "ocean" of low clouds hugging the coast and foothills, or the real ocean, tinted dark blue by the low angle of the sun's rays.

From the Meadows Information Station, mile 19.1 on Sunrise Highway, walk 250 yards north along the highway shoulder to reach the south terminus of the Sunset Trail. Proceed generally northwest, up to and along an undulating crest dotted with the common mix of Jeffrey pines, black oaks and understory vegetation typical of the Laguna Mountains. At 0.9 mile, the trail veers west to curve around a rocky outcrop. There, a view opens of velvet-smooth Crouch Valley, some 500 feet below, and much of coastal San Diego County, weather permitting.

Thereafter, the trail loses about 300 feet of elevation and crosses a tributary of Noble Canyon that drains Laguna Meadow. The water tumbling or trickling down this steep and den-

sely overgrown ravine eventually reaches Pine Valley Creek, Barrett Reservoir, Cottonwood Creek, Rio Tijuana in Mexico, and finally the Tijuana River Estuary just north of the border. Much of the Laguna Mountain crest sheds water which, if not intercepted by aqueducts, flows through Mexico—a little-known fact.

After the ravine crossing, you climb back up to the crest again, with more opportunities to view the broad western horizon. Proceeding farther north, you pass over a hilltop that used to include a radio antenna facility, and descend to the northernmost arm of Laguna Meadow. Turning east, the trail meets, at 4.0 miles, the Big Laguna Trail.

For a somewhat shorter return route, follow the Big Laguna Trail south about 1.5 miles to Big Laguna Lake (the biggest of several shallow, ephemeral lakes hereabouts) which may or may not be filled with water. Since *laguna* means "lake" or "lagoon" in Spanish, the name "Laguna Lake" is redundant. The name seems to originate from the mountains, which were themselves so named because there were lakes (lagunas) on them.

In an average rainy season, the lakes begin

Cross-country skiing at Laguna Meadow

to fill with water or snow by December or January. Carpets of wildflowers—tidy tips, buttercups, goldfields, dandelions, wild onions, and western irises—appear on the meadows surrounding the lakes in April and May. By June, the hot sun causes water levels in the lakes to decline rapidly.

Just past Big Laguna Lake the trail turns decidedly east. Leave it at this point and head straight across the broad meadow, almost due south, toward a brown house at Laguna Ranch. You may have to thread your way through cattle in the meadow—the ranch and the meadow are now on public land, but ranchers retain grazing rights. As you get closer to the ranch, veer right so you can get through a gate in a barbed wire fence some 300 yards west of the ranch house. Continue bearing southwest until you intersect the Sunset Trail near the point where you began your hike.

Trip 9: Big Laguna Trail

Distance	10 miles
Total Elevation Gain/Loss	900'/900'
Hiking Time	5 1/2 hours
Recommended Maps	Cleveland National Forest recreation map; USGS 7.5-min *Monument Peak*
Best Times	All year
Agency	CNF/DD
Difficulty	***

The 6-mile-long Big Laguna Trail, completed in 1991, wends its scenic way over gently rolling hills and grassy dales, never dipping below 5400 feet of elevation nor rising to more than 5900 feet. By combining the BLT with a 4-mile segment of the PCT, as I describe here, you'll cover a relatively flat 10 miles with lots of varied scenery.

The cool, dry days of autumn are a perfect time to follow this route. You'll walk under wind-battered, 200-year-old Jeffrey pines, and spreading black oaks whose golden yellow leaves shimmer in the breeze. Don't let Santa Ana conditions deter you. During strong Santa Anas, the Lagunas are an oasis of coolness, with average temperatures 25-30 less than in the coastal region. All traces of moisture and air pollution are swept away during these episodes, producing surrealistically blue skies that contrast nicely with the sun-bronzed earth.

The Penny Pines parking area, mile 27.3 on Sunrise Highway, is a good place to begin. Start by walking west on the Noble Canyon Trail. After 0.1 mile, there's a split: the signed Big Laguna Trail goes left. After another 0.8 mile through open pine and oak woods, BLT turns south to skirt the margin of Laguna Meadow. By 2.5 miles into the hike, you'll be opposite Big Laguna Lake, which may or may not be filled with water, depending on the season.

Next, the trail turns east toward an arm of Laguna Meadow that contains Little Laguna Lake. When you reach a wire fence at 2.8 miles, don't go through the gap in the fence. Instead, turn abruptly right and follow the fenceline over to the wooded area on the meadow's east side. A spur trail branches left toward Laguna Campground, where water is available if you need it.

The main trail continues south along the meadow edge and then east to follow a shallow ravine. After a turn to the north and a short bit of steep climbing, you cross the graded Los Huecos Road (4.5 miles) and hook up with an old roadbed going east and later north. You ascend easily through chaparral—mostly ceanothus, which puts on a great floral show in the late spring. Look for the shiny-leaved chokecherry bushes, which may bear prodigious quantities of ripe red fruit in the fall.

When the roadbed makes a hairpin turn to the right (at 5.0 miles), stay left on the footpath

On the Big Laguna Trail

that continues through a gap in a wire fence. The path curls down through more pine and oak woods, crosses Sunrise Highway, and continues east, uphill, to join the PCT at 6.0 miles.

Turn left there and return to your starting point by way of a rambling but scenic stretch of the PCT. Along the way you'll pass several overlooks offering desert views, including Foster Point (see Trip 6 above).

Trip 10: Kwaaymii Trail

Distance	0.5 mile
Total Elevation Gain/Loss	100'/100'
Hiking Time	20 minutes
Optional Map	USGS 7.5-min *Mount Laguna*
Best Times	All year
Agency	CNF/DD
Difficulty	*

This walk begins at the Visitor Information Office (mile 23.5 on Sunrise Highway) and loops over a small hill called Pinon Point (or Pinyon Point). The leaflet for this trail describes Indian uses of native plants for food, shelter, clothing, and medicine. Bedrock morteros (deep holes) and metates (shallow depressions) used for grinding acorns may be seen along the trail. The Kwaaymii, the most recent Native American inhabitants of the Laguna Mountains, were a subtribe of the Kumeyaay Indians.

The large pinyon pine on Pinon Point is a Sierra Juarez pinyon, with needles in clusters of five. Nearby is another smaller pinyon of the four-leaved variety. Pinyon pines with one, four, and five needles are distributed throughout

the desert-facing slopes of San Diego and Riverside counties and the Sierra Juarez range of Baja California, but they are relatively rare here in the Lagunas.

Near the large pinyon on Pinon Point are a patch of prickly pear cactus and several holly-leaved cherry bushes. October brings a bountiful harvest of native fruit here—a bit less than sweet to our pampered palates and full of seeds, but no doubt a fitting dessert after a meal of acorn and seed porridge.

Discovering morteros on the Kwaaymii Trail

Trip 11: Desert View Trail

	Distance	1.3 miles
	Total Elevation Gain/Loss	150'/150'
	Hiking Time	1 hour
	Optional Map	USGS 7.5-min *Mount Laguna*
	Best Times	All year
	Agency	CNF/DD
	Difficulty	*

The Desert View Trail starts just inside Burnt Rancheria Campground (there's no charge for parking in the campground as long as you use the lot signed NATURE TRAIL). The trail winds through vanilla-scented Jeffrey-pine forest and then joins the Pacific Crest Trail on a chaparral-covered ridge. As you head north along the ridge, there's a wide-open view of the La Posta Creek canyon, part of a remote southern area of the Lagunas that was swept by wildfire in July 1989. New growth, especially along the creek below, is softening the landscape.

Farther north, a view to the north and west opens: ahead are old radar domes at a former Air Force facility on Stephenson Peak; far off to the right is a slice of the brown desert floor. At a point 0.8 mile from the start, the signed Desert View Trail diverges left from the PCT, descends, and returns through the campground to the trailhead.

Trip 12: Wooded Hill Nature Trail

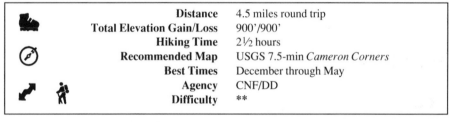

Distance	1.5 miles
Total Elevation Gain/Loss	300'/300'
Hiking Time	1 hour
Optional Map	USGS 7.5-min *Mount Laguna*
Best Times	All year
Agency	CNF/DD
Difficulty	*

The figure-8 path of the Wooded Hill Nature Trail will take you to the highest wooded summit in the Laguna Mountains. (Three slightly higher summits are nearby, but they're entirely brush-covered.) Atop Wooded Hill you can view a 270° panorama that encompasses (when the air's very clear) San Diego, Point Loma, Santa Catalina Island, San Clemente Island, and the Coronado Islands. On the way up you'll catch sight of the white domes of Mount Laguna Observatory, San Diego State University's off-campus site for astronomical research and instruction.

Turn north from Sunrise Highway (mile 21.7) onto a road that leads 0.3 mile to the trailhead. An interpretive booklet for the trail should be available either at the trailhead or at the nearby Visitor Information Office.

Trip 13: Kitchen Creek Falls

Distance	4.5 miles round trip
Total Elevation Gain/Loss	900'/900'
Hiking Time	2½ hours
Recommended Map	USGS 7.5-min *Cameron Corners*
Best Times	December through May
Agency	CNF/DD
Difficulty	**

For the most part, San Diego County's section of the Pacific Crest Trail sticks to high and dry ridgelines and slopes, avoiding most canyon bottoms and streamcourses. On the southern slopes of the Laguna Mountains, however, the PCT passes just 200 yards above a hidden series of waterfalls on Kitchen Creek. Here, water from about 20 square miles of drainage flows through a narrow constriction in the bedrock, and tumbles about 150 vertical feet over water-polished slabs.

In the aftermath of major storms, the sound of the falling water gives away the location of the falls; at other times, finding them may be a bit difficult. A short stretch of moderate scrambling is required to reach them.

A convenient starting point is Boulder Oaks, a major access point along the PCT. Take the Buckman Springs Road turnoff from Interstate 8 and go south on the frontage road—Old Highway 80—two miles to the Boulder Oaks store and campground.

Across the old highway from Boulder Oaks is a broad pathway marked by a PCT post. Follow this as it meanders beside oak-shaded Kitchen Creek and under the twin bridges of Interstate 8. Immediately past the second bridge, find the marked PCT, which abruptly ascends to the right. After a steep climb on tight switchbacks, you begin a gradual, winding ascent up along the brushy slopes above Kitchen Creek.

As the noise from the freeway recedes, you can concentrate on the pervading hum of countless bees and other insects drawn by the sweet fragrances of blue- and white-flowered ceanothus, manzanita, and many kinds of annual wildflowers. The most intense blooming usually occurs in April.

At a point just over 2 miles from Boulder Oaks, the PCT pulls close to the deeply creased canyon containing Kitchen Creek. Look for an obscure path through the low brush north of the trail. This path wanders past a couple of possible small campsites, then drops suddenly about 100 feet to the falls area, located (but not marked) on the topo map between the 3440-foot and 3600-foot contours.

The dry, water-polished rock on either side of the cascade provides fair traction, but beware of any wet streaks that may be slippery.

Kitchen Creek Falls at twilight

Trip 14: Cottonwood Creek Falls

Distance	1.8 miles round trip
Total Elevation Gain/Loss	500'/500'
Hiking Time	1 hour (round trip)
Optional Map	USGS 7.5-min *Mount Laguna*
Best Times	December through June
Agency	CNF/DD
Difficulty	**

Yet another set of falls south of the Laguna Mountain crest invites your exploration. Although these falls on Cottonwood Creek are somewhat less spectacular than those on Kitchen Creek (above), they have the added attraction of swimmable pools.

Public access to the Cottonwood Creek falls is by way of a brushy draw which drains south from Sunrise Highway. Park in either of the two large turnouts between mile 15.3 and mile 15.4 on Sunrise Highway. From the top of the draw, pick up a narrow, partly overgrown trail that goes down to hook up with an old road following powerlines. Along the way you'll find good springtime displays of white ceanothus, beard tongue, and woolly blue curls.

At the bottom of the draw, the powerline road intersects another dirt road. Turn sharply left and go north to where Cottonwood Creek emerges from a narrow canyon. Clamber alongside several cascades to the biggest one, where the stream drops 10 feet into a crystalline pool about shoulder-deep. The water warms to comfortable temperatures by June, though by this time the flow in the creek may be sluggish and unappealing.

The broad banks of the creek just below the falls area provide some nice camping space—if you don't mind packing overnight gear and hauling it on such a short journey.

Cottonwood Creek Falls

Trip 15: Noble Canyon Trail

Distance	10 miles
Total Elevation Gain/Loss	650'/2400'
Hiking Time	5 hours
Recommended Maps	USGS 7.5-min *Monument Peak, Mount Laguna, Descanso*
Best Times	October through May
Agency	CNF/DD
Difficulty	***

The Noble Canyon National Recreation Trail is an extension and reworking of an older trail built in the 1930s by the Civilian Conservation Corps. Since its completion in 1982, the trail has proven very popular among hikers, equestrians, and more recently mountain bikers.

With transportation arrangements set up in advance, you can travel one-way along this trail in the relatively easy downhill direction. You'll find the top end of the trail at the Penny Pines trailhead, mile 27.3 on Sunrise Highway, where parking space is plentiful along the highway shoulder. The bottom end is the developed Noble Canyon trailhead on Pine Creek Road near Pine Valley. Potable water is not available at either trailhead, so plan for your water needs in advance.

Good campsites are fairly abundant along the trail, particularly on shady terraces along the mid-portion of Noble Canyon (remember to establish your camp no less than 100 feet from water). Water flows in the canyon bottom year-round, though it slows to a trickle before the first rains of autumn. Purification is necessary if you intend to rely on it for your drinking or cooking needs.

From the starting point, head west along the marked Noble Canyon Trail. After passing through a park-like setting of Jeffrey pines, you rise a bit along the north slope of a steep hill. From there, the tree-framed view extends to the distant summits of San Jacinto Peak and San Gorgonio Mountain. Next, you descend to cross dirt roads three times, then climb and circle around the chaparral-clad north end of a north-south trending ridge. This seemingly out-of-the-way excursion avoids private inholdings in the national forest, and it opens up interesting vistas to the north and west. Three species of blooming ceanothus brighten the view in springtime.

Next, you descend on a long switchback leg into the upper reaches of Noble Canyon, where the grassy hillsides show off springtime blooms of blue-purple beard tongue, scarlet bugler, woolly blue curls, yellow monkey flower, Indian paintbrush, wallflower, white forget-me-not, wild hyacinth, yellow violet, phacelia, golden yarrow, checker, lupine, and blue flax.

The trail sidles up to the creek at about 3.0 miles, and stays beside it for the next 4 miles. Past a canopy of live oaks, black oaks, and Jeffrey pines, you emerge into an steep, sunlit section of canyon. The trail cuts through thick brush on the east wall, while on the west wall only a few hardy, drought-tolerant plants cling to the exposed schist.

Back in the shade of oaks again, you soon cross a major tributary creek from the east. This drains the Laguna Lakes and Laguna Meadow. Pause for a while in this shady glen, where the water flows over somber, grayish granitic rock and gathers in languid pools bedecked by sword and bracken fern. Look for nodding yellow Humboldt lilies in the late spring or early summer.

You continue within a riparian area for some distance downstream. Mixed in with the oaks, you'll discover dozens of fine California bay trees and a few scattered incense-cedars. The creek lies mostly hidden by willows and sycamores—and dense thickets of poison oak, squaw bush, wild rose, wild strawberries, and other types of water-loving vegetation. The line of trees shading the trail is narrow enough that light from the sky is freely admitted. Greens and browns—and in fall, yellows and reds—glow intensely.

You'll pass some mining debris—the remains of a flume and the stones of a disassembled "arrastra" (a horse- or mule-drawn machine for crushing ore). This dates from gold mining activity in the late 1800s. Next, you'll come upon the foundations of two cabins, then two more cabins in disrepair. Someone long ago planted what is now a huge cypress tree in front of the larger cabin.

Crossing to the west side of the creek, you break out of the trees and into an open area with sage scrub and chaparral vegetation. The trail contours to a point about 100 feet above the creek, then maintains this position as it bends around several small tributaries. Midday temperatures, even in spring, can be uncomfortably warm along this stretch. Yucca, prickly-pear cactus, and even hedgehog cactus—normally a denizen of the desert—make appearances here. There are also excellent vernal displays of beard tongue, scarlet bugler, paintbrush, peony, wild pea, milkweed, wild onion, chia, and larkspur.

At about 7 miles, the trail switches back, crosses the Noble Canyon creek for the last time, and veers up a tributary canyon to the south. The trail joins the bed of an old jeep road, reaches a saddle after about 2 miles from Noble Canyon, then diverges from the road, going right (west) over another saddle. It then descends directly to the developed trailhead facility along Pine Creek Road.

Trip 16: Laguna to Cuyamaca

	Distance	12.2 miles
	Total Elevation Gain/Loss	1250'/2700'
	Hiking Time	7 hours
	Recommended Maps	USGS 7.5-min *Monument Peak, Cuyamaca Peak*
	Best Times	October through May
	Agency	CNF/DD, CRSP
	Difficulty	***

This route, incorporating the new Indian Creek Trail (completed in 1989), provides a fairly direct and convenient connection between the Laguna Mountain Recreation Area and Cuyamaca Rancho State Park. Only a small part of the route is shaded, so plan accordingly if the day is warm. The only potable water found near the route is at Granite Spring, near the end of the trip. It's best, then, to carry all the water you'll need.

A car shuttle can be set up between the Penny Pines trailhead (mile 27.3 on Sunrise Highway) in the Laguna Mountains, and the Sweetwater River bridge parking area (mile 4.8-4.9 on Highway 79) in Cuyamaca Rancho State Park.

If you're going to backpack this route, you'll need to make parking arrangements with the state park, and also obtain a remote camping permit from the Forest Service for camping on national forest land. With prior arrangement, you could also camp at the state park's Granite Spring Primitive Camp, just off the route.

The hike begins pleasantly with a scenic stretch of upper Noble Canyon Trail (see start of Trip 15). After 2.4 miles, turn right on the Indian Creek Trail and descend 0.8 mile to the grassy banks along Indian Creek. After an indistinct crossing of the often soggy creekbed, the trail turns northwest to climb a chaparral-clothed hillside. After about 1.5 miles of steady climbing, the trail tops out at a summit (5440') dubbed Champagne Pass. On the clearest of days, your gaze takes in the western slope of the Lagunas, the eastern slopes of the Cuyamaca Mountains, and a slice of Pacific Ocean freckled with the Coronado Islands.

Next you descend some 800 feet through chaparral and grassland to Deer Park Road in the upper reaches of Pine Valley Creek, 6 miles from the starting point. (An interesting diversion can be made from here: Walk south on Deer Park Road past an old stone house on the right. Next to the road a little farther on you'll find the remains of an arrastra, a circular ore-milling machine powered by horses or mules. Several mine shafts are located nearby, indicated on your topo map. These features date from the mining boom of the late 1800s.)

After crossing Deer Park Road, the Indian Creek Trail continues west 100 yards to join East Mesa Fire Road at the east boundary of Cuyamaca Rancho State Park. Once inside the park, you continue uphill along a sun-blasted, chaparral-covered slope. Near the top of the grade, some large black oak trees provide welcome shade and a good excuse to catch your breath.

East Mesa Fire Road tops out at about 5000 feet, then begins a long and gradual descent across an open meadow. On clear days, beyond the rolling and wind-rippled expanses of grass, Point Loma and the ocean horizon may be seen. Harvey Moore Trail soon joins from the left (north).

From now on follow the route of the Harvey Moore Trail. After passing Granite Spring Primitive Camp, you'll have to veer right to stay on it (East Mesa Fire Road continues toward Highway 79 on a different route). The remaining 3 miles are almost entirely downhill.

Area M-8: Pine Creek

The Cleveland National Forest's Pine Creek Wilderness, created in 1984, encompasses more than 13,000 acres of chaparral-covered slopes and riparian woodland south and west of the Laguna Mountains. A 15-mile stretch of Pine Valley Creek (or "Pine Creek" as many people are referring to it now) meanders through the heart of the wilderness, flanked by sloping walls up to 1000 feet high. Motorists eastbound on Interstate 8 can catch a fleeting glimpse of this impressive gorge when crossing the Pine Valley Bridge, the highest bridge in the Interstate Highway System.

Pine Creek Wilderness is among the most

accessible wilderness areas in California, just 45 minutes east of downtown San Diego via Highway 94 through Jamul, and slightly less time via Interstate 8 through Alpine. If you plan to visit the wilderness area—either for day or for overnight use—don't forget to obtain the necessary wilderness permit from the Forest Service.

A number of trips in the section mapped here (Trips 1, 5, 6, and 7) lie outside the Pine Creek Wilderness boundary, but still inside Cleveland National Forest. You do not need a wilderness permit for these, although a remote camping permit is required if you're going backpacking.

Area M-8: Pine Creek

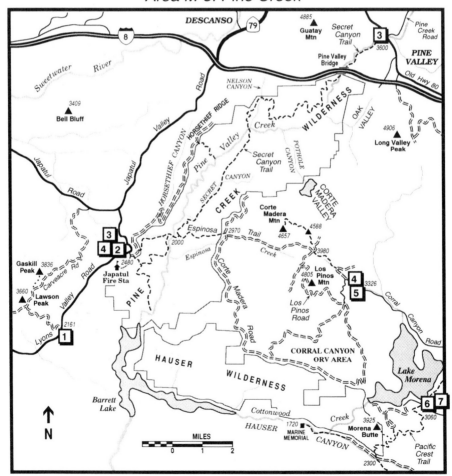

Trip 1: Lawson Peak

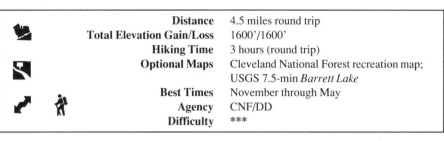

	Distance	4.5 miles round trip
	Total Elevation Gain/Loss	1600'/1600'
	Hiking Time	3 hours (round trip)
	Optional Maps	Cleveland National Forest recreation map; USGS 7.5-min *Barrett Lake*
	Best Times	November through May
	Agency	CNF/DD
	Difficulty	***

Lawson Peak is one of a triad of prominent, granite-topped peaks lying in the southwest corner of Cleveland National Forest. The others are Gaskill Peak and Lyons Peak. Fire-lookout-topped Lyons Peak, formerly listed in this guidebook, no longer has any legal access; Gaskill Peak, on the other hand, can be reached from Lawson Peak at the expense of an hour or two's extra effort, as noted below.

You begin at mile marker 13.0 on Lyons Valley Road (3 miles east of Honey Springs Road and Skyline Truck Trail), where there are two small turnouts for parking.

Start walking on the unsigned Carveacre Road, which is a challenge for off-road drivers, but relatively easy for hikers. The road crests in 2 miles, then descends slightly to meet Wisecarver Road. Lawson Peak lies straight ahead, a massive heap of granite slabs.

The fun begins as you plunge ahead through low brush and boulders east and north of the summit block. Just below the summit on the west side is a near-vertical fissure with abundant hand- and foot-holds. At the top of this is a narrow rock cave. By groping 15 feet or so into the darkness in back of the cave, you'll find an opening above. By mantling up onto a ledge, you'll reach a broad shelf (a nice picnic spot) with a view to the east. Nearby is an easy route to the topmost boulders on the peak.

Standing on the highest boulder is like being on top of the world. To the northwest is Lawson Valley, cut with new roads and dotted with ranches. In most other directions, the view is simply mile upon mile of sun-dappled chaparral and gleaming rock. Lyons Peak and Tecate Peak are prominent on the southwest and south

horizons, while Barrett Lake nestles below an almost unbroken rim of mountains to the east. To the west, if the air's clear, the ocean spreads across the horizon.

If you haven't had your fill of peak bagging, return to Carveacre Road and turn north. After 0.5 mile of road walking, you can find and follow an obscure hikers' trail up the south ridge of Gaskill Peak. Attaining Gaskill's summit, which is slightly higher but less dramatic than Lawson's, requires in the end a short, but somewhat tricky bit of rock climbing. A large flat area of granite lies just northeast of the summit—perfect as a "lunch rock" and suitable as a private, secluded campsite as well.

Summit block of Lawson Peak

Trip 2: Horsethief Canyon

Distance	3.2 miles round trip
Total Elevation Gain/Loss	500'/500'
Hiking Time	2 hours (round trip)
Optional Maps	USGS 7.5-min *Barrett Lake*, *Viejas Mountain*
Best Times	November through June
Agency	CNF/DD
Difficulty	**

The guttural croak of a soaring raven cracked the stillness as my companion and I sauntered down the dusty path. A groggy dragonfly flitted through a beam of morning sunlight. Cool air, slinking down the night-chilled slopes, caressed our faces and set aflutter the sycamore leaves overhead. Arriving at Pine Valley Creek, we felt puffs of warm, dry air pushing down the gorge—a Santa Ana wind flexing its muscles.

We cupped the clear, cold water in our palms and dashed it across our heads.

If you want this kind of escape from the cares of the city, then do what we did: take the Espinosa Trail down Horsethief Canyon. The trailhead, at mile 16.4 on Lyons Valley Road, is quick and easy to reach—either from the north (Japatul Road from Alpine) or from the south (Skyline Truck Trail from Jamul). From the

Pine Valley Creek

trailhead parking lot, a sign directs you north along a gated dirt road for about 300 yards. You then veer right down a ravine on the signed Espinosa Trail.

After a fast, 400' elevation loss, the path bends right (east) to follow live-oak- and sycamore-lined Horsethief Canyon. True to its name, this corral-like canyon was used in the late 1800s by horse thieves to stash stolen horses in preparation for their passage across the international border. The canyon bottom is dry most of the year, but agreeably shaded throughout.

After another mile and not much more descent, you reach the sandy bank of Pine Valley Creek, which in winter and early spring brims with runoff from the creek's headwaters in the Laguna Mountains.

If yours is a casual trip, this is as far as you should go. If the spirit moves you, you might

wade across the creek and continue east on the Espinosa Trail toward higher ground (see Trip 3 below), or you could scramble up the Pine Valley Creek gorge as far as you like. Beyond the large pool just upstream from the trail crossing is a picturesque jumble of car-sized boulders and several mini-waterfalls. Watch your step on the slippery rock, and watch out for poison oak and rattlesnakes. If the water level is dangerously high, don't try following the creek upstream at all.

If you're hooked on loop hikes, you can try the following, less-scenic return route: Proceed downstream on the west bank of Pine Valley Creek for 0.7 mile. At a point opposite the Espinosa Creek confluence, turn right (west) on an old roadbed paralleling a ravine. Follow its steep course upward through chaparral and over a summit to the trailhead parking lot.

Trip 3: Secret Canyon Trail

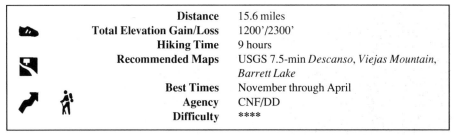

Distance	15.6 miles
Total Elevation Gain/Loss	1200'/2300'
Hiking Time	9 hours
Recommended Maps	USGS 7.5-min *Descanso, Viejas Mountain, Barrett Lake*
Best Times	November through April
Agency	CNF/DD
Difficulty	****

This ambitiously constructed trail, through tough terrain and dense chaparral most of the way, takes you circuitously down the gorge of Pine Valley Creek. Completed in 1992, the trail takes advantage of an old, never-completed flume that would have shunted water from a proposed reservoir in Pine Valley over to King Creek (a tributary of the San Diego River) on the west side of the Cuyamaca Mountains. The Secret Canyon Trail follows some of the longest and best-preserved sections of this circa 1895 engineering effort.

Begin at the new Secret Canyon trailhead staging area (entrance at mile 3.5 on Old Highway 80). You'll end at the Espinosa trailhead on Lyons Valley Road.

For 2 miles, the trail follows the meandering

Pine Valley Creek through a rather broad but twisting gorge. At 1.8 miles you pass under the gargantuan Pine Valley Bridge. Its twin ribbons of interstate highway are held more than 400 feet above the canyon bottom by four massive pillars.

About 300 yards past the bridge, the trail gains a foothold on the brushy slope to the right and starts climbing in earnest to a point about 250 feet above the creek. There it joins the old flume ditch, which in places is accompanied on the down-slope side by remarkably intact walls of dry-laid stone. The latest (photorevised 1988) edition of the *Descanso* topo map shows the general course of both the trail and the flume bed over the next several miles. Since many of the side ravines were never bridged, the trail on occasion darts up and down to connect the nearly flat segments of the flume bed. At about 6.0 miles, there's a rough up-and-down stretch at the point where the topo map shows a nonexistent tunnel. Then it's easy going again until 6.9 miles, where the trail leaves the flume bed and abruptly descends into oak-shaded Nelson Canyon. After rising slightly on the slope west of Nelson Canyon, the trail zigzags down and crosses Pine Valley Creek, 9.0 miles.

On the east side of the now-rather-wide Pine Valley Creek gorge, a gently inclined stretch of trail takes you through monotonous chaparral to a saddle overlooking Secret Canyon at 10.8 miles. You then descend and follow Secret Canyon's trickling creek downstream through grassy hollows where spreading oaks cast inviting pools of shade. The oaks are of two varieties—coast live oak and Engelmann oak.

At 12.5 miles, near Secret Canyon's confluence with Pine Valley Creek, the trail starts angling up a slope to the left. You meander along the east canyon wall of Pine Valley Creek and intersect the Espinosa Trail at 13.8 miles. Follow the Espinosa Trail west across Pine Valley Creek and up Horsethief Canyon (see Trip 2) to the trailhead parking lot along Lyons Valley Road. The final stretch gains 400 feet quickly, so save some energy for it.

Here are some further suggestions if your tastes run to challenging cross-country travel, rather than long miles of trail walking: You're welcome to try boulder-hopping along all or part of the stretch of Pine Valley Creek paralleled by the Secret Canyon Trail. In addition to the spot where the Secret Canyon Trail crosses Pine Valley Creek below Horsethief Ridge, there's access to the creek by way of the still-viable Horsethief Ridge Trail. It descends from the unpaved (and closed to motor vehicles) Horsethief Ridge road.

Boulder-hopping along Pine Valley Creek ranges from rather easy when the water level is low, to dicey and dangerous after major storms. In winter the water is achingly cold, for the creek carries snowmelt from the Laguna Mountains. In warm weather you'll probably want to wade right through the deepest pools.

The 4-mile stretch of the canyon between the Horsethief Ridge and Espinosa trails is best. The creek flows over polished bedrock slabs and tumbles over several small waterfalls, accompanied most of the while by scattered willows, cottonwoods and sycamores.

If you decide to follow Pine Valley Creek south from the I-8 bridge, don't miss an interesting side trip up the short, steep canyon that drains Oak Valley. Floodwaters tearing through this mini-gorge have scoured out a number of huge "potholes" in the bedrock. The Forest Service is considering building a trail that would run along the side of this canyon and loop back under the I-8 bridge.

Trip 4: Espinosa Trail

Distance	7.8 miles
Total Elevation Gain/Loss	1250'/2100'
Hiking Time	4 hours
Recommended Maps	USGS 7.5-min *Morena Reservoir*, *Descanso*, *Viejas Mountain*
Best Times	November through May
Agency	CNF/DD
Difficulty	**

If you can arrange to be dropped off at the east end of this route and picked up later at the west end, this can be an enjoyable and rather easy trip across the mountains. Do it in the early spring if possible, when the chaparral blooms and water bubbles down even the most insignificant ravines.

The east entry is approached by way of

Interstate 8 and Buckman Springs Road. At mile 6.6 on Buckman Springs Road (3 miles south of I-8), turn west on Corral Canyon Road and proceed 4.8 miles on narrow pavement to a hairpin turn. The unsigned, gated Kernan Road goes northwest from the turn. Park nearby off the road. Your friends can drive around to the Espinosa Trail's west terminus at mile 16.4 on Lyons Valley Road and meet you later.

Squeeze around the gate and walk 0.5 mile up Kernan Road along the Morena Creek drainage. Where the road bends right in a horseshoe curve, pick up the Espinosa Trail and continue northwest. After one more mile of climbing, you top a saddle and cross Los Pinos Road. Continue straight ahead (west) and begin a sharp descent toward Espinosa Creek. The next 3 miles of the Espinosa Trail are part of an approved off-road-vehicle route. In the wet season, Espinosa Creek trickles under a canopy of live oaks and splashes over at least one waterfall hidden in the brush. To the right, framed by twisted oaks, the sheer south face of Corte Madera Mountain thrusts skyward.

When you reach Corte Madera Road, jog north for 0.2 mile on it, then go west again on the continuation of the Espinosa Trail, now free of ORV's. The trail cuts across a chaparral-covered flat, and then descends viewfully into the Pine Valley Creek gorge.

Down at the bottom, cross the creek and continue west along the oak-shaded bottom of Horsethief Canyon for one mile. Then bend sharply left (south) to follow the steep path up to the trailhead parking lot along Lyons Valley Road.

Trip 5: Corte Madera Mountain

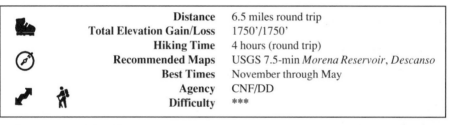

Distance	6.5 miles round trip
Total Elevation Gain/Loss	1750'/1750'
Hiking Time	4 hours (round trip)
Recommended Maps	USGS 7.5-min *Morena Reservoir, Descanso*
Best Times	November through May
Agency	CNF/DD
Difficulty	***

Here is one of San Diego County's prime view spots, affording a panorama that sometimes stretches from Santa Catalina and San Clemente islands to the Sierra Juarez plateau in Baja California. Corte Madera Mountain's sheer south face is noticeable as an abrupt drop in the mountain profile as seen from many parts of metropolitan San Diego; at one point there's a near-vertical dropoff of about 300 feet.

Begin along Corral Canyon Road—see Trip 4 above for directions. Upon reaching Los Pinos Road, on the saddle 1 mile up the Espinosa Trail, turn right and continue 0.3 mile to another saddle, this one a half mile southeast of boulder-studded, Coulter-pine-dotted peak 4588. Leave the road there and find and follow a path that works its way up past peak 4588 and across another saddle just northwest of the peak.

Continue following the path northwest, then southwest along a crest to the undistinguished summit plateau of Corte Madera Mountain. The view north includes a fabulous vista, available nowhere else on public land, of privately owned Corte Madera Valley. A beautiful lake and oak-studded meadows fill the valley. The name Corte Madera ("woodyard") apparently refers to the use of this area as a source of timber during the building of the San Diego area missions.

Corte Madera Mountain's summit plateau is covered by large sheets of granitic rock and patches of chaparral. From the southernmost point on the plateau you can peer over the abrupt face into the canyon drained by Espinosa Creek. To the southeast is Los Pinos Mountain, topped by a fire lookout, one of the three remaining in San Diego County used on a regular basis.

If you care to do a little further exploring, try following the informal network of horse trails cut into the north slope of Corte Madera Mountain. These are most often used by riders who live in the private homes below. The trails meander down to about the 4000' contour in Corte Madera Valley, where the private property begins.

Trip 6: Morena Butte

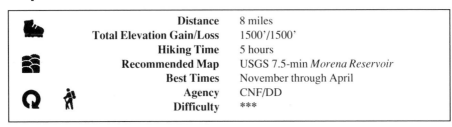

	Distance	8 miles
	Total Elevation Gain/Loss	1500'/1500'
	Hiking Time	5 hours
	Recommended Map	USGS 7.5-min *Morena Reservoir*
	Best Times	November through April
	Agency	CNF/DD
	Difficulty	***

Morena Butte's three-peaked summit plateau presides over a diverse landscape of V-shaped canyons, rock-strewn ridges, and grassy depressions known as *potreros* (pastures). All three peaks are attractive photographically, as they consist of great slabs and boulders of pink-tinted granitic rock weathered into sometimes surreal forms.

The starting point for this hike (and for Trip 7 below) is Lake Morena County Park, 12 miles south of Pine Valley via Interstate 8, Buckman Springs Road, and Morena Village. Park your car and start hiking at the Pacific Crest Trail parking lot at the entrance to the county campground.

Follow the PCT as it ascends west on the slope overlooking Morena Reservoir. During wet cycles, the lake expands to nearly fill this 2-square-mile former potrero; while during drought, the water surface shrinks to about one-tenth that size. Fine views of the blue water can be had for a while, but presently the trail swings away, generally south over and around several hilltops. Good displays of blooming ceanothus liven things up in the spring, otherwise the chaparral-draped slopes can appear quite drab.

At 1.8 miles the trail starts descending generally west into a shallow tributary of Hauser Creek. You cross the ravine at 2.7 miles and gently ascend to a saddle on the southeast shoulder of Morena Butte (3.0 miles). From that point find and follow a rough path going northwest up the ridge 1 mile to the summit area. Climb all three of the rocky peaklets on top for great views in various directions.

Return to where you left the PCT, retrace your steps for 0.2 mile, then stay left on a path (old roadbed) that slants north, gains about 100 feet, and attains a broad divide. There you meet a dirt road that will take you northwest through a beautiful valley, graced by live oaks and Coulter pines, right beneath the stony gaze of Morena Butte. Continue to Morena Reservoir's shoreline road, and follow it 2 miles back to your starting point.

On Morena Butte

Trip 7: Hauser Canyon

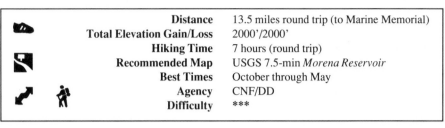

	Distance	13.5 miles round trip (to Marine Memorial)
	Total Elevation Gain/Loss	2000'/2000'
	Hiking Time	7 hours (round trip)
	Recommended Map	USGS 7.5-min *Morena Reservoir*
	Best Times	October through May
	Agency	CNF/DD
	Difficulty	***

The linear, V-shaped gash of Hauser Canyon cuts across one of the really remote parts of the county. Years ago the public could descend into the canyon by way of a dirt road from Lake Morena Drive and reach a Forest Service campground. Today, the east end of this road is blocked by a locked gate and the west end is washed out. Nowadays the canyon is visited only by hikers and, sometimes, undocumented aliens trying to slip north undetected.

The stroll down oak- and sycamore-lined Hauser and Cottonwood creeks will be your reward for putting up with a long, somewhat uneventful approach (and return) on the Pacific Crest Trail. Begin by hiking the PCT, as in Trip 6 above, to the saddle southeast of Morena Butte. From there you lose 900 feet of elevation as you zigzag down the north wall of Hauser Canyon (passing, incidentally, through a corner of Hauser Wilderness). At 4.3 miles, the trail intersects Hauser Creek Road, down along the creek. Leave the PCT at this point and follow the road west, down-canyon.

At 5.8 miles Cottonwood Creek comes in from the north. Its flow depends almost solely upon releases at Morena Dam, about 2 miles upstream. A small waterfall and pool, sculpted into the bedrock, are just above the confluence. Nearby you'll find a pint-size rock cave.

Below the confluence, you must pick your way through a tangle of riparian vegetation. Just pick your way along the bank, or splash along through the shallow water. The site of the old Hauser Creek Campground is an oak-shaded bench along a bend in the creek at 6.3 miles. Nearby are a concrete dam and a pond that once harbored bass (and perhaps still does). After another 0.4 mile, you'll come upon the Marine Memorial—a memorial to the nine Marine Corps fire fighters who perished at that spot during a 1943 wildfire.

Beyond the memorial, the waters of Cottonwood Creek trickle down to Barrett Lake, a county reservoir closed to public use.

Oak canopy, Hauser Creek

Area M-9: Border Ranges

Most admirers of San Diego's beautiful setting of mountain and sea are somewhat familiar with the long, pillowy range of mountains on the city's southeastern horizon. Rising from the flatlands of Otay Mesa, they are officially named the San Ysidro Mountains—but almost everyone knows them as Otay Mountain, which is the name of the highest summit.

Otay Mountain's western slopes offer unexcelled views of San Diego, San Diego Bay, Point Loma, the Silver Strand, Tijuana, and Mexico's Coronado Islands. Seen on a clear winter morning, this wide panorama is almost aerial in perspective, and must be seen to be believed.

Otay Mountain lies within a large block of BLM-controlled land known as the Otay National Cooperative Land and Wildlife Management Area. The slopes are host to two dozen rare or endangered plants, many of which are locally common, but found nowhere else in the United States or in the world. The most impressive of these is the Tecate cypress, which grows in scattered stands on the north slopes. Several species of rare wildlife, including the California gnatcatcher, make their home here, too.

The BLM has just developed a comprehensive plan for its roughly 50,000 acres of land along the Mexican border, which include most of Otay Mountain, parts of Tecate Peak near Tecate, and parts of Hauser Mountain near Campo. Long forgotten by the public, these lands will increasingly be opened to recreational uses such as hiking, camping, horseback riding, mountain biking and hunting. A trail to be called the Border Mountain Trail, separate from roads, may one day stretch from Tecate to Otay Mesa.

For now, at least, you can enjoy the following three hikes—on unpaved roads—that lead to the summits of Otay Mountain and Tecate Peak.

Area M-9: Border Ranges

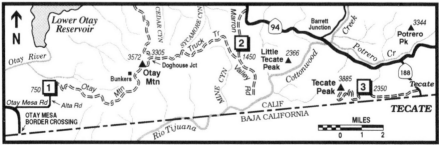

Trip 1: Otay Mountain—West Approach

👞	**Distance**	14 miles round trip
	Total Elevation Gain/Loss	3100'/3100'
	Hiking Time	7 hours (round trip)
▚	**Optional Maps**	USGS 7.5-min *Otay Mesa, Otay Mountain*
	Best Times	October through May
↗	**Agency**	BLM/PS
	Difficulty	***

Otay Mountain is penetrated by three graded dirt roads that join together at Doghouse Junction on the summit ridge. These roads serve communications installations on the mountain crest and provide access for fire-fighting equipment when needed. This trip describes the west approach up Otay Mountain Truck Trail; Trip 2 below covers the east approach.

Good timing can make this hike a memorable experience, rather than simply a long day's slog. Try to pick a crystal-clear morning following the passage of one of the bigger winter storms. On the clearest mornings the view from Otay Mountain stretches all the way to the snow-capped summits of the San Gabriel, San Bernardino and San Jacinto mountains—all more than a hundred miles to the north.

To reach the starting point, take Interstate 905 east from either I-5 or I-805. It becomes Otay Mesa Road atop Otay Mesa. Just before the main road curves south to the Otay Mesa border crossing, turn left (continue east) on Otay Mesa Road. After 1.5 miles, turn north on Alta Road and continue 0.9 mile to an unmarked road on the right (0.1 mile past the entrance to the Donovan state prison). There's space to park ahead, before you reach a cluster of farm houses. The unpaved Otay Mountain Truck Trail begins at a gate just ahead, which may or may not be open to vehicular traffic.

The first couple of miles are uninspiring, but soon the first Tecate cypresses appear. The young cypresses are quite slender, while the more mature specimens, some more than 20 feet tall, assume a bushy form.

After about 4 miles (roughly 2500') the road traverses a north slope thickly grown with an almost pure stand of cypress. At this level, the

coastal low clouds often collect during the night and morning and give up some of their moisture.

The road continues up along the crest, swinging back and forth across a swath denuded of trees and large shrubs. This is the International Fuelbreak, created many years ago as a containment barrier for wildfires, particularly those sweeping north.

At 6 miles you come upon an old concrete structure and other remains nearby. During World War II, massive gun emplacements, ammunition batteries, and lookouts were established here to defend against an anticipated Japanese naval assault.

Finally, after about 7 miles, a paved spur road swings up the slope to the left, leading to an unsightly clutter of antennas on the summit ridge. Near the summit are some nice outcrops of grayish-green metavolcanic rock. A band of this metavolcanic rock stretches northwest from Otay Mountain to San Miguel Mountain and beyond. It is a remnant of the island-arc volcanoes that predated the rise of the Southern California batholith and the formation of the Peninsular Ranges.

Trip 2: Otay Mountain—East Approach

🥾	**Distance**	15 miles round trip
	Total Elevation Gain/Loss	2500'/2500'
	Hiking Time	7 hours (round trip)
🔲	**Optional Map**	USGS 7.5-min *Otay Mountain*
	Best Times	October through May
↗	**Agency**	BLM/PS
	Difficulty	***

One of the most spectacular wildflower displays I have ever witnessed was found one April day along the northeast flank of Otay Mountain. The road to the summit was lined with a changing palette of blooming plants: yellow and red monkey flower, morning glory, yerba santa, chaparral pea, wild pea, clematis, nightshade, mountain misery, and wild hyacinth. On one slope recently swept by wildfire, there were tens of thousands of bush poppy plants, each bearing hundreds of big, delicate, four-petaled flowers—millions of flowers in all, swaying in the breeze.

The eastern approach of Otay Mountain is slightly longer than the western approach, but it involves slightly less elevation gain and loss. To reach the starting point, drive 1.5 miles east of Dulzura on Highway 94 to Marron Valley Road. Proceed 2.1 miles south on a graded surface to a gate just beyond the South Bay Rod and Gun Club shooting range. Park here and begin the long trek.

Hike for 0.6 mile south of the gate, descending about 200 feet, then turn right (west) on Otay Mountain Truck Trail. At about 1.6 miles, pass through a wire gate (please keep closed). Bear left (west, uphill) at the next intersection. In the next 4.5 miles, you ascend along mostly north-facing slopes, partly in shadow during the cooler months. The Tecate cypress prefers these north slopes; not many big ones are seen, but large numbers of seedlings are naturally regenerating wherever fires have swept through. Scattered scrub oaks and a few large manzanitas intermix with the bigger cypress trees.

At Doghouse Junction (6.7 miles), bear left (south). The road traverses a steep, sunny slope providing views south into sparsely populated areas of Baja California between Tijuana and Tecate. After another 0.6 mile, turn right (north) on the road to the summit.

Trip 3: Tecate Peak

🥾	**Distance**	10 miles round trip (via the road only)
	Total Elevation Gain/Loss	1900'/1900'
	Hiking Time	5½ hours (round trip)
🔲	**Optional Map**	USGS 7.5-min *Tecate*
	Best Times	November through May
↗	**Agency**	BLM/PS
	Difficulty	***

Tecate Peak straddles the U.S./Mexico border, overlooking the twin towns of Tecate, California and Tecate, Baja California. Kumeyaay Indians called this peak "Kuchumaa," and believed that a holy power, for healing or harm, emanated from the mountain's granitic boulders. According to oral historical accounts, shamans from tribes involved in disputes would meet at the summit for peace conferences. Recent archaeological evidence suggests that the mountain was also used for fertility ceremonies. Even today, descendants of the Kumeyaay, who have been granted vehicle access to the upper slopes of the mountain, make periodic journeys to its summit.

The Tecate Peak slopes lie largely in the public domain, on lands under the jurisdiction of the BLM and the California Division of Forestry. In 1958 a dirt road was constructed on the eastern slope to serve an antenna site on the summit. A locked gate along this road bars unauthorized vehicles, but not hikers, so you can enjoy a pleasant and usually traffic-free hike to the top.

This is a good late afternoon/early evening trip. Since the road approaches from the east, you can avoid most of the hot sunshine by being in the afternoon shadow of the mountain. You can take in a spectacular sunset at the top, then watch the twinkling lights of Tecate, Mexico, as you make your descent. If you time your visit to coincide with a waxing gibbous or full moon, you probably won't need to use your flashlight.

To reach the starting point from San Diego, drive 35 miles east on Highway 94, then turn south on Highway 188 toward the Tecate border crossing. When you reach the sign reading INTERNATIONAL BORDER 1500 FEET, turn west on an unnamed dirt road. The road quickly swings south, then turns west again to follow the border fence for about 1.5 miles. It then turns northwest to climb the lower slopes of Tecate Peak. The road surface ahead may be rutty. The locked gate is 2.8 miles from Tecate; below it, parking is limited to a few wider spots in the road.

At first you'll hike past chamise, ceanothus, laurel sumac, and yerba santa. Higher up, there's low-growing manzanita and a curious shrub called southern mountain misery. The sticky, fernlike foliage of the mountain misery exudes an aroma similar to witch hazel; clusters of white flowers, resembling strawberry blossoms, appear on it in early spring.

At a point about 1 mile above the gate, you have the option of cutting off about 0.4 mile of tedious road walking by following the top edge of a huge, tilted granite slab bordering a ravine to the right. After about 100 yards of climbing, you can rejoin an upper level of the roadway. This is the most worthwhile of several possible

Atop Tecate Peak

cuts on the way to the summit.

The commanding view from the summit includes most of San Diego County and vast stretches of northern Baja California. To the east there's an almost aerial view of the twin border towns. You can see the sharp delineation between Tecate, California (population 88), and Tecate, Mexico, with a rapidly expanding population of nearly 100,000. The landmark Tecate brewery is visible near the center of town.

Borrego Valley

THE DESERT

Area D-1: Coyote Canyon

Coyote Canyon is the biggest rift between two major mountain complexes in the Peninsular Ranges—the San Ysidro Mountains and the Santa Rosa Mountains. The canyon is underlain by the San Jacinto Fault Zone, a splinter of the San Andreas Fault Zone. Being a natural passage through the mountains, it was for a time an important route of travel.

Pedro Fages was the first European to pass through; his 1772 trip in pursuit of deserters from the presidio at San Diego took him as far north as the San Joaquin Valley. In 1774, and again in 1775, Juan Bautista de Anza led parties of soldiers and settlers up the canyon while en route from Sonora, Mexico, to settlements in northern California.

Although many proposals for a paved highway through Coyote Canyon have been advanced, steadfast opposition has kept it free of pavement. A primitive jeep road down the canyon from Terwilliger Valley (near Anza in Riverside County) to the north edge of Borrego Valley remains the only vehicle access route. This road was built in the 1930s, and has not been maintained for more than two decades. It suits most users fine that Coyote Canyon remains a place difficult, but not impossible, to get into.

Because of its beauty and semi-isolation, Coyote Canyon has become one of the more popular destinations in Anza-Borrego Desert State Park. Coyote Creek's year-round flow supports three dense riparian areas: Upper Willows, Middle Willows, and Lower Willows.

Formerly the Coyote Canyon road went right through the middle of the jungle-like Lower Willows. In 1988 the road was rerouted around Lower Willows, making this particular oasis especially attractive for hikers and horse-riders.

Between Lower and Middle Willows, extending west to the base of the San Ysidro Mountains, is a broad alluvial basin called Collins Valley. Jeep roads and horse trails cross the valley floor, providing direct access to the major tributary canyons on the west side: Salvador Canyon, Sheep Canyon, South Fork Sheep Canyon, Cougar Canyon, and Indian Canyon. These canyons, along with several more to the south (see Area D-2) are part of a vast roadless area designated as state wilderness. Here, the intrepid hiker will find solitude, adventure, and rugged beauty.

Beyond Collins Valley, Coyote Canyon and its tributaries extend quite far into Riverside County. Information about the upper tributaries of Coyote Canyon can be found in Lowell and Diana Lindsay's guidebook, *The Anza-Borrego Desert Region.*

Coyote Canyon's "road"—at times little more than the creekbed itself—is infamous. Protruding rocks, soft sand, and stream crossings have conspired to render inoperative many an automobile driven too far. (It's worth noting that most towing insurance policies do not cover the rescue of vehicles from "off-highway" locales such as Coyote Canyon.) With care, you can usually cover the first few unpaved miles in a regular auto, but only sturdy, high-clearance,

4-wheel-drive vehicles are appropriate for travel beyond the first or second road crossing of Coyote Creek. In the trip descriptions to follow, it is assumed that you will start your hike at certain trailheads accessible by 4-wheel drive. If you have to park short of these trailheads, you may have to backpack in (or perhaps hitchhike) several miles to reach the starting points.

The sprawling desert town of Borrego Springs is the gateway to Coyote Canyon and most other areas in the northern part of Anza-Borrego Desert State Park. The town itself is about two hours' drive from most parts of coastal San Diego County by way of a variety of routes.

To reach Coyote Canyon from Christmas Circle in Borrego Springs, go east 0.5 mile on Palm Canyon Drive, then north on DiGiorgio Road 4.8 miles to the end of the pavement. Now set your odometer at 0.0 (all mileages below refer to this zero point), and proceed slowly on the unpaved road ahead. You'll soon cross the Coyote Creek wash west to east—this usually dry crossing spot can become a muddy morass of wheel tracks after heavy rains. On the far side you continue northwest up alongside the base of Coyote Mountain.

At 3.2 miles there's a small parking turnout for Desert Gardens, a picnic spot in the midst of ocotillos and other low-desert flora. At 3.8 miles you'll come to the first (normally wet) crossing of Coyote Creek. There's plenty of parking space on hard-packed sand just before this crossing, and many choose to drive no farther than this. (On the west side of the first crossing,

a dirt road branches south. This road can be used as a shortcut to or from Borrego Springs, but it goes through a notorious patch of sometimes wet and sometimes dry soft sand.)

The second crossing comes at 4.8 miles—often the limit for non-4-wheel-drive vehicles. At 5.6 miles the road veers sharply left (west), crosses the creek, and begins a steep and in places very rough ascent up a ravine. Once over a 1420' pass, the road passes near a monument commemorating the passage of the Anza party in 1774, and descends to the margins of Santa Catarina Spring, where sandy roads branch west toward the primitive campground at the mouth of Sheep Canyon, and northwest toward Salvador Canyon and Middle Willows.

No permit is required for day or overnight use of the Coyote Canyon area or, for that matter, any other area, wilderness or otherwise, within Anza-Borrego Desert State Park. Do, of course, become familiar with the park regulations first. The park has a unique open-camping policy that allows you to set up camp virtually anywhere (but not near remote springs and water holes—the wildlife depends on them). You can have campfires, as long as they're confined in metal containers and you bring your own wood. For your cooking needs, campstoves are the most practical.

Coyote Canyon and its tributaries are closed to *all* entry between June 15 and September 16 to protect the watering rights of bighorn sheep. No other area in the park is subject to this restriction.

Trip 1: Lower Willows

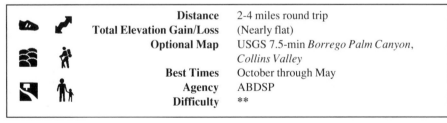

	Distance	2-4 miles round trip
	Total Elevation Gain/Loss	(Nearly flat)
	Optional Map	USGS 7.5-min *Borrego Palm Canyon*, *Collins Valley*
	Best Times	October through May
	Agency	ABDSP
	Difficulty	**

Soggy Lower Willows, along with its primary source of water—Santa Catarina Spring—together comprise Anza-Borrego's

richest riparian habitat. This short trip will introduce you to this surprisingly lush and jungle-like area. Don't forget your binoculars—the

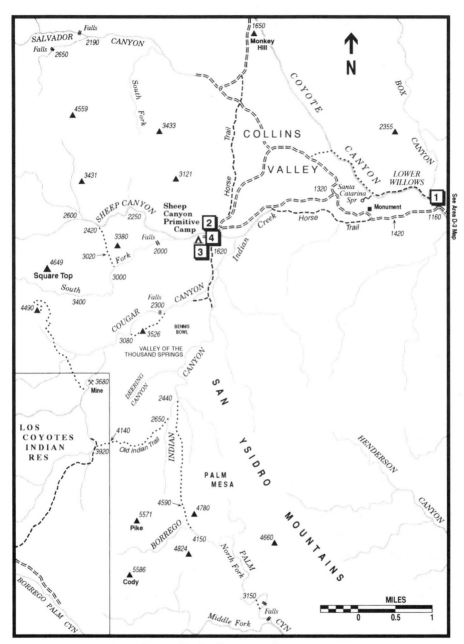

Area D-1: Coyote Canyon

birding is excellent. You'll be tramping through some muddy areas and probably wading in the stream, so wear old shoes and bring an extra pair to leave in the car.

Measured from the end of the pavement at DiGiorgio Road, the starting point for this hike is 5.6 miles northwest up the main Coyote Canyon jeep road. This is where the newly constructed bypass route turns west to climb up a steep ravine. Park here and continue up the main canyon on remnants of the old jeep road— now a trail for hikers and equestrians. Where trucks and 4-wheel drives once waddled, wheezed, and snorted through the stream, there are now only the sounds of bubbling water, birds, and insects. The rampant growth of vegetation, largely willows, mesquite, tamarisk, and arrowweed, has obliterated most parts of the old road. Listen for the monosyllabic hoot of the phainopepla, a winter-resident bird that flits about with white wing patches flashing in the bright sunlight.

After about 1 mile, an ill-maintained path veers left toward Santa Catarina Spring, which comprises several oozing acres. The air is heavy with humid odors, and colorful insects—grasshoppers, beetles, katydids, preying mantises—seem to be everywhere. Much of the canyon bottom here was blackened by wildfire in 1988. Since then, areas fed by surface water have experienced an amazing recovery. Cottonwoods and palms in the burned zone have sprouted new leaves and fronds, and tangles of wild grape vines once again drape many of the trees still standing.

If you continue on the trail up along Coyote Canyon's creek, you'll come to the end of the dense willows after a total of almost 2 miles. By going far enough northwest, you can bear west about 0.3 mile to reach the main Coyote Canyon jeep road. If you want to extend your trip by way of a loop, you can follow that road south up to the bluff overlooking Santa Catarina Spring, and east down the steep ravine back to your car.

Trip 2: Sheep Canyon

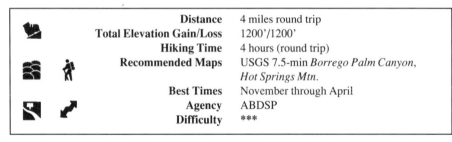

	Distance	4 miles round trip
	Total Elevation Gain/Loss	1200'/1200'
	Hiking Time	4 hours (round trip)
	Recommended Maps	USGS 7.5-min *Borrego Palm Canyon*, *Hot Springs Mtn.*
	Best Times	November through April
	Agency	ABDSP
	Difficulty	***

Each of Coyote Canyon's major tributaries has its own unique character, and Sheep Canyon is no exception. Palms are scarce here, but sycamores and cottonwoods thrive. Your footsteps will play counterpoint to the gurgle and spatter of water over polished boulders. Shady grottos provide coolness and shade at frequent intervals along the way. Depending on the current wet or dry cycle, the canyon's stream may or may not be flowing in the fall season, but there's almost always plenty of water in winter and spring.

Though parts of Sheep Canyon are rugged and overgrown with lush vegetation, foot traffic

in the lower end has hewn out a followable, if primitive, footpath. From Sheep Canyon Primitive Camp it is only 2 miles—and a net gain of 900 feet—to a point where you enter a broad, bowl-shaped valley. This valley is a good destination for backpackers (there are plenty of campsites around), and also a good base camp for further exploration of points all around the compass. I'll mention several possible side trips in the narrative below.

From the primitive campground, go upstream along the banks of the wash (or stream as the case may be). Take care to bear right at the major canyon fork at 0.3 mile, staying in the main canyon. As the bed of the canyon twists and turns, you'll cross the shallow stream several times and climb up and over the rocky canyon walls in order to detour around several small waterfalls. Most of these detours are easier to make on one side of the canyon than the other, so look carefully for footprints or the rudiments of a trail to determine the best route.

At 1.2 miles (2250'), a small canyon leads north to a saddle: on its far side is the South Fork of Salvador Canyon. Cottonwoods have begun to appear, and they will gradually replace the sycamores as you continue to climb. There's not much evidence of a trail now: you simply negotiate the easiest route across great slabs of fractured granitic rock.

Next, the canyon floor widens slightly, and you make your way directly through the streambed, or across grass- and shrub-covered flats to either side. At 1.5 miles the canyon turns abruptly to the right (west).

At 1.6 miles (2420'), a steep ravine climbs sharply south to a saddle between the two forks of Sheep Canyon. South of this saddle lies a broad valley at 3000' elevation in South Fork Sheep Canyon (see Trip 3). From the top of the saddle, two peak climbs are possible: The first is a boulder-strewn 3380' summit overlooking both forks, easily within reach to the northeast. The second is to the west—the massive, flat-topped 4649' promontory I'll call "Square Top," a conspicuous landmark seen from Collins Valley and points east. Square Top can be climbed from the east and possibly the south sides: attempts on the north and west sides will be doomed to failure by a combination of huge boulders and dense chaparral just below the summit.

At 1.9 miles, Sheep Canyon emerges into a broad bowl where two major and several minor tributaries come together. Possible campsites are abundant here. For day hikers, it's a good place to enjoy the view of rugged peaks in every direction before turning around. Around the margins of the bowl, seasonal springs can be found in several of the small tributaries. They're often marked by small cottonwood trees or other riparian vegetation.

Trip 3: South Fork Sheep Canyon

	Distance	3 miles round trip (to valley at 3000')
	Total Elevation Gain/Loss	1500'/1500'
	Hiking Time	4 hours (round trip)
	Recommended Maps	USGS 7.5-min *Borrego Palm Canyon*, *Hot Springs Mtn.*
	Best Times	November through April
	Agency	ABDSP
	Difficulty	****

Mile for mile, the terrain covered on this hike is more technically difficult than that on any other trip described in this book. Skilled scramblers need not use ropes, but certain precautions must be observed.

Careful route finding is the key to safe passage through this canyon. Some routes (especially going downhill) may look promising, but lead to steep rock exposures so that much time can be wasted in backtracking. Other routes can lead to deadends in the canyon bottom where it is difficult (or impossible) to climb out in the absence of outside help, so don't jump or slide down rocks if you can't determine the feasibility of the route ahead. Because of these difficulties, it is recommended that you don't backpack through this canyon without first having traveled it with a light day pack.

The rewards are a close-up view of an idyllic waterfall, glimpses of a half-dozen more, and the pleasure of exploring a hidden valley seldom visited by humans. Less water flows through the South Fork than the main fork of Sheep Canyon. Try to arrive here soon after a major storm, when the stream bubbles with vigor and crashes over the falls.

Begin as in Trip 2, but stay to the left at 0.3 mile, entering South Fork. A well-beaten trail goes up along the bank, but peters out rapidly as boulders and underbrush become a hindrance. Find a way through the brush and climb over rounded granite slabs, passing two palm groves, until you reach (at 0.6 mile, 2000') the base of a sublime 30' waterfall—arguably the most beautiful cascade in Anza-Borrego. Framed by full-skirted palms both top and bottom, and a lush carpet of grass below, this is a point of interest well worth reaching even if you don't intend to continue farther up the canyon.

From just below the waterfall, climb the steep, rocky slope to the right (north side of the canyon). Climb sharply upward until you can traverse at an easier gradient, staying parallel to and about 200 feet above the canyon bottom.

The slope is infested with cactus, agave, and sharp rocks, but if you stay at the right level, the footing is relatively stable. You'll hear the splashing of water in several virtually inaccessible grottos below.

Continue along the north wall of the canyon for about 0.3 mile, then contour into the canyon bottom at about 2600 feet. Now thread your way around immense boulder complexes, staying generally close to the north wall. Note your route carefully so that you can retrace it when you return.

Turning south, you enter a valley at 3000 feet with several flat, sandy areas on the west side. This is a worthy enough destination for a day hike: there are good views of distant peaks and ridges, and small pools in the stream to soak the feet in. Backpackers can reach this valley by

Lower fall, South Fork Sheep Canyon

way of a longer and less problematic route through the main Sheep Canyon and over a saddle between the two forks (see Trip 2 above).

Further exploration up South Fork is just as rewarding as it is challenging. Here are some highlights:

The canyon turns west at 3120 feet. Typical high-desert vegetation appears there—ribbonwood, scrub oak, and yucca on the slopes; palms, sycamores, cottonwoods, and alders along the stream. At 3250 feet, there's a narrow, grassy bench providing the last marginal campsites in this canyon. Amazingly, an in-

cense-cedar grows here, miles away from its normal habitat high up in the mountains. Scattered palms extend several hundred feet upstream. This is truly an extraordinary overlap of mountain and desert flora.

Above 3400 feet there's a series of small falls, then huge boulder mazes and heavy brush. (Refer to Area M-3, Trip 2, for a route into this area from the Los Coyotes Indian Reservation.) From these upper reaches of South Fork, a very difficult, brushy traverse can be made into the main Sheep Canyon via the saddle west of Square Top.

Trip 4: Cougar Canyon

Distance	3 miles round trip (to pool at 2300')
Total Elevation Gain/Loss	900'/900'
Hiking Time	3 hours (round trip)
Recommended Map	USGS 7.5-min *Borrego Palm Canyon*
Best Times	November through April
Agency	ABDSP
Difficulty	***

Cougar Canyon is a place where new worlds open up at every turn. There are more beautiful sights to see along a half-mile of this canyon than in a full day's hiking in many other parts of Anza-Borrego.

Cahuilla Indians were using seasonal camps in the area around the mouth of the canyon as recently as about 150 years ago, and the evidence left behind in the form of bedrock morteros and ceremonial caves gives another interesting dimension to a hike here.

If you plan to stay overnight, the flat, open areas just below the mouth of the canyon make spacious and convenient campsites. A few marginal camping areas do exist in the canyon proper, but these have been overused and are really too close to the canyon stream to be considered appropriate places to set up camp.

Mileages in this description start from the road closure on the spur trail (the old Indian Canyon jeep road) going south from the mouth of Sheep Canyon. Begin by walking south on this eroded and partly overgrown jeep trail. After crossing Cougar Canyon's streambed three times, you'll reach a point a little beyond

the mouth of Cougar Canyon (0.7 mile). Find the informal path that veers right (west) up Cougar's alluvial fan. A little northwest of this point, on a bench overlooking the stream, is a rock cave reputed to have been used as an Indian temescal, or sweat-house.

Follow the path west and cross the stream once more (0.9 mile). Now on the north bank, the path climbs to about 50 feet above the stream as the canyon walls close in rather tightly. Another rock cave yawns on the hillside.

Staying on the path well above the stream, it seems almost a shame to miss the beautiful scenery down below along the sycamore-shaded creek. But soon, steep walls of granite and gneiss force you to descend anyway. Go up the cobbled bed of the stream to the beginning of a palm grove, then climb up to a sandy, shaded bench on the left bank (1.3 miles). On a rock facing the bench is a huge psychedelic "eye"—rock art, circa 1970. Just beyond the eye, upstream, is a deep, shaded pool fed by a silvery waterfall.

The path, now obscure, continues up the south wall of the canyon to avoid a narrow section just beyond the eye. After climbing over a series of rock buttresses, you'll come to a point overlooking a feathery cascade of water flowing down a slab of banded rock in the canyon bottom. Just beyond this you can descend to the streambed again, and work your way up-canyon to a large cottonwood tree nestled beside a sculpted granite wall. Using the limbs of this tree to hoist yourself up and over, you'll come upon the most beautiful spot of all—a clear, deep pool surrounded by sheer, polished granite walls, fed by a 20' waterfall.

This pool and waterfall (1.5 miles, 2300') mark the end of progress in Cougar Canyon proper without resorting to technical climbing aids. A long detour is necessary to bypass the next 0.6 mile. If you're interested, here's the way:

Back up to the point overlooking the feathery cascade. Now go straight up the south wall, dodging brush and boulders, until you reach a point on the ridgeline east of peak 3526. Here you have a bird's-eye view of palm groves in Bennis Bowl and Valley of the Thousand Springs, and a view of some nearly inaccessible palms in Cougar Canyon. Follow this jagged ridgeline west, pass over peak 3526, and traverse just south of two smaller peaklets. Then drop 250 feet northwest through a gully to reach the bed of Cougar Canyon at the 3080-foot contour. From there it's possible to continue up the stream banks for some distance. For more information, see Area M-3, Trip 2.

In Lower Cougar Canyon

Area D-2: San Ysidro Mountains

West of Borrego Springs, the fluted walls of the San Ysidro Mountains rise to a height of over one vertical mile. Slashing back from the edge of this escarpment are a number of beautiful canyon systems containing palms, sycamores, cottonwoods and other riparian vegetation. Best-known of these is Borrego Palm Canyon, first set aside as a park in the early 1930s. This was the small nucleus that eventually grew to encompass 600,000 acres—the Anza-Borrego Desert State Park. Today, tens of thousands of people every year hike up Borrego Palm Canyon to view the palms.

Borrego Palm Canyon may be the largest and most beautiful, but the other, less popular canyons nearby are worth visiting too—especially if crowds turn you off. Most of the hikes below start from either the state park Visitor Center or Borrego Palm Canyon Campground. The others begin along Montezuma Highway, no more than a few miles away.

A stop at the Visitor Center is highly recommended. Aside from the excellent interpretive displays, you can experience an audio-visual show that will surely whet your appetite for exploring the Anza-Borrego Desert region. During the springtime bloom, the Visitor Center can be jam-packed, so try to be there either at opening time, 9 a.m., or near closing time, 5 p.m.

Borrego Palm Canyon Campground is a good base camp for day-hiking the San Ysidro Mountains area, but be aware that camping reservations must be made weeks in advance during the busy winter and early spring seasons.

Trip 1: Borrego Palm Canyon Nature Trail

	Distance	3 miles
	Total Elevation Gain/Loss	450'/450'
	Hiking Time	1½ hours
	Optional Map	USGS 7.5-min *Borrego Palm Canyon*
	Best Times	October through May
	Agency	ABDSP
	Difficulty	*

In the first mile, there's nothing but sun-blasted vegetation, either thorny or low and prostrate. As you round a bend, you suddenly catch sight of a patch of iridescent green cradled in the yawning mouth of the canyon ahead. Hundreds of noble palms stand there, each holding high a crown of feathery, fan-shaped fronds. Water splashes over boulders and gathers in pools, delighting all the senses. It's enough to make anyone as yet unimpressed with the desert an instant convert to the ranks of "desert rats"!

You can learn more about the Colorado Desert flora on this trail than anywhere else in the park. Be sure to pick up the interpretive leaflet at the Visitor Center, or upon entering Borrego Palm Canyon Campground. You begin hiking at the west end of the campground, where a special trailhead parking area has been estab-

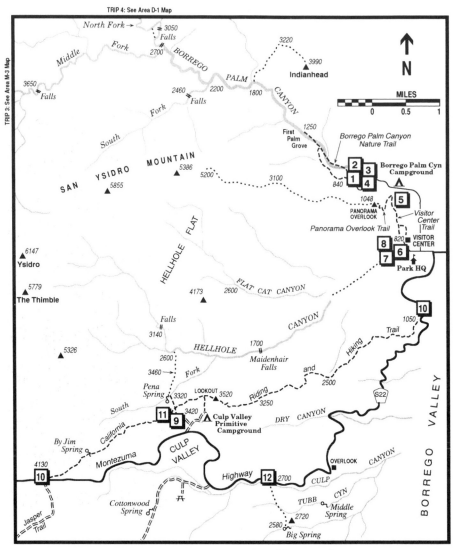

Area D-2: San Ysidro Mountains

lished. A pond holding transplanted desert pupfish is nearby. The trail crosses the seasonal stream, and starts winding up the rocky alluvial fan toward the canyon's mouth. Along the lower part of the trail are various cacti, mesquite and catclaw (with the parasitic desert mistletoe), indigo bush, desert lavender, creosote bush, brittlebush, ocotillo, desert-willow, chuparosa,

and sage. These may look drab most of the year, but they can really light up in a rainbow of colors by March or April of a wet year.

Soon after the palms first become visible, the trail enters the portals of the canyon. Desert-varnished rock walls soar 3000 feet up on both sides. After a second stream crossing, the trail goes up a series of steps hewn in the rock, passes a gauging station and a waterfall, crosses the stream once again, and enters the shade of the palms.

The palms are of one variety, *Washingtonia filifera*, the only palm indigenous to California. Although they are generally well-adapted to wildfire, several blackened and headless trunks in this grove show that some have failed to survive periodic fires. A few alders and sycamores struggle for light among the massive, straight trunks of the palms.

The trail terminates at a point just below a small waterfall and pool at the upper end of the palm grove, 1.5 miles from the trailhead. On the return leg, you can try the alternate trail that winds along the upper edge of the alluvial fan. Here you can study how plants are stratified according to habitat. Higher on the slope, less water is absorbed by the soil, so the drought-tolerant ocotillo dominates.

The so-called first grove at 1.5 miles is the starting point for boulder-hopping journeys of any length into the remote recesses of upper Borrego Palm Canyon. Sturdy footwear and long pants are recommended for any such forays, as you'll be brushing past poison oak and spiny vegetation, and scrambling over potentially ankle-busting terrain.

One such extended trip could take you into the South Fork, wherein lies a 30' stair-step waterfall. At 3.0 miles (from the campground trailhead) and 2040' elevation, you'll find several flat areas above the canyon stream suitable for trail camping. At 3.3 miles, the South Fork branches obviously to the south-west, away from the main Middle Fork. After floundering around amid thorny mesquite and squishing through the swamp-like canyon bottom, it's possible to reach, at 3.7 miles, the base of the South Fork waterfall.

Upper canyon treks like this (and Trips 2, 3 and 4 below) are not to be taken lightly. The farther you venture up the canyon, the more rugged the terrain becomes and the more remote you are from any kind of help.

Fan palms in Borrego Palm Canyon

Trip 2: Indianhead Mountain

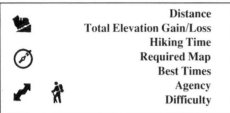

	Distance	7 miles round trip
	Total Elevation Gain/Loss	3200'/3200'
	Hiking Time	7 hours (round trip)
	Required Map	USGS 7.5-min *Borrego Palm Canyon*
	Best Times	November through April
	Agency	ABDSP
	Difficulty	****

The north wall of Borrego Palm Canyon culminates in a spectacular, jagged promontory known as Indianhead. This is a conspicuous landmark seen and admired from most locations in Borrego Valley, and one of the few named summits in the San Ysidro Mountains. Map makers, it seems, haven't bothered to measure or estimate its height—its elevation is not recorded on topographic maps.

There are many ways to climb Indianhead, nearly all involving very steep ascents from the desert floor. My favorite route (detailed here) is somewhat longer, but safer. This can be a challenging day hike, or involve a night's stay in Borrego Palm Canyon. With a base camp established well up in the canyon, you'll have the opportunity to do the climb in the early morning, when the air is clearest and the temperature moderate.

Begin as in Trip 1 above. Beyond the first grove (1.5 miles), but before the first major bend in the canyon (to the north), you'll scramble over some large, light-colored granitic boulders, soon picking up a fair trail on the south side of the creek. Mesquite, catclaw, willow, and desert-willow crowd in along the banks. Palm trees resume as you round the second bend (1.8 miles). Near this point there's a change in the exposed rock: the granitic rock is abruptly replaced by tan- and orange-tinted schist and gneiss. In several places, the creek flows over colorful slabs of this rock and collects in small pools shaded by palms both young and old. Small campsites are fairly abundant in the wider parts of the canyon, especially on the north side.

You reach the turnoff point for Indianhead at 2.5 miles (1800'), where a tributary canyon comes in from the north. Climb northeast straight up the ridge just east of this tributary.

After about 0.7 mile, you'll reach a 3220' saddle northwest of Indianhead. From here make your way southeast around huge boulders and over slab rock to reach the highest point on Indianhead's flat summit.

Now the entire sweep of the San Ysidro Mountains lies before you. In the north, beyond lesser ranges, the snow-capped San Jacinto Mountains float like a mirage. To obtain the best view of the bottom of Borrego Palm Canyon, scramble about 0.1 mile south of the high point, and work your way out to a jagged outcrop. You can sit there, legs dangling, and look almost straight down upon the crowns of hundreds of palms.

Ocotillo blossoms

Trip 3: Middle Fork Borrego Palm Canyon Traverse

![]	**Distance**	10 miles
	Total Elevation Gain/Loss	0'/4100'
	Hiking Time	12 hours
	Required Map	USGS 7.5-min *Hot Springs Mtn.*, *Borrego Palm Canyon*
	Best Times	November through April
	Agency	LCIR, ABDSP
	Difficulty	*****

What dyed-in-the-wool hiker has hiked lower Borrego Palm Canyon and hasn't wondered what it would be like to explore the canyon in its entirety? Well, here's your chance. You'll experience Palm Canyon's main (middle) fork from top to bottom. But be forewarned: mile after mile of slippery rock, small waterfalls, and thickets of brush and alder will necessitate a very slow, painstaking, and difficult descent. Needless to say, this is for expert hikers only. Long pants and sturdy boots are essential. Also take along a 30' piece of cord to use for lowering your pack down one or more of the falls. Middle Fork is a perennial stream with fair-to-good water quality, depending upon the amount of grazing upstream on the Los Coyotes Indian Reservation.

You begin in the valley at the head of the Middle Fork on the Los Coyotes reservation (see the introductory text for Area M-3, and Trip 2 within that section for details on entry into the reservation). Walk southeast on a dirt road past some old buildings and a cemetery at San Ignacio (don't linger around these private sites). The pastoral valley on the right, lined with huge cottonwoods, is used for cattle grazing. Continue down the road under a canopy of live oaks, until you reach the point (1.3 miles) where the road swings south—away from the creek. You have two choices: leave the road to follow the creekbed to a confluence at 4070 feet, or stay on the road south about 0.2 mile, then drop southeast into a western tributary of Middle Fork and go down it to the confluence. The two

Upper Middle Fork, Borrego Palm Canyon

alternatives are of equal length, and both involve some serious bushwhacking and awkward detours around waterfalls. Either way, this is the most difficult and hazardous stretch of the trip.

Below the confluence of the western tributary (2.0 miles, 4050') you enter a botanical transition zone of high-desert and mountain vegetation. The slopes are covered with ribbonwood, scrub oak, mountain mahogany, manzanita, chamise, ceanothus, and sugar bush. A few pinyon pines dot the north-facing slopes, wherever moisture can stay in the soil for long periods of time. In a narrow band along the stream, willows and cottonwoods thrive, along with moisture-loving shrubs and herbs such as wild rose, nettles, miner's lettuce, cattails, and wild peony.

The creek meanders on a gentle gradient for a mile below the confluence, with grassy campsites along the inner banks. You're now passing from a zone containing the common Cretaceous granitic rocks that make up the core of the Peninsular Ranges, to an area with older (pre-Cretaceous) granitic and metamorphic rocks exposed. You'll walk past colorful outcrops of orange-banded gneiss and other metamorphic rocks in the next 6 miles or so.

At 3.0 miles (3650'), the water shoots over

a 15' vertical fall. Below this the creek drops steeply through a narrow gorge. Alder trees appear, and they conspire with the willows to impede your progress. It's easiest to walk right down the middle of the creek most of the time, underneath the tangle of tree limbs. Cottonwoods appear at about 3.8 miles (3300').

At 5.3 miles (2900'), just above the first palm tree, an easy traverse north over a ridge into the North Fork is possible. From here to the confluence of North Fork (5.7 miles, 2700'), both the creek and banks in Middle Fork are overgrown by a junglelike growth of vines that act like trip wires.

Below the confluence, the canyon becomes more open and less thickly vegetated. Slippery, water-polished rock is now the biggest difficulty. This can be a technically demanding and slow stretch during high water. At about 6.2 miles (2450') you'll traverse around two sets of falls.

By the time you reach the confluence of the South Fork (6.7 miles, 2200'), the sparser vegetation of the low desert has begun to appear on the canyon walls, and palms line the canyon in greater numbers. The going gets progressively easier now (see Trips 1 and 2 above for more details).

At 8.5 miles (1300') you come upon the

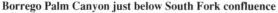

Borrego Palm Canyon just below South Fork confluence

lowest grove of palms, where you pick up the Borrego Palm Canyon Nature Trail. Curiosity satisfied, you can saunter down this "tourist trail," smug in the knowledge that you, unlike the untold thousands who only glimpse the beauty of the canyon, have truly seen it all.

Trip 4: Indian Canyon/Borrego Palm Canyon Traverse

Distance	11 miles
Total Elevation Gain/Loss	3100'/3100'
Hiking Time	13 hours
Required Map	USGS 7.5-min *Borrego Palm Canyon*
Best Times	November through April
Agency	ABDSP
Difficulty	*****

This is a grand tour of one of Anza-Borrego's most remote, rugged, and beautiful areas. In the midsection of this trip, you'll pass through a pristine wilderness where the tracks of a mountain lion are far more common than the impressions of a lug-soled boot.

The trip is best done as an ambitious (strenuous) two-day backpack. Lightly loaded internal-frame packs are recommended for ease of movement. A light rope will come in handy for lowering packs in a few places. Water may be scarce: plan on the possibility of a dry camp.

Transportation logistics are a bit problematical. The drive between the start and end points is 15 miles, mostly on the rugged jeep road through Coyote Canyon. If your vehicle won't make it past Lower Willows, you'll have to walk at least four extra miles across Collins Valley.

Mileages in this description start from the Cougar Canyon trailhead (see directions in Area D-1, Trip 4). Follow the path south past Cougar Canyon and toward the wide mouth of Indian Canyon. At 1.3 miles, Indian Canyon bends right (southwest) and narrows. You pass a palm-studded bowl on the west side—Valley of the Thousand Springs—and an old tin mine near the mouth of Deering Canyon (2.0 miles).

By now the path has faded almost to insignificance. Follow the brush-choked streambed as it curves around in a gooseneck, and continue south to the point where two tributaries join from the southeast. Fill your water bottles here for a possible long, dry stretch ahead.

Climb steeply south up the ridge dividing the upper of the two tributaries from the main Indian Canyon. This ridge continues steadily uphill for 2000 vertical feet, with only moderate brush to contend with and good footing all the way. As you climb, hidden palms become visible in the tributary below, and the distant view expands to encompass Collins Valley and most of Coyote Canyon.

When the ridge tops out, traverse south and then climb slightly to a saddle (4.0 miles) just northwest of peak 4780. The remaining 7 miles to the mouth of Borrego Palm Canyon are all downhill, but more difficult than the 4 miles you've just covered.

Continue going south: descend obliquely down a brushy slope, and drop into the North Fork of Borrego Palm Canyon. The floor of the canyon is delightfully shaded by a dense growth of ribbonwood and scrub oak, which in places forms a canopy over the narrow, rocky bed.

After 0.3 mile in the canyon, you'll come to the top of a series of waterfalls (4150'). On the left (north) side, look for morteros and metates on several orange-colored metamorphic rock slabs. There are at least 45 of these, including two that are worn completely through the thinnest slab. This is one of the most impressive—and remote—old Indian milling sites in the county. Access into this area was by way of a trail, now almost completely overgrown, west to San Ignacio on the Los Coyotes Indian Reservation. The remains of this trail, which is still shown on the *Borrego Palm Canyon* topo map, are occasionally used by hikers.

Bypass the waterfalls and continue down the gravel-and-bedrock floor of the canyon. After passing a major fork leading north toward Palm Mesa (no palms are there), the canyon trends south. There are several small (usually dry) falls to descend ahead. Flat deposits of sand become more abundant—but wait till you reach a wide, level patch of sand at about 3400 feet if you're looking for a good campsite.

At 3150' elevation, you must leave the canyon bottom and climb south up and over a low saddle. From the top of the saddle you descend 200 feet over a brush- and agave-strewn slope to return to the canyon bottom. This maneuver bypasses a gooseneck containing a 50' dry fall.

For the next 0.3 mile, the canyon floor is mostly bedrock, with potholes that may contain water. Just before the confluence of the Middle Fork of Borrego Palm Canyon, there's another set of dry falls—the "crux" of this challenging trip. You'll have to negotiate a route over the loose metamorphic slabs on the nose between the two forks. (A reasonable alternative is to backtrack about 0.1 mile, climb up and over the ridge to the west, and drop into Middle Fork at a point 0.5 mile above the confluence.)

Your water problems, if any, are solved now (assuming you have the means to purify the stream water), because the Middle Fork runs year round. See Trips 1, 2 and 3 above for the details on the last 4.3 miles down the canyon to Borrego Palm Canyon Campground.

Trip 5: Panorama Overlook

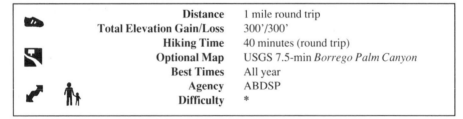

Distance	1 mile round trip
Total Elevation Gain/Loss	300'/300'
Hiking Time	40 minutes (round trip)
Optional Map	USGS 7.5-min *Borrego Palm Canyon*
Best Times	All year
Agency	ABDSP
Difficulty	*

Starting near campsite 71 in Borrego Palm Canyon Campground, this well-used trail climbs sharply up one of the ridge spurs of San Ysidro Mountain, offering a superb vista of Borrego Valley and its spectacular backdrop of mountains. The flat area at the top of the trail is called Panorama Overlook (or Panorama Outlook on some maps). Any map of the Anza-Borrego region will help you identify the major topographical features visible along the horizon from northeast through the south: Coyote Mountain and the distant Santa Rosa Mountains; Fonts Point and the Borrego Badlands; Pinyon Ridge and a slice of the Vallecito Mountains. Facing west, you must crane your neck to follow the continuation of the rocky ridge you're standing upon. This culminates about 4000 feet higher, on the crest of San Ysidro Mountain (Trip 6 below gives further details if you want to climb higher).

Panorama Overlook is an excellent spot to witness the sunrise on the crisp mornings of fall and winter. Late afternoons are nice too: you can watch the mountain shadows slowly stretch across Borrego Valley as the sun sinks unseen.

This trail is one of the few in Anza-Borrego short enough for summer hiking. Summer afternoon thundershowers over the desert floor can be interesting to watch from here, but only if they're a safe distance away.

Trip 6: San Ysidro Mountain

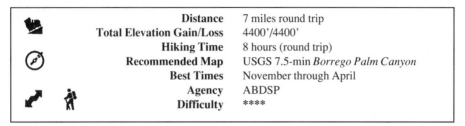

Distance	7 miles round trip
Total Elevation Gain/Loss	4400'/4400'
Hiking Time	8 hours (round trip)
Recommended Map	USGS 7.5-min *Borrego Palm Canyon*
Best Times	November through April
Agency	ABDSP
Difficulty	****

The eastern brow of San Ysidro Mountain overlooks Borrego Valley from an elevation of nearly one mile. Here, in the cool pinyon-pine-and-juniper belt, you can experience a startling pseudo-aerial perspective of Anza-Borrego quite unlike that seen from any other land-based vantage point.

On this hike horizontal distance is trivial and vertical gain is everything. It's a taxing but immensely satisfying journey. Every step upward takes you closer to the heavens, and farther from the civilized world. The roads, dwellings, and windbreak-bordered fields etched on the floor of Borrego Valley always remain visible through the clear desert air, but they become more and more toylike and abstract—as if viewed from space—as you climb.

This is a tough hike, no matter how you do it. The gradient at times approaches 3000 feet of gain per mile of horizontal distance, often over a rugged landscape of weathered granitic boulders. No water is available anywhere along the route. Dayhikers should allow a full dawn-to-dusk day for the round trip: backpackers need almost this much time for the ascent alone—especially in view of the amount of water that must be carried. Navigation is easy in the uphill direction, but a topo map and compass are useful for reference during the return leg, because it's possible to stray off the main ridge.

A convenient place to begin this trip, especially if you are backpacking, is the Visitor Center, where free parking is available. From the parking lot you can clearly see the route ahead. The transparent desert air compresses distance and height, and an illusion of perspective makes it appear as if the truck-sized boulders high on the ridge were really much

smaller. The effort required to reach the top seems—well—trivial.

Head directly across the desert floor toward the spur ridge to the northeast 0.5 mile away (or use the Visitor Center Trail to angle over in that direction). Pick up the switchbacks of the Panorama Overlook Trail, then continue beyond the overlook using the faint trail up the ridge. This trail peters out rather quickly.

You encounter a wide range range of desert vegetation as you climb; first, the creosote bush/brittlebush/ocotillo/cactus community typical of the lower desert alluvial fans and slopes; then agave and widely scattered shrubs like sugarbush, scrub oak, and juniper; and finally pinyon pine.

Beyond Panorama Overlook, you're on granitic rock or decomposed granite (sandy soil) throughout. Above a small flat on the ridge at 3100 feet, the slope becomes distinctly steeper. Large monoliths and stiff vegetation impede progress.

After topping out at 5200 feet, you'll find some flat campsites nearby. It was here that I had a memorable experience: watching an orange-tinted full moon rise over the Salton Sea, awash in the purple glow of evening twilight.

Further exploration along the undulating ridgeline of San Ysidro Mountain is possible, but slow and difficult due to thick brush and boulders. To return the easy way, simply retrace your steps back down the ridge. More difficult return routes include those across Hellhole Flat and down either Flat Cat or Hellhole canyons.

Trip 7: Flat Cat Canyon

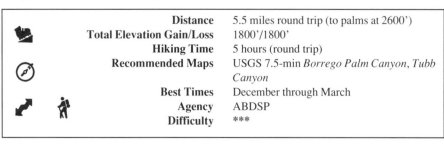

Distance	5.5 miles round trip (to palms at 2600')
Total Elevation Gain/Loss	1800'/1800'
Hiking Time	5 hours (round trip)
Recommended Maps	USGS 7.5-min *Borrego Palm Canyon*, *Tubb Canyon*
Best Times	December through March
Agency	ABDSP
Difficulty	***

Flat Cat Canyon is the curious name given to a rugged gorge just north of lower Hellhole Canyon. Anza-Borrego rangers found a dead bobcat (presumably *very* dead) in this canyon, and followed the honorable Western tradition of assigning colorful names to "colorful" places. As viewed from the alluvial fan below, Flat Cat Canyon looks like a boulder-choked ravine, seemingly unpromising. But its upper reaches hold a surprise or two.

Wear long pants and sturdy shoes; the canyon presents some serious bushwhacking and scrambling challenges. Begin at the Anza-Borrego Desert State Park Visitor Center, where parking (day and overnight) is available. Note the tall flagpole here. The Visitor Center is largely underground, and a sighting of this flagpole will be the best way to find your car on the return leg of the hike.

From the Visitor Center parking lot, head straight for the mouth of Hellhole Canyon, the big canyon to the southwest. Don't enter Hellhole Canyon. Instead, at 1.4 miles from the Visitor Center, bear right (west) and ascend Flat Cat Canyon.

Climb for about a mile, gaining about 1000 feet. The sandy wash at the bottom of the canyon provides smooth going except when choked with vegetation—notably thorny desert apricot and catclaw bushes. Marginal trails of animals and occasional hikers thread the canyon walls, providing serviceable alternate routes. Flat Cat Canyon is hewn from granitic rock: note the contrast between the dark, desert-varnished rock high on the canyon walls, and the whitish, flood-scoured boulders on the lower slopes.

At 2100' elevation, your ears will discover a most welcome sound—the trickle of water. A little above this, you come upon a place where the water slides over a 20' precipice. Two hundred feet higher, you top a small rise and discover—palms!

Below the first group of palms is a flat little terrace suitable as a campsite for four or five people. Just above these palms, on the north side of the canyon, be sure to look for an unusual example of exfoliation. Frost wedging and other erosive forces have carved the rock on the canyon wall into concentric layers, resembling those of an onion. Higher still, where the canyon evenly divides (2600'), is the biggest grove—about two dozen palms.

Young antelope ground squirrel

Trip 8: Lower Hellhole Canyon

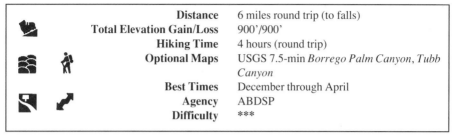

Distance	6 miles round trip (to falls)
Total Elevation Gain/Loss	900'/900'
Hiking Time	4 hours (round trip)
Optional Maps	USGS 7.5-min *Borrego Palm Canyon*, *Tubb Canyon*
Best Times	December through April
Agency	ABDSP
Difficulty	***

In the midst of what is regarded as one of America's hottest and driest deserts, it seems a bit surprising to find a place where mosses, ferns, sycamores, and cottonwoods flourish around a sparkling waterfall. Maidenhair Falls is such a place, and it lies just 3 miles (a couple of hours away by foot) from the Anza-Borrego Desert State Park Visitor Center.

From the lot, head straight across the alluvial fan toward the mouth of the big canyon to the southwest—Hellhole Canyon. The sandy surface of the fan supports a variety of vegetation, stratified according to elevation. Indigo bush, chuparosa, cheesebush, burroweed, creosote bush, desert lavender, and buckhorn cholla are the common plant species of the lower fan. They're largely replaced by jojoba, brittlebush, ocotillo, and teddy-bear cholla on the upper fan. Everywhere, jackrabbits flit among the bushes, startled by your approach.

In a wet year you may encounter the first water half a mile or more down the fan from the canyon's mouth. Stay generally left of the watercourse (or dry wash) until the south slope pinches in so tightly that you have to move to the right (north) side of the canyon. Generally, you'll want to stay away from the boulder-filled and vegetation-choked canyon bottom. Sooner or later you'll get involved in difficult scrambles over large boulders and fallen trees, and unpleasant encounters with wicked catclaw thorns. The dead snags and fallen trees in your path are a result of a 1975 wildfire that burned the entire Hellhole Canyon drainage. Some sycamores and cottonwoods have returned since then.

Palms, too, are present in the canyon bottom, but sparsely distributed. About 200 yards past the densest cluster of palms, the canyon walls pinch in tight. Tucked away in a corner of the canyon bottom—hard to find—you'll discover the grotto containing Maidenhair Falls. The falls plunge about 25 feet into a shallow pool. Tiers of maidenhair fern adorn the grotto, and sopping wet mosses cover the places the ferns don't.

Further travel up-canyon from Maidenhair Falls involves constant bushwhacking—slow going with a backpack. For an easier way into the upper reaches of Hellhole Canyon, see Trip 11 below.

Ocotillo on alluvial fan

Trip 9: Culp Valley Loop

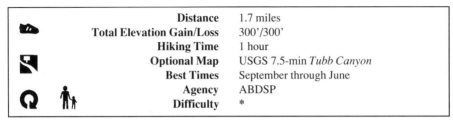

Distance	1.7 miles
Total Elevation Gain/Loss	300'/300'
Hiking Time	1 hour
Optional Map	USGS 7.5-min *Tubb Canyon*
Best Times	September through June
Agency	ABDSP
Difficulty	*

While the low desert swelters, the temperature hovers in a more moderate register at Culp Valley, 3000 feet higher. This is the only designated camping area in Anza-Borrego where the heat on the cooler days of May, June or September is quite bearable. July and August daytime temperatures are probably too warm for most people's tastes—typically the 90s and 100s.

Stark, gray boulders are piled up all around the floor of Culp Valley, sharply etching the horizon. The west wind blows capriciously, often whistling eerily through the rocks. Nearby, out of sight from the valley, is a hillside spring surrounded by an oasis of green grass and small trees. It's this kind of contrast that makes hiking here especially rewarding.

To reach the starting point, drive to mile 9.2 on Montezuma Highway (2.8 miles east of the highway summit near Ranchita; 9.4 miles west of Borrego Springs) and turn north on the unpaved entrance road to Culp Valley Primitive Camp. The campground is truly no frills—just a few nooks and crannies where you can park your car overnight. Our little hike can start from the end of the road that forks west toward Pena Spring.

From the roadend, walk downhill on the remnants of a jeep road that used to lead to Pena Spring. After 0.3 mile, you'll reach a thicket of large sugarbush shrubs. Go west through shoulder-high yerba santa and other shrubby vegetation to the spring, which lies amid a soggy

Split Rock near Culp Valley vista point

hillside meadow. Yerba mansa flowers poke up through the grass blades where the ground is saturated. Rabbits, coyotes, and other animals partake of the clear, cold water, which emerges from a small, raised pipe.

After visiting the spring, backtrack up the road 0.2 mile to the intersection of the California Riding and Hiking Trail, marked by a small wooden post. Go east on this, climbing up, then along, a rather flat-topped ridge that offers good views of Culp Valley, Pinyon Ridge and San Ysidro Mountain, and tantalizing glimpses of the big gorge to the north—Hellhole Canyon. Here you'll find typical high-desert vegetation mixed with common chaparral: juniper, catclaw, desert apricot, various cacti, buckwheat, Mojave and Lord's Candle yucca, and white sage.

After 0.5 mile on the CRHT, you'll come to the intersection of a trail going down to the campground, 0.3 mile south. About 100 feet north of this point are some rock outcrops offering a great view of the Hellhole Canyon gorge, Borrego Valley, and the great wall of mountains beyond the valley. The pinyon-fringed, flattish summit of Rabbit Peak is conspicuous as the highest point visible on the long crest of the Santa Rosa Mountains.

East another 0.2 mile on the CRHT is the marked Vista Point ("Lookout" on some maps), offering a more panoramic but somewhat less spectacular view than you saw earlier. Northwest down the slope from the Lookout Point is a huge, weathered boulder split cleanly down the middle; it's fun to squeeze through the slot, or "chimney," up to the top.

Lastly, backtrack a little and follow the trail toward the campground, and dirt roads over to your parked car.

Trip 10: California Riding and Hiking Trail

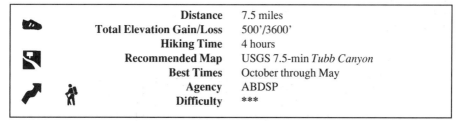

	Distance	7.5 miles
	Total Elevation Gain/Loss	500'/3600'
	Hiking Time	4 hours
	Recommended Map	USGS 7.5-min *Tubb Canyon*
	Best Times	October through May
	Agency	ABDSP
	Difficulty	***

This delightful one-way (preferably downhill) route has a long and varied history. Originally a well-beaten Indian trail, it was used for many decades by cattlemen moving herds from the Mesa Grande area near Lake Henshaw to winter and spring grazing grounds at the mouths of Hellhole Canyon and Borrego Palm Canyon. After World War II the trail became a branch of the California Riding and Hiking Trail. Today, while the statewide CRHT has largely fallen into disrepair, this particular desert segment continues to be frequently used (if not maintained much).

Car shuttling is easy for this trip, as both ends of the trail intersect the same road—Montezuma Highway. The top of the trail is at mile 6.8, across the highway from the junction of the signed Jasper Trail. The bottom end is at mile 16.0, about a mile up from the edge of Borrego Valley. The road shoulder is narrow at the bottom end, precluding parking, but there's a turnout 0.2 mile north.

Topside, pick up the trail, marked by faded, yellow-topped posts, and follow it northeast over a low saddle. The vegetation here is mostly common chaparral—mountain mahogany, chamise, sugarbush, and scrub oak—but there are some high desert plants too, such as juniper, desert apricot, buckhorn cholla cactus, and beavertail cactus. After descending slightly to By Jim Spring, you'll find a trickle of water (in winter and spring) and the ruins of pipes and a tank. The trail continues on or close to a ridgeline for the next mile.

At about 2.0 miles the trail passes just below peak 4068, and a spectacular view of Culp Valley and the distant Borrego Valley opens up. From there the trail descends sharply, crosses the trail to Pena Spring (which offers the only dependable water near the route), and climbs toward the signed Vista Point, 3.5 miles.

From there on, the trail sticks mostly to the top of the ridge dividing Hellhole Canyon and Dry Canyon. You pass some flat, sandy areas—possible campsites—at 4.2 miles (3250'). Beyond, the trail descends sharply again, tend-ing to the left (north) side of the ridge, with good views across Hellhole Canyon and out over Borrego Valley. At 5.5 miles (2500') you skirt a ravine that really comes alive with wildflowers in the early spring.

Near the bottom of the trail, the vegetation grades into that of the low desert: ocotillo, creosote bush, and brittlebush. When in full bloom during March or April, the brittlebush spreads great patches of yellow color across the stony slopes.

Trip 11: Upper Hellhole Canyon

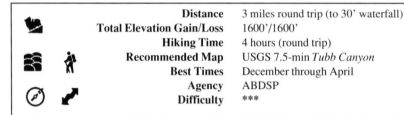

Distance	3 miles round trip (to 30' waterfall)
Total Elevation Gain/Loss	1600'/1600'
Hiking Time	4 hours (round trip)
Recommended Map	USGS 7.5-min *Tubb Canyon*
Best Times	December through April
Agency	ABDSP
Difficulty	***

The easiest entry into the upper reaches of Hellhole Canyon is not by simply going up from the mouth of the canyon past Maidenhair Falls. Nor is it by descending the South Fork below Pena Spring, though this is an interesting and challenging hike in its own right. Rather, it is by dropping down the ridge to the north of Pena Spring. This is a steep and at times slippery descent, but one accomplished in a fraction of the time required on the other routes. In this description, I will describe the way to a 30' waterfall in a northern tributary of Hellhole Canyon.

Begin this hike at the Pena Spring trailhead, as in Trip 9 above. Hike down to the spring first, then go north cross-country 0.4 mile, gaining almost 200 feet, to reach a flat part of the ridgeline overlooking Hellhole Canyon. Now head straight down (north) toward a large cottonwood tree in the canyon bottom ahead. In just over 0.2 mile of horizontal distance on the map, you lose 800 feet. If you choose your route carefully, the footing is quite stable on dirt and sparse grass, and over boulders. Be aware of the possibility of dislodging rocks, especially if traveling with others. Proceed very carefully if carrying a heavy backpack. In wetter years the stream down in the bottom carries water the whole year round.

Travel along the Hellhole Canyon bottom is very difficult due to vines, boulders, and fallen trees. About 100 yards downstream from the cottonwood tree, the canyon bends and widens, offering good camping possibilities. The tributary with the waterfall, however, lies upstream about 100 yards.

Go up the bottom of the tributary about 150 yards, passing several mini-waterfalls, until forced by dense vegetation to gain the slope on the right (east) side. Traverse for about 300 yards on the rocky slope until you can drop again into the canyon bottom at a point close to a multilevel cascade. Then make your way over large boulders and slabs to a grotto containing the 30' fall. The water shoots over in a thin stream, perfect for a shower on a warm day—but be careful of slippery rocks.

Further exploration beyond the waterfall is problematical if you remain in the canyon, but relatively easy if you gain the slopes and ridgelines. Hellhole Flat is one possible destination. So too are The Thimble (5779') and the highest summit on San Ysidro Mountain (6147').

Until recently, a herd of feral cattle flourished in the upper reaches of Hellhole Canyon and its tributaries. Because these cattle were competing for forage with the bighorn sheep and other native wildlife, many attempts were made to remove them—all unsuccessful until 1987 when funds were made available for their evacuation by helicopter. This gives a modern dimension to the same predicament faced by the old-time cattlemen around the turn of the century: so many strays wandered into this canyon that it became known as a "hellish" place from which to retrieve cattle—hence the name "Hellhole."

Trip 12: Tubb Canyon

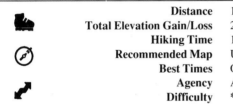

Distance	1.5 miles round trip	
Total Elevation Gain/Loss	200'/200'	
Hiking Time	1 hour (round trip)	
Recommended Map	USGS 7.5-min *Tubb Canyon*	
Best Times	October through May	
Agency	ABDSP	
Difficulty	*	

Big Spring in a tributary of Tubb Canyon ("Tub" Canyon on some maps) is one of the more reliable water producers in the Anza-Borrego Desert. As such, it is an important watering hole for local wildlife. Tracks on the sandy pathways leading to the spring show evidence of visits by coyotes, mountain lions, and bighorn sheep.

Unmarked on the state park map, and unknown to most park visitors, this isolated spring is actually very easy to reach on foot. The best place to begin is the small parking turnout on the north side of Montezuma Grade (Highway S-22) at mile 11.2. Walk due south across 400 yards of flat terrain, and cross over a gentle saddle. At this point you'll pick up a faint wildlife trail that descends into a sandy wash—the head of Tubb

Canyon. After about 200 yards downstream the trail leaves this wash and passes over a low saddle to the south. Big Spring lies beyond, in the bottom of Tubb Canyon's south branch.

At the spring, the water gushes through tall thickets of seepwillow and thorny tangles of catclaw and mesquite—so it's hard to reach the water with one's hide intact. A few small willows and cottonwoods raise their crowns above it all. Enhancing the scene is the massive presence of Pinyon Ridge, rising to the south.

Before going back to the highway, climb the small hill (2720') east of the saddle you just passed over. This is one of the panoramic viewing sites used every summer by volunteers in the Anza-Borrego Desert bighorn-sheep-count program.

Area D-3: Coyote Mountain/ Rockhouse Canyon

The Anza-Borrego Desert State Park extends over such a large area that duplication of place names is common. For example, the Rockhouse Canyon and Coyote Mountain in the north sector of the park are distinct from the Rockhouse Canyon (near Bow Willow) and the Coyote Mountains (near Ocotillo) in the south sector.

The northern Coyote Mountain is a barren, brownish ridge separating lower Coyote Canyon from Clark Valley and Clark (dry) Lake. Geologically, it is a spur of the Santa Rosa Mountains which has drifted away from the main crest by fault action. Coyote Mountain and its extension of lower hills to the northwest form a wedge between the San Jacinto Fault in Clark Valley and the Coyote Creek Fault in Coyote Canyon.

Rockhouse Canyon drains a large alluvial basin at the foot of the Santa Rosa Mountains. It meanders southwest between precipitous walls, then strikes a course southeast along the San Jacinto Fault. Clark Valley lies at the mouth of Rockhouse Canyon.

Trips 2, 4 and 5 below start along the only vehicle route penetrating Rockhouse Canyon. Standard passenger cars, if driven carefully, can usually maneuver up about 9 miles of this progressively more primitive unpaved road. Here's how to get to the starting points of these trips:

At mile 26.7 on Borrego-Salton Seaway (Highway S-22), just east of Pegleg Monument, turn north on Clark's Well Road. Pavement soon ends. Bear right, avoiding the spur road on the left to a highway-maintenance gravel pit. After 1.5 miles (from S-22), the road divides

again. Take the left fork, the Rockhouse Truck Trail. In a short while it skirts the west edge of Clark Lake, which is where Trip 2 starts. (After heavy rains, a short section of the road ahead can become muddy and impassable.) Next, the road swings around a spur of Coyote Mountain, and continues toward the mouth of Rockhouse Canyon. At 9.2 miles from S-22, you come to the junction of jeep roads into Butler and Rockhouse canyons—starting point for Trips 4 and 5. Only high-clearance vehicles are suitable for further travel up either canyon.

Clark Valley from Coyote Mountain

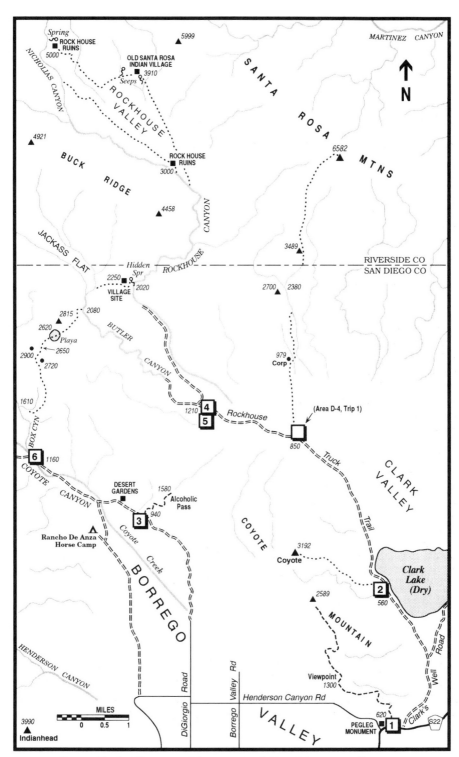

Area D-3: Coyote Mountain / Rockhouse Canyon

Trip 1: Coyote Mountain—South Spur

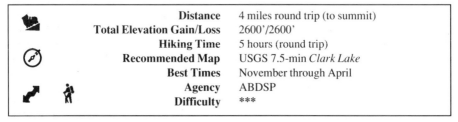

	Distance	4 miles round trip (to viewpoint)
	Total Elevation Gain/Loss	750'/750'
	Hiking Time	2 hours (round trip)
	Optional Map	USGS 7.5-min *Clark Lake*
	Best Times	November through April
	Agency	ABDSP
	Difficulty	**

A spectacular view of upper Borrego Valley—with its patchwork of tamarisk windbreaks, fields, citrus orchards, and palm nurseries—is the highlight of this hike. You begin at Pegleg Monument, nestled against the south spur of Coyote Mountain, and climb steadily on an old jeep road for two miles until you reach a point on the steep southwest escarpment offering the best view.

The Monument, 7 miles northeast of Borrego Springs on Highway S-22, commemorates Pegleg Smith, a prospector and spinner of tall tales, and his famous lost gold. Adding stones to the big rock pile here, it is said, brings luck to the treasure hunter.

Vegetation along the way is sparse—mostly ocotillo, creosote bush, and brittlebush. When in bloom in the early spring, however, the brittlebush can create splashes of yellow color up and down the hillsides and ravines.

Beyond the viewpoint at 2.0 miles, the road continues winding up along ridges and through hidden valleys for another 2.5 miles until it fades out completely near peak 2589. The summit of Coyote Mountain (3192') lies another mile north. The route outlined in Trip 2 below is faster and more direct.

Trip 2: Coyote Mountain—East Approach

	Distance	4 miles round trip (to summit)
	Total Elevation Gain/Loss	2600'/2600'
	Hiking Time	5 hours (round trip)
	Recommended Map	USGS 7.5-min *Clark Lake*
	Best Times	November through April
	Agency	ABDSP
	Difficulty	***

According to Coyote Mountain's informal summit register, relatively few people undertake the straightforward but somewhat arduous ascent. Many routes are possible, but most seem to climb the east slope. This is basically a walk-up ascent, though quite steep. Outcrops of solid, desert-varnished rock provide good footing on the lower slopes. Higher up, a veneer of small stones underfoot makes walking a little difficult.

To reach the starting point, drive 3.5 miles north of Highway S-22 on Clark's Well Road and the Rockhouse Truck Trail. Park in a clearing on the left, near the foot of Coyote Mountain.

On foot, simply go straight up the steep slope to the west. Scattered shrubs and succulents—like brittlebush, cholla cactus, agave, and creosote bush—cling tenaciously to soil pockets amid the rocks.

As you climb, a pattern of lines becomes visible on the dry lake bed below, not unlike the famous intaglios of the Nazca Plain in Peru. These include the outlines of an antenna array of the defunct Clark Lake Radio Observatory, and a nearby landing field. Beyond the dry lake, the panorama of the west escarpment of the Santa Rosa Mountains, its rugged ravines, and its classic (from a geologist's view point) alluvial fans, is almost stupefying.

The broad, rounded summit at 3192 feet is topped by a surveyor's marker. The view is entirely panoramic, but it doesn't include much of the valleys below. You must move well away from the summit in order to look down. If you're looking for a place to bed down for the night, some small, possibly windswept campsites can be found 0.2 mile southwest of the summit.

Trip 3: Alcoholic Pass

Distance	2 miles round trip (to pass)
Total Elevation Gain/Loss	650'/650'
Hiking Time	1 ½ hours
Optional Map	USGS 7.5-min Borrego *Palm Canyon*
Best Times	November through April
Agency	ABDSP
Difficulty	**

For centuries Indians used Alcoholic Pass as a convenient short cut between Coyote Canyon and Clark Valley. In time, a well-beaten trail was worn across the precipitous slopes west of the pass. Around the turn of the century, the Clark brothers, early cattlemen who homesteaded in Coyote Canyon, used this trail to transport some primitive well-drilling equipment to the site now known as Clark Well in Clark Valley. Near the top of the pass, the old Indian trail squeezed between two boulders so closely spaced that the burros had to be unpacked before going through. Today, you can still follow the obvious trace of this historic pathway.

The starting point for this hike is along the main Coyote Canyon dirt road, 2.8 miles north of the end of the pavement at DiGiorgio Road. There is a small roadside turnout here, suitable for one or two cars. East of this turnout is a steep ravine leading up toward the pass. The old Indian trail does not ascend this ravine directly, but instead rises on the ridge immediately south of it. You'll find the base of the trail about 150 yards to the right (south) of the mouth of the ravine.

You climb on a somewhat rough and rocky path, gaining altitude quickly. In a few places, foot travel and erosion have worn the bed of the trail to a depth of two feet. Looking behind you to gauge your progress as you climb, you'll be inspired by the ever-widening, almost aerial, view of Coyote Canyon and the surrounding mountains.

In the upper reaches of the pass, the trail levels somewhat and is a bit hard to follow. Just head for the pile of boulders at the top of pass. There you'll catch sight of the massive wall of the Santa Rosa Mountains, topped by the dusky, pinyon-covered summit of Rabbit Peak.

The remainder of the old Alcoholic Pass route goes east along the sandy bed of a wide wash and eventually reaches the desolate floor of Clark Valley. The Rockhouse Truck Trail is 3 miles northeast of the pass; you could arrange for someone to meet you at some point on the truck trail if you wanted to hike one-way from Coyote Canyon to Clark Valley.

Trip 4: Jackass Flat/Butler Canyon

Distance	10 miles
Total Elevation Gain/Loss	1000'/1000'
Hiking Time	6 hours
Recommended Maps	USGS 7.5-min *Clark Lake NE*, *Collins Valley*
Best Times	November through April
Agency	ABDSP
Difficulty	***

A visit to an ancient Cahuilla Indian village site is the highlight on this long loop hike over mostly gentle terrain. Hidden Spring, about halfway around the loop, nearly always has some surface water, but cannot be considered a good source for drinking needs.

From Highway S-22 drive 9.2 miles up Clark's Well Road and the Rockhouse Truck Trail to the junction of roads into Rockhouse and Butler canyons. On foot follow the Rockhouse road north across a low bank and into the broad wash of Rockhouse Canyon. The next 4 miles are somewhat uneventful, though the canyon deepens impressively. The San Jacinto Fault parallels this section of canyon. At about 3 miles, there is a road closure sign. Continue another mile to Hidden Spring, identified by a sign on the left. A small basin holds about two or three gallons of insect-infested water.

From the spring walk 150 feet back down along the canyon wall to a thicket of mesquite trees. A path through the mesquite will guide you to a deeply worn, eroded trail angling south and upward across a 200' high bluff. Just over the top, on the eastern edge of Jackass Flat, are the remains of a Cahuilla Indian village occupied as recently as the late 1800s. You may chance upon some old fire pits, pieces of pottery, and flakes of a metamorphic rock known as wonderstone, which was once used for stone tools. (Remember that you must leave everything in place.)

Now head west about a mile to the head of Butler Canyon. You'll return by following this canyon, assisted by gravity all the way. As the canyon walls narrow, you may notice miniature pine cones lying about. These washed down from pinyon-dotted Buck Ridge, some 3 miles north and about 2000 feet higher. Buck Ridge and other mountains of similar height in the desert were important pinyon-nut-gathering areas for the Cahuilla Indians.

Follow the course of Butler Canyon as it descends gently for 4 miles through a spectacular serpentine gorge carved out of granitic rock. Beyond the mouth of this gorge you'll pick up wheel tracks leading back to your car.

Trip 5: Rockhouse Canyon and Valley

Distance	25 miles
Total Elevation Gain/Loss	4000'/4000'
Hiking Time	16 hours
Required Maps	USGS 7.5-min *Clark Lake NE*, *Collins Valley*
Best Times	November through April
Agency	ABDSP, BLM/EC
Difficulty	****

Rockhouse Canyon and the broad, sloping alluvial basin drained by it—informally known as Rockhouse Valley—constitute one of southern California's truly forgotten places. Not much more than a century ago, Indian villages thrived here. After the Indians moved to the nearby Santa Rosa Indian Reservation around 1900, a few hardy prospectors made forays into the area, traveling along the ancient footpaths, and in some cases living in the old rock houses built by the Indians. Today, there is still no road beyond the lower reaches of Rockhouse Canyon. The closest inhabited place is several miles away.

Although this grand tour of Rockhouse Canyon and Valley can be rushed through in a single, very long day, it's better to set aside two or three days to explore the area adequately and at a reasonable pace.

To reach the starting point, usually accessible by all but low-slung cars, drive 9.2 miles north from Highway S-22 on Clark's Well Road and Rockhouse Truck Trail. Park near the junction of roads into Butler and Rockhouse canyons (I'm assuming you'll start here—however a high-clearance, 4-wheel-drive car or truck might get you 3 miles farther on wheels).

On foot, walk 3 miles up Rockhouse Canyon to the road closure, and keep going another mile to Hidden Spring. Over the next 3.5 miles,

Rockhouse Canyon is a narrow gorge flanked by soaring rock walls. You'll be on soft sand—alluvium washed down from the valley above—most of the time.

At a point just south of the San Diego-Riverside county line, you'll come upon a granite dike forming a 20' dry fall. Well before this area was declared a state wilderness, jeep-club members built a road over this obstacle and used a winch to haul vehicles over it—though it's difficult to see how! Huge boulders litter the canyon floor now, a result of big flash floods in the late 1970s. Amateur road builders would need dynamite to clear a path today.

At the county line, you leave Anza-Borrego Desert State Park and enter BLM land. After you pass a major tributary to the east and a smaller tributary also to the east, the canyon broadens and you enter Rockhouse Valley. Here you'll spot some junipers, indicators of the high-desert realm.

Next stop is the hard-to-find lower rockhouse ruins. Try this: follow the main wash up the west side of the valley until you reach the base of a boulder-strewn ridge 0.6 mile northwest of the valley entrance; then go 0.2

Rockhouse ruins above Nicholias Canyon

mile due north to find the three rock houses, all of which are roofless. They're spaced along a low, elongated ridge with a view of the entire valley. Mud used as mortar still clings to some of the walls. Each house had a cozy fireplace inside.

The water source for this settlement was said to be a spring next to a lone cottonwood tree 0.5 mile east. Both the tree and the spring seem to have been victims of the tropical storms of the late 1970s; only a dry, sandy wash is in evidence there today. (The "Cottonwood Spring" indicated on USGS topo maps northwest of the ruins is apparently an error.)

From the lower rock houses, head cross-country due northwest through sparse vegetation (mostly catclaw, agave, and golden cholla cactus) toward a low, rounded hill spur at the upper end of the valley, 2.5 miles away. This spur forms the east wall of Nicholias Canyon, your next destination. When you reach the base of the spur, swing left (west) around it and pick up an informal trail that goes down to the creek in Nicholias Canyon. Plenty of water flows here during the winter and early spring. Follow either bank upstream, passing some old, rusted mining debris.

Up-canyon, after a bend to the right (northeast), you'll come upon a magnificent creek-hugging grove of alders and cottonwoods. These are beautiful in April when the new, delicate leaves shimmer in the breeze. Warm light floods in from the pinyon-studded, scrubby slopes surrounding the grove. This is an enchanting spot to camp—some brush-free campsites on sloping ground can be found on the west bank. Nearby you can explore the major source of the water, which is a spring 200 yards east of the main canyon in a tributary ravine. Good water may be obtained there.

Above and south of this spring are two more rock-house ruins, even more tumbledown than those seen earlier. You can also make camp on a nearby flat offering a commanding view of Rockhouse Valley, and the distant San Ysidro, Vallecito, and Laguna mountains. Massive Toro Peak, the crown summit of the Santa Rosa Mountains, looms in the north. (Adventurous

climbers wishing to bag this peak can proceed up the ridge west of Nicholias Canyon. Nicholias Canyon itself, with its dry falls and boulder obstacles, is a slower and more technically difficult route. Plan on a full day's climb, with plenty of bushwhacking and talus scrambling.)

From the last rock-house ruins, go east to a sandy flat containing a scraggly row of cottonwoods (here's yet another possible camping spot). Follow the shallow drainage east of this flat; when it deepens, pick up the well-worn but partly overgrown trail on the left (north) side. The trail switchbacks downward, crosses a major southward-draining ravine, and then strikes a path southeast down a broad ridge. (This is one of several trails in Rockhouse Valley shown on circa-1900 topographic maps.)

A path straight ahead leads directly back to Rockhouse Canyon, but you can depart from it to make one more stop: the Old Santa Rosa Indian village. At about the 4000' contour, turn east and work your way over low ridges and sharp gullies toward the two "seeps" marked on the topo map in sections 17 and 18. The first, in a canyon at 4200 feet, has had evidence of Indian use—morteros and ollas (earthen jugs), the latter removed years ago. The second seep, backed up against the rocky slopes of the Santa Rosa Mountains at 3910 feet, is the site of the old village. Two rock-house foundations are still intact here. It's hard to imagine a more wild and remote dwelling site. The seep is covered with a growth of mesquite, with no water on the surface.

Obscure trails radiate from the old village to all parts of the valley. At least two, still traceable, ascend ridgelines about 1 mile east-southeast of the village and connect with a trail into Martinez Canyon on the east slope of the Santa Rosas. There are springs at the mouths of two canyons near the base of these trails. Much time could be spent exploring this fascinating area—little changed over the last century.

From the old village site, the last leg of this trip is straight across the valley to the head of Rockhouse Canyon. From there you simply follow your footprints back to the starting point.

Trip 6: Box Canyon To Hidden Spring

	Distance	12 miles round trip
	Total Elevation Gain/Loss	2500'/2500'
	Hiking Time	10 hours (round trip)
	Required Maps	USGS 7.5-min *Borrego Palm Canyon,*
		Collins Valley, Clark Lake NE
	Best Times	November through April
	Agency	ABDSP
	Difficulty	****

Hidden Spring, according to Lester Reed, author of *Old Time Cattlemen and Other Pioneers of the Anza-Borrego Area,* served as a hub for Indian trails leading to at least half a dozen destinations. Among them was a route leading to the Lower Willows of Coyote Canyon via Box Canyon. Mr. Reed, himself an old cattleman, once followed this trail on horseback from Coyote Canyon to a tributary of Box Canyon, but apparently never returned to trace the entire route. Following general directions from his book, however, I have located significant parts of it.

The route traverses rough and isolated country, no less pristine than it was centuries ago when Cahuilla Indians passed this way on seasonal migration or food-gathering expeditions. If you haven't sharpened your skills at cross-country travel and trail-finding, you'll certainly have plenty of practice here.

It's possible to rush over this out-and-back trip in a single day, but a two-day backpack will allow you more time to look around. Campsites are abundant, but water is not. The meager supply at Hidden Spring cannot be counted on.

A one-way trip along this route is possible if you arrange to be picked up at the roadend in Rockhouse Canyon (a long, rugged drive by 4-wheel-drive vehicle). Another possibility is to continue hiking down Rockhouse Canyon and loop back through Alcoholic Pass (see Trip 3 above).

You begin the trek at the mouth of Box Canyon, just northwest of where jeep road bypass turns west to avoid going through Lower Willows. This is 5.6 miles beyond the end of pavement at DiGiorgio Road (see Area D-l introductory text). Bad road conditions and dif-

ficult fords may require that you park your car as much as two or three miles short of this point.

Follow the sandy, boulder-choked bed of Box Canyon northeast out of Coyote Canyon. After 0.8 mile, just beyond a narrow section of canyon where the walls pinch tightly, a tributary canyon branches to the right (east). Keep left, in the main canyon. After another 0.5 mile, a second tributary canyon branches right (east). Turn right, and in 100 yards go right again where this tributary divides. Proceed for another 0.3 mile, then leave the canyon bottom and climb to a low saddle on the ridge to the right (south).

Here you pick up a deeply worn trail, marked frequently by ducks. Apparently disused in modern times, this trail is heavily encroached by desert vegetation, including formidable thickets of teddy-bear cholla cactus. In the manner of most Indian trails, this one strikes a path on the ridgeline above the canyon, rather than following the canyon itself. Since the Indians were master pathfinders and trail builders and keen observers of nature, they knew that flash floods would rearrange canyon bottoms, and that ridge trails would not be affected much by erosion. Having trails on ridges with clear lines of sight also facilitated easy route-finding in a world with no maps and direction-finding instruments.

Follow trail fragments up the ridge, bearing mostly left of the ridgeline, until you pass a 2720' knoll. Then bear right and cross a broad 2650' saddle, heading northeast. A playa (flat basin), several acres in extent, lies straight ahead. After heavy rains, a number of compact, shallow depressions (of mysterious origin) on the playa hold supplies of not-very-appealing-looking water. The playa is fringed by a dense growth of creosote bushes and surrounded by a low wall of hills. There's a splendid sense of isolation here, and it's no wonder—the nearest road or maintained pathway lies nearly 3 miles away.

Cross the playa and pass over a low spot in the hills to the northeast. Continue generally northeast, following occasional ducks and a hint of trail, and negotiate a steep descent into Butler Canyon. Avoid descending directly on the nose of the ridge that divides Butler Canyon and a deeply cut western tributary: the canyon wall is undercut below.

Once in Butler Canyon, follow it north onto the vast expanse of Jackass Flat. Then head for the Indian village site on its eastern lip, just above Hidden Spring (see Trip 4). Before you reach the main village site overlooking Rock-house Canyon. you'll notice signs of former habitation—fire pits and potsherds—on the sandy areas of Jackass Flat. Within the main village area, you'll find the top of the steep, eroded trail leading down to Hidden Spring.

"Truckhaven Rocks"—sandstone outcroppings

Area D-4: Santa Rosa Mountains

From the 8716' summit of Toro Peak in Riverside County, the main crest of the Santa Rosa Mountains undulates southeast past Rabbit and Villager peaks, then drops steadily to the desert floor at the edge of the Borrego Badlands. A complex of lesser ridges and promontories lies east of the main crest. Geologically, the Santa Rosas are identified as being an eastern arm of the Peninsular Ranges.

The northern summits of the Santa Rosa Mountains are high enough to support a variety of conifers, but the south half of the range—San Diego County's share—is quite desolate. The southern Santa Rosas are rugged, almost lacking in sources of water, virtually trail-less, seldom-visited, and (to the ill-prepared hiker) unforgiving. Yet it's here, more than almost any other place within the county, that you can really get away from it all. Perched on some high and dry peak, you can gaze out over hundreds of square miles of mountains and desert with a feeling that you own it all.

Other than Trip 1, which begins in Rockhouse Canyon, all hikes below start along the Borrego-Salton Seaway (County Highway S-22), northeast of Borrego Springs. Except for the area around the Calcite Mine (Trips 8 and 9), where vehicular traffic is allowed on certain roads and in certain washes, the southern Santa Rosas are classified as a state wilderness within Anza-Borrego Desert State Park. As elsewhere in the Anza-Borrego Desert area, you're on your own—no permits are required. Remember, however, to observe the state park regulations, which are designed to protect all features within the park.

Refer to John Robinson's *San Bernardino Mountain Trails* for information about hikes in the northern part of the Santa Rosas, particularly the higher, forested areas within Riverside County.

Cairn at summit of Peak 6582

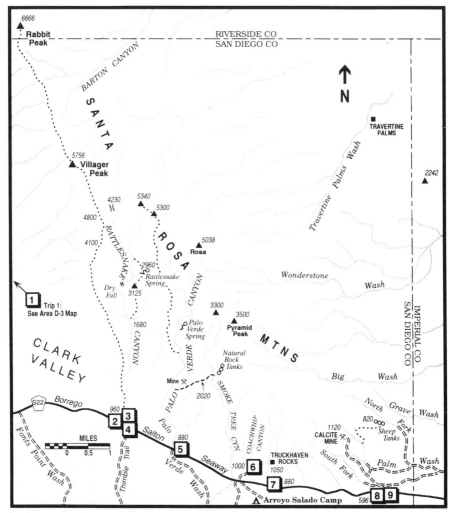

Area D-4: Santa Rosa Mountains

Trip 1: Peak 6582

	Distance	12 miles round trip
	Total Elevation Gain/Loss	5800'/5800'
	Hiking Time	13 hours (round trip)
	Required Map	USGS 7.5-min *Clark Lake NE*
	Best Times	November through April
	Agency	ABDSP, BLM/EC
	Difficulty	*****

Peak 6582 (labelled "Dawns Peak" on some maps) is the highest point on the main Santa Rosa crest between Toro Peak (8716') and Rabbit Peak (6666'). With one or two visits per year over the past two decades, it is one of the least climbed—and least accessible—peaks in the Anza-Borrego Desert. A few adventurers have passed over its summit while traveling along the crest from Toro to Rabbit and beyond. Others have ascended from upper Clark Valley—my description below is one of several possible variations of that route.

It takes strong determination to withstand miles of waterless, rocky terrain and thousands of feet of steady elevation gain for the privilege of standing atop a bump on a ridge barely distinguishable from others of similar stature nearby. But like many desert peaks, this one holds a special fascination. An elaborate pillar of stones, erected sometime before 1970, graces the summit—a monument to some unknown hiker or hikers who not only climbed the peak but also put in hours of skilled labor.

Although this trip can be done in one long, exhausting day, a two-day trip makes more sense. A base camp established halfway up, and a quick ascent of the peak using light packs, is the method that proved successful for every one of the ten people I once had the pleasure of leading on this route. The lack of water (except during rainfall or when snow is present at higher elevations) makes any trip longer than two days undesirable.

Refer to the Area D-3 introductory text for details on road access into upper Clark Valley (also note that this particular trip is plotted on the Area D-3 map). Find parking space along the Rockhouse Truck Trail, somewhere be-

tween 6.8 and 7.3 miles north of Highway S-22. Don't forget to take a compass bearing of at least one nearby landmark to assist in finding your car later.

Start hiking north across the sandy floor of upper Clark Valley. Head for a broad ridge spur (with survey marker "Corp" noted on the topo map) that descends south to meet the floor of Clark Valley—about 1.5 miles away. Below the survey marker, some petroglyphs are inscribed on the jumbled, desert-varnished boulders.

From the petroglyphs, head north-northeast and gain the narrow, rocky ridge between two canyons that leads toward peak 2700. At about the 2200' contour on this ridge, drop into the canyon on the right (east). Follow the rock-strewn canyon bottom, bearing right at a major fork at 2380 feet, and continue about 0.3 mile to a large sandy flat ideally suited (except for lack of water) for camping. The wash and the rocky slopes surrounding this campsite show signs of both bighorn sheep and mountain lions.

Next morning, you can set out before sunrise to bag the peak, carrying light, dayhiking gear. Climb the steep ridge (with loose rocks and cactus) northeast of the campsite, topping out at or near peak 3489. Continue about 1 mile north over rolling terrain, dotted with agave and small shrubs, to the base of the ridge leading up to a point on the Santa Rosa crest 0.1 mile northwest of Peak 6582. In the last mile you gain nearly 3000 feet over jagged terrain. Luckily, scattered pinyon pines afford welcome shade on the way up.

The view from the rounded granite boulders at the summit is magnificent. You'll see most of the Santa Rosa crest, the dusky Palomar and San Ysidro mountains to the west, and long vistas south across Clark Valley to the middle and southern reaches of Anza-Borrego Desert State Park. Don't forget to sign the register hidden beneath the towering cairn.

By noon at the latest, you ought to be off the peak and busy hightailing it back to the campsite. There you can hoist your backpack and start the long trudge to your car. With luck, you'll arrive before dusk.

Trip 2: Rabbit Peak via Villager Peak

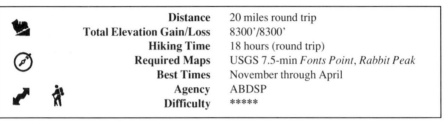

	Distance	20 miles round trip
	Total Elevation Gain/Loss	8300'/8300'
	Hiking Time	18 hours (round trip)
	Required Maps	USGS 7.5-min *Fonts Point*, *Rabbit Peak*
	Best Times	November through April
	Agency	ABDSP
	Difficulty	*****

Despite their remoteness, Villager and Rabbit peaks are among the most popular destinations for peak baggers in the Anza-Borrego Desert. Several dozen people per year attain the summits of these two peaks, and bottles and tin cans containing the peak registers are often overflowing with business cards and other mementos.

Rabbit Peak has two popular routes of approach. A steep, eastern approach from Coachella Valley, beginning near sea level, is described in John Robinson's *San Bernardino Mountain Trails*. Here, I will describe the southern route, up the main crest of the Santa Rosas via Villager Peak. This is longer, more gradual, and arguably more scenic (but overall more difficult) than the eastern approach; and it begins at a point closer to San Diego County residents. A minimum of two full days is needed, with the first night's camp on or near Villager Peak. Alternatively, you can set your sights on Villager Peak only—a hike of 13 miles (11 hours).

Park in the northside turnout at mile 31.8 on Highway S-22. Proceed north toward the east end of a long, sandy ridge 0.5 mile away. The north face of this ridge is a huge scarp along the San Jacinto Fault—said to be one of the largest fault scarps in unconsolidated material in North America. North of this ridge, flash-floods exiting from Rattlesnake Canyon have cut a series of braided washes in a swath about 0.6 mile wide. A ducked trail takes you over this dissected terrain to the base of the long, ramp-like ridge leading to Villager and Rabbit peaks.

The initial climb is very steep, but the route soon levels off to a rather steady gradient averaging about 1000 feet per mile. Stay on the highest part of the ridge to remain on route. Here and there, you'll be on fragments of trail well worn by the passage of both bighorn sheep and hikers. Creosote bush, ocotillo, and glistening specimens of barrel cactus, hedgehog cactus, and silver, golden, and teddy-bear cholla cactus grace the slopes below 3000 feet. Dense thickets of agave at 3000 to 4000 feet may slow you down a bit.

Along the lower part of the ridge you'll come upon several Indian "sleeping circles," which may have been used as windbreaks or to anchor shelters made from local vegetation. At about the 3000' level (3.0 miles) a green patch marking Rattlesnake Spring comes into view in a tributary canyon of Rattlesnake Canyon about 1.5 miles east.

At 4100 feet (4.3 miles), you'll pass along the edge of a spectacular dropoff overlooking Clark Valley. The white band of rock prominently displayed along the face of this escarpment is marble. This is metamorphosed limestone predating the rise of the Southern California Batholith. Just beyond the 4800' contour (5.0 miles), the ridge descends a little to a small, exposed campsite with airy views both east and west.

In the next mile the ridgeline becomes quite jagged. Pinyon, juniper, and nolina (a relative of the yucca) now dominate. The rounded summit of Villager Peak (6.5 miles) offers good campsites amid spreading pinyons.

A predawn start is recommended if you plan to reach Rabbit Peak, return to your packs on Villager Peak, and make the long descent back to your car all in one day. Rabbit Peak is only 3.5 miles away and 900 feet higher than Villager Peak, but the undulating ridgeline between the two adds considerable elevation gains and los-ses both ways. The total gain/loss for the round trip between peaks is a surprising 3300'/3300'.

Rabbit Peak lies just 0.3 mile north of the San Diego-Riverside county line. If the county line were shifted just that far north, Rabbit Peak would be the highest elevation in San Diego County.

The flat summit of Rabbit Peak is dotted with pinyon pines, precluding the kind of panoramic views available from more angular peaks. Still, it's a delightful spot—a kind of sky island aloof from all the rest of Southern California.

Trip 3: Rattlesnake Spring

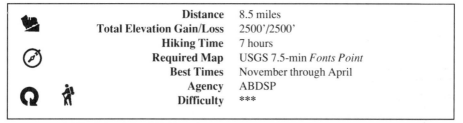

Distance	8.5 miles
Total Elevation Gain/Loss	2500'/2500'
Hiking Time	7 hours
Required Map	USGS 7.5-min *Fonts Point*
Best Times	November through April
Agency	ABDSP
Difficulty	***

Rattlesnake Spring is one of the few reliable sources of water in the southern Santa Rosa Mountains. Several dozen bighorn sheep may depend on it for survival during periods of drought. The spring produces a low volume—it's more like a seep. You shouldn't count on it as a source for your own drinking needs.

On this loop hike, you'll approach the spring via one route and return via a second route comparable in difficulty. Both routes involve a fair amount of scrambling. Feel free to reverse the direction of travel from that described below.

As in Trip 2 above, park at the turnout at mile 31.8 on Highway S-22. Proceed 1.1 mile north to the base of the broad ridge leading to Villager and Rabbit peaks. Bear right around this ridge and follow the main wash into Rattlesnake Canyon. At a point about 1.3 miles farther, a major tributary will be seen to the right (east). Climb the steep slope north of this tributary and gain the ridgeline containing survey point 2971. Continue north over the top of this ridgeline (3125'); bear northeast, avoiding some steep terrain to the north, and then descend into the canyon containing Rattlesnake Spring.

Mesquite groves and a single large cottonwood tree grow in the moist area surrounding the spring. The chalky hillsides to the north of the spring have been stripped bare of vegetation by many a bighorn sheep hoof. Trails radiate in all directions to higher ridges where the bighorn spend their time when not in need of water. Do respect the watering rights of all kinds of wildlife by not camping close to the water.

You can now return by way of Rattlesnake Canyon. The tributary containing Rattlesnake Spring has a set of formidable dry falls at its mouth, so the following detour is recommended: Climb northwest from the spring over sloping terrain to a point in Rattlesnake Canyon below the 2960' contour. Then wend your way down-canyon, passing below the dry falls in the tributary.

Fallen rocks are common between the narrow walls of Rattlesnake Canyon, but several sandy stretches suitable for camping are here too. Just below the 2400' contour, you'll come to the top of a 20' dry fall—the biggest challenge

Bighorn sheep ram at Rattlesnake Spring

on this trip. Lower your packs on a rope and down-climb directly; or detour around the fall on the rocky, cactus-infested slopes either left or right. The latter method is less elegant but probably safer. From this point on, the canyon widens, and the going is quite easy over small boulders and patches of sand.

Trip 4: Mile-High Mountain

Distance	13 miles round trip
Total Elevation Gain/Loss	5500'/5500'
Hiking Time	10 hours (round trip)
Required Maps	USGS 7.5-min *Fonts Point*, *Rabbit Peak*
Best Times	November through April
Agency	ABDSP
Difficulty	****

This unnamed, tan-colored massif, which I have dubbed "Mile-High Mountain" for the elevation of its highest summits, rivals in prominence the main south ridge containing Villager and Rabbit peaks. The unobstructed eastern and southern view from its crest is probably unequalled anywhere in the Santa Rosas; it includes the entire shoreline of the Salton Sea and virtually all of the Coachella and Imperial valleys. From here I once spotted the summits of the Sierra San Pedro Martir, 180 miles away.

The most direct route up is by way of the ridge forming the west wall of Palo Verde Canyon. Park in the turnout at mile 31.8 on Highway S-22, and head northeast across the open desert for 1 mile to the mouth of Palo

Verde Canyon. Follow the main wash up the canyon another 1.5 miles to a sharp bend at 1900' elevation. Now climb the steep slope to the left (west) and gain the ridgeline. (Palo Verde Canyon itself enters a steep bowl just below the usually dry Palo Verde Spring, where further progress is blocked.)

Simply follow this ridgeline north for the next 3 miles or so, gaining 3000 feet. The sequence of vegetation is similar to that on the Villager/Rabbit ridge to the west, described in Trip 2.

There are four distinct, rounded summits at the top, the highest of which is farthest north,

elevation approximately 5340 feet. Peak 5300 is dotted with a few scraggly pinyons, and would accommodate perhaps two or three prone bodies.

Mile-High Mountain is a good hub for routes into many remote corners of the Santa Rosas. West of peak 5340 you can descend into Rattlesnake Canyon (where there are dry falls you must carefully climb around) or into the major unnamed drainage system to the north; or you can gain the Villager/Rabbit ridge. You can also visit survey marker "Rosa" (which has a climber's register) and descend from there into Wonderstone Wash.

Trip 5: Rock Tanks Loop

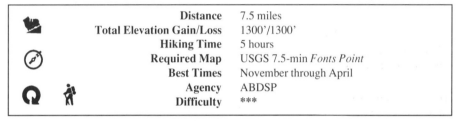

	Distance	7.5 miles
	Total Elevation Gain/Loss	1300'/1300'
	Hiking Time	5 hours
	Required Map	USGS 7.5-min *Fonts Point*
	Best Times	November through April
	Agency	ABDSP
	Difficulty	***

Many experiences—some powerful and some merely annoying—await you on this hike: the palpable force of the desert sun's rays; the desiccated air, catching in the throat; the sharp prick of a cactus spine on the ankle, or the brittle scrape of an ocotillo wand on the elbow; the feeling of vertigo when you step to the edge of an abyss and view the shattered landscape below; and, most powerful of all, the sublime silence.

Here's how to get started with this quintessential desert experience: Park at mile 32.9 along Highway S-22, where a small wash crosses the road. This is Palo Verde Wash, named for the many palo verde trees along it. (These green-limbed, spindly trees are in glorious yellow bloom in April.) Begin hiking generally north along the braided wash, taking care not to stray into a smaller canyon that comes out of the mountains just east of Palo Verde Wash—this is an easy mistake to make. At about 1 mile you'll see a prominent cut in the mountains

ahead—Palo Verde Canyon. At this point it's possible to make a short side trip to see some cottontop cacti (*Echinocactus polycephalus*), which resemble small barrel cacti but grow in dome-shaped clusters. They're quite rare in the Anza-Borrego area. Look for them on the low ridge spurs west of Palo Verde Wash. One amazing specimen spans 5 feet.

At 1.3 miles the canyon walls begin to close in on both sides. Walk near the wall on the right side, and in another 0.2 mile, you'll spot an obscure trail going straight up the rocky slope to the right. The bottom of the trail should be marked by cairns. Ducks placed here and there alongside the trail will guide you over the next 1.3 miles. This trail is the beginning of an Indian route that goes over the Santa Rosa Mountains and down Wonderstone Wash to a spot where wonderstone (a raw material for stone tools) was quarried.

On your left, as you gain elevation, is an old mine tunnel sunk into a prominent vein. Woe to

View of Salton Sea from Pyramid Peak

those who venture in more than a few feet: pack rats have secreted away here a huge collection of cholla-cactus spines.

At 2.1 miles the trail crosses a divide and descends along a precipitous slope overlooking Smoke Tree Canyon. A rock slide has obliterated traces of the old trail, but use by hikers has forged a new trail. When you reach the canyon bottom, make a short side trip up the narrow tributary canyon to the northeast. Here, the scouring of flash floods has worn large depressions in the rock—the Natural Rock Tanks. Pockets like these, called *tinajas*, serve as natural reservoirs of water for weeks or months after major storms. If you're lucky, you may spot bighorn sheep in the area.

North of the tributary containing the rock tanks, remnants of the old Indian trail continue on the slope east of Smoke Tree Canyon all the way to a saddle at the head of Smoke Tree Canyon, just west of Pyramid Peak. You can also reach that saddle by following the canyon bottom all the way to its head. It's possible to make a long side trip up and over the saddle into the remote upper Wonderstone Wash drainage; for detailed information on this, please see pages 207-209 in the first edition of this guidebook.

To continue our loop hike, head straight down Smoke Tree Canyon toward the highway, 3 miles away. The canyon becomes a narrow fissure in two places, where dark conglomerate cliffs hover menacingly overhead, seemingly subject to imminent collapse. (I once noticed, two days after a mild earthquake, numerous basketball-size rocks newly fallen and embedded in the sand just below these cliffs. If you're backpacking, choose a campsite well away from the cliffs.) There's a short scramble down a dry waterfall, followed by a mile or so of intermittent boulder-hopping, and then it's smooth sailing on a nice bed of packed sand all the way to the highway.

Close the loop by walking along the wide shoulder of the highway. Or, if fatigued or just lazy, have one or more members of your party sprint over to pick up the car.

Trip 6: Coachwhip Canyon

	Distance	1 to 4 miles
	Optional Map	USGS 7.5-min *Fonts Point*
	Best Times	October through June
	Agency	ABDSP
	Difficulty	*

Stark, dry, and almost barren, Coachwhip Canyon is somehow—despite these attributes—a very peaceful and appealing place. A beautiful forest of smoke trees, framed by sandstone formations, stands at the entrance. The wind, which can blow like the devil just outside, seldom seems to intrude within the confines of the canyon. Hidden nooks in the side canyons, each unique, invite you to pause, rest, and enjoy.

The wraithlike, gray-green smoke tree, a handsome shrub in any season, puts on quite a show in June, when it is festooned with thousands of indigo-colored blossoms. The smoke-tree forest literally hums then with the wingbeats of bees gathering nectar. It is, of course, terrifically hot at that time of year, so you would want to do your hiking at dawn or dusk.

There are actually dozens of steep-walled ravines here, all draining into Ella Wash. The ravines twist and turn through soft sandstone, each one ending abruptly at the horseshoe-shaped headwall that surrounds the area.

A sandy road, suitable for most cars at its lower end, penetrates an eastern branch of Coachwhip Canyon for about 1.2 miles. (This road intersects Highway S-22 at mile 34.8, just west of the road to Arroyo Salado Primitive Camp.) There are several good spots for car camping along the road.

By exploring some or all the tributaries, you'd walk anywhere from 1 to 4 miles. In a few spots, you can climb high enough up the headwall to get a good view of both the Coachwhip area and the Borrego Badlands beyond. Once on top, you could continue to follow the main ridge 3 miles north to 3500' Pyramid Peak.

View of Borrego Badlands from rim above Coachwhip Canyon

Trip 7: Truckhaven Rocks

	Distance 1.5 miles round trip
	Total Elevation Gain/Loss 200'/200'
	Hiking Time 40 minutes (round trip)
	Optional Map USGS 7.5-min *Fonts Point*
	Best Times October through May
	Agency ABDSP
	Difficulty *

The Truckhaven Rocks are somewhat reminiscent of the outcrops of sandstone at Garden of the Gods in Colorado Springs, Colorado. The tilted slabs of orange-tinted sandstone, which can be plainly seen from Highway S-22, are a favorite haunt of photographers.

Park on the wide shoulder of Highway S-22 at mile 35.5, and head up the wash that leads toward a point a little east of the Truckhaven Rocks. Climbing out of this wash to reach the outcrops, you'll cross a boulder-strewn plain dotted with ocotillo. Here and there, in areas free of large rocks, are patches of "desert pavement," a common surface condition in which small pebbles of roughly uniform size form a flat mosaic. This is a result of fine particles being blown away, leaving the larger particles and pebbles to settle and pack together.

Smoke trees in Coachwhip Canyon

Trip 8: Calcite Mine

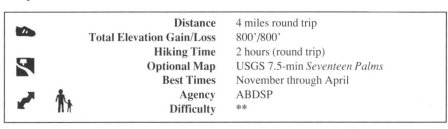

	Distance	4 miles round trip
	Total Elevation Gain/Loss	800'/800'
	Hiking Time	2 hours (round trip)
	Optional Map	USGS 7.5-min *Seventeen Palms*
	Best Times	November through April
	Agency	ABDSP
	Difficulty	**

Thousands of years of cutting and polishing by water and wind erosion have produced the chaotic rock formations and slotlike ravines you'll discover in the Calcite Mine area. The highlight of this hike is, of course, the mine itself. During World War II, this was an important site—indeed the only site in the United States—for the extraction of optical-grade calcite crystals for use in gunsights. Trench-mining operations throughout the area have left deep scars upon the earth, seemingly as fresh today as when they were made.

Park in the roadside turnout at mile 38.0 along Highway S-22; then walk 0.1 mile east to the Calcite jeep road intersection. An interpretive panel here gives some details about the history of the mine. Follow the jeep road as it dips into and out of South Fork Palm Wash, and continues northwest toward the southern spurs of the Santa Rosa Mountains.

Ahead you will see an intricately honeycombed whitish slab of sandstone, called Locomotive Rock, which lies behind (northeast of) the mine area.

About 1.4 miles from S-22, the road dips sharply to cross a deep ravine. Poke into the upper (north) end of this ravine and you'll discover one of the best slot canyons in Anza-Borrego. (Skilled climbers can squeeze through the slot and go up a break on the right side to reach a point above and northwest of the mine area.)

At road's end calcite crystals lie strewn about on the ground, glittering in the sunlight. You could spend a lot of time exploring the mining trenches and the pocked slabs of sandstone nearby. Palm Wash, a frightening gash in the earth, precludes travel to the east.

On the return, try this alternate route: Backtrack 0.5 mile to the aforementioned slot ravine.

Proceed downstream along its bottom. As you pass through deeper and deeper layers of sandstone strata, the ravine narrows until it allows the passage of only one person at a time. When you reach the jumbled blocks of sandstone in Palm Wash at the bottom of the ravine, turn right, walk 0.3 mile downstream, and exit the canyon via a short link of jeep trail that leads back to the Calcite road.

In a tributary of Palm Wash

Trip 9: Palm Wash/Sheep Tanks

	Distance	7 miles
	Total Elevation Gain/Loss	900'/900'
	Hiking Time	4 hours
	Required Map	USGS 7.5-min *Seventeen Palms*
	Best Times	November through April
	Agency	ABDSP
	Difficulty	***

Off the beaten track, this loop hike gives access to a labyrinth of deep gorges and a bench with clear traces of ancient Indian pathways. The upper end of North Fork Palm Wash, about halfway around the loop, offers good camping spots for backpackers.

Begin as in Trip 8 above. At 0.8 mile from Highway S-22, leave the Calcite Mine road and descend a jeep trail into Palm Wash. Head up-canyon (northwest) through the vertical-walled gorge, past fallen blocks of tan-colored sandstone. The walls of the canyon seem to be in a state of arrested collapse, with huge slices of rock fully separated from the walls, ready to surrender to gravity during the next earthquake or flash flood.

At a point 0.6 mile up Palm Wash, a major tributary enters from the left. (This tributary goes past peak 1122 toward the Calcite Mine, and can be used to combine parts of Trip 8 with this trip. From this point you can also, if skilled at bouldering, continue up Palm Wash, climbing past sandstone blocks and huge granitic chockstones, to a point well above the Calcite Mine.) Opposite and a little beyond this tributary, on the right (east) side of Palm Wash, is an easy break through the sandstone wall. Climb this and head north along a sloping bench east of Palm Wash. You'll pick up an Indian trail that leads northwest, then northeast, then finally east toward the Sheep Tanks in the North Fork of Palm Wash. (The south branch of this Indian trail approaches another break in the wall of Palm Wash about 1 mile south-southeast.)

Due east of Locomotive Rock (see Trip 8), which you can see clearly over the gorge of Palm Wash, is a flat, cleared area with two partly collapsed cairns of desert-varnished stones. A sighting across these cairns intersects the north-eastern horizon at a point within 2° of where the sun rises over the Salton Sea on the day of the summer solstice, June 21. More cairns are in the same line farther to the northeast. It is tempting to think this is an Indian solstice marker, but the presence of test trenches nearby probably means that the cairns had something to do with the mine.

Using map and compass, work your way overland to the Sheep Tanks, an important watering hole for bighorn sheep and other wildlife. These are located in a narrow, southern tributary of North Fork Palm Wash that joins North Fork at 700 feet elevation. From above you can look down (very cautiously) into the slot containing several deep *tinajas*. Their capacity is estimated at some 20,000 gallons—about as much as a backyard swimming pool.

A series of sloping sandstone ledges leads down the south wall of the slot to the lowest tank, then out to the North Fork, where you'll find wheel tracks. You may want to avoid the exposed bit of downclimbing by backtracking about 0.3 mile and going north into the upper end of the North Fork. Here, the North Fork has flat sandy spots suitable for camping—except during rainy periods.

Close the loop by walking the North Fork jeep road to Palm Wash, and the Palm Wash jeep road back to the Calcite Mine road.

Area D-5: Borrego Badlands

The Borrego Badlands consist of lake, stream and alluvial-plain deposits that have been severely attacked by the erosive forces of water and wind. The clay soils are so weak, and the plants which might otherwise anchor the soil are so sparse, that flash floods have carved the land into a bewildering maze of sinuous channels, razorback ridges, and mud hills.

The most renowned point of interest here, and one of the best view spots in all of Anza-Borrego Desert State Park, is Fonts Point. Here you can stand on the edge of a receding cliff and look across many square miles of intricately carved landscape.

Relatively few plants thrive in the alkaline soil of the Borrego Badlands, but there are some surprises. Several groups of palms cling tenuously to life in areas where subsurface water is dependable; these may be the tiniest remnants of a much wider distribution of palms present during wetter periods of the past. Small trees—palo verde, desert-willow, and smoke tree—line some of the sandy washes where their roots can take advantage of ephemeral flows of water. The right combination of rainfall and

sunshine occasionally brings forth a profusion of wildflowers, especially sand verbenas, desert asters, dune primroses, desert sunflowers, and desert lilies.

The Borrego Badlands are laced with approved vehicle routes (for licensed vehicles only) and the passage of jeeps and motorcycles can be annoying if you're out hiking on a busy weekend. Nevertheless, there are several areas within the badlands where you can wander cross-country and find peace and quiet. Three such hikes are suggested below.

For any foot travel through the badlands, be sure to take along enough water and a topographic map and compass. While it is almost impossible to wander very far without running into a road, it's easy to lose track of your position and identifiable landmarks. Use the best maps available: the entire area is covered on USGS 7.5-minute quadrangles *Fonts Point*, *Borrego Mountain*, *Shell Reef*, and *Seventeen Palms*. These maps have a contour interval ranging from 20 to 40 feet, which is enough to show a wealth of complex detail in the convoluted landscape.

Borrego Badlands

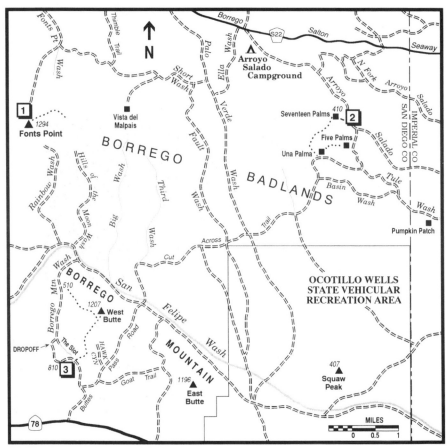

Area D-5: Borrego Badlands

Trip 1: Fonts Point

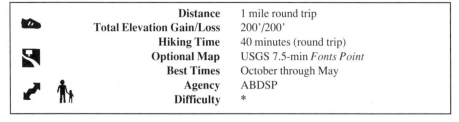

	Distance	1 mile round trip
	Total Elevation Gain/Loss	200'/200'
	Hiking Time	40 minutes (round trip)
	Optional Map	USGS 7.5-min *Fonts Point*
	Best Times	October through May
	Agency	ABDSP
	Difficulty	*

Sure, it's possible to drive to within a frisbee's throw of Fonts Point Overlook and take in the famous view of erosion-scarred mud hills and dry washes. But no, the overlook, per se, isn't really the *best* viewing place.

Try this: Starting from the Fonts Point parking area, walk east alongside (but not on the very brink of) the cliffs for about 0.5 mile. Here and there along this viewful stretch, you can walk (cautiously) over toward the cliff edge, where

Receding cliff near Fonts Point

mile upon mile of convoluted landscape seems to unfold. Up to about one hour after sunrise and one hour before sunset, the razorback ridges cast bold shadows across the honey-colored hills—perfect lighting for photographic-minded visitors. Remember to approach the brink cautiously, especially if you have kids. In a couple of places, large blocks of the cliff face are beginning to cleave.

Driving to Fonts Point can be a bit of an adventure in itself. Ask about road conditions first if you'll be using a two-wheel drive vehicle. From Highway S-22 turn south at mile 29.3, and follow the signs to Fonts Point, 4 miles away. You may have traction problems on the first part of the road, which is sometimes dusted with soft sand.

Trip 2: Seventeen Palms and Vicinity

Distance	2 miles
Total Elevation Gain/Loss	200'/200'
Hiking Time	1½ hours
Recommended Maps	USGS 7.5-min *Seventeen Palms, Shell Reef*
Best Times	December through March
Agency	ABDSP
Difficulty	**

Smack dab in the middle of the most desolate part of the Borrego Badlands stands a remarkable triad of palm oases. The best known of these, Seventeen Palms, is a popular destination for park visitors. The other two lie just a short distance away. They are accessible in a roundabout way via jeep trails, or overland on foot as

described here.

The starting point for this hike is the Seventeen Palms parking area along Arroyo Salado. To get there, turn southeast from Highway S-22 at mile 34.9 onto the dirt road leading through Arroyo Salado Primitive Camp. The 3.5-mile-long unpaved stretch to Seventeen Palms is

Prospectors' post office at Seventeen Palms

seemingly endless maze of dissected mud hills. Make an easy descent into any of the several small washes directly below. Continue downhill 0.3 mile to the Cut Across Trail (jeep trail) in Tule Wash. Turning left (east), you'll soon catch sight of Una Palma (single palm), its forlorn crown peeping above the mudhills. Head directly for it, passing a clump of mesquite along the way. Una Palma does not appear on the USGS topographic map.

From Una Palma head northeast. Topping the first hill, you'll be able to see the only remaining palm at Five Palms Spring, 0.5 mile away. Head directly for it east across the mud hills. If you have been scrutinizing your topo maps, you'll note a remarkable coincidence: all three oases lie at the same elevation!

Complete the loop by following the Tule Wash and Arroyo Salado jeep trails back to Seventeen Palms.

recommended for 4-wheel drives, but often it's in good enough shape for less rugged vehicles as well.

An interpretive leaflet available at the Seventeen Palms parking area recounts some of the old lore associated with this famous watering hole. Decades ago, prospectors and travelers used this oasis for relaying messages. The tradition continues today, and you'll probably find hundreds of notes and business cards in an old barrel beneath the palms. You'll also learn about the complex web of plant and animal life existing in this seemingly lifeless area. Because most animals that depend on the spring are nocturnal, you're asked not to camp in the area. Don't count on the water—if you can locate it—for your drinking needs; it is highly saline.

You start hiking cross-country at Seventeen Palms (410'). A hundred feet north of the northernmost cluster of palms, follow the small ravine that leads west into the mud hills. After about 100 yards, bear southwest across a low maze of washes. Continue southwest into a broad wash that bends southward toward a broad saddle. Topping this rise (510'), you'll have come about 0.5 mile from Seventeen Palms.

From the rise you can look south into a

Trip 3: West Butte Borrego Mountain

	Distance	3.5 miles
	Total Elevation Gain/Loss	700'/700'
	Hiking Time	3 hours
	Recommended Map	USGS 7.5-min *Borrego Mountain*
	Best Times	November through April
	Agency	ABDSP
	Difficulty	**

The twin peaks and eroded ravines of Borrego Mountain lie between the Borrego Badlands on the north and Lower Borrego Valley on the south. The area is laced with a network of unpaved roads of varying quality. In the adjacent Ocotillo Wells State Vehicular Recreation Area, any kind of vehicle may travel cross-country, but here (in Anza-Borrego Desert State Park) motorized travel is limited to street-licensed vehicles, which must stay on the designated roads.

The West Butte, with its sheer-cut ravines and slot canyons, is better for hiking than the East Butte, which lies partly in the vehicular recreation area. Nestled against the southeast side of the West Butte is Hawk Canyon, the premier remote camping spot in this neck of the desert.

West Butte is a fun place to get slightly lost—fun, because all you have to do to recover your bearings is climb up to some higher vantage point. The most striking feature of the hike sketched here is called, ominously, The Slot. We'll save its exploration until the end of this hike.

To reach the starting point, turn north on unpaved Buttes Pass Road from State Highway 78 at mile 87.2. (This point is 1.5 miles east of Borrego Springs Road and 5.2 miles west of Split Mountain Road at Ocotillo Wells.) After 1.0 mile on the dirt road, stay left, following the sign to the "Lookout." Drive another 0.9 mile over an increasingly rough road to a parking area overlooking The Slot.

On foot now, follow old wheel tracks 200 feet east until they end at the top of a ridge. Follow this ridge north, then northeast, directly to the summit of West Butte (1207'), the highest

point within a radius of about 6 miles. You'll have excellent views of the Borrego Badlands and the Santa Rosa Mountains to the north, the Salton Sea to the east, and the Vallecito Mountains to the south.

The summit area is covered with crumbling piles of granitic rock, deeply stained by desert varnish, and there's lots of pegmatite too: thousands of white crystals glitter in the sun. Deep layers of soft sandstone, siltstone, and conglomerate lie to the west. These layers, pushed up long ago by the granitic mass now exposed at the summit, are in the throes of rapid erosion.

Backtrack about 300 yards on the same ridge used for the summit approach. Then turn west and find a faint trail leading west, then

Desert lily, Borrego Badlands

northwest, along the north wall of the deepest westward-draining ravine (try not to descend to the north, an easy mistake). This trail takes you down to a point where you can drop into the ravine at its lower end; from there you walk out to the jeep trail in Borrego Mountain Wash. (You could spend many fascinating hours exploring the maze of ravines in this area. If you do, be aware that the rock is absolutely untrustworthy, sometimes crumbling at the very touch.)

Turn south on the jeep trail following Borrego Mountain Wash and pass an area of wind caves and small arches on the left. On past some sandstone bluffs and colorful clay hills, you'll eventually spot a scarred hillside on your right. This is the "Dropoff," a one-way jeep route into Borrego Mountain Wash from the flatlands above. Keep following the canyon as it narrows and turns east.

You now enter the portals of The Slot. The walls are fashioned from multiple layers of dark gray siltstone, convoluted into bulbous parapets and spires. The Slot narrows as you move into it. Tilted parapets and giant chockstones lie wedged above you, seemingly subject to imminent collapse. The Slot narrows even more. You may have to remove your day pack in order to wedge through. When The Slot widens, there's a fork. Take the right branch, and in just 200 yards you'll be back at your car.

The Slot

Area D-6: Grapevine Canyon/ Pinyon Ridge

This sparsely vegetated area of rounded ridges and long, linear valleys lies between Montezuma Highway (Highway S-22) on the north and State Highway 78 on the south. The highest elevations, about 4500 feet, feature the typical desert/mountain mix of pinyon, juniper, yucca and chaparral shrubs; while the lower elevations, hillsides and washes around 2000 feet exhibit the familiar creosote bush, cacti, agave, and desert willow of the lower desert. In the few moist areas, willow, ironwood and mesquite thrive.

Vehicle routes lace part of this area, but a large block centered around Pinyon Ridge is designated as state wilderness. As in all other parts of Anza-Borrego Desert State Park, wilderness or otherwise, you don't need a permit for either day or overnight use.

The longer hikes described below start and end along either Montezuma Highway or Highway 78. I've also included three of Anza-Borrego's very few maintained trails. All three are near Tamarisk Grove Campground at Highway 78 and Yaqui Pass Road (County Highway S-3).

Car-camping opportunities are abundant throughout the area, not only at the developed Tamarisk Grove Campground and two primitive campgrounds near it, but also along the several unpaved roads.

Area D-6: Grapevine Canyon / Pinyon Ridge

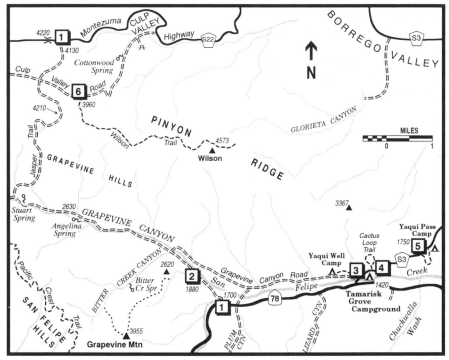

Trip 1: Jasper Trail/Grapevine Canyon

	Distance	11 miles
	Total Elevation Gain/Loss	500'/2900'
	Hiking Time	4½ hours
	Recommended Map	Anza-Borrego Desert State Park map/brochure
	Optional Maps	USGS 7.5-min *Tubb Canyon, Ranchita*
	Best Times	November through April
	Agency	ABDSP
	Difficulty	***

This route, used by jeepers, motorcyclists, mountain bicyclists and equestrians, is also a worthwhile one for hikers. Try it during off-days (weekdays) or during off-hours (early morning or evening) if you don't like the sound of groaning engines. Since the route is largely downhill, and almost entirely on soft sand or soft dirt, it's ideal for jogging too. A section of the old California Riding and Hiking Trail sometimes coincides with and sometimes parallels the route. The description below assumes that you stay (with a couple of exceptions) on the easier-to-follow roadways.

The starting point is the north terminus of the Jasper Trail (a jeep road), mile 6.8 on the Montezuma Highway east of Ranchita. In the first 2.4 miles, the road traverses rolling, brushy terrain, generally heading south. After passing over a rocky ridge at 2.4 miles, the road drops very sharply down a dry canyon for about 0.7 mile; then it turns north up a slope and briefly follows a ridge to avoid a narrow, rocky section of the canyon. On foot, it's easier to go down the bottom of the canyon and join the road again, saving 0.4 mile, not to mention needless elevation gain and loss.

In the next mile, the canyon is flanked by picturesque, near-vertical rock walls. After this stretch, the canyon widens, and the road swings right (west) to avoid another narrow chasm below. Don't make a short cut this time; follow the road as it crosses a flat and drops into the sandy bed of a draw leading to Grapevine Canyon.

Grapevine Canyon was one of the main routes of travel east from Warner Springs and Julian before the construction of Highway 78

through Sentenac Canyon. Several springs along the way served the needs of travelers in the early days of the automobile. Well before that, the canyon was a favorite camping area of aboriginal peoples. Bedrock morteros and other signs, especially around the springs, attest to many centuries of occupation.

Stuart Spring (0.4 mile east of the Jasper Trail junction in Grapevine Canyon) is the first source of water and a good place to fill up canteens. Angelina Spring, 1.3 miles farther, flows for several hundred feet through a tangle of willows. The road rises onto a bluff to the north; but it is more interesting to walk right along the riparian strip on a parallel horse trail.

At a point 2.3 miles beyond Angelina Spring (below the mouth of Bitter Creek Canyon), Grapevine Canyon Road bends left and then continues toward Yaqui Well and Tamarisk Grove Campground. Continue straight; Highway 78 lies ahead, 2 miles away. Arrange to be picked up here—mile 74.1 on Highway 78, just below the mouth of Sentenac Canyon.

Trip 2: Grapevine Mountain/Bitter Creek

	Distance	6 miles
	Total Elevation Gain/Loss	2400'/2400'
	Hiking Time	5 hours
	Recommended Maps	USGS 7.5-min *Tubb Canyon, Earthquake Valley*
	Best Times	November through April
	Agency	ABDSP
	Difficulty	***

This is a good hike to get acquainted with cross-country desert travel and "peak bagging." You'll make intimate visual contact (but I hope not physical contact) with cholla, hedgehog, beavertail, barrel, and fishhook cacti; in addition you'll see agave, catclaw, and mesquite all thorny or prickly. There are boulders to scramble over on occasion and wildlife trails to follow through the low brush.

Winter months bring invigorating cool air to Grapevine Mountain, but the best months are March and April. This is the time to catch the cactus and the succulent blooms. You'll see everything from the pearl-like flower of the diminutive fishhook cactus to the showy magenta and red blossoms of the hedgehog and beavertail cacti.

A convenient starting point for this hike is along the dirt road connecting Highway 78 and Grapevine Canyon Road. This road intersects the highway at mile 74.1, just below the mouth of Sentenac Canyon. Drive 1.3 miles northwest on this road to reach a parking spur on the left. (Flowing water in San Felipe Creek may block the way; if so, you can park, ford the creek on foot, and walk the extra mile to the starting point.)

The parking spur is just east of a prominent unnamed canyon that leads southwest toward the highest slopes of Grapevine Mountain. Follow the sandy wash leading up to the mouth of this canyon. Around the corner is a formidable granite dike blocking direct progress up the canyon. Climb up and over on either the right or left side, through dense thickets of teddy-bear cholla.

Stay with the canyon for another 0.3 mile,

then veer right toward a saddle just south of peak 2620. (If you continue in the canyon, you'll run into a second and more formidable dry fall.) The first twisted junipers appear on the saddle; junipers will be a familiar feature from now on.

From the saddle, head generally south along the ridge, up and over several small summits, all the way to the top of Grapevine Mountain. At one point you can look down into Bitter Creek Canyon and spot the lone cottonwood tree at Bitter Creek Spring.

Fallen survey stakes and ribbons mark the summit. Down below, the broad trough of the San Felipe and Earthquake valleys shimmers at the foot of a backdrop of dark ranges—the Volcan, Cuyamaca, and Laguna mountains.

Continue by descending west into Bitter Creek Canyon. In the first 300 vertical feet, the going is slippery on decomposed rock, with little worthwhile to hold on to other than a few small manzanita shrubs. Footing becomes easier as you take to a narrow ridge bearing northwest. Drop into Bitter Creek, and follow down the sandy bed for as long as it stays open. Small pools of water may be found here after rainy periods.

Soon you'll encounter a tangle of willow, mesquite, and tamarisk in the creek bed. Don't fight it. Instead climb up to the gentle slopes on the east side. Easy-to-follow animal trails will guide you for about a mile to a point where the creek bed is open again.

Near this point, look for the lone cottonwood, mentioned earlier, that marks Bitter Creek Spring. You'll find it in a nook about 100 feet above the creek bed. True to their names, both Bitter Creek and its nearby spring feature

Running the Pacific Crest Trail near Grapevine Mountain

slightly bitter tasting, mineral-rich water. Old broken pipes lead from the spring to an empty bathtub downslope. The spring is a mecca for local wildlife; trails and tracks (including those of mountain lions and bighorn sheep) radiate from it in every direction.

All that remains is an easy stroll down the broad wash of Bitter Creek Canyon, and a short walk back to the starting point via the dirt road.

Trip 3: Yaqui Well Trail

	Distance	1.5 miles
	Total Elevation Gain/Loss	100'/100'
	Hiking Time	45 minutes
	Optional Map	USGS 7.5-min *Tubb Canyon*
	Best Times	All year
	Agency	ABDSP
	Difficulty	*

Follow the yellow painted footprints from Tamarisk Grove Campground to the beginning of the Yaqui Well Trail, across Yaqui Pass Road. This is a self-guiding nature trail with interpretive signs posted beside several repre-sentative desert wash plants. The trail climbs slightly, skirts a hillside covered with dense growths of cholla cactus, and then descends to Yaqui Well, an important desert water hole.

Yaqui Well is one of the premier birdwatching sites in San Diego County. The presence of surface water and fine growths of ironwood, mesquite, and desert willow have created a micro-environment cooler, more damp, and much richer in food sources than the surrounding arid hills. The well has been used by Indians, prospectors, and cattlemen, and is now surrounded by drive-in campsites. A fenced area keeps humans away from the seeps and allows wildlife undisturbed use of the water.

You can stroll back to Tamarisk Grove Campground by way of either Grapevine Canyon Road or the sandy bed of San Felipe Wash.

Trip 4: Cactus Loop Trail

Distance	1 mile
Total Elevation Gain/Loss	200'/200'
Hiking Time	40 minutes
Optional Map	USGS 7.5-min *Tubb Canyon*
Best Times	All year
Agency	ABDSP
Difficulty	*

The trailhead for this short but somewhat steep and rocky path is directly opposite the entrance to Tamarisk Grove Campground. On the first part of the trail, you'll find interpretive signs for a half dozen or so common desert plants. But the real story here concerns the ubiquitous teddy-bear cholla (also called Bigelow cholla and jumping cholla) cactus, which grows to exceptional size (up to 6 feet high) and density here.

The teddy-bear cholla has a well-deserved, fearsome reputation. Its thousands of glistening spines, like soft bristles, invite tactile exploration, but woe be to those who prick themselves even lightly with a single "bristle." Concealed beneath the straw-colored, innocent-looking papery sheath on each thorn is an incredibly sharp, barbed point. The spiny joints of the cholla can detach at the slightest brush by shoe or clothing, often seeming to jump at and "bite" unwary hikers.

E. Yale Dawson writes this about cholla cactus in his book *Cacti of California*:

> The vegetable kingdom has not produced anything else so fearfully armed. But in the desert one thing is worse than any pain of spine in the flesh. It is thirst. I have seen emaciated, dreadfully dehydrated cattle, deprived of water for months in the blistering heat, so mad from thirst that they eat the terrible cholla. They munch these awful morsels of moisture until their lips are pinned together with the spines, and their throats are a veritable pincushion. The spines eventually cause their death.

Incredible as it may seem in light of the above, there are reliable reports of bighorn sheep browsing on cholla cactus. On occasion you may come across a cholla, hedgehog, or other similarly armed cactus plant broken open with fresh teeth marks in the green pulp.

Barrel and teddy-bear cholla cactus

Trip 5: Bill Kenyon Trail

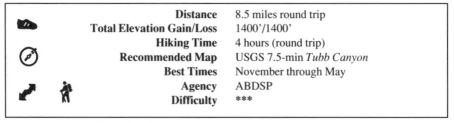

	Distance	1 mile
	Total Elevation Gain/Loss	150'/150'
	Hiking Time	30 minutes
	Optional Map	USGS 7.5-min *Borrego Sink*
	Best Times	All year
	Agency	ABDSP
	Difficulty	*

Walk this easy trail in the early morning or late afternoon, when warm lighting and long shadows soften the landscape. You'll find the marked trailhead at the top of Yaqui Pass, the broad saddle in the mountains between Borrego Springs and Tamarisk Grove. The trail is named in honor of Bill Kenyon, a former Anza-Borrego park supervisor.

Vegetation is varied but sparse around the windswept pass area. Most varieties of indigenous cactus are represented. The best attraction, though, is the marvelous view from the two overlook points along the trail. Dominating the scene is Mescal Bajada, a vast, sloping sheet of alluvial deposits. The stark Pinyon Mountains, the source of the deposits, rise in the background.

You can easily imagine the processes that produced this landscape: Wind and water erosion, aided by alternating hot and cold temperatures, tear at the face of the Pinyon Mountains, opening up ravines and canyons. Great loads of sand and boulders wash out of these openings during floods and build alluvial fans. The fans coalesce to form a sloping skirt (or *bajada*) extending outward from the base of the mountains. Material on the lower edge of the bajada is picked up by flood waters in San Felipe Creek. This debris-laden water flows through one channel and then another, dropping its load gradually and creating a braided pattern of smooth, sandy washes and rubble-strewn "islands" in the bed of the creek.

Flat and uninteresting-looking at midday, Mescal Bajada comes alive with texture and color under the grazing illumination of the low sun. Gray-green seems to predominate, in part because of the dense growth of "mescal" (a.k.a. agave, or century plant) on its surface.

Trip 6: Pinyon Ridge

	Distance	8.5 miles round trip
	Total Elevation Gain/Loss	1400'/1400'
	Hiking Time	4 hours (round trip)
	Recommended Map	USGS 7.5-min *Tubb Canyon*
	Best Times	November through May
	Agency	ABDSP
	Difficulty	***

Dry Pinyon Ridge stands just high enough on the desert rim to support a sparse growth of pinyon-pine trees. Like other similar "islands in the desert sky" such as the Pinyon Mountains and Whale Peak to the southeast, this ridge offers expansive views framed by picturesque foregrounds of eroded boulders and gnarled pinyons.

Happily, the Wilson Trail, an old jeep road along the crest of the ridge, has been converted to a hiking trail. The route leads to almost the exact center of a state wilderness area that is now completely free of motorized travel.

To reach the trailhead, turn west on Old Culp Valley Road from mile 10.4 on Montezuma Highway. The road becomes progressively more difficult to negotiate, especially if the surface has not been freshly graded. Bear right at the fork of a spur road after 0.4 mile. (The left branch leads to a pleasant picnic spot at the foot of Pinyon Ridge) At 1.1 miles from Montezuma Highway, a turnout near Cottonwood Spring (easily identified by tall cottonwoods) offers the last easy place to turn around and park if you decide to drive no farther.

Whether you decide to drive or walk at this point, go another 1.9 miles to the intersection of the Wilson Trail, on the left. There's limited parking nearby.

The Wilson Trail's eroded track meanders south and east over and around a series of rocky knolls on the crest of Pinyon Ridge. Common vegetation seen along the way includes chamise, sage brush, mountain mahogany, scrub oak, sugar bush, manzanita, Mojave yucca, buckhorn cholla cactus, juniper, and, of course, pinyon pine. After 4 miles you'll pass north of "Wilson" peak (4573'). This is a good spot for a panoramic view. Scramble up over the rocks, discover the bench mark, and admire the view. Palomar Observatory's dome gleams on the dark Palomar ridge to the west. The broad sweep of the Santa Rosa Mountains in the northeast serves as a backdrop for Borrego Valley and Coyote Mountain. Far to the east are the Salton Sea and the Chocolate Mountains of Imperial County. The Pinyon Mountains and Whale Peak rise to the southeast; and the Laguna and Cuyamaca Mountains stand to the south and southwest.

If you're looking for a large, flat campsite, you'll find one 0.4 mile east-northeast of Wilson peak (at 4300'). Walk a short distance north from there for a great view of Borrego Valley.

Sacred datura below Pinyon Ridge

Area D-7: Pinyon Mountains

The austere-looking Pinyon Mountains are the northwestern component of a large and complex range, the Vallecito Mountains, lying across the geographic center of Anza-Borrego Desert State Park. (Trips in the Vallecito Mountains proper are covered in Areas D-8 and D-9.)

Although the Pinyon Mountains are largely within state wilderness boundaries, vehicle use is permitted for some distance up several of the sandy washes that drain from them. Most of these motor routes cross Mescal Bajada and intersect Highway 78. Beyond the upper ends of these roads, foot travel will take you into terrain that gets progressively rougher with higher elevation. Besides the hikes suggested

below, there are plenty of other possibilities for exploration. Parts of the Pinyon Mountains have probably never felt the impact of boot or moccasin.

The existence of bighorn sheep in the Vallecito and Pinyon mountains is somewhat of mystery. In 1971 at Blue Spring, and again in 1983 near Harper Flat, water tanks and guzzlers were installed to enhance the bighorn habitat. Before these improvements were made, however, there were no known year-round sources of water. Perhaps in the course of your wandering about these mountains, you may stumble upon an unknown spring, solving this mystery.

Trip 1: Narrows Earth Trail

Distance	0.3 mile
Total Elevation Gain/Loss	50'/50'
Hiking Time	15 minutes
Optional Map	USGS 7.5-min *Borrego Sink*
Best Times	All year
Agency	ABDSP
Difficulty	*

Stop at the Narrows Earth Trail for a brief lesson in geology. Most of the northern Vallecito Mountains consist of granitic rock, part of the Peninsula Ranges batholith that solidified deep underground about 100 million years ago. But here, in an area fractured by faults, it is possible to view some much older metasedimentary rock in close proximity to the granitic rock. These metamorphosed layers of sand and mud represent the oldest kind of rock exposed in the Anza-Borrego Desert.

The interpretive leaflet for this trail is help-

ful, if not essential, to the lesson. Leaflets may be present in a box at the trailhead (or available at the Tamarisk Grove Campground and the Visitor Center in Borrego Springs).

You'll find the trailhead at mile 81.6 on Highway 78, just above "The Narrows" of San Felipe Creek. The canyon behind the trail is designated Powder Dump Wash on topographic maps. For those interested in further exploring, nearby Quartz Vein Wash offers a direct way to climb into the Vallecito Mountains toward Sunset Mountain.

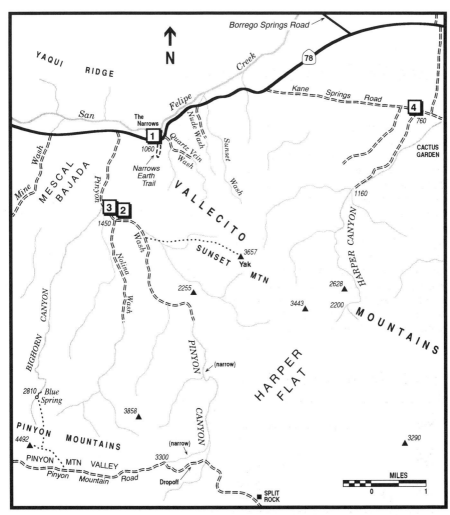

Area D-7: Pinyon Mountains

Trip 2: Sunset Mountain

Distance	6 miles round trip
Total Elevation Gain/Loss	2200'/2200'
Hiking Time	5 hours (round trip)
Recommended Map	USGS 7.5-min *Whale Peak*
Best Times	November through April
Agency	ABDSP
Difficulty	***

Sunset Mountain stands lofty and somewhat isolated from the main Vallecito mountain chain. Seen from Borrego Springs and other points in Borrego Valley, the desert varnished rocks on its rounded flank glow warmly in the evening light. From the west and south the mountain appears more pyramidal and jagged, abruptly rising above the broad, sandy expanses of Mescal Bajada and Pinyon Wash.

An easy and convenient way to climb Sunset

The descent of Sunset Mountain

Mountain is from the west starting at Pinyon Wash. Most ordinary cars can easily reach the intersection of Pinyon and Nolina washes— about 3 miles west of the summit. Turn south at mile 81.0 on Highway 78 onto the Pinyon Wash jeep road and proceed 1.6 miles to the intersection of Nolina Wash. Park off the road on hard-packed sand.

On foot now, follow the Pinyon Wash jeep road east and southeast for about 1 mile. Soon the entire west slope of Sunset Mountain comes into view, and you can picture one or more routes to the top. Among the plethora of possibilities is the broad ridge west of the summit (marked on the topographic map as "Yak"— 3657').

Cross the the small *bajada* at the base of the mountain, and begin the route of your choice. In any event, it will be an arduous climb—a gain of almost 2,000 feet over desert-varnished boulders, loose pebbles, and sinister patches of agave and cactus. The view from the top is worth the trouble, though. The Salton Sea is striking on a clear day—its surface mirroring the blue sky.

If you're going to combine an overnight backpack with a climb of Sunset Mountain, a good place to set up a dry camp is the small wash that passes south of the mountain and north of peak 2255. East of peak 2255 this wash broadens into a shallow, sandy bowl, marvelously insulated from the outside world and protected from the wind to boot. There are at least two obvious routes up Sunset Mountain from there.

Trip 3: Pinyon Mountain—North Approach

![icon]	**Distance**	14 miles
	Total Elevation Gain/Loss	3100'/3100'
	Hiking Time	10 hours
![icon]	**Required Map**	USGS 7.5-min *Whale Peak*
	Best Times	November through April
![icon] ![icon]	**Agency**	ABDSP
	Difficulty	****

Best done as a two-day backpack, this loop trip is still within the scope of an ambitious day hike. Only about a tenth of the total distance covered involves difficult terrain, and most of that is in the first half.

Several dozen bighorn sheep make the Pinyon Mountains their home, and you may have a close encounter with one, as I did recently, in Bighorn Canyon. There being no easy escape route, the surprised ewe clawed her way up an almost sheer granite wall to reach a safer stance on the steep, rock-strewn slopes above. When threatened, bighorn sheep prefer this kind of "escape terrain," on which they're more nimble than any other large animal.

A good place to start this hike is along the Pinyon Wash jeep road. This road intersects Highway 78 at the 81.0 mile marker, and runs south across Mescal Bajada. Drive south 1.6 miles (ordinary cars will usually survive) to the intersection of the Nolina Wash jeep road. Park on hard-packed sand nearby.

Start hiking about 0.3 mile west to pick up one of the washes that drain Bighorn Canyon—the prominent cut in the mountains to the southwest. Don't confuse the mouth of Nolina Canyon, due south, with that of Bighorn Canyon. The going is easy over mostly hard-packed beds of sand for the next 3 miles; then the canyon steepens and there are some short scrambles over small boulder piles. Water may trickle through this section of the canyon for several weeks following a heavy rain.

Blue Spring, 4.0 miles, is the site of a sophisticated water-delivery system for bighorn sheep and other wildlife in the area. Water is drawn from a silted-in catch basin and piped to a series of three 1600-gallon tanks. From there it flows

to an open guzzler. Don't count on this as a source for your drinking needs, especially in a dry year.

Huge outcrops of quartz pegmatite surround and seem to hover menacingly over Blue Spring. Eroded into grotesque shapes by wind and water, they make a long stay here somewhat uncomfortable, particularly after the sun goes down. (In deference to the watering needs of the local wildlife, you should not camp here anyway.)

East of the spring there's a low pass with a tributary of Nolina Wash on the other side. You could use this route as a shortcut back to your car—about 5 miles away.

Our way continues south and much higher.

Mountain lion tracks in Bighorn Canyon

The canyon above Blue Spring becomes very steep and rugged, so it's best to bypass it. From the spring, traverse east for about 100 yards, then go up the ridge leading to the Pinyon Mountain summit, a climb of 1700 feet. You'll be in the pinyon-juniper belt all the way, with plenty of shady spots for rest.

On and near the summit, there are many small, flat areas suitable as campsites, and enough pinyon, nolina and other vegetation to cut the wind. At night, you can watch the twinkling lights in Borrego Valley, gaze at the stars above, and truly feel as if you're "king (or queen) of the mountain."

From the summit, your return is entirely gravity assisted, though you will cover 9 miles instead of the 5 miles covered so far. Descend 500 vertical feet to the jeep road in Pinyon Mountain Valley and follow it eastward as it descends down the head of Pinyon Canyon. After about 2 miles, the road veers south out of the canyon, climbs a bit, and then descends east on a "dropoff" (one-way jeep route); it returns to a tributary wash just above Pinyon Canyon and then veers south toward Hapaha Flat and Fish Creek. Head down the tributary wash to return to Pinyon Canyon.If you don't mind some fun rock scrambling, don't take the road where it exits the canyon—simply stay in the Pinyon Canyon drainage and work your way down the narrow canyon bottom over water-polished slabs of rock. One exciting passage takes you down a sloping dry fall about 35 feet high.

After you reach the mouth of the narrow stretch of Pinyon Canyon, turn north and keep following Pinyon Canyon wash along the west edge Harper Flat. Now classified as state wilderness, Harper Flat is closed to all motor vehicle use. At the northwest corner of Harper Flat, you'll enter another narrow section of Pinyon Canyon. After a couple of twists and turns, you'll come upon the Pinyon Wash jeep road. Follow it an easy 4 miles back to the starting point.

Trip 4: Harper Canyon

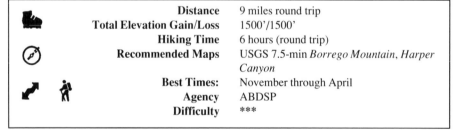

	Distance	9 miles round trip
	Total Elevation Gain/Loss	1500'/1500'
	Hiking Time	6 hours (round trip)
	Recommended Maps	USGS 7.5-min *Borrego Mountain, Harper Canyon*
	Best Times:	November through April
	Agency	ABDSP
	Difficulty	***

Formerly accessible to off-road vehicles, the 4-square-mile expanse of Harper Flat now lies protected within a state wilderness area. Jeep roads approach it from the west and south, but a more interesting route for foot travelers is by way of Harper Canyon on the north.

A patchwork of unmarked access roads at the mouth of Harper Canyon complicates things, so follow these directions carefully in order to avoid taking a wrong turn: Drive south from Highway 78 on the dirt road intersecting at mile 87.2. Go 1.6 miles south to a T-intersection with the old Kane Springs Road. Turn right, drive 0.2 mile west, then veer left on a dirt road trending southwest. (The "jeep trail" marked on the USGS topo maps no longer leads to the mouth of Harper Canyon; instead it leads to a small canyon a mile to the west.)

Those with ordinary cars should find a place to park no farther than 0.5 mile up this southwest-trending road, or back along Kane Springs Road. With 4-wheel-drive you can proceed 1.5 miles to the road's end at the mouth of Harper Canyon. Hiking mileages in this description refer to Kane Springs Road as the starting point.

In the first mile, you skirt the Cactus Garden,

Harper Flat

an area where most common species of cactus on the Colorado Desert are represented, but especially barrel cactus. Some specimens near the road are seven feet tall.

Beyond the roadend, the walls of Harper Canyon narrow, then widen again as tributary canyons split off on both sides. A better name for the canyon would be "Ironwood Canyon." Hundreds of these slow-growing trees line it for 3 miles, providing welcome, if somewhat thin shade during the middle of the day. Desert lavender also grows quite abundantly here. Starting about February, its tiny purple blossoms exude a perfumelike aroma.

At about 3.5 miles the canyon narrows, and you climb over the lower ends of some sharply eroded fins of granitic rock that soar along the canyon wall. Smoke trees and desert willow begin to appear. At 4.5 miles you reach the head of Harper Canyon, and come upon the broad expanse of Harper Flat. Curiously, Harper Canyon drains most but not all of Harper Flat.

If you're making camp here, there are several options for further exploration or travel. Peak 2628 lies directly to the north (scramble up 400 vertical feet), offering superb views of both Harper Flat and landmarks to the north, including the Santa Rosa Mountains and the Salton Sea. Harper Flat itself is rich in ar-

chaeological evidence of Indian use, and is easily investigated on foot. With prearranged transportation, you could devise point-to-point backpacking routes up Harper Canyon and out to points as far away as Blair Valley or Split Mountain.

Area D-8: Blair Valley/Vallecito Mountains

Nestled between the rounded summits of Granite Mountain and Whale Peak is Blair Valley, a focal point of recreational activity in the south part of Anza-Borrego Desert State Park. Nooks in the rock-strewn ridges surrounding the valley serve as popular primitive campsites, and roads and trails radiate out to nearby attractions such as the Marshal South cabin and an Indian pictograph site. Motivated hikers can venture beyond these familiar points of interest and explore summits, such as Whale Peak, that afford some of the best views in Anza-Borrego.

At 2600 feet elevation, Blair Valley gives a taste of the transition zone between low and high desert. Creosote bushes and agave plants thrive in the valley itself, the latter sending up flower stalks by the thousands in April or May. A few hundred feet higher, in the bouldered canyons and on the ridges, juniper, Mojave yucca, ephedra (Mormon tea), jojoba, creosote bush, catclaw, desert apricot, cholla cactus, and

white sage are common. Still higher, toward the summits of Granite Mountain and Whale Peak, pinyon pine, nolina, scrub oak, and manzanita flourish.

County Highway S-2, the long, lonely road paralleling the historic Southern Emigrant and Butterfield Stage routes, provides easy access for hikes starting in the Blair Valley area. Several dirt roads diverge from the highway and climb east into the Vallecito Mountains, where you can car camp or backpack in one of the most peaceful and remote areas of the county.

Another dirt road leads west near the Box Canyon historic site (where in 1847 members of the Mormon Battalion hacked through a passage in solid rock for their wagons) into Mason Valley and up through Oriflamme Canyon. Oriflamme Canyon itself is recognized as a significant mountain-to-desert route of travel during prehistoric and historic times.

Area D-8: Blair Valley / Vallecito Mountains

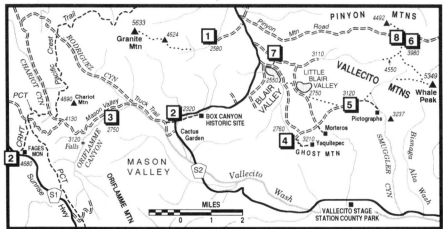

Trip 1: Granite Mountain

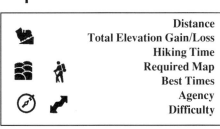

Distance	6.5 miles round trip
Total Elevation Gain/Loss	3200'/3200'
Hiking Time	7 hours (round trip)
Required Map	USGS 7.5-min *Earthquake Valley*
Best Times	November through April
Agency	ABDSP
Difficulty	***

Although there's no trail to the summit, it is possible to climb the mountain from nearly every direction. The Pacific Crest Trail meanders around the mountain's north flank, but never approaches the summit close enough to be much good in facilitating a climb. The following route breathes some life into a task that, on most other routes up this mountain, is a bit of a bore. You'll multiply your satisfaction if you do it on a crystal-clear day—the summit view can be fantastic.

The starting point lies 1.1 miles down a sometimes-rutted dirt road going southwest from Highway S-2 at mile 21.5. From the end of the road, descend into the wash just north, and follow it west through a narrow portal. Complexes of granitic and metamorphic rock are seen along the walls and on the floor of this canyon. Thorny desert apricot bushes grow along the wash bottom, and the slopes are thickly covered with brittlebush, a big producer of yellow, daisylike flowers in early spring. After rains, mosses and grass thrive in the shady spots.

After 0.2 mile the canyon divides. Take the left (major, south) fork, passing over several easy dry falls. At 0.9 mile the canyon splits into three forks. Go about 100 yards into the right

(northwest) fork, and veer left to climb the ridge between the northwest and west forks. You climb moderately at first through sparse growths of cacti and small shrubs. Set your sights on the rocky shoulder 600 feet below and southeast of peak 4624. After attaining this shoulder, work your way steeply upward to peak 4624 over large boulders. Scattered pinyons and junipers appear now.

You'll find flat campsites on the tablelike top of peak 4624, itself a worthy destination for those who don't wish to continue. Earthquake Valley and the Vallecito Mountains lie before you.

Descend west a little and make your way up a difficult slope of brush and boulders to peak 5184. Then follow the easy ridgeline west toward peak 5633, where you may find yourself following deer and mountain lion tracks. After a short, brushy climb you reach the topmost boulder pile—with a truly panoramic view. On the far horizons are Old Baldy in the San Gabriel Mountains (seen just above the head of San Felipe Valley); San Jacinto Peak; a sliver of San Gorgonio Mountain; the Salton Sea; and, beyond Julian in the mountains to the west, Santa Catalina and San Clemente islands!

San Felipe Valley from Granite Mountain

Trip 2: Mason Valley Truck Trail

	Distance	8.5 miles
	Total Elevation Gain/Loss	200'/2400'
	Hiking Time	4 hours
	Recommended Maps	USGS 7.5-min *Cuyamaca Peak, Julian*
		Earthquake Valley
	Best Times	October through May
	Agency	ABDSP
	Difficulty	***

North of the Laguna Mountains and east of the green meadows rimming Cuyamaca Reservoir, Oriflamme Canyon cuts a curved gash in the mountain escarpment—a natural passage leading to the brown floor of the desert. Over many centuries, a well-beaten pathway through Oriflamme Canyon allowed local Indians to migrate easily between winter homes in the desert and summer encampments in the Cuyamaca Mountains. This pathway was also a part of the Yuma Trail, a main travelway between Indian settlements along the Colorado River and fishing villages at San Diego Bay.

In 1772 Pedro Fages, the Spanish military commander of California, led a detachment of three soldiers down Oriflamme Canyon in search of army deserters who had reportedly fled inland from San Diego. This was the first recorded passage by Europeans into California's interior desert. Fages and his men traveled as far east as the present-day shoreline of the Salton Sea, then turned northwest into Coyote Canyon—preceding the first of the famous Anza expeditions by two years.

Starting in 1854, horse and mule riders began to carry mail for the U.S. Army through Oriflamme Canyon. By 1857 the so-called Jackass Mail, part of a mail route from San Antonio to San Diego, made use of the canyon as a short cut. A short time later, the famed Butterfield Stage (St. Louis to California) took over the operation. Only mules could negotiate the Oriflamme short cut toward San Diego; the stagecoaches had to use the much longer and more gradual wagon road up through Box Canyon and past Warner's Ranch (today's Highway S-2 route).

In the 1930s, an unpaved road was constructed on the north slope of Oriflamme Canyon by crews using little more than hand tools. Now known as the Mason Valley Truck Trail, it is currently closed to through auto traffic and serves as a link in the desert branch of the California Riding and Hiking Trail (CRHT). This is the route I describe here—the easiest and fastest way on foot to descend from mountain to desert anywhere in the county. (More difficult and obscure ways down the Oriflamme corridor are described in detail on pages 124-130 in the first edition of this book.)

Since this is a one-way trip, why not persuade your compatriots to drop you off at the starting point and later pick you up at Box Canyon down in the desert. While you hike, they can be sightseeing in the mountains or feasting on apple pie in Julian.

Start at the Pedro Fages monument (mile 36.0 on Sunrise Highway 1.7 miles southeast of Highway 79), where a large turnout is available for overnight parking if needed. Walk 300 yards west along the highway to a cattle grate and find, on the north side, an unlocked gate in the barbed-wire fence. Pass through the gate (please close) and follow the CRHT, which leads east and north into a broad, treeless valley.

At the north end of the valley, pass through a second gate, turn right (east) when you reach the Mason Valley Truck Trail, and proceed through a third gate. Just beyond, the Pacific Crest Trail comes in from the right. Just ahead there's an old water tank in a pleasant grove of planted pines. Springtime displays of blue ceanothus, bush poppies and goldfields, and the white exclamation points of blooming Lord's Candle yucca brighten the otherwise drab slopes.

Now choose between two alternate routes: Our recommended route to the right (Mason Valley Truck Trail/CRHT) descends gradually to a broad saddle between Oriflamme and Chariot canyons. The old road on the left—the current PCT route—is more rugged and dips sharply into the upper reaches of Chariot Canyon; you'd have to climb about 300 vertical feet back up to reach the broad saddle.

At about 3.5 miles, just past the broad saddle, Mason Valley Truck Trail begins a sudden, zigzag plunge down the north wall of Oriflamme Canyon. The furnace breath of the desert is upon you now, but the sound of water rushing through the canyon bottom below atones for that. Down the road another mile or two you'll be able to reach the stream without difficulty. Tree-shaded campsites—and good picnic spots—are found in fair abundance alongside the stream.

Back on the road again, you'll bypass the scanty remains of a work camp used during construction of the truck trail. After that, you emerge onto a broad alluvial fan leading out to Mason Valley. Rodriguez Canyon's jeep trail joins from the left, and the road curves gently right (southeast) to skirt the base of massive Granite Mountain. Cacti of many species are represented here, including a peculiar hybrid resembling both the buckhorn cactus and teddy-bear cholla cactus.

About 0.6 mile past the Rodriguez Canyon junction, the main road is blocked by a gate (private property), but a lesser road continues east and southeast around this parcel and eventually joins Highway S-2 at mile 26.8. A more direct way to reach Highway S2 is via a remnant of the seldom-maintained CRHT. It continues east along the base of Granite Mountain and strikes Highway S-2 at mile 26.5—a good pick-up point. This point is 0.8 mile west of the Box Canyon historical site.

Fages Monument

Trip 3: Oriflamme Canyon

Distance	2.6 miles round trip (to waterfall)
Total Elevation Gain/Loss	500'/500'
Hiking Time	2½ hours (round trip)
Recommended Maps	USGS 7.5-min *Earthquake Valley, Julian*
Best Times	December through April
Agency	ABDSP
Difficulty	***

Oriflamme Canyon's gurgling waters are borne to the open air at a spring high on the east slope of the Laguna Mountains. For 5 miles or so they trickle over polished granite and schist, tumble over small waterfalls, and nourish a line of oaks, sycamores, willows and cottonwoods. At Mason Valley they finally sink into porous sand.

A well-worn cow path, once used to move cattle back and forth between the Lagunas and the desert, threads through the bottom of the canyon. Currently, it is badly overgrown in the narrow, brushy upper canyon; though it probably remains a viable route for determined bushwhackers. On the other hand, it's not too hard to poke into the canyon's lower half, where the water at one point cascades over a 15' precipice. This is a beautiful hike when enough water is flowing—typically after winter rains, and sometimes after sufficiently heavy, late-summer thunderstorms. Be aware that this is prime rattlesnake habitat, so be especially alert and cautious during warm weather.

From mile 26.8 on Highway S-2, turn west on the road signed ORIFLAMME CANYON, which leads to the Mason Valley Truck Trail. With the aid of a 4-wheel-drive vehicle, it's possible to navigate 2.9 miles to the site of a Depression-era road camp (this is 0.8 mile past the Rodriguez Canyon road split). Park off the road and walk down to the alder-shaded creek bank, where you'll discover some old concrete slabs.

From the old camp, find and follow the best path southwest up Oriflamme Canyon on the right bank. The canyon soon becomes narrow, and you'll be forced to walk along the bottom—back and forth across the bubbling stream and over crunchy leaf litter. Look for morteros ground into some of the streamside boulders.

After 1.3 miles (3120') a major tributary comes in from the right (west). Proceed another 0.1 mile south and you'll come upon the sublime, almost hidden 15' cascade and a shallow pool, framed by the twisted trunks of sycamores. Watch out for poison oak growing along the stream hereabouts.

Depending on the condition of the old cow path ahead, you could forge onward to Oriflamme's source about 2 miles up-canyon, and from there ultimately reach Sunrise Highway. If you accept this challenge, you should have the 7.5-minute *Cuyamaca Peak* map for navigating beyond the 15' falls.

Waterfall in Oriflamme Canyon

Trip 4: Marshal South Cabin

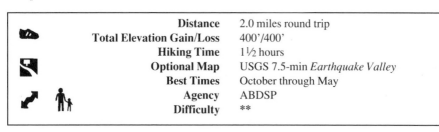

	Distance	2.0 miles round trip
	Total Elevation Gain/Loss	400'/400'
	Hiking Time	1½ hours
	Optional Map	USGS 7.5-min *Earthquake Valley*
	Best Times	October through May
	Agency	ABDSP
	Difficulty	**

The California desert has been home to many an eccentric, but possibly none so audacious as Marshal South. From 1931 until the mid-'40s. Marshal and his poet wife, Tanya, lived atop what was then a very remote mountaintop in the Vallecito area, depending in large part on local resources for food, water, and shelter. Here, they built an adobe cabin, "Yaquitepec"; fashioned an ingenious rainwater collection system; raised three children; and tried to emulate, as completely as possible, the life of the prehistoric Indians.

Marshal South cabin

The ruins of Yaquitepec are today one of Anza-Borrego's noted attractions—and quite easy to reach. At mile 22.9 on Highway S-2, turn east into Blair Valley. Follow the dirt road around the east edge of Blair Valley for 2.7 miles, then turn right (southwest) toward the the foot of Ghost Mountain, site of the cabin. From the road-end parking area a trail climbs in switchbacks up the rocky slope, and turns east along the ridge to the Yaquitepec site. Little remains of the dwelling except some of the walls and the water cistern, but the view from the site is impressive.

South's writings on his family's experiment in primitive living appeared frequently in *Desert Magazine* during the 1940s. These articles are well worth looking up in the library.

Trip 5: Pictograph Trail

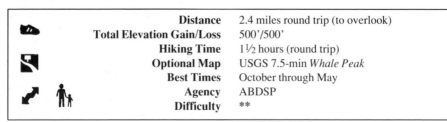

	Distance	2.4 miles round trip (to overlook)
	Total Elevation Gain/Loss	500'/500'
	Hiking Time	1½ hours (round trip)
	Optional Map	USGS 7.5-min *Whale Peak*
	Best Times	October through May
	Agency	ABDSP
	Difficulty	**

The Kumeyaay Indians who made camp around Blair Valley well over a century ago left more than bedrock morteros and potsherds. They also left impressive pictographs—red and yellow painted designs—on the face of a large boulder in Smuggler Canyon. Generations of archaeologists have puzzled over the meaning of these and other pictographs and petroglyphs (etched designs) which appear not only in the Anza-Borrego region but throughout the Southwest. The diamond-chain motif at the Smuggler Canyon site has been linked to puberty rites, but the complete meaning of these rock inscriptions may never be known.

Drive into Blair Valley as described above in Trip 4, but make a left turn (northeast) at 2.7 miles. (At 3.5 miles, a fork goes right—southeast—toward a cluster of large boulders. Walk over, and you'll find Indian morteros on several of the flatter slabs. Note, also, how several of the tallest boulders are pocked with dozens of shallow depressions—called cupules.

Their use was associated with fertility ceremonies and puberty rites.)

At 3.6 miles, a road to Little Blair Valley branches to the left. Stay right (northeast) and continue another 1.5 miles to the end (the topo map shows a nonexistent "petroglyphs" site here).

Continue on foot over the low pass to the east. Once over the top, bear right and stay near the west side of Smuggler Canyon—a wide, sandy wash at this point. You'll find the pictographs on the face of a very large boulder to your right, 0.8 mile from your starting point.

If it's a clear day, don't miss the spectacular view of the surrounding desert from a nearby overlook. Continue southeast down the wide bed of Smuggler Canyon another 0.4 mile to the lip of a dry waterfall. This frames a view of Vallecito Valley to the south. Climb the knoll east of you (peak 3237) for a more inclusive view.

Trip 6: Whale Peak—North Approach

	Distance	4 miles round trip
	Total Elevation Gain/Loss	1500'/1500'
	Hiking Time	3½ hours (round trip)
	Required Map	USGS 7.5-min *Whale Peak*
	Best Times	October through May
	Agency	ABDSP
	Difficulty	***

Whale Peak is probably the most visited major summit in Anza-Borrego Desert State Park. Hundreds of people every year day-hike or backpack into this serene, wooded island in the desert sky. Like Granite Mountain, Whale

Peak yields readily to approaches from nearly every direction. The area around it, however, can prove distressing from a navigational point of view. The peak lies within a complex of similar-looking hogback ridges and gentle valleys, and the peak itself remains hidden from view until you are almost upon it. Count on no sources of water along the way—even storm runoff sinks immediately into the porous, decomposed-granite soil.

The easiest way to climb Whale Peak is from the north at Pinyon Mountain Valley (described here). A long drive on a primitive dirt road is required this way, however. See Trip 7 below for a longer hiking (but easier-on-the-car) approach.

At mile 21.4 on Highway S-2, turn east on the signed Pinyon Mountain Road (high clearance is recommended, 4-wheel drive helps). Stay right (east) at the fork in 0.1 mile, and continue up the alluvial fan. The road is never steep, but there are patches of soft sand and occasional protruding rocks. At 5.7 miles the road tops a watershed divide at 3980 feet in the middle of Pinyon Mountain Valley. Find a place to park in one of the turnouts or spur roads nearby. In his *Anza-Borrego Desert Guide Book*, Horace Parker describes Pinyon Mountain Valley as being "caressed by some of the most invigorating air found anywhere in the world . . . it has the tang and coolness of the high mountains and the warmth and dryness of the deserts."

Head directly up the small canyon to the south. A little hand- and foot climbing is re-

quired to negotiate some large boulders. The canyon soon widens into a sandy flat just below 4400 feet. You can now pick up an informal trail trending southeast over and around several rocky summits. It's unreliable to focus only on following "the" trail, since thousands of hikers, taking different paths, have worn in a variety of routes. Keep track of your position by map and compass. Flat areas for trail camping are quite abundant along the way.

The mature pinyon pine, juniper, scrub oak, manzanita, yucca, and nolina on the north slopes of Whale Peak are San Diego County's best example of the pinyon-juniper woodland community. A similar but much larger expanse exists on the Sierra Juarez plateau just below the Mexican border—some 30-60 miles south.

A little over a mile from the sandy flat, you come to a small valley west-northwest of Whale Peak. From this point scramble directly up the slope to the flattish 5349' summit.

Much time could be spent reading through the climbers' register, but don't ignore the view. In addition to the usual landmarks (the Santa Rosa Mountains, the Salton Sea, etc.), there's a good panorama to the south, including the Sierra Juarez, Signal Mountain, and Baja's Laguna Salada—a huge salt flat that occasionally gets covered by shallow water.

Trip 7: Whale Peak—West Approach

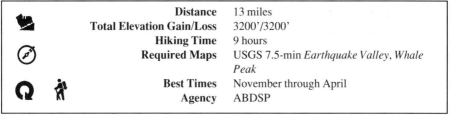

	Distance	13 miles
	Total Elevation Gain/Loss	3200'/3200'
	Hiking Time	9 hours
	Required Maps	USGS 7.5-min *Earthquake Valley*, *Whale Peak*
	Best Times	November through April
	Agency	ABDSP

An interesting mix of experiences awaits you on this trek: a stroll down an old stagecoach path, meandering passages up and down boulder-strewn canyons, even the crossing of a dry lake. Don't forget to take along plenty of water.

You begin at Blair Valley (entrance at mile 22.9 on Highway S-2). Park in the camping area tucked up against a rocky ridge 0.5 mile east of

Highway S-2. Walk north past outlying campsites and climb over the saddle ahead. This is Foot and Walker Pass, separating Blair Valley from Earthquake Valley. Passengers on the Butterfield Stage, which operated along this route in 1858-61, had to walk and sometimes help push the coaches over this rocky pass.

Just north of the pass pick up the dirt road to

Little Blair Valley and go east. After 0.8 mile, bear left (east), while the main road swings south into Little Blair Valley. One mile farther, this spur road ends at the mouth of a small, rocky canyon.

Go up this canyon, taking care to bear right (southeast) at a fork just 0.1 mile ahead. Continue following the drainage up-canyon for another 0.4 mile, whereupon you emerge in a nearly flat valley. Bear east and a little south across the valley (staying with the same drainage), and continue going up a narrow gorge. After climbing about 1000 feet through this gorge, you'll reach a saddle at 4550 feet. This is a pleasant campsite if you're backpacking.

Continue northeast, dropping slightly, until you come to a sandy flat just below 4400 feet. Whale Peak lies 1.5 miles southeast of here—see Trip 6 for details on finding your way to the top.

The trip back to Blair Valley is an interesting variation on the approach route. Go back down the west slope of Whale Peak to a small valley that lies 0.3 mile west-northwest of the summit. Now head generally west, losing elevation steadily, until you drop abruptly into Smuggler Canyon. Follow the canyon out to a broad valley, and turn south toward the pictograph site. (Resist the temptation to continue toward Little Blair Valley by going north of peak 3777—you won't save time this way.) Swing west, picking up the Pictograph Trail and the dirt road leading to it. Once you're in the south end of Little Blair Valley, leave the road and cut straight across easy terrain to the valley's dry lakebed, over a mile away. This creosote-bush-fringed valley often comes alive with wildflowers in March and April. The lakebed itself can become a muddy morass after heavy rain.

Pass over a gap in the boulder-strewn ridge west of the dry lakebed, and voila!—Blair Valley and your starting point lie right below.

Trip 8: Pinyon Mountain—South Approach

	Distance	2 miles round trip
	Total Elevation Gain/Loss	500'/500'
	Hiking Time	1½ hours (round trip)
	Optional Map	USGS 7.5-min *Whale Peak*
	Best Times	October through May
	Agency	ABDSP
	Difficulty	**

A long, bumpy drive up Pinyon Mountain Road puts you within easy hiking distance of the Pinyon Mountains' 4492' high point. The hike itself is easy compared to the drive; it leads to one of the best and most easily reached view spots in the Anza-Borrego Desert.

See Trip 6 for details on the approach by way of Pinyon Mountain Road. From the road summit at 3980 feet in Pinyon Mountain Valley, simply head cross-country up the ridge to the north and west—to the flattish, boulder-studded, 4492' summit. The south slope is almost bald, but good growths of pinyon and nolina are found on the summit and on north-facing slopes, where the sun's drying effect is allayed.

Whale Peak swells across the southern horizon, blocking views in that direction. Opposite, however, is a sweeping vista of the San Ysidro and Santa Rosa mountains, Borrego Valley, the Borrego Badlands, and the Salton Sea.

Area D-9: Split Mountain/Fish Creek

This is the desert at its lowest, hottest, and—to the unappreciative eye—most unfriendly. To those who know it well, however, it is a fascinating labyrinth of rugged canyons, twisted arroyos and mud hills, containing not only some of nature's best examples of earth sculpture, but also a complete sequence of animal fossils spanning a period of several million years. In truth, it's not unfriendly at all. Even the weather is beautiful—at least from late fall into early spring.

Fish Creek is the major drainage system of the area. Numerous washes feed into the upper end of Fish Creek from the south slopes of the Vallecito Mountains and the north edge of the Carrizo Badlands. For more than 2 miles, Fish Creek squeezes between the near-vertical walls of Split Mountain, which divides the rambling Vallecito Mountains on the west from the Fish Creek Mountains to the east. Fish Creek has maintained its course through this gap by cutting downward fast enough to compensate for the rise of the adjacent mountains. Split Mountain's canyon walls reveal layer-cake strata reflecting successive periods of invasion by the sea and reclaiming by the land. Recent faulting has offset some of the layers, creating abrupt discontinuities.

Fish Creek was once a sluggish creek with large potholes in its sandstone and conglomerate floor, some containing desert pupfish. A huge flood in 1916, it is surmised, smothered the creekbed with a thick carpet of sand and destroyed the habitat for the fish. Today's Fish Creek supports only scattered smoke trees, desert lavender, mesquite, and other shrubs. A trademark of the area is the Orcutt aster, a plant whose purple-petaled, yellow-centered, daisylike flowers bloom profuse-ly after the rains come.

Fish Creek and some of its tributaries are open to motor-vehicle use (by street-legal vehicles only). The more remote areas of the drainage system, especially on the north (Vallecito Mountains) side, are classified as state wilderness, and therefore accessible only by foot.

Paved Split Mountain Road leads south from State Highway 78 at Ocotillo Wells, passes the Elephant Trees Area (Trips 1 and 2), and continues south to a dirt road turnoff for Fish Creek Primitive Camp and Split Mountain. Passenger cars normally can make it to the entrance of Split Mountain (starting point for Trip 3). If road conditions allow, high-clearance vehicles usually have no problem on the passage through Split Mountain. Beyond the North Fork confluence (starting point for Trip 4), soft sand becomes more prevalent. Four-wheel drive may be needed to drive as far as Sandstone Canyon (Trip 5).

Mud Hills off Fish Creek

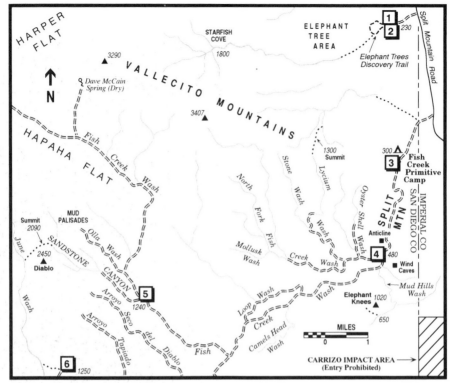

Area D-9: Split Mountain / Fish Creek

Trip 1: Elephant Trees Discovery Trail

	Distance	1.2 miles
	Total Elevation Gain/Loss	100'/100'
	Hiking Time	1 hour
	Optional Map	USGS 7.5-min *Borrego Mountain SE*
	Best Times	October through May
	Agency	ABDSP
	Difficulty	*

The elephant tree is one of Anza-Borrego's most unusual plants. This self-guided nature trail winds through a small group of these trees and calls attention to 20 other plants indigenous to the low, hot, alluvial-fan environment. Numbered posts along the trail are keyed to a leaflet available at the trailhead.

Long considered to be rare north of the border, the few small elephant tree (*Bursera microphylla*) specimens you see here are only a part of a group that includes at least several hundred more to the west (see Trip 2). Elephant

trees are also present in scattered numbers in the south end of the state park near Mountain Palm Springs, and at a small site high in the Santa Rosa Mountains.

The elephant tree is truly a botanical oddity. With a short, stubby trunk, puffy limbs, reddish twigs and sap, tiny green leaves, and purplish fruit, it is right at home with the weird types of vegetation found in Baja's central deserts. Like cacti and succulents, the elephant tree is able to store water internally.

Indians believed the plant was associated

with a great power capable of curing many diseases, especially skin ailments. Shamans kept the sap from the plant hidden away, as it was considered too dangerous to keep openly around a household.

To reach the Elephant Trees Discovery Trail, drive 6 miles south of Highway 78 (at Ocotillo Wells) on the paved Split Mountain Road. A dirt road, negotiable with care by standard cars, goes 0.9 mile west to the trailhead.

Elephant tree and barrel cactus in Alma Wash

Trip 2: Alma Wash to Starfish Cove

	Distance	10 miles round trip
	Total Elevation Gain/Loss	1600'/1600'
	Hiking Time	7 hours (round trip)
	Recommended Maps	USGS 7.5-min *Borrego Mountain SE, Harper Canyon*
	Best Times	December through March
	Agency	ABDSP
	Difficulty	***

If it's solitude you want, this is your trip. Years ago, I hiked in on a cold, silent winter night, under the pale light of a first-quarter moon. I felt as if I were traveling a canyon no one had ever visited before—and that may have been close to the literal truth. In the flashlight's beam I discovered fresh, fist-sized tracks of a mountain lion.

By the light of dawn I discovered the densest population of elephant trees I'd ever seen in one spot. These trees grow on both sides of the canyon, but especially on the north wall, where the tiny leaves of the plants are exposed to the maximum amount of sunshine. Some stand upright 10 or more feet tall, while others, rooted to talus slopes, have limbs that seem to slither along like stunted, battered conifers at timber-line. Once the wiry saplings gain a foothold in small pockets of soil, they survive by rolling with the punches: rock slides merely train the flexible limbs to grow in new directions.

Begin this trip on the Elephant Trees Discovery Trail (Trip 1 above). At post #6, leave the nature trail and bear left into one of the many channels of Alma Wash (which is labelled as such on the state park maps, but not on topographic maps). Follow the braided wash floor southwest around the left (south) side of a low dome, then continue west for about 2 miles up the alluvial fan that debouches from the mouth of a prominent, east-flowing canyon in the Vallecito Mountains. The wash bottom still shows evidence of floods during tropical storms Kathleen (September 1976) and Doreen (August 1977). Note the contrast between the desert-varnished rock on the higher areas of the fan and the gleaming white rock in the recently scoured flood channels. Desert varnish, a reddish or black patina of iron and manganese oxides, takes centuries or millennia to form on

the surfaces of granitic rocks.

Scattered elephant trees appear on the fan as you approach the mouth of the canyon. Conglomerate rock is exposed at its portals, then big slabs of granitic rock—the bare bones of the Vallecito Mountains.

The going is relatively easy—mostly on flat sandy patches, but occasionally over small boulder piles. Creosote bushes intermix with elephant trees on the rocky slopes. From a distance the two plants look similar; the elephant-tree foliage is a slightly darker or grayer shade of green.

After following the canyon for 3 miles, you'll come to junction of several tributaries. Because of its starfish shape on the topo map, I like to call it "Starfish Cove." Campsites on flat beds of sand are abundant here.

Starfish Cove is in the heart of one of the least visited areas of Anza-Borrego. There are numerous peaks and ridges to climb in every direction. On a warm winter day, however, you may be content just to vegetate in the sun and enjoy the splendid solitude.

Trip 3: Split Mountain/Lycium Wash Loop

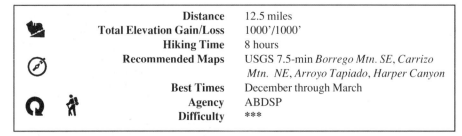

	Distance	12.5 miles
	Total Elevation Gain/Loss	1000'/1000'
	Hiking Time	8 hours
	Recommended Maps	USGS 7.5-min *Borrego Mtn. SE*, *Carrizo Mtn. NE*, *Arroyo Tapiado*, *Harper Canyon*
	Best Times	December through March
	Agency	ABDSP
	Difficulty	***

This long circle trip includes a passage through Split Mountain and a traverse over the arid east extremity of the Vallecito Mountains. For a 3-mile stretch, you'll negotiate some semi-rugged terrain—a scramble through a narrow ravine and a descent along a rocky ridgeline. The rest involves easy walking on jeep roads and along a sandy wash.

Begin at the mouth of Split Mountain, roughly 2 miles south of paved Split Mountain Road. With an early start, you probably won't encounter many vehicles on the several miles of jeep road ahead. The walls of Split Mountain

consist of two stacks of various sedimentary layers, including sandstones and a curious kind of conglomerate called "fanglomerate"—an aggregate of cobbles and sand that originated from deposits on ancient alluvial fans. In places, these layers are tilted or folded into spectacular synclines and anticlines.

Just past Split Mountain's entrance, look for evidence of landslides along the steep cliffs left and right. Notice also the series of vertical fault cracks in the west wall. The fresh debris at the bottom of the cliffs was the result of a 1968 earthquake centered near Ocotillo Wells. The

Visitor Center in Borrego Springs has an interesting videotape of events immediately following this magnitude 6.4 quake.

At about 2.2 miles, just before the "split" in Split Mountain begins to widen, look for a spectacular anticline (an inverted U) of sandstone layers on the west side.

After the split widens, bear right (west) on the jeep road through North Fork Fish Creek. Continue 1 mile through a landscape dominated by clay hills (also called "mud hills" for their consistency when wet) strewn with sparkling chips of gypsum crystal.

Turn right (north) into Lycium Wash, named after the shrub *Lycium*, or boxthorn, which flourishes here and in other badlands washes. Follow Lycium Wash on a meandering course through more mud hills to the end of the jeep road, 2.5 miles past North Fork.

(Serious rock scramblers may want to inves-tigate the fantastic passages through nearby Stone Wash, a west tributary of Lycium Wash. Flood waters in this drainage have carved several steep chutes into layers of conglomerate or fanglomerate. The abundant protruding rocks provide enough handholds and footholds to facilitate a painstaking passage. It is also possible—actually faster—to follow the ridge between Lycium and Stone washes.)

From the roadend in Lycium Wash, continue up-canyon to the mouth of a narrow trench sometimes filled with tinajas. You can bypass the trench by climbing up and over on the right (east) side. The fanglomerate rock soon yields to tilted sandstone layers sculpted by water into fantastic shapes. After scrambling over three low dry falls, you'll come to a big, boulder-choked defile that can be detoured by climbing up and over to the right.

Now make your way north over easier ter-

Greatly folded anticline in sandstone wall of Split Mountain

rain, staying in the biggest drainage as tributaries separate left and right. You'll soon reach a high point along a rounded ridge frosted with darkly varnished granitic rocks. An old cairn of crumbling rocks marks the summit.

Go north from the summit, down along a rocky ridge dividing two north-flowing canyons that later join together. At any convenient place, make a steep descent over loose rocks into either

of these. Then proceed down the sandy wash ahead.

A short cut across the rocky alluvial fan toward the mouth of Split Mountain is tempting, but not a time-saver, as the plain is cut by too many small washes and ravines. Instead simply follow the main wash as it curves east, then southeast toward the road that leads into Split Mountain.

Trip 4: Mud Hills Wash

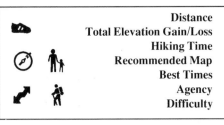

Distance	5 miles round trip
Total Elevation Gain/Loss	300'/300'
Hiking Time	2 hours (round trip)
Recommended Map	USGS 7.5-min *Carrizo Mtn. NE*
Best Times	November through April
Agency	ABDSP
Difficulty	**

This hike will put you within easy reach of ancient fossil-shell reefs so dense that fossils and fossil fragments outweigh the very matrix in which they lie.

You can combine this walk with a stroll through Split Mountain if road conditions block passage by automobile through the Split itself. This would involve an additional 5 miles round trip. We'll assume you can start at the south end of Split Mountain, where parking is available on

hard-packed sand.

Before or after your hike, be sure to check out the "wind caves" on the slope to the east of Fish Creek—just past the south end of Split Mountain. At least three informal trails lead up to several sandstone outcrops, where sandblasting by the wind has hollowed out chambers and skylights. This type of formation is quite common in the Fish Creek watershed and elsewhere in parts of the Carrizo and Borrego Badlands.

Elephant Knees

Just beyond (south of) the starting point, bear left, staying in the main Fish Creek Wash, as the North Fork veers to the right. In another 0.3 mile Mud Hills Wash comes in from the left (south). Walk past the vehicle closure signs and make your way along the smooth bed of this wash. If the wash bottom is wet from rains, you'll accumulate about two inches of mud on your shoes, but that's all part of the fun.

On the right is a spectacular undulating landscape of mud hills, glistening with chips of gypsum. Above this you'll see a flat-topped butte with the formation known as Elephant Knees along its north flank.

About 1.5 miles up meandering Mud Hills Wash, there's a major split. Take the right (southwest) fork, and swing around the south side of the Elephant Knees butte. Here you'll find, scattered along the wash and imbedded within the butte, the fossilized remains of oysters and pectens (scallops) which thrived in a northern extension of today's Gulf of California several millions of years ago.

Further exploration in the immediate area is rewarding, but be sure to keep track of your bearings, especially if you travel overland into the mud hills. Take care not to stray into the Carrizo Impact Area, which is strictly off limits to the public.

Trip 5: Sandstone Canyon—East Approach

	Distance	Up to 7 miles
	Required Maps	USGS 7.5-min *Arroyo Tapiado, Harper Canyon*
	Best Times	November through April
	Agency	ABDSP
	Difficulty	* to ***

Sandstone Canyon has been called the most spectacular small wash in Anza-Borrego Desert State Park. After exploring the main canyon, and any of its many tributaries, it would be hard to argue with that assertion.

For the purposes of this description, a starting point at the mouth of Sandstone Canyon is assumed. Four-wheel drive is usually needed to reach this point, 10.5 miles up the main Fish Creek from Fish Creek Primitive Camp. Jeeps can navigate about two miles up Sandstone Canyon, but its tributaries can be explored only on foot. The uppermost reaches of Sandstone Canyon can be reached from the south via June Wash (see Trip 6).

The walls of Sandstone Canyon consist of horizontally stacked layers of tan and dark brown sandstone. In some places where the sheer walls soar almost 200 feet, there's not much room at the bottom for a car to get through. The canyon bottom is filled with granitic sand and boulders, washed down from the south slopes of the Vallecito Mountains (a largely granitic body). A few large smoke trees inhabit the canyon, along with catclaw, desert lavender, locoweed, and other small shrubs.

At a point 1.2 miles up from the confluence of Fish Creek, a major tributary enters Sandstone Canyon from the right (north). Up this canyon a short distance is a small tinaja below a narrow, almost unclimbable dry fall. In your wanderings about the area, take care not to descend this wash from above in the hopes of reaching Sandstone Canyon.

At 1.7 miles another major tributary enters from the left (west). This narrow slot canyon may be followed for 0.5 mile to the top of the gently sloping plateau above and to the south of Sandstone Canyon. A complex of Indian trails radiates into the Arroyo Tapiado and Arroyo Seco del Diablo drainages, and along the south wall of Sandstone Canyon. Excellent if somewhat frightening views of the bottom of Sandstone Canyon can be seen along the latter trail. You could spend many hours tracing the upper tributaries of Arroyo Tapiado and Arroyo Seco del Diablo, discovering an array of bizarre landscapes strewn with sandstone concretions (erosion-resistant nodules).

At 2.1 miles a third major tributary enters from the right (north). This is an access to the top of the Mud Palisades overlooking Olla Wash. You can go up this canyon 1 mile, bearing right at all forks, and then climb the slope to the right. Technically, the Mud Palisades are a receding cliff, one of several similar features along the south flank of the Vallecito Mountains. The view from the brink encompasses most of the upper Fish Creek drainage and extends to the Imperial Valley and Mexico.

Past the third major tributary, you can go another 1.3 miles to reach the head of Sandstone Canyon—a saddle overlooking June Wash. From there you can scramble up the slope to the southeast to reach "Diablo" peak, where you'll get an inclusive view of nearly the entire Carrizo Badlands.

Trip 6: Sandstone Canyon—South Approach

	Distance	6.2 miles round trip (to head of Sandstone Canyon)
	Total Elevation Gain/Loss	900'/900'
	Hiking Time	4 hours (round trip)
	Required Maps	USGS 7.5-min *Agua Caliente Springs*, *Arroyo Tapiado*
	Best Times	December through March
	Agency	ABDSP
	Difficulty	***

Many an early prospector or traveler tried to find a short cut between the Vallecito Creek corridor (the Southern Emigrant Trail and Butterfield Stage route) and Lower Borrego Valley. Legend says that some of these travelers went "in" and failed to come "out." In the days before accurate maps were available, it was all too easy to become disoriented in the maze of washes within the Carrizo Badlands.

Today, it's not so hard to make a similar traverse, as long as you know how to locate yourself on a topographic map, and find and follow this route:

From mile 41.5 on Highway S-2, southeast of Agua Caliente Springs, turn east on the jeep road signed JUNE WASH (4-wheel drive recommended). A new alignment of this route takes you north along the Vallecito Creek wash, then northeast into broad, sandy June Wash. After about 2 miles, the road veers imperceptibly to the right and follows a tributary wash another mile. There's parking for several cars at the road's end.

Walk over to the main June Wash by heading west for about 0.4 mile. Take note of your route so you can follow it back to your car when you return. Proceed up June Wash over sand and rocks for about 2 miles to just below the 1800' contour, where the canyon narrows and a small, south-flowing tributary joins on the left. Wind-sheltered campsites on flat sand can be found about 100 yards up the tributary.

Continue up June Wash, now over larger boulders, to where the canyon widens after another 0.5 mile. Leave the main wash there, and stay close to the base of "Diablo" peak, which rises on the right. After another 0.3 mile over rocky, cactus-studded terrain, you'll reach a broad saddle at the head of Sandstone Canyon, which lies to the northeast.

The saddle is a major divide between areas that shed water toward Vallecito and Carrizo creeks, and those that drain into Fish and San Felipe creeks. Runoff from the southeast slope of Diablo goes into Arroyo Tapiado and Arroyo Seco del Diablo. Diablo is thus a "triple divide peak." It's no wonder that early travelers were perplexed by the complexity of this landscape.

Your options are numerous now. You could ascend Diablo to the southeast. You could des-

cend into Sandstone Canyon and follow it all the
way (13.7 miles) to the mouth of Split Mountain. With careful map and compass work, you
could also enter one of the upper tributaries of
Arroyo Seco del Diablo or Arroyo Tapiado, and
follow either roughly 15 miles out to Vallecito
Creek wash.

Wall of Split Mountain

Area D-10: Agua Caliente Springs

Take in a deep breath of clean, dry air. Bask in the larger-than-life brilliance of the desert sun. Sink into the womblike comfort of warm spring water. At Agua Caliente Springs you can have your cake and eat it too—hike first, then enjoy a relaxing soak in the hot springs.

A county park has been established here in the midst of state park lands on the edge of the Tierra Blanca Mountains. The big campground and nearby store, along with the bathing pools, have made Agua Caliente Springs a focal point of activity in the southern Anza-Borrego area.

A splinter of the Elsinore Fault is responsible for the upwelling of 98°F, mineral-rich water. The Elsinore Fault passes through the Lake Elsinore area and Warner Springs, where hot springs are also found.

There are two options for hot-water soaking at Agua Caliente Springs: a large indoor jacuzzi (open 9-3), where the water temperature is boosted to more than 100°; and a shallow, outdoor pool (open daylight hours) at a temperature

averaging about 95°. A small "Indian Pool" fed by cold water lies up on the hillside (this pool was closed as of this writing).

Two short trails out of Agua Caliente Springs, described below, penetrate the stark hills to the west and south. A third trip, for hardy hikers only, starts almost a mile higher in the Laguna Mountains.

Agua Caliente Springs lies off Highway S-2, 27 miles northwest of Interstate 8 at Ocotillo, and 22 miles southeast of Highway 78. Driving time is about the same along either route from the central San Diego and South County areas. The northern route (Highway 78) is faster from North County.

Area D-10: Agua Caliente Springs

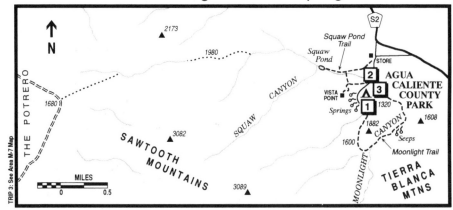

Trip 1: Moonlight Trail

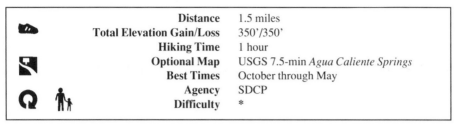

	Distance	1.5 miles
	Total Elevation Gain/Loss	350'/350'
	Hiking Time	1 hour
	Optional Map	USGS 7.5-min *Agua Caliente Springs*
	Best Times	October through May
	Agency	SDCP
	Difficulty	*

This well-marked but somewhat steep and rugged trail climbs over a rock-strewn saddle, drops into a small wash mysteriously named Moonlight Canyon, descends past some seeps and a little oasis of willows in the wash bottom, and finally circles back to Agua Caliente Springs. You'll find the trailhead near the shuffleboard court at the south end of the campground. Although moonlight treks on this trail are possible, a good flashlight wouldn't hurt after dark.

True to their name, the Tierra Blanca ("white earth") Mountains are composed of light-colored granitic rock that tends not to develop desert varnish. The rock fractures easily, and its component mineral crystals break down into coarse sand.

From the high point on the trail, 300 feet above the campground, you can climb an additional 250 feet to reach Peak 1882, offering a superb view of Carrizo Valley and the Vallecito Mountains.

Another, much longer side trip may be made up-canyon (south) in Moonlight Canyon to a point overlooking the Inner Pasture, an isolated valley ringed by the Tierra Blanca and Sawtooth mountains. This is one way to reach a big chunk of BLM-managed public land lying along the west edge of Anza-Borrego Desert State Park (see Area D-11, Trip 7 for more details).

Trip 2: Squaw Pond Trail

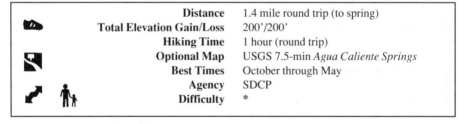

	Distance	1.4 mile round trip (to spring)
	Total Elevation Gain/Loss	200'/200'
	Hiking Time	1 hour (round trip)
	Optional Map	USGS 7.5-min *Agua Caliente Springs*
	Best Times	October through May
	Agency	SDCP
	Difficulty	*

You can pick up this trail at the campfire circle near the county park's entrance. You wind over a low ridge, passing a spur trail leading to a vista point a little higher on the ridge, then descend to a sandy wash in Squaw Canyon. Turn left and make your way past thickets of mesquite—vibrant green when leafing out in March, and festooned with creamy yellow-green flower spikes April through June.

The nutritious pealike pods of the mesquite ripen in September, and are eaten by numerous mammals, including humans. The 19th century American botanist C. C. Parry, who is commemorated in the scientific names of several important native plants, wrote this about early Cahuilla Indian usage of mesquite:

A due mixture of animal and vegetable diet is also secured in the mesquite bean, the pods of which are largely occupied with a species of weevil. The whole pod and its contents are pounded into a fine powder, only the woody husk of the seed being rejected. The process of baking is equally primitive. A squaw takes, generally from her head, a cone-shaped basket of close texture; the meal, slightly sprinkled with water is packed in close layers into this hat or pot as the case may be; when full it is carefully smoothed off and then buried in the sand exposed to a hot sun. The baking process goes on for several hours, till the mass acquires the consistency of a soft brick, when it is turned out, and the hat resumes its proper position on the head. The solid cake so made (if we could forget the process) is sufficiently palatable, containing a gummy sugar which dissolves in the mouth and is unquestionably nutritious.

While pondering the value of native plants, you'll soon come to Squaw Pond—a small spring in a marshy area with several large willow trees and a single palm tree. At least one diamondback rattlesnake makes a living on the small furry creatures that come here to drink. Coyotes and bobcats also frequent this little oasis. On the nearby hillsides you can admire the natural gardens of barrel and teddy-bear-cholla cactus—without a doubt of no nutritive value to any creature but the bighorn sheep.

Just beyond the spring, in a jagged ravine to the south (the main Squaw Canyon), is a tiny cave, a *tinaja*, and a usually dry waterfall. Further exploration is possible up any of the several branches of the canyon.

Trip 3: Mount Laguna to Agua Caliente

	Distance	11 miles
	Total Elevation Gain/Loss	300'/5100'
	Hiking Time	9 hours
	Required Maps	USGS 7.5-min *Mount Laguna, Monument Peak, Agua Caliente Springs*
	Best Times	November through April
	Agency	BLM/EC, ABDSP
	Difficulty	****

Get set for an incredible journey. Botanically and climatically, this is the equivalent of traveling from Canada to Mexico. From the edge of cool pine forest, you descend to a land desiccated by the hot sun and inhabited by austere-looking plants. Depending on the time of day, the temperature increases by perhaps 50°F and air you breathe becomes noticeably denser and drier.

This route offers the only relatively easy way to travel from the top of the Lagunas to the desert floor without trespassing on private property. You'll cross national forest land, a big parcel of BLM land, a strip of Anza-Borrego Desert State Park, and finally Agua Caliente County Park. The BLM land is part of the federal 35,000-acre Sawtooth Wilderness Study Area. The area is seldom visited, rugged in its upper reaches, and extremely remote from the usual pathways of travel.

This hike is strictly a one-way downhill af-

fair, unless for some reason you have the desire (and stamina) to scramble up 3000 feet of loose rock and scree. Backpacking is an option, although day-hiking with light but sufficient gear is probably more rewarding and trouble-free. Plan your water needs carefully, as there is no guarantee of its availability. An early start is important if you're day-hiking; it's essential in November and December, when darkness falls by about 5 p.m.

Have someone (preferably with a good book to read) take you to the starting point, and pick you up later at Agua Caliente Springs. The starting point is found by taking the "Vista Point" turnoff from Sunrise Highway at mile 23.8. (This turnoff is distinct from the turnoff to Desert View Picnic Area, 0.1 mile south.) Drive up the Vista Point road exactly 0.25 mile to the first parking area overlooking the desert. The continuation of this road leads to a telecommunications site (formerly an Air Force radar station) on Stephenson Peak.

At the Vista Point, you'll be able to see most of the route ahead. The green patch in the distance is the *cienaga* at Vallecito Valley. You will turn to the right before reaching Vallecito Valley and go over a divide into Agua Caliente Springs, which is hidden from this vantage point by the Sawtooth Mountains.

The key to an easy descent on this cross-country route is to avoid going straight down. Instead, angle down and to the left (northeast) through low chaparral until you reach a ledge occupied by a gnarled pinyon pine rooted tenuously in bare rock. Step behind this tree, keep angling down along the ledge, and cross a ravine. You should now be able to pick up one of several deer trails lacing the brushy mountainside.

Resist the temptation to drop too fast. Stay generally about 300 or 400 feet lower than (south of) the ridgeline that is directly east of Stephenson Peak. You'll traverse slopes dotted with mountain mahogany, scrub oak, and ceanothus shrubs, and occasionally traipse through colorful patches of lupine.

After a total of about 1.5 miles, you'll have reached a point where it seems best to drop into the bottom of the drainage below. If you're here in April, you'll be able to see, even from a distance, some large yellow-yellow shrubs in the canyon bottom. This is a colony of fremontia, or flannel bush, one of the showiest of California native plants. Some of these spindly shrubs bear thousands of big, waxy, yellow flowers.

A small stream flows through the canyon at this point, flanked by dense clusters of California bay, willow and scrub oak. Follow the water where convenient, or push through the vegetation on the banks. This vegetation includes white sage and desert apricot, typical inhabitants of the higher desert. At the 3160' contour, the canyon widens, and you'll pass under a broken plastic pipe suspended over the canyon by a barbed-wire strand. Follow this pipe north to a dry watering trough, and pick up a disused jeep road leading north into "The Potrero," the large scrub-covered alluvial basin that abuts against both the Laguna and Sawtooth mountains. The Potrero was once known as Treasure Canyon, after a story about a cattle rustler and a bandit who robbed miners from the

Indian Pool at Agua Caliente County Park

rich California gold fields and reportedly hid the loot there.

You now face a long and somewhat tedious march down the length of The Potrero. The disused road merges with a better road, and this road continues about 2 miles toward a prominent rocky hill. At 0.4 mile past the hill, bear right, and go about 0.3 mile to pick up a well-traveled dirt road aligned due north. After 0.5 mile, veer right at the fork and continue northeast about 1.5 miles to the point where the road swings abruptly left (northwest). Now you're beginning to see low-desert vegetation like creosote bush, indigo bush and ocotillo.

Where the road swings abruptly northwest, leave it and head cross-country east-northeast over an easy saddle into a tributary of Squaw Canyon. (Take care not to blunder into one of the drainages that go north into Vallecito Creek.) In Squaw Canyon you will pick up the Squaw Pond Trail, leading to the camping area at Agua Caliente County Park. In this last part of the hike, the only thing driving you on may be lounging in the infinitely relaxing, spring-fed pools.

The edge of the Carrizo Badlands, which includes some of the rawest desert anywhere, lies an easy 3 or 4 miles farther east from Agua Caliente Springs. This fact opens up the possibility of experiencing, in a single day's walk, environments ranging from cool pine forests to hot, barren badlands. There are few places in the world where such a trip is possible.

Area D-11: Bow Willow/In-Ko-Pah Mountains

The area between County Highway S-2 in the south end of Anza-Borrego Desert State Park and the BLM's McCain Valley Cooperative Management Area constitutes some of the most wild, beautiful and serene territory in San Diego County. Here, the Tierra Blanca and In-Ko-Pah mountains serve as a bridge between the hot sands of the low desert and a vast stretch of chaparral-dotted tableland southwest of the Laguna Mountains. Amid the tortured folds of these mountains are fan-palm oases, hidden waterfalls, and many species of plants that would seem more at home in places hundreds of miles to the north or south. Here, for example, water-loving trees like cottonwood and bay are found only a few miles from stands of elephant trees, which are common in the most arid parts of Baja California.

Bow Willow Campground (entrance at mile 48.3 on Highway S-2), the only semideveloped camping area in Anza-Borrego's south end, is a good staging area for hikes into the Tierra Blancas and the eastern In-Ko-Pahs. There is ready access from here into Bow Willow and Rockhouse canyons. Dirt roads lead to Mountain Palm Springs (turnoff at mile 47.1) and Indian Gorge (turnoff at mile 46.1), which are starting points for trips to side canyons, desert valleys and peaks.

Topside, there's McCain Valley Road, a well-graded dirt road that runs some 14 miles north and west from Old Highway 80 near the town of Boulevard. (To reach it, leave Interstate 8 at the Highway 94/Boulevard exit, go 0.5 mile south, then go 1.9 miles east on Old Highway 80.) This road is the only public access into the McCain Valley area, which is managed for mul-

tiple uses by the BLM. Most areas west of this road are open for restricted and unrestricted off-road vehicle use, while most areas east of the road are closed to all vehicle use in order to protect bighorn sheep habitat. With the exception of a few hunters chasing game in certain seasons, the east margins of the McCain Valley Cooperative Management Area are essentially hikers' domain. Cottonwood Campground is a good place for car-camping, and serves as a jumping-off point for hikes into the wild areas lying north and east.

Several interesting but rugged one-way hikes may be undertaken between McCain Valley and the desert floor. One such hike is specifically described below in Trip 7, while others are suggested in Trips 5, 6 and 8.

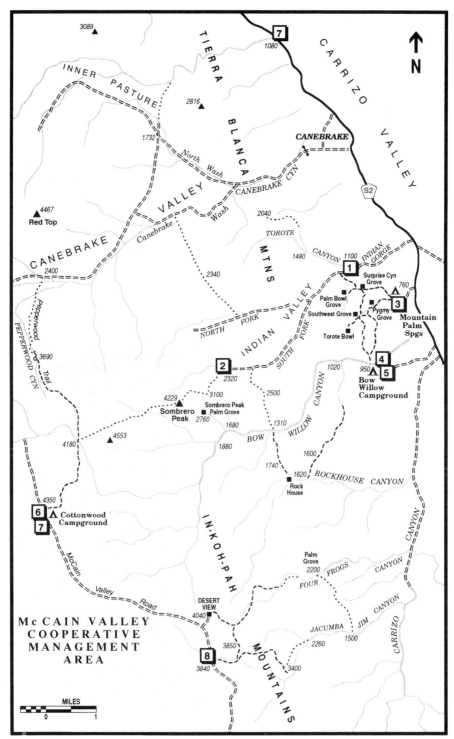

Area D-11: Bow Willow / In-Ko-Pah Mountains

Trip 1: Torote Canyon

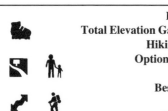

Distance	4 miles round trip
Total Elevation Gain/Loss	1000'/1000'
Hiking Time	2½ hours (round trip)
Optional Maps	USGS 7.5-min *Sweeney Pass*, *Arroyo Tapiado*, *Agua Caliente Springs*
Best Times	November through April
Agency	ABDSP
Difficulty	**

Dozens of elephant trees cling to the walls of this interesting canyon. In Mexico, this tree is called *torote*, which means "twisted," in reference to the haphazard way in which the limbs twine upward.

A series of secluded valleys, each seemingly cut off from the rest of the world, lie up-canyon a mile or two. A broad expanse of sand, a few sparse shrubs, cobbled walls in the distance, and the vault of sky overhead: an hour spent quietly contemplating such purity and simplicity can bring on a feeling of profound peace.

Drive up the road into Indian Gorge (turnoff at mile 46.1 on Highway S-2), and proceed 1.8 miles to the mouth of Torote Canyon on the right (north), where it is possible to pull off the road onto what is usually hard-packed sand. On foot, scramble up the rock-strewn bed of the canyon, passing the elephant trees that seem to cling tenaciously to the steep walls.

After 0.8 mile you enter the first valley, an almost-flat, sand-drowned expanse stretching nearly half a mile. Within this valley the canyon divides, with the main branch (Torote Canyon) climbing sharply up a bouldered crease on the left (northwest). Keep right, in what seems to be the main part of the valley, and proceed north into a small, narrow canyon, a tributary of Torote Canyon. Within 200 yards this broadens into a second valley, similar to the first. Continue northwest to the second valley's end, and climb to the low pass that appears straight ahead. Reaching it, you'll discover a canyon just below that drains east toward the desert floor. To your left (west) you can contour over rocks into this canyon, and within 200 yards reach the east end of still another sand-drowned valley. This one is richly endowed with desert vegeta-

tion, and hosts a lively population of jackrabbits.

This is as good a place as any to turn back and retrace your steps. If you do go on, though, you can make your way west over a divide, descend a rocky canyon, and reach the big valley above Canebrake Canyon.

Smoke tree in Torote Canyon

Trip 2: Sombrero Peak—East Approach

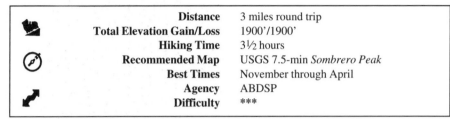

	Distance	3 miles round trip
	Total Elevation Gain/Loss	1900'/1900'
	Hiking Time	3½ hours
	Recommended Map	USGS 7.5-min *Sombrero Peak*
	Best Times	November through April
	Agency	ABDSP
	Difficulty	***

Cone-shaped Sombrero Peak rises head and shoulders above the east lip of the McCain Valley plateau, overlooking a hundred-square-mile expanse of rock-strewn mountains and gorges, sun-baked valleys, and distant badlands. Conversely, the peak itself is a prominent and familiar landmark widely observed from the desert below.

There is but one relatively easy way to climb to the summit from the desert side, involving a rather long approach by car up Indian Gorge and Indian Valley. (Another way to climb this mountain is from the west—see Trip 6.)

From Highway S-2, turn west and drive through Indian Gorge. After 2.0 miles, the walls of the gorge part, and you enter Indian Valley. In another 0.7 mile, the road splits, with branches going into the north and south forks of Indian Valley. Keep left at this junction and drive into the south fork about 3 miles to the road's end near the mouth of a canyon dotted

(higher up) with a few palms. On a slope above this drainage, archaeologists have identified an Indian ceremonial site keyed to the rising position of the sun at summer solstice.

From the roadend, climb straight up the ridge to the south until you reach a flat at elevation 3100 feet. As a side trip from here, you could traverse over to Sombrero Peak Palm Grove, a dense cluster of palms with no surface water in evidence. Continue west, then southwest up the ridgeline to Sombrero's boulder-studded summit—scrambling over modest-sized rocks all the way. On top, the best view is east, where Bow Willow Canyon and its tributaries yawn open in the blazing sun.

On your return to Indian Valley, don't be tempted to descend the east slope toward Sombrero Peak Palm Grove; house-sized boulders and scratchy thickets of scrub oak will stop you!

Trip 3: Mountain Palm Springs

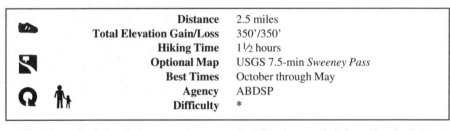

	Distance	2.5 miles
	Total Elevation Gain/Loss	350'/350'
	Hiking Time	1½ hours
	Optional Map	USGS 7.5-min *Sweeney Pass*
	Best Times	October through May
	Agency	ABDSP
	Difficulty	*

The Mountain Palm Springs area boasts, without a doubt, the most charming palm oases south of Borrego Palm Canyon. The palms here are gregarious, growing in dense clusters, often with pools of water at their feet. Many have never been burned: they still hold full skirts of

dead fronds around their trunks, the better to serve the local population of rodents and snakes. In late fall and early winter, the sticky, sweet fruit of the palms hangs in great swaying clusters, sought after by birds and the sleek coyotes that prowl up and down the washes.

The palm groves are distributed along several small washes that drain roughly a square-mile area on the east side of the Tierra Blanca Mountains. Water lies close to the surface in several of the ravines. A primitive camping area sits on the alluvial fan just below the point where the washes come together. A short dirt road leads to this campground from mile 47.1 on Highway S-2.

Consider the loop hike described here as a fairly complete tour of the area; but do be enticed to extend your explorations in the form of side trips or extended loop trips if the spirit moves you.

Begin by walking up the small canyon southwest of the primitive camp. Past some small seeps you'll come upon the first groups of palms—Pygmy Grove. Some of these small but statuesque palms grow out of nothing more than rock piles.

A long pause is in order at Southwest Grove, a restful retreat shaded by a vaulted canopy of shimmering fronds. A rock-lined catch basin fashioned for the benefit of the local wildlife mirrors the silhouettes of the palms. A couple of elephant trees cling to the slopes just above the grove, but for a better look at these curious plants, you can climb a spur trail to Torote Bowl, where a bigger group of elephant trees will be found. Further travel (cross-country over boulders) can take you to a single large specimen, perhaps 15 feet tall and 20 feet wide, 0.6 mile west-southwest of Torote Bowl, and 0.4 mile south of "Palm" peak.

From Southwest Grove, pick up the well-worn, but obscure trail that leads north over a rock-strewn ridge to Surprise Canyon Grove in Surprise Canyon. Up-canyon from this small grove lies Palm Bowl, filled with tangled patches of mesquite and fringed on its western edge by more than a hundred palms. On warm winter days, the molasseslike odor of ripe palm fruit wafts upon the breeze, and phainopepla hoot and flit among the palm crowns, their white wing patches flashing.

Northwest of Palm Bowl Grove, an old Indian pathway leads over a low pass into Indian Gorge—another tempting diversion. To conclude the loop hike, however, you return to

Spring at Southwest Grove

Surprise Canyon Grove and continue down-canyon to the campground. On the way, you pass North Grove, hidden in a side drainage on the left.

Trip 4: Bow Willow/Rockhouse Canyon Loop

	Distance	7.5 miles
	Total Elevation Gain/Loss	1100'/1100'
	Hiking Time	4½ hours
	Recommended Maps	USGS 7.5-min *Sweeney Pass*,
		Sombrero Peak
	Best Times	November through April
	Agency	ABDSP, BLM/EC
	Difficulty	***

A simple shack fashioned of rock, cement and corrugated metal might be unremarkable anywhere else, but in the midst of thousands of acres of wild desert, it becomes a significant point of interest. The old cattlemen's line shack in Rockhouse Canyon is a case in point: hikers routinely travel miles overland to visit it.

This rather popular if somewhat rugged hike includes some stretches of well-worn but poorly marked trails. Ducks and wooden stake markers are of some help in following the route. Topo maps are very handy if you do go off course.

A 1.5-mile-long graded dirt road, intersecting Highway S-2 at mile 48.5, leads in to Bow Willow Campground, where the hike begins. Walk 0.5 mile up-canyon; on your left (south) is a small alluvial fan leading up to a rocky draw in the mountains. Clamber upward through this draw, passing a single palm tree (whose source of water is mysterious), gaining about 200 feet. You'll come up to a sandy wash that winds upward to a gently sloping plateau area of broken rock formations. Hardy desert plants, like cholla cactus, ocotillo and creosote bush, cover the area. After you stay with the wash for about a mile, ducks and wooden markers guide the way generally south-southwest over an almost imperceptible divide (1600'), then down more steeply onto the broad floor of Rockhouse Canyon.

The jeep road shown on the topo map is gone now; simply head up-canyon 0.5 mile to an elliptical valley thickly covered with cholla and ocotillo. Nestled against the rocky hillside on the south side of this valley is the line shack, which leans against the face of a large boulder. The decrepit interior of the shack houses the remains of a fireplace and the usual rusty bedsprings.

East of the shack, at the mouth of a canyon, is a watering trough and the remains of a pipeline to a seasonal spring and waterfall 0.4 mile up-canyon. A pleasant hour or two can be spent exploring this canyon and the next canyon to the west.

The line shack marks the halfway point of the hike. Return by going directly over the low pass to the north into Bow Willow Canyon. An old cattle trail—probably once an Indian trail—traverses this pass. Once in Bow Willow Canyon, the walking is very easy over open stretches of firm sand.

Trip 5: Bow Willow Canyon

	Distance	7.5 miles round trip (to palms)
	Total Elevation Gain/Loss	750'/750'
	Hiking Time	4 hours (round trip)
	Optional Maps	USGS 7.5-min *Sweeney Pass, Sombrero Peak*
	Best Times	November through April
	Agency	ABDSP
	Difficulty	***

The intriguing name "Bow Willow" seems to be associated with the supple wood of the desert willow, used by Indians to fashion hunting bows. Hundreds of these fragrant, bushy trees are scattered along Bow Willow Canyon's lower end. A small spring at the mouth of the canyon serves a modest campground and a seasonal ranger station.

Vehicles were allowed on the sandy bed of Bow Willow Canyon until the early 1980s, when flash flooding obliterated the road and half the campground. Thereafter, park officials decided to keep the canyon vehicle-free. In 1985 new campsites, replacing those washed away, were built on a gentle slope out of reach of floodwaters.

The now-silent lower canyon is perfect for cool-weather hiking. Its white ribbon of sand winds, fjordlike, some 3 miles between steep walls heaped with desert-varnished boulders. In the upper canyon, the terrain becomes more rugged: the canyon divides into several branches cut deeply into the In-Ko-Pah mountains.

Start walking at the campground, 1.5 miles west of Highway S-2. Walking in the wash is easy since the sand is made up of rather large crystals deriving from easily decomposed granitic rocks above. As you stroll along, look for elephant trees—a few cling inconspicuously to the south wall. The canyon bends abruptly south, then gradually resumes a western course. The massive east flank of Sombrero Peak can be seen ahead, resplendent in early morning sunshine.

After 2.7 miles, a low pass over the ridge to the south-southeast can be seen. This is the route from Rockhouse Canyon (see Trip 5). On the opposite (north) side, a faint trail up and over the north wall leads to the South Fork of Indian Valley—a vigorous climb for the adventurous.

Our way straight ahead (west) now becomes increasingly choked with obstacles—low brush, rocks, and, during most of the year, a bubbling stream. The first scraggly palms appear at about 3.0 miles; but much finer specimens are seen farther on. Year-round water in the upper canyon nourishes dense growths of mesquite, catclaw, willow and tamarisk in or near the streamcourse. Detour around this tangle of vegetation by staying high on the banks.

At about 3.7 miles (1680'), a dry tributary comes in from the northwest. (This tributary can be used to reach Sombrero Peak Palm Grove, an enigmatic, solitary cluster of palms on the flank of Sombrero Peak.) This junction is as good a place as any to have lunch before returning. Listen for the sound of falling water, and you'll be drawn to one of the secret grottos found in the canyon.

A major fork lies upstream (1880'), with V-shaped branches going west and southwest. The right fork is steeper, with less water, while the left fork enjoys a nearly perennial flow of water over massive boulders. In both branches (which ultimately lead to more gentle terrain atop the McCain Valley plateau) scattered cottonwood and alder trees lend a touch of softness to the harsh glare of naked granite.

Trip 6: Sombrero Peak—West Approach

	Distance	9 miles round trip
	Total Elevation Gain/Loss	1300'/1300'
	Hiking Time	6 hours (round trip)
	Required Map	USGS 7.5-min *Sombrero Peak*
	Best Times	October through May
	Agency	BLM/EC
	Difficulty	***

Dust off your map-and-compass skills—you'll really need them on this approach to Sombrero Peak via the rolling McCain Valley plateau. The peak stays largely hidden behind growths of chaparral and intervening ridges until you're practically upon it. To make matters more difficult, many of the roads and jeep trails shown on the most recent USGS topo map of the area are totally overgrown and some new roads have appeared in the interim.

A good place to begin is Cottonwood Campground, 12.7 miles northwest of the Mc-Cain Valley Road/Old Highway 80 intersection. It's nestled in a pleasant strip of oak woodland along an upper tributary of Bow Willow Creek. Bedrock morteros nearby show that the Indians liked this area too.

Pick up the hiking and horse trail (a disused dirt road) 0.1 mile north of the campground entrance. Heading east at first, the trail soon swings generally north, crossing two small tributaries of Bow Willow Canyon. After about 1 mile, a 0.3-mile-long public easement begins, taking you through a corner of a private inholding within the BLM lands.

At 2.0 miles from the campground you should leave this trail (which continues north into Pepperwood Canyon) and swing east over a gentle divide north of peak 4553. Once over the divide, work your way entirely cross-country east-northeast across a shallow tributary of Bow Willow Canyon and up along an east-trending ridge. Try to choose an easy route through the maze of tall, widely spaced chaparral shrubs. From higher ground, the conical summit of Sombrero Peak may pop into view.

Eventually, you'll come to a "Sombrero Peak" sign at the base of the last pitch. A short,

tough scramble up a heap of huge boulders puts you on the summit. Your route-finding challenge is now only half over; on the return you'll need to navigate back toward peak 4553 and find the trail leading back to Cottonwood Campground.

Using a variation of the approach described here, expert hikers can use Bow Willow Canyon to reach the desert floor. These canyons are boulder-strewn and rugged, graced with palms and cottonwoods, and semi-perennial streams.

Sombrero Peak

Trip 7: Pepperwood Trail to Canebrake

	Distance	14.0 miles (to Highway S-2)
	Total Elevation Gain/Loss	450'/3700'
	Hiking Time	8 hours
	Required Maps	USGS 7.5-min *Sombrero Peak, Agua Caliente Springs*
	Best Times	November through April
	Agency	BLM/EC
	Difficulty	***

On a cool day this is one of the most delightful downhill hikes in the county. Except for a 2-mile scramble down the eroded and overgrown remnants of the Pepperwood Trail in Pepperwood canyon, little effort is required to keep moving. Below Pepperwood canyon, the route traverses the lonely reaches of Canebrake Valley and the Inner Pasture; these two form a large, U-shaped alluvial plain surrounded by the stark, boulder-strewn slopes of the Tierra Blanca and Sawtooth mountains. Much of this area is encompassed within the BLM's Sawtooth Mountains Wilderness Study Area.

The riparian area along the upper part of Pepperwood canyon is a worthy enough destination of itself, as a trail of footprints attests. Traffic down the lower end of the Pepperwood Trail is virtually nil, though. Few people visit Canebrake Valley and the Inner Pasture either, save for ranchers who have been granted grazing allotments. If the BLM ever acts on a longstanding proposal to reconstruct and extend the Pepperwood Trail and develop a trail camp, more people will surely be drawn this way.

Begin, as in Trip 6 above, at Cottonwood Campground. Proceed east and then generally north on the trail (former jeep road) toward Pepperwood canyon. At 2.0 miles and 2.7 miles, trails (old roadbeds) diverge left and right, respectively. Stay on the main route, which veers northwest over a divide and begins a steep descent between two tributaries of Pepperwood canyon.

As you descend, the trail becomes steeper and more obscure, until finally it is only a narrow path kept recognizable through occasional use by hikers and wildlife. The soil is a loose, decomposed granite that flows downslope with

your every step.

Before long, there's a pungency in the air that brings a sense of *deja vu* to those familiar with the Coast Ranges of Northern California and Oregon: this is the unmistakable fragrance of the pepperwood tree (California bay, or bay laurel). When crushed and sniffed, the leaves give off an odor that is pleasant but, if overdone, the cause of a headache. The line between pleasure and pain is a fine one, yet who can resist going the limit?

Stumbling down past the first pepperwoods, you reach the canyon bottom and a stretch of flat sand (4 miles, 3720'). A seasonal waterfall is just upstream, shaded by pepperwoods and cottonwoods. Downstream about 200 yards is a year-round spring in the flat bed of the creek. This area is a good place to turn around if you wish to go no farther.

Beyond the spring, faint trails lead down the steep walls of both sides of the canyon. Try to follow the trace of the original foot trail (as plotted on the *Sombrero Peak* topo map) on the ridge east of the canyon bottom. This leads, after some moderate scrambling over loose rocks and through low brush, to the floor of Canebrake Valley.

A search of the south side of the valley might turn up, among the strangely eroded granitic rock formations, many Indian morteros and a ceremonial site related to fertility rites. Without lots of time to spare, however, you should continue north to pick up the dirt road that will take you, after several miles, to Inner Pasture.

Strangely enough, Inner Pasture is drained by two major washes—North Wash, which flows through Canebrake Canyon, and another, unnamed wash that cuts through the Tierra

Blanca Mountains to the northeast. It seems only a matter of a short time, geologically, before one or the other wash captures the entire drainage.

This unnamed wash can be your exit. You'll reach mile marker 41.0 on Highway S-2 after a walk of about 3 miles. The easy stroll down this wash is a fitting climax to a long day's (or weekend's) hike. In the late afternoon sun, the shattered walls of granite on either side glow softly, offering a silent benediction.

There are at least three other ways to exit. From a south arm of Canebrake Valley, it is possible to reach Indian Valley's north fork via a rocky pass; this is the BLM-proposed route for the lower end of the Pepperwood Trail. From Indian Valley one could walk out to S-2 or get a prearranged ride. Another, more obvious, route is right through Canebrake Canyon itself, but private lands within the canyon make this route inadvisable without permission. By finding a low gap in the ridge north of Inner Pasture, you could also exit by way of Moonlight Canyon into Agua Caliente Springs.

Palms at Suprise Canyon Grove

Trip 8: Four Frogs/Jacumba Jim Loop

	Distance	9 miles
	Total Elevation Gain/Loss	3200'/3200'
	Hiking Time	8 hours
	Required Maps	USGS 7.5-min *Sombrero Peak*, *Sweeney Pass*
	Best Times	November through April
	Agency	BLM/EC
	Difficulty	****

The palm-lined canyons known informally as "Four Frogs" and "Jacumba Jim" lie in the heart of the BLM's Carrizo Gorge Wilderness Study Area, a region whose east boundary abuts a large expanse of state wilderness in adjacent Anza-Borrego Desert State Park. The area supports a sizable herd of bighorn sheep most of the year. During the springtime lambing season, the sheep cross Carrizo Gorge and take up residence in the Jacumba Mountains. The strenuous, cross-country loop hike described here touches

both canyons and gives a good overview of this rugged area.

Unlike most long trips in this book, this one starts "at the top," with most of the work—a 2400' elevation gain over gut-wrenching terrain—at the end. You'll dip deeply into your energy reserves for this one. Do it in a single long day, or take your time and backpack in.

A good place to begin is the intersection of McCain Valley Road and the former Lost Valley Road. Drive 8.0 miles north of Old Highway

80 to reach this unmarked road/trail and find a place to park.

Past a steel gate, the abandoned road takes you 0.5 mile east to an overgrazed meadow and the eroded remnants of a cattle pond. Above it, cross a flood-torn gully, proceed north on traces of a jeep trail over a viewful summit (0.9 mile), and continue down a slope into a wide draw. Stay in the draw (northeast) as old roadbeds intersect from the left. At 1.9 miles a good trace of jeep road detours you up and across the slope to the north, avoiding a sharp dropoff. After returning to the draw, pick your way down along the bottom for another mile. A thin stream of water flows here about half the year.

At 3.5 miles easy walking ends as you come to a spectacular abyss at the head of Four Frogs canyon. Negotiate a route downward over the tops of the truck-sized boulders and slabs, and you will soon see clusters of palms below. Little or no surface water is present at the biggest grove (2200'), but it's nice to stop here for shade.

A good two thirds of the trip, in terms of effort, remains ahead. Head due east from the grove, first contouring, then climbing obliquely, to a small flat (2450') on the ridgeline above. Now, taking the path of least resistance, proceed generally south-southeast 0.5 mile across the glaring slopes to a flattish area, again at 2450 feet, covered with scattered low shrubs. This can be used as an excellent dry campsite, with a panoramic view of Carrizo Canyon and its many tributaries. Bighorn sheep "beds" (scuffed areas) and scats are common in this area.

Next continue generally south-southeast, descending sharply into Jacumba Jim canyon. You may notice a low wall of stones, possibly an Indian hunting blind, on the way down. Upon reaching bottom, turn west and make your way up toward the first set of palms. The springs in this canyon are among the most dependable in the In-Ko-Pahs, and a vigorous supply of water cascades over the polished rock after rainfall. Above the first palms, however, the canyon becomes choked with vegetation, and it is necessary to clamber over the rocks on slopes north of the creek to make decent progress.

Water trickling over numerous small falls can be heard below.

Many more palms are found above 2260 feet, where a tributary canyon comes in from the right (west). At this point it's time to begin climbing in earnest. Swing southwest onto the ridge between the two forks and climb up the sandy slope. Make your way through large and small semidesert shrubs (scrub oak, juniper, sugarbush, mountain mahogany) and a few palms. After about 0.7 mile, past an obstacle course of large rocks, you'll reach an old jeep road that leads northwest and west toward the washed-out pond and the meadow east of your car.

Fishhook cactus in bloom

Area D-12: Carrizo Badlands

Much of southern Anza-Borrego is blanketed by the low, hot, and intricately dissected terrain known as the Carrizo Badlands. Spectacular examples of erosion in soft claystones, mudstones and sandstones are found throughout the area. You'll see clay hills, mud caves, small arches and windows, receding cliffs, sinuous washes, and deep-cut ravines.

Five million years ago, today's badlands were nothing but ooze at the bottom of a shallow sea that occupied the southeastern corner of California. The same geological forces that built up the Peninsular Ranges to the west raised and tilted these soft sedimentary deposits. Erosion has acted almost as quickly to tear them down. The forces of wind and gentle rainfall, acting slowly, have done their part to smooth a few rough edges; but it is the catastrophic events—the rare flash floods and earthquakes—that have played and will continue to play the major roles as shapers of this chaotic-looking landscape.

The Coyote Mountains, bordering the Carrizo Badlands on the south, have a core of ancient granitic and metamorphic rocks overlain by marine sediments. Erosion has cut down through the softest sediments, leaving harder sandstones and fossil-shell reefs exposed. Fossil Canyon, Painted Gorge, and other areas on the east end of the range in Imperial County (not covered in this book) are well worth exploring. On the west end of the range, older metamorphic and granitic rocks are exposed in places such as Canyon Sin Nombre and Mine Peak.

In the western Carrizo Badlands, centered on Arroyo Tapiado, many fossils of land creatures, dating back one to two million years, have been found, including bones of mammoth, sabertooth cat, rhinoceros, camel, and dire wolf.

County Highway S-2, the road that finally opened up southern Anza-Borrego to easy access by conventional autos in the early '60s, is still the only way to reach the areas described here. Most San Diego County residents will find it easier to come by way of the south end of Highway S-2—from Interstate 8 at Ocotillo.

As in the Borrego Badlands, most of the major Carrizo Badlands washes are open to street-legal vehicles. Hikers, however, have exclusive access to the hundreds of miles of smaller drainages.

Area D-12: Carrizo Badlands

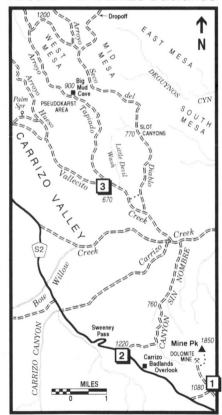

Trip 1: Mine Peak

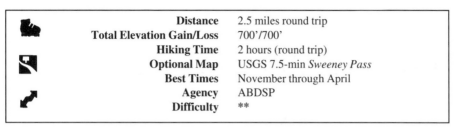

	Distance	2.5 miles round trip
	Total Elevation Gain/Loss	700'/700'
	Hiking Time	2 hours (round trip)
	Optional Map	USGS 7.5-min *Sweeney Pass*
	Best Times	November through April
	Agency	ABDSP
	Difficulty	**

Mine Peak (1850') is the highest point on the west end of the Coyote Mountains. On a clear day the view from the summit seems to go on forever, with the wrinkled Carrizo Badlands in the north, the cobbled Tierra Blanca, In-Ko-Pah, and Jacumba mountains to the west through south, and the flat, hazy Yuha Desert and Salton Sink to the southeast and northeast.

Turn east at mile 53.4 on Highway S-2 onto the West Dolomite Mine Trail. Drive 0.7 mile, then turn sharply left (north). Go 0.2 mile to a large parking area and stop. After this, the road sharply deteriorates.

On foot now, cross a wash and continue up the road 0.6 mile to an abandoned dolomite mine. From here it's a simple matter of scrambling straight up the ridge, due north, to the rounded summit of Mine Peak.

**Concretions in tributary
of Canyon Sin Nombre**

Trip 2: Canyon Sin Nombre

	Distance	5 miles round trip
	Total Elevation Gain/Loss	550'/550'
	Hiking Time	3 hours (round trip)
	Optional Map	USGS 7.5-min *Sweeney Pass*
	Best Times	November through April
	Agency	ABDSP
	Difficulty	**

One of the best examples of a slot canyon in Anza-Borrego's south end is off of Canyon Sin Nombre (Canyon without a Name). Canyon Sin Nombre serves as a rugged route for vehicle travel between Highway S-2 above Sweeney Pass and Carrizo Creek, but it's seldom busy. Hiking down this canyon, especially when a low sun brings out the variegated colors of its walls, is pure delight.

Park in the small turnout at mile 51.3 on Highway S-2, and begin by following the vehicle tracks that descend steeply down a sandy slope toward the head of Canyon Sin Nombre. As you approach the head of the canyon, admire the beautiful barrel cacti on the flats and slopes nearby: many grow to heights of 5 feet or more. Notice how they lean south— toward the sun at its brightest.

The entrance walls are only a foretaste of the hodgepodge of shapes and colors to come. The twisted brown and gray layers are Julian Schist, a metasedimentary rock commonly found around Julian, where it is associated with gold-bearing ore. Small pieces of petrified wood can

be found near here. Just beyond, some granitic rock is exposed. On the right (east) wall, about 0.3 mile farther, notice the crumpled swirl of sedimentary layers.

Farther on, the canyon broadens somewhat, and the walls are fashioned from a more uniform-textured mudstone and sandstone. At a point 1.3 miles into the canyon—at the 760' contour—a tributary cuts deeply into the cliflike left (west) wall. This becomes a narrow slot canyon, with walls perhaps 150 feet high. A squeeze through, climbing all the while, brings you to the top of the cliffs overlooking Canyon Sin Nombre.

The easiest way to return is the same way you came. Further exploration in this area might include a trek up the trace of an Indian trail running southwest along the hills west of Canyon Sin Nombre in the direction of Sweeney Pass; this trail can be picked up above the slot canyon. You might also try poking into one of the many concretion-littered tributaries east of Canyon Sin Nombre and north of Mine Peak.

Trip 3: Arroyo Tapiado/Arroyo Diablo Loop

	Distance	16.5 miles
	Total Elevation Gain/Loss	600'/600'
	Hiking Time	8 hours
	Recommended Map	USGS 7.5-min *Arroyo Tapiado*
	Best Times	December through April
	Agency	ABDSP
	Difficulty	****

This is one of the longest hikes described in this book, but one of the flattest and most relaxing—relaxing, that is, if you pick the right day

or days. Avoid weekends, particularly holiday weekends, if you can. Otherwise you'll share these arroyos with too many motor vehicles.

It's only by walking that the otherworldly beauty of this area can really be appreciated. Opportunities for side trips abound, so much so that you could easily spend two days on this circuit. If you're backpacking the route, secluded campsites well off the roads can be found in the upper reaches of both Arroyo Tapiado and Arroyo Seco del Diablo.

The highlight of the trip comes early: the Arroyo Tapiado cave formations. Some of the caves are pitch dark; bring two flashlights per person and a hard hat or a rock-climbing helmet if you intend to explore them.

To reach the starting point, find the signed Palm Spring turnoff at mile 43.0 on County Highway S-2. This is opposite (east of) Canebrake Canyon. Go east, passing the spur road to Palm Spring, and continue (if road conditions allow) down Vallecito Creek wash. Park at the intersection of the road into Arroyo Tapiado, 4.5 miles from S-2.

On foot, proceed north in the wash of Arroyo Tapiado (meaning "mudwall wash"). After 2.0 miles you reach the beginning of a deep, twisting gorge. The next 2 miles will take you through what geologists call pseudokarst topography. Like the *karst* topography found in many parts of the world, pseudokarst contains caves, subterranean drainage systems, sinkholes, and blind valleys that end in swallow holes, where water descends underground. Unlike karst, which results from the dissolution of limestone or similar material by water, this topography is the result of an unusual process: First, flood waters gouge out slotlike tributary canyons in the soft claystone walls of the main arroyo (Arroyo Tapiado). Second, landslides fill in the slots. Third, flood waters dig tunnels through the lower levels of the landslide debris.

Some of the caves (subterranean stream channels) in the area are over 1000 feet long, with rooms up to 80 feet high and 30 feet wide. Others are tall and narrow, much like a meandering slot canyon with a roof overhead. Some have multiple levels, and one contains a 45' subterranean dry fall. Sinkholes (skylights) illuminate the interiors of some caves. Most cave passages eventually lead upstream through a swallow hole to a "blind" valley.

The bigger and more mature caves are quite stable, with ages on the order of thousands of years. Except during an earthquake or flood, the hard-packed floors of these caves should offer safe passage. It is very dangerous, however, to wander around topside in the pseudokarst valleys (those with sinkholes) and blind valleys (those ending in swallow holes). There would be no exit if one were to fall into some of these holes—or incipient holes. (This may explain the reported disappearance of travelers in the last century who tried various shortcuts across the Carrizo Badlands.)

Several tributaries on the left, just past 2.0 miles in Arroyo Tapiado, are worth investigating. Huge berms of slumped debris lie across most of them; climb these berms and cautiously

Big Mud Cave in Arroyo Tapiado

peer into frighteningly deep pits that lie at the foot of dry falls.

A small grove of mesquite on the left at 2.7 miles is the clue to finding the entrance to one of the longer caves. Halfway through this cave is a tiny skylight, perhaps 50 feet up. Another cave entrance on the left at 2.9 miles offers an easy passage of several hundred feet to a wide swallow hole. This cave also features a large sinkhole in the roof of its midsection, and a curious oxbow, or alternate passage.

On the right at 3.1 miles you'll find the entrance to the "Big Mud Cave," the collapsed remnants of a former cave passage. It's an easy and worthwhile side trip, and you don't need a flashlight: Walk through the huge punctured cavern at the front and continue up the narrow wash bridged by many arches. After about 0.5 mile, on the left, you can climb out of the wash for a look at the mazelike terrain above. Stay on the ridgeline, don't wander through the valleys, and keep track of your footprints—you must reenter the same wash to get back safely!

Don't miss the slot-like passage just south of the Big Mud Cave entrance, on the same canyon wall. After squeezing through, let your eyes adjust to the dark and behold an amazing sight.

Other passage entrances penetrate the walls of Arroyo Tapiado and some of its tributaries. So do "pipes," or upper-level conduits, which spew forth waterfalls during rare flash floods.

Arroyo Tapiado widens after 4.0 miles and sets a straighter course northwest. The canyon divides at 6.3 miles; take the right fork, following the sign indicating "Arroyo Diablo." At 6.7 miles, the road goes up the slope to the right and meanders southeast to join Arroyo Seco del Diablo at 9.0 miles. (A "dropoff" jeep route to Fish Creek intersects nearby, offering a direct connection to the Split Mountain area of the Carrizo Badlands.)

Shallow at first, Arroyo Diablo deepens steadily between golden-colored walls of sandstone—quite unlike the gray-green claystone walls you saw in Arroyo Tapiado.

Sandstone concretions, most shaped like balls or bullets, lie half-imbedded in the water-polished walls. Others have completely weathered out and lie on the ground. Between 11.0 and 13.0 miles, there are many interesting tributaries to explore if you have time. The one at 12.3 miles (west side) divides into a maze of narrow slot canyons chock-full of concretions, each one a unique sculpture. (Leave 'em as they lie—even rocks are protected in the state park.)

Down near the mouth of Arroyo Diablo are some mesquite groves, and a small seep in the floor of the canyon. When you emerge onto flat land just beyond the mouth, save some time and distance by leaving the wheel tracks and turning west to pick up the jeep road in Vallecito Creek wash.

Mud cracks in Arroyo Seco del Diablo

Area D-13: Carrizo Gorge

A north-south-trending fault zone is responsible for the series of ridges and canyons at Anza-Borrego's south end. Carrizo Gorge, the most dramatic of these, divides the Jacumba Mountains to the east from the In-Ko-Pah Mountains to the west. These mini-mountain ranges are links in the Peninsular Ranges from the Laguna Mountains in the northwest to the Sierra Juarez of Baja California.

Carrizo Gorge is best known for the railroad that threads along its eastern wall: the San Diego & Arizona Eastern. Built in 1907-1919, the railroad carried freight, and for a time passengers, between San Diego and the Imperial Valley. The gorge section features 11 miles of twisting track, 17 tunnels, and numerous wooden trestles. The spectacular Goat Canyon trestle, completed in 1933 as part of a realignment of the original route, is a noted county landmark. Hurricane Kathleen badly mangled the line in 1976, and cut off traffic through the gorge for five years. After reopening in 1981, the line was quickly severed again, this time by a fire that burned out several smaller trestles. Today the Carrizo Gorge section remains out of service, but there's never-ending speculation on its possible future uses. The tracks could someday carry sightseeing tourists through the gorge, or they might end up carrying cars filled with San Diego's solid waste destined for some future Imperial Valley landfill.

Hiking along the SD & AE tracks through Carrizo Gorge is expressly forbidden. The route is posted and patrolled. The railroad also owns a strip of land on either side of the tracks. It is the opinion of Anza-Borrego rangers, however, that hikers are permitted to cross the tracks at right angles within the state park.

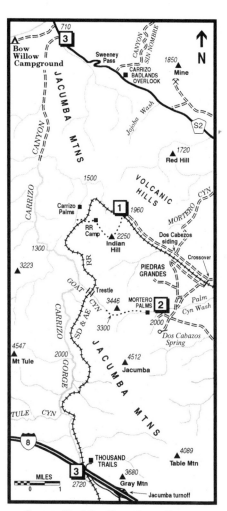

Area D-13: Carrizo Gorge

Trip 1: Indian Hill/Carrizo Palms

🥾	**Distance**	6.5 miles
	Total Elevation Gain/Loss	900'/900'
	Hiking Time	4½ hours
⊘	**Required Map**	USGS 7.5-min *Sweeney Pass*
	Best Times	November through April
↻ 🚶	**Agency**	ABDSP
	Difficulty	***

A variety of interesting historical, botanical and geological features are seen along this route. Even if you don't want to attempt this entire loop, you'll find much to fascinate you on an abbreviated hike.

You can begin at a point along the SD & AE tracks near Dos Cabezas siding. Do not take the Mortero Wash and Jojoba Wash jeep roads to reach this point in your standard auto! A route on much firmer ground, the so-called Dos Cabezas Road, is better. From Interstate 8, drive 4.1 miles up Highway S-2 to an unsigned dirt road on the left. Go south on this road and veer right after 1.1 miles. Continue another 6.1 miles, staying north of the tracks, to Dos Cabezas siding. From the siding, continue driving 2.2 miles on the north side of the tracks until you reach the road's end, which overlooks a wash.

On foot, backtrack about 200 yards, cross the tracks (west of here the tracks are posted against trespassing—don't walk along them or loiter around them), and head south-southwest across an alluvial plain dotted with cacti and shrubs. Several rocky hills consisting of desert-varnished granitic boulders punctuate the surface of the plain. One of these is Indian Hill—which is incorrectly labelled on the Sweeney Pass topo map. The true Indian Hill, a site of former Indian occupation, has a fire-blackened cave and morteros on its northeast side.

Next point of interest is the remains of a circa-1912 railroad camp used during the construction of the railroad. The ruins are located 0.1 mile south of the center of section 20. Use your topo map as a guide. Here you'll find the walls of an old shed constructed of mortar and blasting-powder cans.

Back up about 0.1 mile and follow remnants of an old jeep road west toward a hillside over-

looking the railroad tracks. Cross the tracks and descend over a rugged slope into a tributary of Carrizo Canyon; then go north in the sandy bed of the canyon past several seeps and small palm groves. There's good camping here and there in flat, sandy areas sheltered from the wind.

The seep and large grove of palms at the 1720' contour is one of the spots labelled "Carrizo Palms" on the topo map. During 1912 through 1919 railroad workers installed a pump here to boost water up to the camp.

After another mile, you'll come to a major confluence. Go right (east, upstream) into a narrow canyon with colorful rock formations, and scramble over a series of bedrock exposures and easy dry falls. After 0.5 mile the bed becomes sandy again; continue one more mile south to the tracks. Don't follow the tracks; instead cross them, continue south, and drop into an east-draining wash. Pass under the tracks and you'll soon arrive at a point just below your parked car.

Mortero Palms

Trip 2: Mortero Palms To Goat Canyon

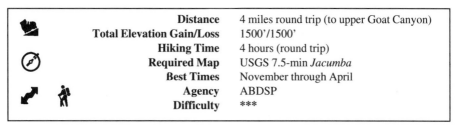

	Distance	4 miles round trip (to upper Goat Canyon)
	Total Elevation Gain/Loss	1500'/1500'
	Hiking Time	4 hours (round trip)
	Required Map	USGS 7.5-min *Jacumba*
	Best Times	November through April
	Agency	ABDSP
	Difficulty	***

Along the crest of the Jacumba Mountains lies several hidden bowls, surrounded by austere, rock-strewn peaks. To spend a night here on a bed of sand, immersed in an achingly profound silence, with nothing but a sky filled with stars overhead is to experience the desert in all its wonder and simplicity.

Not far away from one of these bowls is a landmark revered by railroad buffs the world over. This is the 200-foot-high, 600-foot-long trestle over Goat Canyon on the San Diego & Arizona Eastern line. It has been called the longest curved railroad trestle and one of the highest wooden trestles in the world.

You start this hike at the Mortero Palms trailhead, rather close to the rock formation known as Dos Cabezos ("two heads"). As in Trip 1, take the Dos Cabezos Road south and west from Highway S-2. At a point 5.7 miles from S-2, go south across the tracks on a paved

crossover. Continue on the south side of the tracks for 0.1 mile, veer left (southeast, away from the tracks) and proceed 0.9 mile to a road fork. Bear left there, and stay left again after another 0.3 mile. Drive 0.4 mile farther (past an isolated, rocky hill on the left), and turn right toward Mortero Palms. Go 0.5 mile to the road's end overlooking a wide wash.

Take care to hike up the main (Mortero Palms) canyon to the west, not the tributary canyon to the south. A path follows the south bank for a while, avoiding the vegetation-choked streambed. Soon you begin climbing over granitic boulders. Look for a half-dozen morteros, namesakes of the palm grove, in the center of the drainage 100 yards below the beginning of the palms. A path also threads the north canyon wall—but you miss the morteros if you follow it.

The palm grove is one of the densest in

Goat Canyon trestle

Anza-Borrego, arising from seeps amid a jumble of huge boulders reminiscent of the rock formations at Joshua Tree National Monument. On warm days this is a seductively cool spot, and it takes some will power to get moving again to tackle the short but steep stretch of canyon ahead. Traverse left or right, or climb the water-polished rocks directly if you're a real daredevil.

At the 2440' contour it's easier to leave the canyon bottom temporarily and go up on the slope to the north through stands of teddy-bear cholla. Drop back in at about 2750 feet, but leave the canyon again at the 2840' contour. Proceed west and southwest across a small sad-

dle and continue west over a divide into the Goat Canyon drainage.

Descend to a delightful, juniper-dotted bowl at about 3200 feet, a good place to spend the night. Further exploration in the area might include a visit to Jacumba peak (4512') south along the crest of the Jacumba Mountains, or a descent down Goat Canyon for a look at the famous trestle. At about 2700 feet in Goat Canyon, there's an excellent—if not at all close-up—view of the bridge, framed by the steep walls of the canyon. Keep in mind that it is illegal to loiter around the railroad line. Viewing is best done from afar.

Trip 3: Carrizo Gorge

Distance	18 miles (I-8 to S-2)
Total Elevation Gain/Loss	0'/2000'
Hiking Time	14 hours
Required Maps	USGS 7.5-min *Jacumba, Sweeney Pass*
Best Times	November through April
Agency	ABDSP
Difficulty	*****

The trek down the length of Carrizo Gorge is long, rugged, difficult, and memorable. It is one to be undertaken cautiously, with the right equipment and clothing. Essential are long pants and sturdy, waterproofed boots.

This trip is best done as a two-day backpack, though one very long day is sufficient for speed demons who travel lightly. The last 6 miles, on jeep tracks in the sand, can be done at night. If you're backpacking, keep the weight of your pack to a minimum. Consider leaving your stove, tent, and other luxury items behind. Several roomy rock caves may be used for shelter in the canyon's midsection. There's likely to be a fair amount of water in parts of the canyon, but carry drinking water anyway—or in lieu of that, a water-purification filter.

Although the SD & AE tracks along the east wall of Carrizo Gorge seem an easier alternative to the rugged, twisting bed of Carrizo Canyon, you're not allowed to walk them. Hikers who have been caught walking the tracks have had to pay heavy fines.

First, set up your car shuttle or drop-off/pick-up arrangement. The starting point is reached by taking the Jacumba exit off Interstate 8. Go west on the frontage road (Carrizo Gorge Road) to where it crosses under I-8. This is the assumed starting point—unless you can obtain permission from the Thousand Trails resort, just ahead, to park and start hiking from there. The end point is mile 48.6 on Highway S-2.

Staying south of I-8, walk across the SD & AE tracks, and parallel the freeway for 200 yards until you reach the I-8 bridge over Carrizo Creek. Go north under the bridge and on down the broad drainage. Presently you enter a real canyon. The creek carries a respectable flow of water during the wet season, and you may be up on the banks most of the time in an effort to avoid having your boots fill with water. At 2.0 miles, the creek cascades over a tumble of car-sized boulders; you may have to detour over the jagged rocks on the left (west) side, a climb of 150 feet, class 3 rock climbing. This is the only really serious technical obstacle on the trip.

The next 10 miles offer bushwhacking, boulder-hopping and mud-stomping in abundance. The sharp thorns of mesquite and catclaw; the needlelike tips of a particularly wicked type of bunch grass; dense thickets of *carrizo*, or cane, a bamboolike reed; and slippery rocks will all conspire to slow your progress. Feral cattle used to keep paths through the mesquite clear, but they were airlifted out of the canyon in the late 1980s. Mercifully, however, there are some easy stretches across sand and rock too.

The gorge has served as a trap for railroad debris which has tumbled off the slopes, and for flotsam and jetsam washed down from the Jacumba area during past floods. At about 4.0 miles, four sets of railroad wheels and axles lie in the canyon. You can look up to see rails drooping over two of the ravines like limp clotheslines, their underpinnings burned away.

At about 6.0 miles, above a landscape of rusted tin cans from a former railroad camp, there is a beautiful teddy-bear-cholla forest with specimens up to 10 feet tall. Barrel cacti up to 8 feet high are also seen a short distance down the gorge.

Goat Canyon, a tributary, enters from the right (east) at 8.5 miles. Climb 200 feet up the ridge to the north of this canyon for a great view of the famous curved trestle. Several rock caves are nearby, some with signs of Indian occupation, and nearly all with evidence of more recent visits by undocumented aliens (the gorge is sometimes used by Mexican workers moving north).

The gorge (now called Carrizo Canyon) widens past Goat Canyon, though it is not until about 12 miles that you can walk continuously on smooth sand. Four-wheel drives can sometimes make it up the canyon about 6 miles, but don't count on that for someone who might try to pick you up at the bottom. By walking all the way out, you end up at the Carrizo Creek crossing (mile 48.6) on Highway S-2.

Another possible endpoint for this trip is Bow Willow Campground. To reach it, leave Carrizo Canyon about one mile short of the highway and head directly northwest toward the dirt road into Bow Willow Canyon.

Giant cholla cactus

Area D-14: Jacumba Mountains

East of Jacumba, pressed against the California-Baja California border, is a series of scenic peaks and valleys in the Jacumba Mountains affording vistas of two counties and two nations. The BLM manages the area, which lies entirely south of Interstate 8, for wildlife protection and primitive recreation. Jeep roads penetrate its periphery, but the heart of it lies so untouched that it qualifies for consideration as a potential federal wilderness area.

Although American map makers consider this rugged area to be a part of the Jacumba Mountains, it is more closely associated with the 100-mile-long Sierra Juarez, Baja's northernmost link in the chain of Peninsular Ranges. As on the scenic Sierra Juarez crest to the south, you'll see great stacks of weathered boulders, with pinyon pines and other high-desert vegetation growing wherever sand or soil can collect.

Each of the three trips below is within Imperial County, just east of the San Diego County line. They are included in this book because they're so easily accessible from San Diego (about 90 minutes by car) and right next to Anza-Borrego Desert State Park.

To reach the starting point for Trips 1 and 2, exit Interstate 8 at In-Ko-Pah Park Road (east of Jacumba). Drive southwest 0.2 mile along the frontage road, Old Highway 80, then turn left on an unmarked dirt road. Ordinary cars should park no farther than 0.8 mile up this road, at a large turnout. Sturdy 4-wheel drives can continue farther, prudently, up the steep road toward the patchwork of jeep roads and primitive campsites. The hiking descriptions below assume that you park in the large turnout.

A nice alternative (or complement) to the USGS topographic map listed below for Trips 1 and 2 is the Mexican government "La

Rumorosa—I11D63," 1:50,000 scale map. Unlike the USGS map, which is blank below the border, the Mexican topo shows features on both sides. It is not legal, of course, to cross the border into Mexico except at official ports of entry.

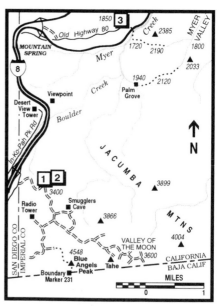

Area D-14: Jacumba Mtns

Trip 1: Blue Angels Peak

	Distance	5 miles round trip
	Total Elevation Gain/Loss	1300'/1300'
	Hiking Time	3 hours (round trip)
	Recommended Map	USGS 7.5-min *In-Koh-Pah Gorge*
	Best Times	October through May
	Agency	BLM/EC
	Difficulty	**

Blue Angels peak, one of several crags along a high north-south ridge spanning the two Californias, happens to be the highest point in "Alta" California within six miles of the international border. The peak is surely one of the windiest spots in southern California—especially in spring, when hot air rising up from the low desert to the east draws in a strong flow of cooler air from the coastal regions.

From the parking area 0.8 mile from Old Highway 80, walk up the road to a saddle at 3830 feet. A jeep road branches left to Smuggler's Cave, an old hideout of bandits and smugglers, now a fire-blackened, grafitti-emblazoned wreck. Proceed another 0.1 mile south and bear right (west). Continue south and finally east to the roadend, staying left at two road junctions at 1.1 and 1.4 miles. An old mining prospect lies at the end of the road.

Blue Angels peak is to the southeast, hidden behind a false peak capped by a massive block of granite seemingly poised to roll. Scramble up over lichen-encrusted boulders and past scraggly pinyons to find the bench mark on the summit.

On the return trip, make a short detour to discover International Boundary Marker 231, a handsome 10' steel obelisk, in the middle of a flat that is south and a little west of the peak. These markers are numbered consecutively along the border from #1 at the Gulf of Mexico shoreline east of Brownsville-Matamoros to #258 at the Pacific shoreline.

Border marker south of Blue Angels Peak

Trip 2: Valley of the Moon

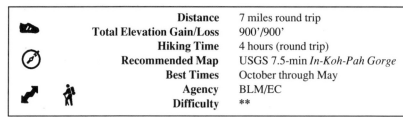

	Distance	7 miles round trip
	Total Elevation Gain/Loss	900'/900'
	Hiking Time	4 hours (round trip)
	Recommended Map	USGS 7.5-min *In-Koh-Pah Gorge*
	Best Times	October through May
	Agency	BLM/EC
	Difficulty	**

Strolling through the appropriately named Valley of the Moon, you would almost think that a square-mile chunk of Joshua Tree National Monument had been transported here—minus, of course, the famous Joshua trees. Huge granitic outcrops, seamed with horizontal and vertical cracks, ring the valley.

Begin this hike as in Trip 1 above, but bear left at the intersection 0.1 mile beyond the saddle. Descend sharply and bear southeast toward a small peak ("Tahe") containing the Elliot Mine, an abandoned amethyst mine. Keep straight and avoid the spur roads to campsites tucked up against coves in the rocks, but turn left (east) just before the main road continues

sharply uphill to the mine. Bend east and south around the base of "Tahe," then veer east and enter the Valley of the Moon.

The sandy floor of the valley is dotted with Mojave yucca, catclaw, Mormon tea and buckwheat. You can continue toward an old water tank in the northeast corner of the valley, or follow any of the jeep roads that wind around the statuesque boulder heaps to the south. Photographers should be here early or late in the day, when the sun bathes the stone battlements in a warm light, and sharply defined shadows march across the valley.

In the Valley of the Moon

Trip 3: Myer Valley/Boulder Creek

	Distance	4.0 miles
	Total Elevation Gain/Loss	1000'/1000'
	Hiking Time	3 hours
	Required Map	USGS 7.5-min *In-Koh-Pah Gorge*
	Best Times	November through April
	Agency	BLM/EC
	Difficulty	***

Have you ever driven down Interstate 8 east of Jacumba, and, eyeing the immense boulder piles that rise on both sides, wondered what it would be like to clamber over them? Here's your chance. Follow these directions, and in just a few minutes you can be parked off the freeway, and on your way into a primeval landscape visited only by an occasional adventurer like yourself.

Exit I-8 at Mountain Spring. At a point midway in the "island" between the eastbound and westbound lanes of the freeway, turn east on a rough dirt road. In 0.2 mile this road joins the abandoned concrete ribbon of old U.S. Highway 80. Drive east, dodging fallen boulders on the roadway, for an additional 1.3 miles and park near the road's end—just before the brink of a road cut made for the eastbound lanes of I-8.

Scramble down the slope (this is probably the most difficult part of the hike!) about 100 feet to the sandy bed of Myer Creek. Pass under the lanes of I-8 through the large culvert to the west and continue 0.1 mile in the wash until you come to the base of a rocky gully on the left (east). Scramble up the coarse-grained granitic boulders in this gully; after 400 feet of elevation gain you join a sandy wash. Continue east and top a saddle 0.2 mile south of peak 2385. Pass over the saddle, and descend an easy drainage leading to Myer Valley. The half-square-mile valley gently slopes to the north. It is so thickly grown with creosote bush, ocotillo, and other plants whose color intensifies after periods of rainfall that it can look from a distance as if it were covered by a verdant carpet. There is a maze of old jeep roads in the valley from the days when vehicles could navigate up Myer Creek from the Ocotillo area. Flash floods

obliterated that route, and the valley has been closed to all vehicle use by the BLM.

Upon reaching the edge of the valley, you can turn south and skirt the west edge of the valley, following a minor wash. Pick up traces of an old jeep trail about 0.3 mile southwest of peaklet 2033. Follow this west-southwest to the top of a broad divide, then drop into a ravine that leads west into a north-flowing tributary of Boulder Creek. After some moderate scrambling, you'll arrive at a beautiful palm oasis, complete with a year-round spring. A sculpted dry fall and a nice set of Indian morteros are nearby.

From the palm oasis, it's an easy 1.2 miles back to the culvert under I-8, via Boulder and Myer creeks downhill in wash bottoms all the way. Several small groups of palms provide welcome shade if needed.

At 0.3-0.4 mile below the palm oasis, two canyons come in on the left, inviting side trips. The first of these, a rugged tributary to the south, is fascinating, with immense boulders, hidden cottonwoods and palms, and secluded campsites. Some difficult scrambling is required to fully explore it. The second of these, upper Boulder Creek canyon to the southwest, is vegetation-choked and unremarkable.

APPENDIX 1: BEST HIKES

BEST BEACH HIKE

La Jolla Shores to Torrey Pines Beach (Area B-2, Trip 1). Here the primeval Southern California coastline survives more or less intact.

BEST SUBURBAN HIKES

Torrey Pines State Reserve (Area B-2, Trip 3). Breathtaking views of the coastline, eroded landforms, and the rare Torrey pine.

Blue Sky Ecological Reserve (Area C-2, Trip 2). A quintessential example of riparian woodland and oak woodland.

Los Penasquitos Canyon (Area C-3, Trips 2 & 3). Largest undeveloped canyon bottom close to San Diego. Rolling hills, meadows, and a delightful, tree-lined stream.

Cowles Mountain (Area C-5, Trip 1). The summit has the best view of metropolitan San Diego.

BEST MOUNTAIN HIKES

Lower Doane Valley/Lower French Valley (Area M-2, Trip 4). Trickling streams, dark forests, and sunny meadows.

Azalea Glen Trail (Area M-6, Trip 6). Oak and conifer forests and a trickling stream.

BEST DESERT HIKES

Borrego Palm Canyon Nature Trail (Area D-2, Trip 1). Discover a fan palm oasis amid soaring canyon walls.

Mountain Palm Springs (Area D-11, Trip 3). A half dozen palm groves secreted in boulder-strewn hills.

BEST CANYON HIKES

Noble Canyon (Area M-7, Trip 15). A year-round mountain stream in a narrow, shaded canyon.

Pine Valley Creek (Area M-8, Trip 2). Beautiful rock exposures, lots of water in winter and spring. Easy to reach via Horsethief Canyon.

Sheep Canyon (Area D-1, Trip 2). Palms, sycamores, lush vegetation, and waterfalls.

BEST WATERFALLS AND SWIMMING HOLES

Cedar Creek Falls (Area M-4, Trip 3). San Diego County's most spectacular waterfall; deep "punchbowl" beneath.

Cougar Canyon (Area D-1, Trip 4). Waterfalls and deep pools in a pseudotropical desert setting.

BEST PEAK CLIMBS

Stonewall Peak (Area M-6, Trip 8). Easy trail; good overview of Cuyamaca and Laguna mountains from the pointed summit.

Garnet Peak (Area M-7, Trip 3). Easy climb; fabulous view on the Laguna escarpment.

Villager and Rabbit peaks (Area D-4, Trip 2). Long, rugged, desert peak climb; views across half the width of California and deep into Mexico.

BEST WILDFLOWERS

Torrey Pines State Reserve (Area B-2, Trip 3). Nearly all varieties of wildflowers common to the coastal region are represented here.

East Mesa Loop (Area M-6, Trip 13). Wildflowers of the mountain meadows and chaparral.

Big Laguna Trail (Area M-7, Trip 9). Wildflowers of the mountain meadows and pine forest.

Borrego Palm Canyon Nature Trail (Area D-2, Trip 1). Most common varieties of desert wildflowers bloom here.

BEST AUTUMN COLORS

Fry Creek Trail (Area M-2, Trip 6). Conifer and oak forest.

Kelly Ditch Trail (Area M-6, Trip 1) Conifer and oak forest; trickling streams.

West Mesa Loop (Area M-6, Trip 14). Conifer and oak forest; meadows.

Sunset Trail (Area M-7, Trip 8). Black oak and pine forest.

BEST BIRD AND WILDLIFE WATCHING

San Elijo Lagoon (Area B-1, Trip 2). Birds of shoreline and coastal lagoon habitats.

Tijuana River Estuary (Area B-4, Trip 1). Local and migrant bird life.

Silverwood Wildlife Sanctuary (Area C-6, Trip 3). An Audubon preserve harboring birds and wildlife of the chaparral zone.

Barker Valley (Area M-2, Trip 11). Deer, bobcats, mountain lions, and eagles can be seen in this area.

Dyar Spring/Juaquapin Loop (Area M-6, Trip 11). One of the largest deer herds in San Diego County roams this area unmolested.

Lower Willows (Area D-1, Trip 1). Birds, small mammals, and insects thrive in the jungle-like growth.

Borrego Palm Canyon Nature Trail (Area D-2, Trip 1). Bighorn sheep are commonly seen here in summer.

Yaqui Well (Area D-6, Trip 3). Good birding in this small desert oasis.

Squaw Pond Trail (Area D-10, Trip 2). This desert oasis draws coyotes, bobcats, birds, bats and rattlesnakes.

BEST RUNNING TRAILS (• indicates routes also good for mountain biking)

La Jolla Shores to Torrey Pines Beach (Area B-2, Trip 1). Beach all the way except for a few cobbled areas. Recommended during low tide only.

Lake Poway Loop (Area C-2, Trip 1). Pleasant loop around a small lake. One steep and several mild grades.

• Iron Mountain Trail (Area C-2, Trip 6). Mostly moderate grade up from Poway Road to superb viewpoint. North part of this loop too steep for most mountain biking.

• Los Penasquitos Canyon (Area C-3, Trips 2 & 3). Mostly flat dirt road. Pleasant scenery, cool breezes, peace and quiet.

• Rose and San Clemente canyons (Area C-4, Trips 1 & 2). Wide trails shaded by oaks and sycamores.

Cowles Mountain (Area C-5, Trips 1-4). The quintessential mountain workout in the San Diego area. Superb views.

Sweetwater Trail (Area C-8, Trip 1). A classic California landscape of golden, rolling hills. Narrow trail with some short, steep grades.

Oak Grove to High Point (Area M-2, Trip 10). To the highest point on Palomar Mountain via road and trail. Experts only.

• Cuyamaca Peak (Area M-6, Trip 7). Paved road all the way, but steep.

Stonewall Creek/Soapstone Grade Loop (Area M-6, Trip 9). Mostly gentle fire roads, some steep grades on trails.

West Mesa Loop (Area M-6, Trip 14). Pleasant, shady route on fire roads.

• Mason Valley Truck Trail (Area D-8, Trip 2). Run from the mountains to the desert on an old dirt road.

Noble Canyon Trail (Area M-7, Trip 15). Narrow, but mostly smooth trail. Downhill direction preferred. One long, steep stretch.

• Otay Mountain (Area M-9, Trips 1 & 2). Steady ascent on good dirt roads. Unusual cypress groves, good views all the way.

• Jasper Trail/Grapevine Canyon (Area D-6, Trip 1). High desert to low desert on mostly smooth, sandy jeep trails.

• Arroyo Tapiado/Arroyo Diablo Loop (Area D-12, Trip 3). Through the badlands washes on flat, smooth jeep trails.

APPENDIX 2: RECOMMENDED READING

Hiking, Backpacking, and Mountaineering

Darvill, Fred, *Mountaineering Medicine*, Wilderness Press, 1992.
Ganci, David, *Desert Hiking*, Wilderness Press, 1993.
Graydon, Don (ed.), *Mountaineering: The Freedom of the Hills*, 5th edition, The Mountaineers, 1992.
Manning, Harvey, *Backpacking: One Step at a Time*, Vintage Books, 1980.
Moser, David and Schad, Jerry (eds.), *Wilderness Basics, The Complete Handbook for Hikers and Backpackers*, The Mountaineers, 1992.
Winnett, Thomas and Melanie Findling, *Backpacking Basics*, Wilderness Press, 1988.

San Diego Area Guidebooks

Anderson, Priscilla and Scott, *Fido's Field Guide to San Diego*, Maps and Travel, 1991.
California Coastal Commission, *California Coastal Access Guide*, 4th edition, University of California Press, 1991.
Hewitt, Lonnie and Barbara Moore, *Walking San Diego*, The Mountaineers, 1989.
Johnson, Paul R., *Weekender's Guide* (Anza-Borrego), Anza-Borrego Desert Natural History Association, 1987.
Lindsay, Diana and Lowell, *The Anza-Borrego Desert Region*, 3rd edition, Wilderness Press, 1991.
Mendel, Carol, *San Diego!. . . City and County*, Carol Mendel, 1985.
Mendel, Carol, *San Diego On Foot*, Carol Mendel, 1985.
Parker, Horace (G. Leetch, ed.), *Anza-Borrego Desert Guide Book*, revised edition, Anza-Borrego Desert Natural History Association, 1979.
Peik, L. and R., *Campers Guide to San Diego County Campgrounds*, Peik Enterprises, 1981.
Robinson, John W., *San Bernardino Mountain Trails*, 4th edition, Wilderness Press, 1990.
Ruland, Skip, *Backpacking Guide to San Diego County*, revised edition, Calif. Backpacking Co., 1984.
Schad, Jerry, *Backcountry Roads & Trails, San Diego County*, 4th edition, Centra Publications, 1993.
Schaffer, Jeffrey P., et al. *The Pacific Crest Trail, Volume 1: California*, Wilderness Press, 4th edition, 1989.

History and Natural History

Bailey, H. P., *The Climate of Southern California*, University of California Press, 1966.
Chase, J. Smeaton, *California Desert Trails*, Houghton Mifflin Co., 1919. (Out of print)
Ellsberg, Helen, *Mines of Julian*, La Siesta Press, 1972.
Jaeger, Edmond C. and Smith, Arthur C., *Introduction to the Natural History of Southern California*, University of California Press, 1971.
Lindsay, Diana E., *Our Historic Desert: The Story of the Anza-Borrego Desert*, Copley Books, 1973.
Pryde, Philip R., *San Diego: An Introduction to the Region*, 3rd ed., Kendall/Hunt Publishing Co., 1992.
Reed, Lester, Old Time *Cattlemen and Other Pioneers of the Anza-Borrego Desert Area*, Anza-Borrego Desert Natural History Association, 1986.
Stein, Lou, *San Diego County Place-Names*, Tofua Press, 1975.

Geology

Abbott, P. (ed.), *Geologic Studies of San Diego*, San Diego Association of Geologists, 1982.

Kennedy, M. P., and G. L. Peterson, *Geology of the San Diego Metropolitan Area, California*, Bulletin 200, California Division of Mines and Geology, 1975.

Kern, Philip, *Earthquakes and Faults in San Diego County*, Pickle Press, 1989.

Kuhn, Gerald G. and Francis P.Shepard, Sea Cliffs, *Beaches, and Coastal Valleys of San Diego County*, University of California Press, 1984.

Sharp, Robert P., *Coastal Southern California* (geology guide), Kendall/Hunt Publishing Company, 1978.

Weber, F. H., *Geology and Mineral Resources of San Diego County*, California, County Report 3, California Division of Mines and Geology, 1963. (Contains large-scale geological map of San Diego County.)(Out of print)

Biology

Bean, L. J. and S. S. Saubel, *Temalpakh: Cahuilla Indian Knowledge and Usage of Plants*, Malki Museum Press, 1972.

Beauchamp, R. Mitchel, *A Flora of San Diego County*, California, Sweetwater River Press, 1986.

Belzer, Thomas J., *Roadside Plants of Southern California*, Mountain Press Publishing Co., 1984.

Clemons, Duffie, *Plants of Anza-Borrego Desert State Park*, Anza-Borrego Desert Natural History Association, 1986.

Dawson, E. Yale, *Cacti of California*, University of California Press, 1971.

Jaeger, Edmond C., *Desert Wild Flowers*, revised edition, Stanford University Press, 1969.

Jaeger, Edmond C., *Desert Wildlife*, Stanford University Press, 1961.

Johnson, Paul, *Cacti, Shrubs and Trees of Anza-Borrego*, Anza-Borrego Desert Natural History Association, 1982.

Munz, Philip A., *California Spring Wildflowers*, University of California Press, 1961.

Munz, Philip A., *California Desert Wildflowers*, University of California Press, 1962.

Munz, Philip A., *California Mountain Wildflowers*, University of California Press, 1963.

Peterson, P. Victor, *Native Trees of Southern California*, University of California Press, 1966.

Raven, Peter H., *Native Shrubs of Southern California*, University of California Press, 1966.

Unitt, Philip, *Birds of San Diego County*, San Diego Society of Natural History, 1984.

Yocum, Charles and Ray Dasmann, *Pacific Coastal Wildlife Region*, revised edition, Naturegraph Publishers, 1965.

APPENDIX 3: LOCAL ORGANIZATIONS

(all telephone numbers are area code 619)

Anza-Borrego Desert Natural History Association
P.O. Box 311
Borrego Springs, CA 92004
(Activities associated with Anza-Borrego Desert State Park)

Adventure 16 Wilderness Outings
4620 Alvarado Canyon Road
San Diego, CA 92120
283-2374
(Basic mountaineering instruction and backpacking trips in San Diego County)

Audubon Society of San Diego
2321 Morena Blvd., Ste. D
San Diego, CA 92110
275-0557
(Nature and bird walks; also operates the Silverwood Wildlife Sanctuary)

California Native Plant Society, San Diego Chapter
P.O. Box 1390
San Diego, CA 92112
(Offers outings to view native plants)

Cuyamaca Rancho State Park Interpretive Association
12551 Highway 79
Descanso, CA 92016
(Activities associated with Cuyamaca Rancho State Park)

Laguna Mountain Volunteer Association
3348 Alpine Blvd.
Alpine, CA 91901
445-6235
(Activities associated with the Descanso Ranger District of Cleveland National Forest)

San Diego Hiking Club
P.O. Box 161068
San Diego, CA 92176
(Day hikes and backpacking trips throughout San Diego County; wilderness information)

San Diego Peaks Club
c/o Paul Freiman
4868 Austin Dr.
San Diego, CA 92115
692-1367
(Sponsors moderate to difficult peak climbs in San Diego County and beyond)

San Diego Society of Natural History
(Natural History Museum, Balboa Park)
P.O. Box 1390
San Diego, CA 92112
232-3821
(Interpretive outings throughout San Diego County)

Sierra Club, San Diego Chapter
3820 Ray St.
San Diego, CA 92104
299-1743
(Hiking and backpacking outings throughout the San Diego region; plus a wilderness basics training course in winter-spring.)

Walkabout International
835 5th Ave.
San Diego, CA 92101
223-9255
(Sponsors mostly urban walks, but some hikes in San Diego's backcountry)

APPENDIX 4: AGENCIES AND INFORMATION SOURCES

(all telephone numbers are area code 619, except as noted)

Parks and Agencies

Anza-Borrego Desert State Park (ABDSP)
P.O. Box 299
Borrego Springs, CA 92004
Recording: 767-4684
Visitor Center: 767-4205
Administration: 767-5311

Blue Sky Ecological Reserve (BSER)
486-7238

Border Field State Park (BFSP)
237-6766

Bureau of Land Management (BLM/EC)
El Centro Resource Area
333 South Waterman Ave.
El Centro, CA 92243
352-5842

Bureau of Land Management (BLM/PS)
Palm Springs-South Coast Resource Area
400 S. Farrell Dr., Suite B-205
Palm Springs, CA 92262
323-4421

Cabrillo National Monument (CNM)
293-5450

California Parks and Recreation Department
San Diego Coast District (CP/SDC)
729-8947

Cleveland National Forest Supervisor's Office
10845 Rancho Bernardo Road
San Diego, CA 92127
673-6180

Cleveland National Forest
Palomar Ranger District (CNF/PD)
1634 Black Canyon Road
Ramona, CA 92065
788-0250

Cleveland National Forest
Descanso Ranger District (CNF/DD)
3348 Alpine Blvd.
Alpine, CA 91901
Recording: 445-8341
Office: 445-6235

Cuyamaca Rancho State Park (CRSP)
12551 Highway 79
Descanso, CA 92016
765-0755

Dixon Lake Recreation Area (DLRA)
741-4680

La Jolla Indian Reservation (LJIR)
742-1297

Lake Poway Recreation Area (LPRA)
679-4393

Los Coyotes Indian Reservation (LCIR)
P.O. Box 248
Warner Springs, CA 92086
782-3269

Los Penasquitos Canyon Preserve (LPCP)
533-4067

McGinty Mountain Preserve (MMP)
c/o Santa Rosa Plateau Preserve (Nature Conservancy)
(714) 677-6951

Marian Bear Park (MBP)
525-8281

Mission Trails Regional Park (MTRP)
533-4051

Palomar Mountain State Park (PMSP)
765-0755

San Elijo Lagoon Regional Park (SEL)
753-5091

San Diego County Parks and Recreation Department (SDCP)
5201 Ruffin Road, Suite P
San Diego, CA 92123
Information: 694-3049
Camping reservations: 565-3600

San Diego (city of) Open Space Division (SDOS)
525-8281

San Dieguito River Park (SDRP)
595-5398

San Pasqual Battlefield State Historic Park (SPBSP) 238-3380

Silverwood Wildlife Sanctuary (SWS)
443-2998

Tijuana Estuary Visitor Center (TEVC)
575-3613

Tecolote Canyon Natural Park (TCNP)
525-8281

Torrey Pines State Reserve (TPSR)
755-2063

Map Sources

Most of the agencies listed above are good sources of maps and map/brochures for areas under their own jurisdiction. For general navigation and exploratory hiking in the Cleveland National Forest, you should have a copy of the Cleveland National Forest recreation map. This periodically updated map delineates public and private lands, and shows the locations of vehicle gates (either locked or subject to seasonal closures) on the forest-service road system.

Desert travelers should obtain the Anza-Borrego Desert State Park map/brochure for vehicle navigation. A nearly equivalent map of the Anza-Borrego region is bundled with the Lindsay's book *The Anza-Borrego Desert Region*.

In addition, you can obtained a photocopied series of 15-minute USGS topographic maps of the Anza-Borrego desert region from the Anza-Borrego visitor center in Borrego Springs.

Tom Harrison publishes a shaded, topographic map of Cuyamaca Rancho State Park, and another map at a smaller scale covering most of the San Diego backcountry.

For one-stop shopping for all kinds of local maps and guides, visit one of the following retail map stores. Each offers a complete selection of the USGS topographic maps referred to in this book.

Map World
123-D N. El Camino Real
Encinitas, CA 92024
942-9642

Map Centre
2611 University Avenue
San Diego, CA 92104
291-3830

A good selection of maps and guidebooks are also available from the following outdoor equipment outfitters:

Adventure 16
4620 Alvarado Canyon Road
San Diego, CA 92120
283-2374

Recreational Equipment, Inc.
3029 University Ave.
San Diego, CA 92104
295-7700

Adventure 16
143 S. Cedros
Solana Beach, CA 92075
755-7662

Miscellaneous

Project Hug-a-Tree
(send SASE)
6465 Lance Way
San Diego, CA 92120

San Diego County Sheriff
(Emergencies—dial 911)
565-5200

California Division of Forestry
(To report fires: 442-1615)
588-0364

California Department of Transportation (CalTrans)
Road condition hotline for all California state and interstate highways:
(800) 427-7623

INDEX

Afoot and Afield in San Diego County
2nd edition
1996 Update

Area C-1, page 42:

The Elfin Forest Recreation Reserve (earlier known as the Mount Israel Recreation Area) is now open with about 15 miles of dirt roads and trails for use by hikers, equestrians, and mountain bikers. You will find the entrance near mile 6 on Harmony Grove Road, 3 miles west of the outskirts of Escondido. Hours are 8 a.m. to dusk daily. For more information, call 753-6466.

The San Dieguito River Park is building and clearing trails in the Lake Hodges area near Escondido. The new Highland Valley Trail runs about 2.5 miles east along the east arm of Lake Hodges, starting from a point near the intersection of Highland Valley and Pomerado roads. A concrete footpath going under Interstate 15 at Lake Hodges now links the north-shore Lake Hodges segment of the Coast-to-Crest Trail to points near North County Fair shopping center. A new interpretive trail, the Piedras Pintadas ("painted rocks") Trail, 3.6 miles round trip, runs from West Bernardo Road and around the south end of the reservoir. San Dieguito River Park offers guided walks on these and other trails. Call the park office, 235-5445, for details.

Area C-1, Trip 1, page 44:

Wilderness Gardens Preserve reopened for public use in May 1994. Some trails are newly cleared, but the upper part of the Meadows Trail is overgrown and may not be reopened. Picnic areas abound, but camping is no longer allowed. The preserve's hours are limited: 9:30 a.m. to 4:00 p.m. on Thursdays, Fridays, and Saturdays only.

Area C-1, Trip 2, page 45:

Two miles of wide, new trail now traverse the mountainous, east part of the Hellhole Canyon Open Space Preserve. You can piece together a loop hike of 8 miles that runs along the view-rich northwest shoulder of Rodriguez Mountain.

Area C-2, page 50:

A new trail from the Mt. Woodson Estates subdivision (due north of the Woodson Mountain summit) ascends southwest and joins the older trail atop the ridge west of the summit.

Area C-6, Trip 4, page 83:

The rambling trail trending south and east of the Mt. Gower Open Space Preserve trailhead has been extended for about two more miles. The summit ridge of Mt. Gower is now relatively easy to reach by this route.

Area C-7, Trip 2, page 86:

A proposed land swap between the Sweetwater Authority, which operates Loveland Reservoir, and Cleveland National Forest would result in the closing of Government Cove to hiking and fishing. It is expected that another area of the reservoir shoreline will be opened to public visitation and fishing. Contact Cleveland National Forest for the latest update.

Area M-1, page 90:

Parts of the Dripping Springs, Magee-Palomar, and Wildhorse trails are severely overgrown at the present time. Volunteers have been working to clear the lower part of the trail system, near Dripping Spring Campground. Count on intense bushwhacking, route-finding effort, and a pace of less than one mile per hour if you plan to use the upper parts of these trails—especially the Magee-Palomar Trail.

Area M-3, page 109:

The campgrounds at Los Coyotes Indian Reservation have been intermittently closed of late. Access to the reservation may be restricted, so call first. This affects Trips 1 and 2 in Area M-3, and also Trip 3 in Area D-2.

Area M-3, Trip 3, page 113:

Indian Flats Road has been renamed and posted "Lost Valley Road." The road is now paved from Highway 79 to Indian Flats Campground, though it remains very narrow.

Areas M-5 and M-6:

Several incidents involving mountain lions stalking or menacing campers, hikers, and mountain bikers have occurred in the Julian and Cuyamaca Rancho State Park areas during recent years. In December 1994, a woman was attacked and killed by a mountain lion while hiking near Cuyamaca Peak. This was the thirteenth known fatal attack by a cougar in the United States and Canada in this century. Experts are uncertain why the normally elusive mountain lions here and at other spots in California are becoming more aggressive. An intensive study of mountain lions is underway in Cuyamaca Rancho State Park. No trails have been closed permanently, but the following precautions are urged for all persons entering mountain lion country:
• Hike with one or more companions.
• Keep children close at hand.
• Never run from a mountain lion. This may trigger an instinct to attack.
• Make yourself "large," face the animal, maintain eye contact with it, shout, blow a whistle, and do not act fearful. Do anything to convince the animal that you are not its prey.
• Carry a hiking stick and use it, or pitch stones or other objects at the animal if it continues to advance.

Areas M-7, M-8, and M-9:

In mid-1996, Operation Gatekeeper, the federal government's attempt to stave off illegal immigration from Mexico into the United States, resulted in an eastward shift in migration patterns (from Tijuana/San Ysidro to points well east of there) and a dramatic increase in migrant foot traffic northward across some of the mountainous regions of San Diego County. As of this update, these regions include Otay Mountain (Area M-9), Pine Creek Wilderness (Area M-8), and to a lesser extent the Laguna Mountains M-7. Residents of the backcountry and hikers and campers using these

areas (including the Pacific Crest Trail) have reported thefts of gear and other unpleasant encounters with desperate travelers. The environmental degradation caused by the passage of large groups of migrants across these sensitive lands and the greatly increased incidence of wildfire along the border has become a nationally publicized issue.

Operation Gatekeeper involves the building of a sturdy fence many miles eastward along the international border. If and when this fence is extended as far east as the desert, the migration routes will likely shift into Imperial County. Since safety issues are currently a special concern for anyone visting the southern mountain region of San Diego County, it would be a good idea to contact Cleveland National Forest (Descanso Ranger District) for the latest update.

Area M-8, Trip 3, page 171-72:

The Secret Canyon Trail is well used and open on its north end (south to the Pine Valley Bridge), but severely overgrown in many places south of there, as of 1996. Check with Cleveland National Forest beforehand if you want to hike the entire length of the trail.

Area D-2, Trips 6, 7, and 8, pages 197-99:

Hikers using these routes now have the option of starting from a new parking lot/trailhead located on the west side of Montezuma Highway, 0.7 mile south of Anza-Borrego park headquarters. Overnight parking is allowed here. If you use this trailhead, the mileages listed in the trip descriptions will be slightly different.

Area D-2, Trip 10, page 201-202:

A new, lower extension of the California Riding and Hiking Trail has been completed. The trail now ends at a new parking lot/trailhead located on the west side of Montezuma Highway, 0.7 mile south of Anza-Borrego park headquarters. If you end your hike here, you add another mile of distance plus 200 feet of further elevation loss.